T. E. HULL
University of Toronto

D. D. F. DAY
North York Board of Education

AN INTRODUCTION TO PROGRAMMING AND APPLICATIONS
WITH BASIC

ADDISON-WESLEY PUBLISHERS
Don Mills, Ontario

Reading, Massachusetts · London · Amsterdam · Sydney · Tokyo

Canadian Cataloguing in Publication Data

Hull, Thomas E., 1922-
    An introduction to programming and applications
with BASIC

Includes index.

ISBN 0-201-03029-2

1. Electronic digital computers - Programming.
2. Basic (Computer program language) I. Day,
David D.F., 1941-   II. Title.

QA76.6.H82   001.6'42   C79-094341-7

Portions of this book were originally published in *An Introduction to Programming and Applications with Fortran* by T. E. Hull and D. D. F. Day © 1978 by Addison-Wesley (Canada) Limited.

The quotation on Part III opening is from *Grooks II* by Piet Hein. Copyright 1968 by Piet Hein; quoted by permission.

ISBN 0-201-03029-2
ABCDEFGHIJ-AL-79

To our families

Preface

The purpose of this book is to explain the fundamentals of programming and to show how computers can be used in a wide variety of application areas.

The book is in three parts:

Part I consists only of Chapter 1 and is intended to provide an overview of three basic topics, namely

a) *algorithms,* which are the fundamental idea in computing,

b) *stored-program computers,* which are the essential mechanisms that enable us to implement algorithms both reliably and extremely rapidly,

and (with the greatest emphasis)

c) *a convenient way of describing algorithms,* which we call a *pseudo-code,* and which is the most important starting point in preparing to run a program on a computer.

Part I should be covered fairly quickly on first reading. Then it can be studied again in more detail, or referred back to later, according to one's background or inclination.

Part II consists of Chapters 2–7, plus two summaries. It is intended to be a relatively detailed introduction to programming in Basic, with an emphasis on how the pseudo-code that was introduced in Part I can be rendered in Basic.

There is no standard Basic language and the differences among various versions of the language that have been developed are quite considerable. We usually restrict our attention to the original version that was developed by Professors Kemeny and Kurtz at Dartmouth College. However, when appropriate, we mention extensions that may be useful if such features are available in the particular version being used by the reader.

A summary of Basic is also included at the end of Part II, along with a summary of how the algorithmic pseudo-code constructs introduced in Section 1.3 can be rendered in Basic. The pages containing these summaries are marked for easy reference.

Part III consists of Chapters 8–14 and is devoted to applications in a variety of areas. It is intended that the problems be realistic and reasonably significant. In many cases the problems are open-ended and can be explored to whatever depth one might wish.

Appendixes A and **B** give details about a hypothetical machine. They contain too much detail about stored-program computers for the purposes of Part I, but the material is available in the appendixes for those who wish to pursue the subject in greater depth. It is also available for later reference in Part III, particularly in the last chapter of Part III where the simulation of a hypothetical computer, as well as certain translators, are discussed in some detail.

Appendix C contains material on number representations that would be of interest in some circumstances, but which is too detailed for inclusion in Chapter 9, where questions affected by machine arithmetic are given special consideration.

Small amounts of material are occasionally repeated in different sections of this book. This is done so that the treatment of various topics will be reasonably self-contained, and also so that various streams can be followed through the book without breaks in the continuity. In particular, any material from the appendixes that is essential for a particular chapter is repeated in that chapter, except that too much of Appendixes A and B is needed in Chapter 14 to warrant so much repetition.

Many of the problem descriptions in this book are somewhat vague. This is partly because it is not possible to be absolutely precise without becoming machine dependent. But there is a more important reason. Some of the problems have been deliberately left vague because that is the way in which we are usually presented with problems in real life. In fact, the first step in tackling a realistic problem, once it has been identified, is to produce a reasonably precise definition of what is required. One often hears complaints that students are not taught to formulate problems. The reason may be that they are usually presented with problems that are already precisely stated.

We cannot overemphasize the need for great care in studying the solution of worthwhile problems. Various methods of solution should be considered and compared. The final program should be thoroughly tested and completely documented. These steps cannot all be taken with every problem, of course, but every now and then one problem should be singled out for careful treatment. Occasionally, it is also a good idea for a group of students to work together on the same problem. They should agree on exactly what has to be done and then divide up the work, perhaps assigning a subprogram to each member of the team.

No special mathematics is required in most of this book beyond what is normally learned in high school. However, the calculus is used in a few places in Chapters 8 and 9, but mainly in order to derive results that can still be taken on faith and used by someone not familiar with the mathematics. Mathematical results are mentioned in some of the other applications as well, for example, in solving equations or in the use of statistics. In such cases, the necessary formulas are quoted and explained. The corresponding problem areas are treated thoroughly and all aspects are given careful consideration, but no attempt is made to derive the mathematical formulas themselves.

Most of the material in this book has already been used in introductory courses. (Much of it is based on an earlier book by the same authors, entitled *Computers and Problem Solving,* Addison-Wesley, Canada, 1970. Parts I and III of the present book are essentially identical to the corresponding parts of our companion book, *An Introduction to Programming and Applications with Fortran,* Addison-Wesley, Canada, 1978.)

It has proved useful to have available an interpreter for SIMON and an assembler for SAP, the languages described in Appendixes A and B. Information about these processors and their availability can be obtained from the authors.

Introductory course:	**Part I** • Do as quickly as you wish, • mainly some of the pseudo-code in Section 1.3. **Part II** • Do all of this part, • also a few examples chosen from Part III.
Follow-up course on applications:	**Part I** • Review this material, • especially Sections 1.3 and 1.4. **Part III** • Do a selection of topics from this part. • Refer to the summaries in Part II whenever necessary.

Parts I and II, along with a selection of just a few problems from different chapters of Part III, provide enough material for a course lasting one term. The rest of Part III can provide more than enough material for a follow-up term on computer applications. Our experience in such a follow-up course has been particularly successful when students are given an opportunity to tackle a relatively small number of problems in considerable depth, especially when they are encouraged to help with the problem specifications, and perhaps formulate considerably different, and often more enlightening versions of the problems for themselves.

We are greatly indebted to the many persons who have helped, both directly and indirectly, with the preparation of the material in this book, and particularly to the large number of friends who have influenced our thinking about programming languages in such a fundamental way during recent years.

We would like especially to thank our colleagues Dave Andrews, Imre Farkas, Ric Hehner, Ric Holt, and Les Mezei for their many very helpful comments and suggestions. We also wish to thank Professor N. P. Archer of McMaster University, and Frank Neal of Erin, Ontario, for providing constructive criticism of the original version of Part II. We are also very thankful once again for the patience of our families, and we are grateful for the excellent cooperation we have continued to receive from the staff of Addison-Wesley. Finally, we wish to thank Rosemary Bell and Teresa Miao for their typing of Part II both carefully and cheerfully.

Toronto   T.E.H.
March 1979   D.D.F.D.

About the Authors

THOMAS E. HULL is Professor of Computer Science and Mathematics at the University of Toronto, and formerly Chairman of the Department of Computer Science. His current interests are primarily in the development of software for scientific computation and in programming languages.

After receiving his Ph.D. in Applied Mathematics from the University of Toronto in 1949, Dr. Hull taught at the University of British Columbia, where he was also director of the Computing Center from 1957 to 1963. He returned to the University of Toronto in 1963. He is an active member of several professional societies and an editor of the ACM Transactions on Mathematical Software. For several years he was the Canadian representative to the International Federation for Information Processing. He was also a member of the Computer Science Study Committee of the Ontario Department of Education and has helped to develop computer science programs in high schools and community colleges, as well as at the university level. Dr. Hull has given lectures on numerical analysis and computing at many places throughout Canada, the United States, Europe, and Australia. He is a Fellow of the Royal Society of Canada.

Dr. Hull is author or co-author of numerous articles in the fields of applied mathematics and computer science, as well as a text of the School Mathematics Study Group entitled *Algorithms, Computation and Mathematics* and the 1968 report of the ACM Curriculum Committee on Computer Science. He is also the author of *Introduction to Computing,* Prentice-Hall, Englewood Cliffs (1966), of *Introduction to Algorithms,* W. J. Gage, Toronto (1967), with G. T. Nicholls and R. C. Wong, and of *Computers and Problem Solving,* Addison-Wesley (Canada), Toronto (1970), with D. D. F. Day.

DAVID D. F. DAY is Superintendent of Computer Services at the North York Board of Education. The staff which he directs provides computing services to 165 schools, as well as to the administrative departments of the school board.

After receiving his B.A. in mathematics from the University of Toronto in 1963, Mr. Day taught secondary school mathematics and computer science in Toronto and North York. In his former position as Curriculum Consultant in Computing for North York, he was involved in developing courses of study and assisting teachers of computer science and data processing in the preparation of materials. He has conducted workshops and given in-service training for teachers, and he participated in the development of systems to support the teaching of Computer Science. In addition, he has authored a large number of informal booklets and papers on computing, as well as co-authoring *Computers and Problem Solving* with T. E. Hull.

Contents

A well laid plan is ever to my mind most profitable.
Herodotus

PART 1

Algorithms, Computers, and Programming

Algorithms are discussed briefly in the first section of this chapter. The notion of an algorithm is the fundamental idea in computing, and it is therefore appropriate to begin with such a discussion. We do not attempt to provide a rigorous definition of algorithms. We introduce the idea in an intuitive way, along with some examples. We also point to the kinds of questions that arise naturally in connection with algorithms, and that will be illustrated in more detail in later chapters when we study algorithms in practical applications.

Computers are machines for implementing algorithms and we therefore devote the second section of this chapter to a brief glimpse at stored-program computers. It is not necessary at this stage to consider many details. We expose only the main features of these machines, in order to show how they are related to algorithms, and to give some indication of the role they play in actual practice. In any event, some readers may already have been exposed to the characteristics of particular machines. Anyone who would like to have further information about the nature of stored-program computers will find further details in Appendixes A and B.

Our main goal throughout this book is the development of algorithms for solving practical problems which are to be implemented on computers. For this purpose we need a convenient and easily understood way of describing the algorithms. We concentrate on one aspect of this question in Section 1.3, where we il-

lustrate the way in which we describe the "structural" aspect of algorithms that appear in later chapters. The purpose of Section 1.3 is to outline a reasonably good way of describing this aspect of the algorithms we develop, and to try to make their descriptions relatively independent of the details of a particular programming language. To transcribe one of these descriptions into a program in a particular programming language (such as Basic, Fortran, or PL/I) is a relatively straightforward task. The details for transcribing them into Basic are contained in the material of Chapters 2–7.

Algorithms are designed to manipulate data, such as numbers and arrays of numbers, as illustrated in the introductory examples of this chapter. However, in the further applications of later chapters we run across a number of other kinds of data (such as logical values and characters) and other kinds of data structures that are more complicated than simple arrays. It is the purpose of Section 1.4 to develop this "data" aspect of algorithms somewhat further by providing a brief preview of the additional kinds of data and data structures to be found in later chapters. Again, the details for Basic are given in Chapters 2–7.

Finally, in Section 1.5, we round out our introduction with a summary of a number of additional points that should be kept in mind in the course of developing algorithms and programs in subsequent chapters. These points are a part of good programming practice, and are concerned with the importance of such obviously desirable characteristics as correctness and efficiency of algorithms, careful testing, documentation, and so on. These points are collected in the last section of this introductory chapter because they are applicable in all of the following chapters. It is hoped that it will not be necessary to repeat these points, as such, but that their importance will be amply illustrated in the examples that follow in later chapters.

1.1 ALGORITHMS

We are all familiar with the idea of using step-by-step procedures for solving problems. Everyday examples include the directions we give a friend on how to find his way to a particular meeting place (as in Fig. 1.1), the instructions on how to assemble the parts of a piece of equipment we have just purchased, or the recipe for a special gourmet dish.

Although everyday procedures are usually precise enough for practical purposes, most of them could not be classified as absolutely precise or unambiguous ("It's large and dark brown—you can't miss it!" "Let stand for about 30 minutes." "Add a pinch of salt."). However, there are many step-by-step procedures for solving problems that are completely *unambiguous* and *finite,* and it is procedures of this kind that are called *algorithms.* One example is the procedure we are all familiar with for finding the sum of a column of integers. Another is a particular sequence of steps that one might follow in order to sort a list of items. An example of the latter is given later in this section.

Algorithms must solve problems. We say they must be *effective.* It is usually intended that an algorithm be able to solve *any* problem from some particular class of problems, such as finding the sum of *any* column of integers, not just one particular column. It is also essential that the solution be found in a finite number of steps. (This last requirement rules out limit processes, such as those that are used in the calculus, despite the fact that such processes are quite well defined and unambiguous.)

One way of trying to ensure that the steps are unambiguous is to insist that they be such that they can

Go north from the corner of Main Street and Center Street to the third stop light. Then go one block further and turn right, just beyond a large shopping plaza on your right. Then go two blocks and turn left. It's about the fifth or sixth building on your right. It's large and dark brown—you can't miss it! Number 19, I believe.

FIG. 1.1 Example of a step-by-step procedure for "solving the problem" of explaining to a friend how to get to a particular meeting place.

be carried out by a machine, to help convey the idea that the steps can be carried out "mechanically," without, for example, the imprecision caused by "judgment" or "chance." Of course we then have to specify the kind of machine we have in mind, but, it turns out, all that is required is that the machine be able to carry out sequences of precisely defined steps such as performing arithmetic operations on numbers and determining the order in which a sequence of operations is performed as a result of comparing one number against another. More details will be given in Section 1.2.

One of the first persons to give a precise definition of an algorithm was A. M. Turing. In 1936 he defined an algorithm in terms of what could be accomplished by an idealized machine which he described and which is now referred to as a Turing machine. He introduced this idea almost 10 years before he and others became involved in the design of the first modern-day computers, which were constructed in the late 1940's. The idealized Turing machine appears, at least on the surface, to be very different from present-day computers. However, what can or cannot be done on one is, at least in principle, the same as what can or cannot be done on the other.

Because of what has just been said, it would seem appropriate to consider algorithms to be essentially synonymous with what can be carried out on a computer. However, it has become customary to make a distinction between the algorithm itself and a particular computer program which is intended to implement the algorithm. The algorithm is the ideal, more abstract, and more general procedure, whereas the program may be subject to a number of restrictions which arise mainly because of characteristics of the machine being used, such as the size of the machine's storage facility, or the size of the numbers that can be stored. This distinction will be illustrated frequently in what follows. However, we will often use the terms interchangeably, if the distinction is not important.

Although precise definitions of algorithms did not appear until the 1930's, and their application on the enormous scale that they are used today did not become possible until the development of computers at an even later date, it must be acknowledged that the basic idea of an algorithm has been known for thousands of years. We use an old and very famous algorithm, known as Euclid's algorithm, as our first example.

The purpose of Euclid's algorithm is to find the greatest common divisor of two positive integers. The basic idea of the algorithm is described in Fig. 1.2.

Let us consider an example. Suppose the original two numbers are 210 and 154. Dividing the smaller of these into the larger gives a remainder of 56. Since this

First divide the smaller of the two numbers into the larger. Then, if the remainder is not zero, the original two numbers are replaced by the remainder and the smaller of the original two, and the process is repeated. Eventually, a remainder of zero is produced. At this point, the smaller of the two numbers being considered is the required greatest common divisor.

FIG. 1.2 A prose description of Euclid's algorithm which is a procedure for finding the greatest common divisor of two positive integers.

is not zero, we replace the original two numbers with 56 and 154. Dividing the smaller of these two into the larger gives a remainder of 42. This is not zero either, so we replace the two numbers just considered with 42 and 56. Dividing now gives a remainder of 14, which is not zero, so we replace the two numbers just considered with 14 and 42. This time, however, dividing does lead to a remainder of zero so that, according to the rule given earlier, we should take 14 to be the re-

quired greatest common divisor. (Is the result correct?)

We have deliberately presented Euclid's algorithm and the worked out example in prose form, in order to emphasize the obvious inadequacy of this way of describing algorithms. It would be particularly inadequate for algorithms of any substantial size. Another approach that is often used is to describe the algorithm with the help of a *flowchart,* as illustrated in Fig. 1.3. A flowchart shows the overall "flow" of the process in a much more graphic way, something for which a mixture of English prose and traditional mathematical notation is not well suited.

With the introduction of the flowchart, we have added a few embellishments to our description of the algorithm which will become part of whatever technique we finally use for describing algorithms. The most important of these embellishments is the introduction of names for the numbers involved (A and B for the two numbers being considered at each stage and R for the

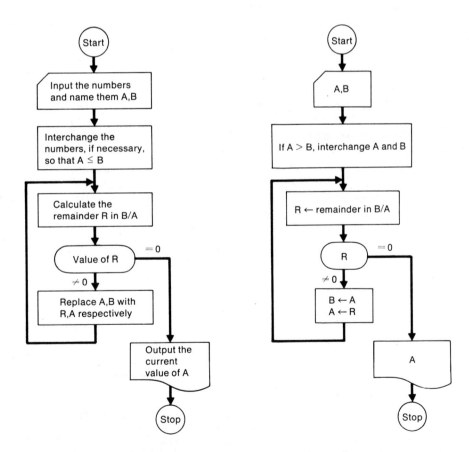

FIG. 1.3 Flowcharts for Euclid's algorithm. The shape of the "input" box is motivated by the shape of a punched card, and that of the "output" box is intended to suggest paper that has been torn from a printer. An oval shape is used at a point where the flow of control can take more than one direction. The second flowchart is merely an abbreviation for the first; the reverse arrow (←) can be read as "is assigned the value of."

remainder). Another embellishment is the explicit recognition of input and output, which makes the description a bit more machine oriented, and also draws attention to a property that is common to most algorithms, which is that they transform a given input into the required output.

Despite their visual appeal, there are at least two important disadvantages in the use of flowcharts. One is that they are not in a form that is convenient for implementation on a computer. The other is not so obvious, but it is that the unrestricted use of arrows for showing the flow of control in a flowchart may provide too much temptation to the user to develop very complicated algorithms that are difficult to understand and analyze.

Another way of describing Euclid's algorithm is shown in Fig. 1.4. It lacks much of the visual appeal of the flowcharts in Fig. 1.3, but it does happen to be in a form that is more convenient for implementation on a computer.

In Section 1.3 we will introduce a way of describing algorithms that combines most of the advantages of Figs. 1.3 and 1.4 without their disadvantages. We will see, as one of the examples given there, that the description of Euclid's algorithm in Fig. 1.4 can be modified in a way that retains its convenience for machines but also makes it considerably more appealing for people. In the meantime, we would like to consider one other example of an algorithm and then conclude this section by mentioning a few other aspects of algorithms in general.

As a second example of an algorithm we describe a procedure for sorting. Specifically, we start with a list of numbers, and, in Fig. 1.5, we describe an algorithm for rearranging these numbers into nondecreasing order.

This description may appear to be a bit more complicated and perhaps less well defined than the corresponding one given for Euclid's algorithm. Is it clear how the case when there is only one number in the list is handled? What about when there are only two? The

Search all numbers beginning with the first for the smallest and interchange it with the first. Then search all numbers beginning with the second for the smallest and interchange it with the second. Then search beginning with the third, and so on. This process is to be continued until we have run out of numbers to search (which may of course have happened right at the start, if there was only one number to begin with).

FIG. 1.5 A prose description of an algorithm for sorting a sequence of numbers into nondecreasing order.

phrase "and so on" might presume too much on the part of the reader.

The flowchart in Fig. 1.6 is somewhat more precise than the prose description in Fig. 1.5 and should help to clarify these questions. In Fig. 1.6, it is assumed that the list of numbers is $a_1, a_2, \ldots, a_n$. (Provision for the input of these numbers and their later output in rearranged order could also have been included in the flowchart.) Note how the "number of times around the loop" is controlled by the "counter" i. The number of times is exactly $n - 1$.

A question might be asked regarding either Fig. 1.5 or Fig. 1.6 about using the term "Search." Is it clearly understood what is meant by that term, or should

1. Input the numbers and name them A,B.
2. Interchange the numbers, if necessary, so that A ≤ B.
3. Divide A into B and call the remainder R.
4. If R = 0, transfer to step 7.
5. Otherwise (when R ≠ 0) replace A,B with R,A respectively.
6. Return to step 3.
7. Output the current value of A.
8. Stop.

FIG. 1.4 An alternative description of Euclid's algorithm. It lacks much of the visual appeal of the flowcharts in Fig. 1.3, but it is closer to a form that is convenient for implementation on a computer.

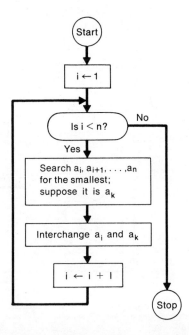

FIG. 1.6 A flowchart for the algorithm described in Fig. 1.5. Here it is presumed that the original list of numbers is $a_1, a_2, \ldots, a_n$, and that the purpose is to end up with a rearrangement of this list that is in nondecreasing order. (Initially the "counter" i is assigned the value 1. Then, after each search and interchange, the value of i is increased by 1, and this new value is assigned to i.)

it in turn be defined by a separate algorithm or subalgorithm? This last point raises the question about just what we can assume is known in describing algorithms and what we cannot assume, and it is here that reference to a particular machine is helpful, reference to either a Turing machine or to a computer, because what we can assume is exactly what the machine can do. In any event, it is clear once again that we also need to pay careful attention to the problem of describing algorithms, that is, to a convenient algorithmic language, since descriptions like those given above will soon get out of hand if we attempt much more complicated algorithms. As indicated earlier, we will consider a more convenient way of describing algorithms in Section 1.3.

Before finishing this section there are a few more points we would like to mention by way of rounding out a general discussion of algorithms. We first point out once again that algorithms usually start with some information (such as two positive numbers in the case of Euclid's algorithm, an array of *n* numbers in the case of the sorting algorithm), and the algorithm produces something (a single positive number from Euclid's algorithm, a permutation of the array with a particular property from the sorting algorithm). The algorithm therefore defines a function or a mapping from some domain of possible inputs to a range of possible outputs, as illustrated in Fig. 1.7.

It is of course possible for two different algorithms to define the same function. In this case we say the algorithms are *equivalent,* and it is sometimes of considerable interest to determine which of two equivalent algorithms is the *more efficient,* or, better still, to determine the *most efficient* algorithm for evaluating a particular function. Of course, it will be necessary to define

what we mean by efficiency before we can attempt to study such questions.

One of the fundamental results that was established by Turing and others is that there are functions for which there exist *no* algorithms capable of evaluating them. Nowadays there is a great deal of interest in classifying the algorithmically solvable problems according to the efficiency with which they can be solved. The term usually used to describe this study is Computational Complexity and it is a part of what is often called the Analysis of Algorithms.

One final point concerns the *correctness* of algorithms. We would certainly want our algorithms to be "correct" in *some* sense or other! One view of this question is to consider the function already prescribed (for example, the greatest common divisor can be defined, or a sorted permutation of an array can be specified), and then the algorithm is considered correct if it evaluates the given function. This view is a very useful one and is the one intended in Exercise 1.1. However, there are other possibilities, and we should be clear in each case as to what is meant by the "correctness" of an algorithm. For example, there are many situations in which we merely mean that the algorithm follows a sequence of steps we intended it to follow; but "what we intended" must itself have been described in some way, so this definition of correctness would amount to saying that a particular algorithm is correct if it is the same as another (although the other might nevertheless have been described quite differently). Alternatively, we might mean that one algorithm is correct if it is merely equivalent to another. Because "correctness" can have so many different interpretations, it might be better to speak of proving properties of algorithms rather than proving their correctness in one sense or another. However, for the sake of brevity we will frequently use the term "correctness" and either explain the sense in which we are using the term, or assume that the context makes the meaning sufficiently clear.

EXERCISE 1.1

1. Give a list of some step-by-step procedures for accomplishing particular tasks that arise in everyday life (such as the instructions for assembling a piece of equipment, or the recipe for a cake). Identify two or three such procedures that are finite and completely unambiguous (such as the procedure for finding the sum of a column of integers) and that can therefore be called algorithms.

2. Prove that the result produced in this section as an application of Euclid's algorithm is the correct solution to the problem, i.e., show that 14 is indeed the greatest common divisor of 210 and 154.

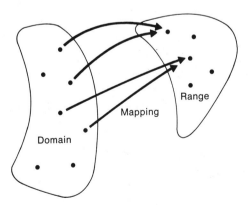

FIG. 1.7 An algorithm defines a mapping from a domain of possible inputs to a range of possible outputs. Two algorithms that define the same mapping (or function) are said to be equivalent.

3. Prove that Euclid's algorithm is correct, i.e., that it will always produce the greatest common divisor of whatever two positive integers are prescribed at the start.

4. Describe an algorithm that is equivalent to Euclid's. Using the number of arithmetic operations as the measure of efficiency for such algorithms, can you determine if your algorithm is more efficient than Euclid's, or is it less efficient?

5. The "search" part of the sorting algorithm in Figs. 1.5 and 1.6 can be broken down into simpler steps in a number of ways. Describe one such way, both in prose form and by means of a flowchart.

6. Use some particular cases to test the sorting algorithm. Be sure to test extreme cases such as when $n = 1$ or 2.

7. Prove that the sorting algorithm is correct. Are there any restrictions on what arrays can be handled?

8. Can you suggest a sorting algorithm that is equivalent to the one described in this section? Is it more efficient, or less efficient, in terms of the number of comparisons needed to sort n numbers?

9. One way of determining whether or not a given positive integer N is prime is to first test whether or not N is 1, 2, 3, or a multiple of 2, and then to divide in turn by each of the odd integers 3, 5, 7, ..., that are less than N. This could require as many as about $N/2$ divisions. Using a maximum number of divisions as a measure of the efficiency of an algorithm, can you suggest a more efficient algorithm for this task? Give a precise description of your algorithm. What is the domain of the function in this example? What is its range?

1.2 STORED-PROGRAM COMPUTERS

Almost all users of computers write the algorithms (or programs) they wish to implement in a *higher-level* language, such as the Basic language described in Chapters 2–7 of this book. There are many other such languages, as well as a number that have been especially designed for particular application areas such as data processing or simulation.

Programs written in such higher-level languages must be translated into the *machine language* of the computer on which they are to be implemented before they are ready to be executed by the machine. Fortunately, the translation is done automatically, by other programs, and the user does not have to become involved in the details of machine-language programming.

Nevertheless, there are good reasons for the user to have at least some familiarity with machine-language programs. First of all, the introduction of stored-program computers was a very revolutionary development, with far-reaching consequences, and some appreciation of exactly what such machines can do, as well as what they cannot do, is worth a certain amount of effort. It is surprising how little effort is needed for at least a basic understanding, compared to what one would require in a number of other areas of scientific development. One can soon begin to appreciate the advantages computers have in terms of speed (millions of operations per second), reliability (many days without malfunction), and cost (perhaps only a few dollars per minute). One also soon begins to appreciate how tasks which appear to be quite complex can be broken down into sequences of very simple steps that the machine is capable of carrying out. On the other hand, one also soon sees how totally dependent the machine is on being provided with these sequences of steps—these algorithms—and one becomes aware of the very distinct limitations to what can be accomplished with computers.

Another good reason for the user to have some familiarity with machine-language programs, to know what is going on "behind the scenes" as it were, is that he is then able to understand and perhaps cope with some of the many restrictions that otherwise seem to be somewhat arbitrarily built into higher-level languages. He may also be in a better position to assess some of the trade-offs regarding efficiency of different higher-level programs if he knows something about the kind of machine-language program into which his higher-level program is being translated. In numerical computations it is also important to have at least some appreciation of the kind of arithmetic (the rounding convention, for example) that is carried out by the particular computer one is using. It is admittedly rather difficult to find out exactly what is going on "behind the scenes" at most computer installations, but that does not make it less worthwhile to know.

Anyone wishing to study at least the basic ideas about machines and machine-language programming can examine the material on a hypothetical computer called SIMON in Appendixes A and B. The information in the appendixes is self-contained. It has been separated from the rest of the text so that its detailed study can easily be postponed if one wishes. We also want to refer to this material quite independently in later chapters; for example, we need to refer to it when we discuss the simulation of a computer in Section 14.1 and the development of translators in other sections of Chapter 14. Incidentally, it should also be mentioned that "programmable" calculators have the kind of features described in the appendixes for our hypothetical machine.

Before concluding this very general discussion of computers and machine-language programming, we would like to display one example of a SIMON program. A complete understanding of this example would depend on the material developed in Appendix A. But perhaps some feeling for the nature of machine-language programs can be derived from a brief study of this one example, after some consideration of the first three sections of Appendix A but without going into all the details developed in those sections.

The example in Fig. 1.8 is a SIMON program for Euclid's algorithm. The flowchart is placed alongside the machine-language program in order to show the correspondence between one reasonably understandable way of describing an algorithm and the almost incomprehensible way in which it has to be described for a machine. The notes beside the machine instructions are intended to explain what the individual instructions mean. It is no wonder that a great deal of effort has been put into developing techniques for translation from higher-level languages into machine languages!

It should be acknowledged that the machine-language program could be shortened to some extent. For example, the instruction in location 018 is not necessary, since the value of R is already in the accumulator, but, in the form given, the program corresponds more directly with the flowchart than it would if we tried to shorten it.

Incidentally, this example illustrates one of the ways in which an algorithm and a program for its implementation can differ. The algorithm as described in

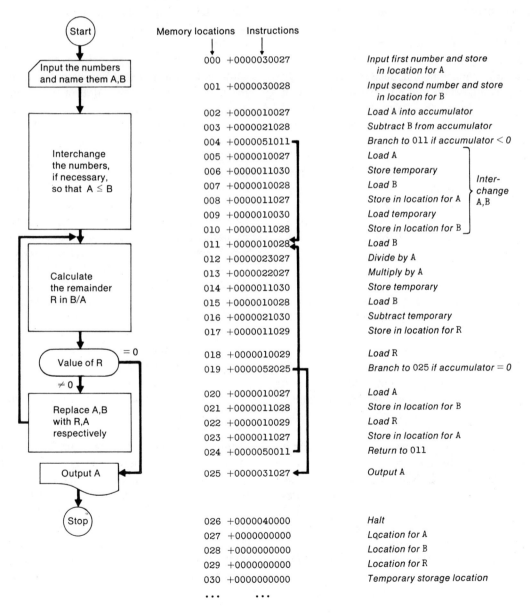

FIG. 1.8 A SIMON program for Euclid's algorithm.

Figs. 1.2–1.4 (and hence the flowchart in Fig. 1.8) is valid for all pairs of positive integers, whereas the machine-language program in Fig. 1.8 is restricted to integers of no more than 10 decimal digits. The domain of the program is restricted to pairs of positive integers of this size. (This is not to say that there could not be a SIMON program which would be valid over a larger domain. In fact, it would be a straightforward, although tedious matter to construct a program with a larger domain.)

We have been concentrating on the relationship between higher-level languages and machine languages. The picture would not be a balanced one from the user's point of view if we did not also mention program libraries. We do not wish to give the impression that the correspondence between what the user writes in his higher-level language and the machine-language program produced by the translator is a simple one, in the sense that each statement made by the user is translated into only a few machine-language instructions. On the contrary, it is important that an extensive library of programs, or subprograms, that have already been written and tested be available to the user. Almost any program a user writes will call upon subprograms, already available in the computer's memory, for carrying out at least part of what the user requires. A simple example of such a subprogram would be one for calculating an approximation to the square root of a number. The computer system (machine, higher-level language, translator, etc.) must be able to support this kind of activity.

EXERCISE 1.2

For detailed questions about SIMON programs, refer to the exercises that are available in Appendixes A and B.

1.3 DESCRIBING ALGORITHMS

Since our main purpose in this book is to discuss the development of useful algorithms that can be implemented on computers, we need a convenient way of describing the algorithms themselves.

From our examples in Section 1.1 it would appear that English, or a combination of English and traditional mathematical notation, is not adequate. For one thing traditional mathematics is not well adapted to describing the dynamic aspects of algorithms, as opposed to the static relationships in other mathematical areas. The use of English and mathematics alone was inconvenient in describing even relatively simple algorithms, such as an algorithm for finding greatest common divisors or for sorting a list of numbers. This approach would also not provide algorithms in a form that is appropriate for implementation on a computer.

Flowcharts provide some improvements, especially in exhibiting the flow of control quite clearly. But they have their disadvantages, including the fact that they also are not appropriate for implementation on a computer. What we plan to do is to use a method of description that is somewhat more along the lines illustrated in Fig. 1.4, although, as it stands, the method used in Fig. 1.4 is not very satisfying visually. It also has the potential for producing complicated programs, by unrestricted use of statements that transfer control to particular steps, just as flowcharts allow unrestricted use of arrows that could produce complicated control structures.

What we plan to do is to describe algorithms at a language level that is somewhat "higher" than the higher-level languages like Basic, but which can be easily rendered in these other languages. That is, we will try to describe the algorithms in a way that captures only the essence of the algorithms themselves, but at the same time in a way that can be easily transformed into the more detailed specification of the programming language we are using (or, to be more precise, of the appropriate version of the language we are using). We will not try to formalize this "higher" language, even though this could lead to making the transformation a process that could be carried out automatically. The main reason for not formalizing our method of description is that we want to maintain the informality and flexibility that we believe is necessary at this level. (As in mathematics, it is of course necessary to observe quite a few conventions, but it is not necessary, or even desirable, to insist on completely rigid rules to govern all details about how mathematical proofs are presented.)

Our plan is to rely heavily on English and mathematics, especially in short sentences as we did in Fig. 1.4, but to extend this approach in two ways. First, we adopt a very small number of informal conventions, primarily to provide for "flow of control"—the dynamic aspects of the algorithms. Second, we organize the layout of an algorithm, especially the indentation of the lines, in a way that helps to exhibit its overall structure; such "paragraphing" is considered good practice in any event, with whatever language one happens to be using. We will refer to the new language as a *pseudo-code*.

We return again to the example of Euclid's algorithm and, in Fig. 1.9, we describe it in the new form. A comparison of Fig. 1.9 with Fig. 1.4 will show that the new version is indeed the same algorithm that was considered earlier in Section 1.1. However, the main points that we want to emphasize at this stage about Fig. 1.9 are the features it illustrates about how we plan to describe algorithms in later chapters of this book.

First of all, the individual pieces of the description (individual lines in the case of Fig. 1.9) are composed

```
Input A and B
If (A > B) interchange A and B
Loop
        Find remainder R in B/A
. . . . If (R = 0) exit loop
        Replace B,A by A,R respectively
End loop
Output A
Stop
```

FIG. 1.9 A pseudo-code description of Euclid's algorithm; it is assumed that A and B are positive integers.

of English and mathematical notation. Second, the "flow of control" is governed by an implied sequencing of the steps in the algorithm from top to bottom, unless it is explicitly altered by a *control construct,* such as Loop-End or Exit in this case. Third, the indentation of what appears between "Loop" and "End" draws attention to the overall flow of control. Fourth, the use of dots to mark a possible exit from the loop also "catches the eye" and helps to draw attention to the overall structure of the algorithm. It must be admitted that some people object to the use of exits from a loop, unless the exits take place at the beginning or the end of the loop. We will allow exits from anywhere within a loop, because we believe such circumstances arise quite naturally in the development of algorithms. However, we recognize that such exits can add to the complexity of algorithms and should therefore be used only sparingly.

We will use the repetition construct Loop-End in a variety of forms. One of the most common is when some action is to be repeated a certain number of times. For example,

```
d = 0
Loop for i = 1, 2, . . . , 100
      d = d + xᵢyᵢ
End
```

will cause d to acquire the value of the dot product

$$x_1y_1 + x_2y_2 + \cdots + x_{100}y_{100}.$$

Here we have followed a number of conventions that, while still mathematical in a sense, are influenced by notations that are common to a number of programming languages. For example, the use of "=" in "d = 0" stands for assignment, so that "d = 0" stands for "Assign to d the value 0." Similarly, "d = d + x_iy_i" stands for "Assign to d the new value obtained by adding x_iy_i to the current value of d." (If we wish, we could just as well have written "Let d = 0" instead of "d = 0", or we could have written "d ← 0". Such alternatives would have more clearly distinguished the use of = as an assignment from the use of = as a relation, as it was used in Fig. 1.9. Here we are depending on the context to make the distinction.)

There are circumstances in which we will want to *nest* one loop within another. For example,

```
Loop for i = 1,2, . . . ,N
.   Loop for j = 1,2, . . . ,N
.        Sᵢⱼ = Uᵢⱼ + Vᵢⱼ
.   End
End
```

will cause the matrix S to become the sum of the matrices U and V. Here we have inserted a column of dots to line up the corresponding outer "Loop" and "End"; the dots don't really help in this example, but with longer loop constructs, and perhaps greater depths of nesting, such a use of dots can be very helpful in displaying the overall structure of the algorithm.

Another form in which it will sometimes be convenient to use the Loop-End construct is exemplified by

```
Set initial value for i
Loop while i satisfies some condition
      ——————
      Do something that changes i
      ——————
End
```

For example, the calculation of the dot product could be rewritten as

```
i = 1
d = 0
Loop while (i ≤ 100)
      d = d + xᵢyᵢ
      i = i + 1
End
```

The "while" form does not improve matters in this example. In fact, it makes the description slightly more complicated. However, there are situations in which the "while" form is convenient, especially with programming languages that happen to have such a form available.

The "while" form provides an alternative way of describing Euclid's algorithm. The Loop-End of Fig. 1.9 can be replaced by

```
Find remainder R in B/A
Loop while R ≠ 0
      Replace B,A by A,R respectively
      Find remainder R in B/A
End loop
```

Note that the "exit" from the middle of the construct has been avoided. However, the "Find remainder . . ." statement has had to be duplicated, and this sort of duplication could be a nuisance in some situations, especially if the part being duplicated is relatively long.

Before leaving the Loop-End construct we should return to the question of exits. This question obviously becomes more complicated if we are going to allow exits from inner loops. There must be a way of indicating which loop is being exited. One way of doing this is to attach a name to the appropriate loop and describe the algorithm as illustrated in the pseudo-code outline of Fig. 1.10. As indicated earlier, exits should probably be avoided if possible. However, as already indicated, we believe there are circumstances in which they do arise naturally and should then be used. For example, if an error condition is detected in the course of a calculation, there may be no reasonable alternative to follow except to simply terminate that part of the calculation.

Another way of indicating exits from a control construct that is sometimes helpful when more than one point of exit is to be allowed is illustrated in Fig. 1.11. This way of indicating exits can also be used for coping with exits from nested loops. The idea is to give at the beginning of a loop a list of "events," such as FOUND (indicating that a particular search procedure has been successful) or ERROR (indicating that an error condition has turned up), that can cause execution of the loop to terminate.

We have so far indicated a number of ways in which we might use an iteration construct, along with the possibility of exits, in describing algorithms. We have been careful to give a representative view of how the construct is to be used in this book. But we have also deliberately tried not to be too rigid about how such a construct ought to be used. This is because there are as yet no generally accepted rules about how such a construct should be used, and it may often be a matter of personal taste as to how one prefers to use such a capability. It is also true that we cannot avoid keeping in mind the programming language into which we will eventually translate our algorithm. This is bound to have some effect on the way we develop our program initially at the "higher" level, although we

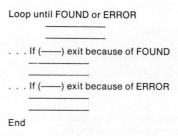

FIG. 1.11 Another illustration of how exits from a loop might be denoted. FOUND and ERROR can be considered different events that cause execution of loop to be terminated.

should at the same time remind ourselves that too much influence of this kind can seriously distort the way in which we think about our algorithms. Some compromise is obviously necessary, but it is probably best to concentrate first on the algorithm itself and a clear description of it, and then use fairly straightforward, though perhaps tedious techniques for rendering our algorithm in the particular programming language we plan to use. The main purpose of Chapters 2–7 is to show how this can be done in Basic.

We turn now to the other main control construct we plan to use in our pseudo-code, namely a *selection* or *case* construct. An example is outlined in Fig. 1.12. The indentation of part of the program after each alternative indicates the part of the program that is to be executed when that particular alternative has been selected; in particular, this indentation will distinguish the use of "If" in the context of a selection construct from the way it can be used in "one-liners," as, for example, it was used earlier in illustrating exits.

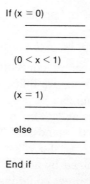

FIG. 1.12 A pseudo-code outline of a selection construct. It is understood that the alternatives, or cases, which are shown in this example in parentheses, are tested in order. The first one that is true causes the following portion of the program, and only that portion, to be executed. The use of "else" is optional. (If none of the specified alternatives is true, the entire construct is skipped.)

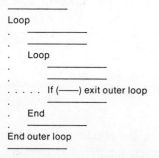

FIG. 1.10 An outline of an algorithm that illustrates how an exit from an inner loop might be specified.

We will also permit exits from selection constructs, just as we did with repetition constructs. Some of the answers to Exercise 1.3 provide examples.

Some users may prefer to add the word "then" after the alternatives, and some may prefer to precede the second and subsequent alternatives with "else if." Once again, we do not want to be too rigid about the notation.

A use of the selection construct that we will occasionally find helpful is immediately after a loop with exits marked by "events." For example, the loop in Fig. 1.11 might be followed by a selection construct in which two alternatives are (FOUND) and (ERROR), so that appropriate action can be taken, depending on which event caused the loop to be terminated.

One more major idea needs to be discussed before completing this section. This is the idea of what we will usually refer to as *refinement*. The term can be applied either to the development of an algorithm or to its presentation, and it refers to developing or describing an algorithm in stages, beginning at a very high level and systematically "refining" parts of the algorithm until, finally, it is in sufficiently detailed form for implementation on a computer.

Our plan to describe algorithms with the pseudocode discussed in this section, and then to render them in the greater detail of a particular programming language, is one example of "refinement." However, the term is more frequently used to describe a situation in which some part of an algorithm is described rather briefly and then expanded in more detail elsewhere. The expansion itself may contain parts that need still further expansion, and so on.

The process of refinement is absolutely essential to our being able to comprehend large algorithms, or to the breaking up of large algorithms into smaller components for assignment to different individuals for completing portions of the program. The idea is a familiar one in mathematics, where the proof of a theorem can often be described in a relatively small number of steps, with some of these steps being "subtheorems" or "lemmas" which must themselves be described in further detail elsewhere, and which in turn might lead to still further refinements. In programming, the further details are often provided by "subprograms" or "procedures," some of which may have been previously developed and perhaps used in other contexts.

In Fig. 1.13 the sorting algorithm discussed earlier in this chapter (Figs. 1.5 and 1.6 and Question 5 of Exercise 1.1) is described in a way that illustrates the explicit use of refinement. This is, of course, not an example of a large algorithm, but does illustrate the use of refinement. The point is that the top-level description

```
/Assume a₁,a₂,. . . ,aₙ are available/
Loop for i = 1,2,. . . ,n − 1
        Search aᵢ,aᵢ₊₁,. . . ,aₙ for the smallest and
                suppose it is aₖ (see below)
        Interchange aᵢ and aₖ
End loop
/a₁,a₂,. . . ,aₙ are now rearranged in non-
        decreasing order/

Where by "Search aᵢ,aᵢ₊₁,. . . etc." we mean
        smallest = aᵢ
        k = i
        Loop for j = i+1,i+2,. . . ,n
                If (aⱼ < smallest)
                        smallest = aⱼ
                        k = j
                End if
        End loop
End where
```

FIG. 1.13 The algorithm discussed earlier for sorting *n* numbers, but written in such a way as to illustrate the use of "refinement." The statement "Search a_i, a_{i+j}, . . . , etc." is used in the top-level description of the algorithm, and later "refined."

of the algorithm (the first Loop-End in Fig. 1.3) is short and easily understood. Perhaps we can even agree that it is "obviously" correct, providing of course that the "Search . . ." statement is correct. It then remains to examine the refinement of the "Search . . ." statement to see that it is indeed correct, so that the entire algorithm is then seen to be correct.

Figure 1.13 illustrates one other notation that we will find convenient, namely, the use of some special way of setting comments off from the rest of the algorithm. In Fig. 1.13 we have used slashes for this purpose. It should be pointed out that such comments can sometimes contain quite explicit statements about the current status, at a particular point in an algorithm, that are important in proving algorithms correct. For now we merely point out that the first comment about the availability of $a_1, a_2, . . . , a_n$ defines the domain of the algorithm, while the final comment, in effect, defines the range, and the two comments together define the mapping between domain and the range. The correctness of the algorithm is determined by whether or not it correctly evaluates the function so defined.

The discussion in this section, of iteration, selection, and refinement, has been intended only to provide a useful guide to understanding how the "structural" aspects of algorithms are described in subsequent chapters. We have the essential ingredients for the purposes of our later applications, and we have at the same time left enough flexibility so that our approach can be easily adapted to particular needs and, if necessary, to the requirements of particular programming languages.

The iteration and selection constructs described in this section are intended to provide all of the control structure that is needed for well-designed algorithms. It should be noted in particular that no provision has been made for the "unrestricted" flow of control that we pointed out was possible with flowcharts and with the technique used in Fig. 1.4. The iteration and selection constructs enable us to describe what are often referred to as *well-structured* algorithms, although, as already noted, there are differences of opinion about whether or not algorithms with the relatively free use of exits that we have allowed should be called well structured. The refinement facility, on the other hand, enables us to describe algorithms in a *top-down* manner which, as mentioner earlier, is essential to our being able to handle or even comprehend algorithms of any considerable size.

EXERCISE 1.3

1. Describe an algorithm for finding the greatest common divisor of two positive numbers that differs from (but is equivalent to) Euclid's algorithm.

2. Suppose that n numbers $c_1, c_2, \ldots, c_n$ are available and describe an algorithm that will find their sum.

3. Give refinements for the statements

a) Interchange A and B, if necessary, so that A $\leq$ B
b) D = smaller of A and B

4. Assume that an n by n matrix is available, along with a vector of length n, and describe an algorithm that will determine the product of the matrix and the vector.

5. Assume that two n by n matrices are available and describe an algorithm for finding their product.

6. Assume that a matrix of order 100 is available. Describe an algorithm that will search this matrix, row by row, until it finds the first zero element. If this element is the (i, j)th element, have the algorithm output the values of i and j. What does the algorithm do if there is no such element?

7. Consider the situation described in Question 6 but this time have the algorithm output a list of the (i, j) values for *all* zero elements, not just the first it reaches.

8. Describe an algorithm that will input a sequence of numbers, one after the other, until one of the numbers is negative. The algorithm should count the number of 1's, the number of 2's, and the number of 3's, as well as the total number of numbers, before it reaches the negative number. After reaching the negative number, the algorithm is to output the four counts.

9. Assume that a sequence of one hundred numbers, say $a_1, a_2, \ldots, a_{100}$, is available. Describe an algorithm that will do what the one in Question 8 does, except that it will output the required counts after reaching the last number, if it has not already reached a negative number by then.

10. Describe an algorithm that will input a sequence of numbers (representing kilowatt-hours) and which will, for each such number, calculate and output the total cost. Each of the first 100 KWH costs 10 cents, each of the next 100 costs 6 cents, each of the next 200 costs 8 cents, and each KWH over 400 costs 10 cents. The algorithm is to terminate when a negative number is input.

11. Suppose n pairs of numbers, $a_1, b_1; a_2, b_2; \ldots; a_n, b_n$, are available at the start of an algorithm. A number x is input and a "table look-up" is to be carried out, which means that the a_i which equals x is to be found and the corresponding b_i is to be output. Describe an algorithm that will accomplish this task. Have your algorithm do something sensible if the value of x cannot be found among the a_i.

12. Describe an algorithm that will carry out the task described in the preceding question, except that it is to do so for a sequence of inputs. Assume that termination is caused by the input of zero.

13. Suppose that a sequence of numbers is to be input until a negative value is reached. Describe an algorithm that will count and output how many are in a table such as the one described in Question 11, and how many are not.

14. Describe an algorithm for sorting n numbers that is different from (but equivalent to) the algorithm described in Fig. 1.13.

15. Give an algorithm that will input one number and, after determining whether or not the number is a prime, will output an appropriate message.

1.4 OTHER DATA STRUCTURES

In the preceding section we concentrated mainly on an overview of how we describe the flow of control in an algorithm, as well as on the important idea of refinement. We paid relatively little attention to the data that was being handled by the algorithms. We restricted ourselves to cases in which the data consisted of numbers. We considered individual numbers (as with Euclid's algorithm) and arrays of numbers (as with the sorting algorithm).

When we get involved in the details of a particular programming language, we soon find that even these kinds of data, which are mathematically quite simple, can become complicated in various ways. This is partly because the numbers must be represented on machines in finite precision, and partly because the designers of machines and languages have sometimes not been consistent in their implementations. Unfortunately, the complications must be kept in mind in designing one's algorithms, and they can be quite crucial when we get to the point of transcribing an algorithm into a particular language, as we shall see in Chapters 2–7.

However, the purpose of the present section is to discuss briefly a number of other kinds of data (besides numbers) and other kinds of structures (besides arrays) that arise frequently in the course of developing algorithms for solving problems in various application areas. Which of these happen to be available in the programming language we use depends on the language. If what we want is not available, we have to construct what we need out of whatever does happen to be available. And how this is done may depend on the application to a considerable extent; it may be easy to do or it can be quite awkward at times.

Most higher-level languages make provision for *logical* values, or *boolean* values (there are other names for them as well). The possible values are "true" or "false," and the logical variables can take on only one or the other of these two values. An expression such as "$A > B$" also has such a value (assuming that A and B have numerical values) and can be assigned to a logical variable. Logical operations such as negation, conjunction (the "and" operation), and disjunction (the "or" operation) can be performed with logical variables. Thus, if P and Q are logical variables, while A and B are numerical, the assignment statement

$$P = Q \text{ and } (A > B)$$

assigns the value "true" to P if Q is "true" and A is greater than B; otherwise it assigns the value "false" to P.

As another example of nonnumerical values, we should also consider *character* variables. It is often important to be able to manipulate *strings of characters,* as in searching a portion of text for certain words or in editing some material stored in the computer. A recognition of the need to handle character values, and strings of character values, has been increasing, and most higher-level languages make provision for this facility. Besides allowing variables to have values which are characters, it should be possible to perform certain operations on them, such as comparing two for equality, searching a string for a particular character, deleting or inserting a substring, and so on.

Another form in which data often appears in practice is one consisting of a number of individual items, somewhat like an array, but where the items are not all of the same kind (i.e., all numbers, or all characters) as they are with an array. Such a form is often called a *record.* As an example, a record kept by a company might contain all the relevant information for an employee. Some items in the record, or *fields* as they are often called, might be the employee's name, address, marital status, and so on; other items might pertain to his position in the company, his department, salary, insurance category, etc. The kinds of operations we want to perform on records normally involve updating, searching, insertion, deletion, and so on.

Numerical data, and arrays of numerical data, are directly available in all higher-level programming languages that have been designed for general-purpose use, although, as already indicated, their exact forms unfortunately differ between different languages (and, at least in some details, between different implementations of what is intended to be the same language). The other forms of data that we have mentioned (logical, character, and record) appear directly in some general-purpose languages, but have to be constructed in one way or another in others.

There are many other forms in which one might want to work with data. In the chapter on simulations, for example, the need to handle *queues* arises quite naturally in the simulation of various kinds of traffic, such as automobiles arriving at an intersection, people lining up at service counter, telephone calls waiting to get through a crowded exchange, and so on. In such situations we may need a way of representing queues, and of carrying out the appropriate operations on queues, such as adding a new item to the end of the queue or removing an item from the head of the queue.

As another example, consider the problem of representing the kind of *graph* that arises in graph theory, as described in more detail in Section 13.1. Mathematically, such a graph is a collection of *nodes,* some pairs of nodes being joined by *edges.* A simple example with only 5 nodes is shown in Fig. 1.14. The nodes are numbered 1 through 5 and, as can be seen, the pairs (1,2), (1,3), (1,4), (2,5), and (3,4) are joined by edges. One way of representing this graph for the purposes of a particular algorithm is to use a list of these edges. An alternative is to use what is called an *adjacency matrix,* which is a matrix whose (i,j)th entry is nonzero if nodes i and j are joined by an edge but which is otherwise zero. These are just two of a number of possible representations of the graph; the one used in a particular application will depend to a large extent on the application itself, as well as on the programming language and the system that supports it. Considerations of efficiency in terms of both storage and operations may also be important.

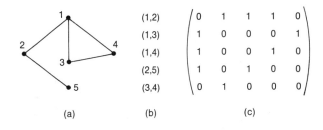

FIG. 1.14 A graph is shown in (a), along with a representation by a list of edges in (b), and an alternative representation by an adjacency matrix in (c).

Graphs with the property that they have no closed paths (such as the path from nodes 1 to 3 to 4 and back to 1 in Fig. 1.14) are known as *trees*. They play a particularly important role in a number of application areas, as we shall see. One simple illustration is shown in Fig. 1.15 where an arithmetic expression is represented as a tree.

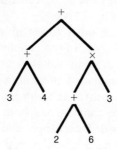

FIG. 1.15   The arithmetic expression $(3 + 4) + (2 + 6) \times 3$ is depicted as a tree. Here the nodes of the tree are operators, while the "leaves" are numbers. The node at the top in this diagram is the "root" of the tree.

The data we wish to work with may be in the form of queues, graphs, or trees, which have just been mentioned, or in the form of stacks or certain kinds of lists, which will be discussed shortly, or sets, and so on. Such forms appear directly only in specialized languages that have been designed for particular applications, but ordinarily must be constructed out of whatever else is available in the general-purpose language we have decided to use, as already indicated in the case of graphs. Along with arrays and records, these forms are usually called *data structures,* because they owe their importance in each case mainly to the particular structure they have and to the operations to be performed on them, rather than to the nature or *type* of the individual items that make up that structure.

Most further details of how new data types or data structures are represented must be left to the appropriate chapters. However, two of them, *stacks* and certain

kinds of lists, arise in such a variety of contexts that it will be worthwhile considering them now. They also provide good examples of how data structures can be represented by, or constructed from, whatever is available in all higher-level, general-purpose languages.

A stack is a list of items somewhat like a queue, except that the rule governing entry and exit is last-in-first-out (LIFO), whereas with a queue the rule is first-in-first-out (FIFO). We shall see that stacks arise in quite a variety of application areas.

One well-known situation where a stack is useful is in the evaluation of arithmetic expressions, and a stack is used for this purpose in the design of some hand calculators. One possible set of rules is the following:

1. numbers are placed on the stack and removed from it on a LIFO basis,
2. each arithmetic operation is performed on the top two numbers on the stack (which are themselves removed from the stack) and the result is placed on the stack.

For example, consider the evaluation of the expression

$$(3 + 4) + (2 + 6) \times 3.$$

The sequence of steps is shown in Fig. 1.16, along with the corresponding positions of the numbers in the stack.

A stack is relatively easy to implement in any programming language. The stack itself can be represented by an array of items, as shown in Fig. 1.17. Depending on the circumstances of the problem, the ith item can be the ith component of a single array, or all the ith components of a number of arrays, or, if the language provides for records, the ith item in the stack can be the ith record in an array of records. A special variable, sometimes called a *pointer* variable, keeps track of the current location of the top of the stack. When the stack is empty the pointer variable has the value zero; as each item is added to the stack (*pushed* onto the stack) the pointer variable is incremented by one, and as each item is removed from the stack (*popped* from the stack) the pointer variable is decreased by one. Depending on the application, it may or may not

Place 3 on stack	Place 4 on stack	Add	Place 2 on stack	Place 6 on stack	Add	Place 3 on stack	Multiply	Add	Remove result
				6		3			
	4		2	2	8	8	24		
3	3	7	7	7	7	7	7	31	31

FIG. 1.16   Use of a stack in the evaluation of the expression $(3 + 4) + (2 + 6) \times 3$.

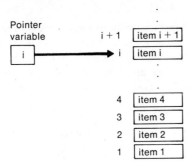

FIG. 1.17 A stack can be represented by an array of "items"; a pointer variable points to the top of the stack.

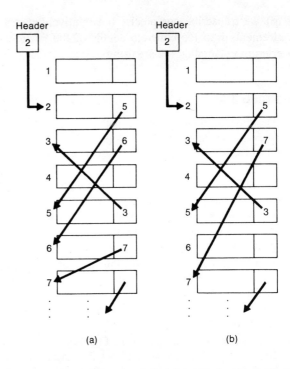

FIG. 1.18 An example of a linked list. The header indicates where the list begins; the pointer in each component indicates where to find the next component. When the component in location 6 of list (a) has been removed we obtain list (b).

be important to check for stack overflow (i.e., to test the pointer each time it is to be incremented to make sure it is not about to become too large), or to check for an empty stack when attempting to remove the top item.

As another example of a data structure that occurs quite frequently in practical applications we mention *linked lists*. They occur in a variety of forms, only one of which will be discussed briefly here. It is illustrated in Fig. 1.18. Each component in a list might consist of, say, the corresponding components of a number of single arrays, or perhaps a row of a matrix (i.e., of a doubly subscripted array) or of a record. One item in each component is a *pointer* which gives the location of the next component in the list, while a *header* variable gives the location of the first component in the list. Figure 1.18 shows the change that has to be made to delete the component in location 6 from the list. Conversely, if the unused components were joined together in another linked list, it would be a straightforward matter to cause insertions to be made in the list, at whatever point we might choose, simply by changing appropriate pointers and by making sure the inserted component contains the information to be inserted.

An algorithm for maintaining certain kinds of *files* that require updating, as well as insertions and deletions, can now be imagined. A typical outline is shown in Fig. 1.19. The actual implementation of the algorithm would require translation of the file itself and the available space into separate linked lists, while instructions such as "insert" and "delete" would be translated into manipulations of pointers, etc., along the lines suggested earlier.

Our discussion of data structures has been necessarily rather brief. Our purpose was to give an overview of what we illustrate in considerable detail in later chapters. The key idea at this stage is to specify the data

structure which is appropriate to the particular problem we are analyzing, and to incorporate it into the algorithm we are designing; it is important that the properties we require of the data structure be specified precisely. Then, as a second step (but not completely separate of course, because we must have it in mind all

```
Open file and available space
Loop until end of transactions
    Read next transaction
    If (update)
            Find appropriate component
            Update information
        (insert)
            Copy required data to first component
                in available space
            Insert in file
        (delete)
            Find appropriate component
            Delete
        (end of transactions)
. . . . . . . . . Exit from loop
        End if
End loop
Close file
Stop
```

FIG. 1.19 Pseudo-code outline of file maintenance algorithm.

along) we transcribe our precise but relatively abstract requirements into the concrete details of the particular programming language we are using.

EXERCISE 1.4

1. Describe an algorithm which will start with a positive integer N (> 3) and which will assign a value to a logical variable L, the value "true" if N is a prime and "false" if not.

2. Describe an algorithm that will start with a numerical value x and an array of numerical values a_i, $i = 1, 2, \ldots, n$, and which will assign "true" or "false" to L, depending on whether x is equal to one of the a's or not.

3. Describe an algorithm for converting an adjacency matrix, as described in Fig. 1.14, into a form in which 1 and 0 are replaced by "true" and "false," respectively. Also describe algorithms for converting from the representation of a graph in the form illustrated in Fig. 1.14(b) to the representation in 1.14(c), and vice versa.

4. The switching circuit shown in Fig. 1.20 is an example of something that can be represented by a "logical" or "boolean" expression. As indicated, each individual switch is represented by a variable which is "true" if the switch is closed, or "false" if open. The circuit itself is closed or open depending on the value of the corresponding expression. Draw a circuit that is represented by the expression

A and (B or C)

and another that is represented by

(A and B) or (C and (D or E or F)).

Are these two circuits closed or open when C and F are "true" but A, B, D, and E are "false"?

5. Suppose that an array of records is available, and that each record contains information about the age, sex, and income of an individual. Describe an algorithm that will determine the number of individual males in their 30's who are earning between \$20,000 and \$30,000.

6. Suppose that an array of characters is available and that it is required to find whether or not this array contains a particular subarray. Describe an algorithm for carrying out this task. Specify precisely what your algorithm produces. Indicate what modifications would be necessary if

the array of characters was to be input, one character at a time.

7. Suppose that an array of characters is available. Without making use of a stack, describe an algorithm that will search the array and determine whether or not the parentheses in the array are "properly balanced" in the mathematical sense. For example, the parentheses in

$$A + (B + (C \times D + E) + F/(G + H))$$

are properly balanced, whereas those in

$$A + (B/(C + D)$$

and in

$$A \text{ or } B) \text{ and } (C$$

are not.

8. Indicate how you would describe refinements that explain exactly what you mean by a statement such as "Push this character onto the stack" or "Pop a character from stack 3".

9. Show how a stack can be used in an alternative approach to Question 7. Assume that the characters are being input, one at a time, rather than being available in an array.

10. Explain at least one way of using an array, or arrays, to represent large tridiagonal matrices efficiently. (A matrix is tridiagonal if its elements a_{ij} are zero unless $j = i - 1$, i, or $i + 1$, as illustrated in Fig. 1.21.) Describe algorithms for adding and multiplying matrices in one such form.

11. a) Explain how you can represent a queue with an array. What is the major difficulty? Describe algorithms for adding an individual item to the end of the queue and removing an item from the front.
   b) Describe how a linked list can be used to represent a queue, and give algorithms for adding to and removing from the queue.

12. How can a *deque* be represented and handled? (A deque is a "doubly ended queue," i.e., a queue to which items can be added to, or removed from, either end.)

13. Suppose that an array a_i, $i = 1, 2, \ldots, n$ is available, along with a single item x. Describe an algorithm that will insert x onto the end of the array (i.e., as a_{n+1}) if it is not already one of the a's. What would have to be done if the a's were sorted and x had to be inserted in such a way that the order was preserved? Describe another algorithm that will delete x if x is among the a's.

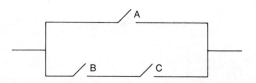

FIG. 1.20 The switching circuit shown is represented by the "logical" or "boolean" expression A or (B and C), where the individual switches, A, B, C, are "true" if closed or "false" if open.

$$\begin{pmatrix} X & X & O & O & O & O & O & O \\ X & X & X & O & O & O & O & O \\ O & X & X & X & O & O & O & O \\ O & O & X & X & X & O & O & O \\ O & O & O & X & X & X & O & O \\ O & O & O & O & X & X & X & O \\ O & O & O & O & O & X & X & X \\ O & O & O & O & O & O & X & X \end{pmatrix}$$

FIG. 1.21 An example of a tridiagonal matrix. The x's represent nonzero elements.

14. Suppose that a linked list of components is available, along with another linked list of available space. Describe algorithms for insertion and deletion. Give precise specifications of what your algorithms actually do.

1.5 FURTHER REMARKS

The first two sections of this chapter were devoted to introducing the idea of an algorithm and explaining, very briefly, how digital computers provide a means for implementing algorithms. Then in the next two sections, we concentrated on an outline of how we plan to describe algorithms that we want to develop for execution on a computer. In Section 1.3 we emphasized the flow of control and refinement aspects, and in Section 1.4 the data aspects of algorithms, as they can be described at a relatively high, but still reasonably precise level of abstraction. Such descriptions must still be translated into the more detailed specifications required by a particular programming language, which is in turn translated automatically into the machine language of a particular computer before the algorithms can be executed.

Before turning to chapters on Basic and on various application areas, we would like to round out this overview of algorithms, computers, and programming by drawing attention to a number of other aspects of programming that are important in practice and that should be kept in mind as we deal with the problems arising in subsequent chapters.

1. *Correctness.* We have already mentioned the "correctness" of algorithms in connection with a number of examples. We have referred to some fairly clear-cut situations in which algorithms could be considered correct if they evaluated the functions they were supposed to evaluate. However, we also pointed out that this point of view needed to be modified in some situations. Another specific example of a situation in which this point of view needs to be modified occurs in numerical calculations, where the results are usually only approximations to those of an exact mathematical function, and the correctness of the program is defined only to within certain error bounds. As still another example of where some modification is needed we will find that it is not usually very helpful to think of simulation programs as programs for evaluating functions.

Despite the complications associated with understanding exactly what is meant by the correctness of algorithms, it is important to be as clear as possible in describing the purpose of a particular algorithm. It must be admitted that it is not practical to insist on a detailed and rigorous proof of the correctness of every program we use. Nevertheless, there is general agreement that standards must be improved over what has previously been prevalent and, in fact, a great deal of progress has been made in recent years. Much of this progress has been due to an insistence on making sure that programs are more carefully organized so that their structure is simple and clear (i.e., so that they are *well structured*) and also to an insistence on more thorough testing of the final products.

The situation is not as different from what occurs in mathematics as may appear at first sight. It would not have been possible to develop and use mathematics in worthwhile application areas if no step could be allowed without a detailed and rigorous proof of its correctness. (When the famous nineteenth-century electrical engineer named Heaviside was accused of not giving rigorous proofs of the techniques he had developed for the operational calculus, he replied that he did not refuse to eat simply because he did not completely understand the processes of digestion!) On the other hand, we should also acknowledge that much of what is possible in mathematics is due to the availability of a large number of well-established results on which other results can be built. With programming we are still a long way from having a comparably extensive and well-established "library" of carefully proven, efficient, and thoroughly tested subprograms. Parenthetically, it can be pointed out that the standards of rigor in computing have to be somewhat higher than in mathematics: it usually does not matter particularly if a comma is missing in the proof of a mathematical theorem, but a missing comma could be disastrous in a computer program!

2. *Robustness.* Sometimes there is a temptation to concentrate a bit too much on considering the correctness of a program in terms of what it does when its input is valid. But we also want the program to behave "correctly" when it is inadvertently presented with invalid data. Ideally we would like it to fail gracefully, perhaps by continuing if possible, or stopping if necessary, but in any event giving an appropriate indication of the source of difficulty. For example, should we modify Euclid's algorithm so that it will do something sensible if A or B is negative or zero?

Such "robust" behavior can of course be considered a part of correctness—it is just that the domain of the algorithm is then expanded to include invalid as well as valid input, and its behavior under all possible circumstances is specified. We have chosen to mention this part of the "correct" behavior of a program under the separate heading of "robustness" only to emphasize the importance of this aspect. We will consider examples of robustness with some of the problems discussed in later chapters.

3. *Efficiency.* Besides correctness (including robustness) of a program, it is of course important to consider its efficiency. We have already raised a few questions about efficiency in connection with some of the algorithms discussed earlier in this chapter. However, this aspect will be one of our major concerns in later chapters. We will find that this leads to a number of interesting theoretical questions involving the comparison of operation counts for different algorithms, as well as the need for experimental measurements.

4. *Documentation, Maintenance, and Portability.* In mentioning these three topics only very briefly, we do not mean to imply that they are of relatively minor importance. On the contrary, we consider them to be extremely important. However, it is difficult to say much about them in an introductory chapter—except to say that they are important! We cannot expect to provide complete documentation with every program, just as we do not expect a proof of correctness with each program. However, we do expect to state clearly what each program does, and how to use it, and, in the chapters that follow, we will occasionally expand this information so that it will be clear what is needed to document a program fully. One of the purposes of good documentation is to make it easy to maintain a program, that is, to make corrections if they should become necessary, or to make modifications to the program and to its docu-

mentation at the same time, if changes should become desirable or necessary.

Portability is required when a program is intended to be run on different machines, or even under different compilers on the same machine. Inevitably there are differences between machines, or between compilers, and even small differences may cause a program that runs well in one situation to run quite differently, or even to fail altogether, in another.

Portability is a difficult problem to deal with in a text such as this, because it can depend so critically on what are often relatively minor details of programming language implementations. As much as possible, we will try to avoid difficulties that arise in transporting programs from one machine to another by using only standard programming conventions, and by pointing out where necessary any machine-dependent features that exist in our programs. We realize that this still leaves many difficulties unresolved, but we feel that we should mention the problem and at least take the modest precautions just indicated.

In any event, both the maintenance and portability of a program are of considerable practical importance. Programs are valuable. A substantial intellectual and financial investment is required for the development of a major program.

Answers to Selected Questions in Part I

CHAPTER 1

Exercise 1.1

1. Other examples of everyday procedures include the following:

    a) instructions for assembling a piece of furniture from parts supplied by the manufacturer,
    b) instructions for knitting a sweater,
    c) steps taken in getting ready for a party,
    d) steps to be followed in multiplying two numbers together,
    e) actions to be taken in carrying out a calculation with the aid of a hand calculator,
    f) trying all possibilities in a certain puzzle to see if the puzzle has a solution.

Examples (d) and (e) would appear to satisfy the requirements of an algorithm. So would (f) if there were only a finite number of possibilities to be tried and we were sure we had a systematic way of trying them all without missing any of them; it would still be considered an algorithm even if the number of possibilities was so large that it was impractical to consider this method of solution.

2. The greatest common divisor of 210 and 154 must be less than or equal to 154. One way to show that 14 is the greatest common divisor would therefore be simply to try all the other possibilities between 15 and 154 inclusive. This would be a valid approach, but of course it would be very tedious. It would be much faster to notice that, since 14 is a divisor of both 210 and 154, then the greatest common divisor must be a multiple of 14; we need therefore try only the multiples of 14 that are between 15 and 154 inclusive. Perhaps the process can be speeded up still further.

3. Assume that A and B have already been interchanged if necessary so that $A \leq B$, and suppose that Q is the quotient when B is divided by A. Then

$$B = Q \times A + R.$$

It can be seen from this equation that any common divisor of B and A must be a divisor of R, and similarly that any common divisor of A and R must be a divisor of B. Thus the greatest common divisor of A and R must also be the greatest common divisor of B and A. In this way we see that the process described in Euclid's algorithm, of repeatedly replacing B and A with A and R, preserves the greatest common divisor. To complete the proof it is only necessary to see that the process must eventually terminate (the value assigned to A decreases by at least 1 each time), and to see that it produces the greatest common divisor of B and A when it does finally terminate (A divides into B exactly, with a remainder of zero).

4. A more obvious but more tedious way of finding the greatest common divisor of two positive integers is to try the smaller. If it does not divide into both A and B, then try the next smaller integer. If that fails as well, try the next smaller still, then the next, and so on. The process must terminate eventually, since 1 does divide both A and B. The value for which the process terminates is the greatest common divisor. (If the greatest common divisor of two numbers is 1, the numbers are said to be relatively prime.) In most cases any algorithm based on this idea will obviously be much less efficient than Euclid's.

Two somewhat different algorithms based on this idea are shown in the figure (see next page). Notice how the trial divisor D is initially assigned the value of the smaller of A and B, and then later is reduced by 1 after each unsuccessful trial. (D ← D − 1 is interpreted as "D is assigned the value of D reduced by 1.")

The first version shown in the figure is more complicated than the second, but, on the other hand, the first would usually require fewer divisions and comparisons and therefore be more efficient.

5. One way to search $a_i, a_{i+1}, \ldots, a_n$ for the smallest is as follows. Suppose that s is going to denote the smallest and k its subscript. Start the process by tentatively assigning the value of a_i to s, and the value of i to k. Of course, if $i \nless n$, the process is finished. Otherwise, s is compared to the next in the sequence a_{i+1}, then to a_{i+2}, etc. After any comparison that shows the value of the "a" is smaller than s, appropriate new values are assigned to both s and k. The figure on the next page gives a flowchart for this process.

6. Try some simple examples, including some with negative values and also some duplicates. For example, try 2, −3, 2, 3.14.

7. The proof can be divided into two stages. First convince yourself that the algorithm described in Fig. 1.6 does what it is supposed to do. Then show that the "Search" part described in the answer to Question 5 works properly. Be sure to check that the algorithm is correct when $n = 1$ or 2; special cases like these are often the ones for which poorly designed algorithms break down. If the algorithm is correct for all values of n, including $n = 1$ and 2, then there are no restrictions on what arrays can be handled.

8. A number of equivalent sorting algorithms will be considered in Section 12.2. The algorithm described in Section 1.1 requires approximately $n^2/2$ comparisons to sort n numbers. Some of the algorithms described in the later section can require as few as $n \log_2 n$ comparisons to do the same task. (Note that $n \log_2 n$ is much smaller than $n^2/2$ when n is large; for example, when $n = 1000$ their ratio is only .02.)

9. There are many different algorithms for determining whether or not a number is a prime. One obvious way to

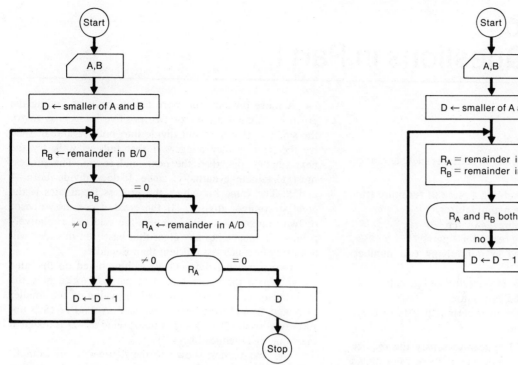

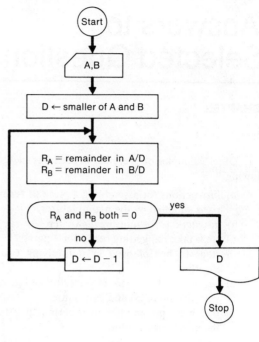

Figure accompanying answer to Question 4 of Exercise 1.1.

speed up the algorithm described in this question would be to divide in turn by each of the odd integers less than or equal to $N^{1/2}$, since there is no need to try those greater than $N^{1/2}$ as well. This reduces the maximum number of divisions to approximately $N^{1/2}/2$, which is much less than $N/2$ if N is large. The domain in either case is the set of positive integers, and the range consists of the two possible outputs, namely "yes" and "no." (What can go wrong if N is not tested initially to see if it is 1, 2, or 3?)

Exercise 1.3

1. The algorithms given in the answer to Question 4 of Exercise 1.1 can be described along the lines outlined in this section as follows:

```
Input A and B
D = smaller of A and B
Loop
.    R_B = remainder in B/D
.    If (R_B = 0)
.            R_A = remainder in A/D
.......If (R_A = 0) exit loop
.    End if
.    D = D − 1
End loop
Output D
Stop

Input A and B
D = smaller of A and B
Loop
      R_A = remainder in A/D
      R_B = remainder in B/D
...If (R_A = 0 and R_B = 0) exit loop
      D = D − 1
End loop
Output D
Stop
```

Figure accompanying answer to Question 5 of Exercise 1.1. When completed, a_k is the smallest of $a_i, a_{i+1} \ldots, a_n$.

A variation on the second of these is as follows:

```
Input A and B
D = smaller of A and B
R_A = remainder in A/D
R_B = remainder in B/D
Loop while (R_A and R_B are not both 0)
    D = D − 1
    R_A = remainder in A/D
    R_B = remainder in B/D
End loop
Output D
Stop
```

Notice that the need for an "exit" disappeared, but that the statements about the computation of R_A and R_B have had to be repeated. Which variation is to be preferred will depend in part on the programming language we intend to use.

2. /S is to be the required sum of $c_1, c_2 \ldots, c_n$/
```
S = 0
Loop for i = 1, 2, . . . , n
    S = S + c_i
End loop
```

3. a) Where "Interchange A and B, if necessary,
    .   so that A ≤ B" means
    .   /In the following T is used as a
    .   "temporary" variable to retain the
    .   value of B while B is assigned the
    .   value of A/
    .   If (A > B)
    .   T = B
    .   B = A
    .   A = T
    .   End if
    End where

   b) Where "D = smaller of A and B" means
    .   If (A < B)
    .   D = A
    .   else
    .   D = B
    .   End if
    End where

4. /Assume that the matrix components are
    m_{ij} and the vector components are v_i/
```
Loop for i = 1, 2, . . . , n
    p_i = 0
    Loop for j = 1, 2, . . . , n
        p_i = p_i + m_{ij}v_j
    End loop
End loop
Stop
```
/The components of the required product
    are p_i/

5. /Assume that the components of the two
    matrices are a_{ij} and b_{ij}/

```
Loop for i = 1, 2, . . . , n
.     Loop for j = 1, 2, . . . , n
.     .      c_ij = 0
.     .      Loop for k = 1, 2, . . . , n
.     .          c_ij = c_ij + a_ik b_kj
.     .      End
.     End
End
Stop
```
/The components of the required
        product are c_{ij}/

6. /Assume that the components of the
        matrix are a_{ij}/
```
Loop for i = 1, 2, . . . , 100
    Loop for j = 1, 2, . . . , 100
        If (a_ij = 0)
            Output i, j
. . . . . . . . . .Exit outer loop
        End if
    End
End outer loop
Stop
```

With this algorithm, nothing is output if no zero element is found. How would you modify the algorithm so that a message would be output if no zero element is found?

7. Use the same algorithm as in the answer to Question 6, except that the Exit line is omitted.

8. $n_1 = 0$ /n_1 is the count of the number of 1's/
   $n_2 = 0$ /n_2 is the count of the number of 2's/
   $n_3 = 0$ /n_3 is the count of the number of 3's/
   $n = 0$ /n is the count of the total number of
                numbers/
```
Loop
    Input number
    If (number < 0)
. . . . . . . . . .Exit loop
    (number = 1)
        n_1 = n_1 + 1
    (number = 2)
        n_2 = n_2 + 1
    (number = 3)
        n_3 = n_3 + 1
    End if
    n = n + 1
End loop
Output n_1, n_2, n_3, n
Stop
```

Alternatively we could replace the Loop-End with:

```
Input number
Loop while (number ≥ 0)
    If (number = 1)
        n_1 = n_1 + 1
    (number = 2)
        n_2 = n_2 + 1
    (number = 3)
        n_3 = n_3 + 1
```

```
        End if
        n = n + 1
        Input number
    End loop
```

Note once again that the need for an "exit" has been avoided, but it was necessary to repeat the input statement.

9. The algorithm can be exactly the same as the one for Question 8, except that

```
    Loop
```

is replaced by

```
    Loop for i = 1, 2, ..., 100
```

10.
```
    Loop
        Input KWH
        If (KWH < 0)
........Exit loop
        (KWH < 100)
            Cost=10×KWH
        (KWH < 200)
            Cost=10×100+6×(KWH−100)
        (KWH < 400)
            Cost=10×100+6×100+8×(KWH−200)
        else
            Cost=10×100+6×100+8×200
                            +10×(KWH−400)
        End if
        Output KWH, Cost
    End loop
    Stop
```

It would be a nuisance to modify such an algorithm if the rates had to be changed. Can you suggest ways in which such modifications could be made relatively easy?

The correctness of the pseudo-code solution given above depends critically on the assumption that the alternatives are tested in order. Thus, for example, the alternative KWH < 200 cannot be reached unless KWH ≥ 100. For greater clarity it might therefore be better to rewrite the alternatives so that such implied conditions are made explicit. The alternative (KWH < 200) could be replaced by (100 ≤ KWH < 200), and the others changed in a similar way.

11.
```
    Input x
    f = 0   /This indicates that x has not yet been
                    found in the table./
    Loop for i = 1, 2, ..., n
        If (x = aᵢ)
            Output bᵢ
            f = 1
.......Exit loop
        End if
    End loop
    If (f = 0)
        Output x and the phrase "is not in table"
    End if
    Stop
```

Alternatively we could use:

```
    Input x
    Loop for i = 1, 2, ..., n or until FOUND
...If (x = aᵢ) exit because of FOUND
    End loop
    If (FOUND)
            Output bᵢ
        else
            Output x and the phrase "is not in table"
    End if
    Stop
```

12.
```
    Loop
        Input x
...Exit if (x = 0)
        f = 0
        Loop for i = 1, 2, ..., n
            If (x = aᵢ)
                Output bᵢ
                f = 1
........Exit inner loop
            End if
        End inner loop
        If (f = 0)
            Output x and the phrase "is not in table"
        End if
    End
    Stop
```

13.
```
    nᵢₙ = 0     /nᵢₙ are in the table/
    nₒᵤₜ = 0    /nₒᵤₜ are not in the table/
    Loop
        Input x
...  Exit if (x < 0)
        Set f = 1 if x in table, otherwise 0
        If (f = 1)
                nᵢₙ = nᵢₙ + 1
            (f = 0)
                nₒᵤₜ = nₒᵤₜ + 1
        End if
    End loop
    Output nᵢₙ  and phrase "are in the table"
            nₒᵤₜ and phrase "are not in the table"
    Stop

    Where "Set f = 1, etc." means
        f = 0
        Loop for i = 1, 2, ..., n
            If (x = aᵢ)
                    f = 1
........Exit loop
            End if
        End loop
    End where
```

14. For example, see Questions 2 and 4 of Exercise 12.2.

15. Input N
   If (N = 1)
        Output "Not a prime"
     (N = 2 or 3)
        Output "Is a prime"
     (2 divides N)
        Output "Not a prime"
     else
        D = 3
        Loop while (D $\leq$ N$^{1/2}$)
           If (D divides N)
               Output "Not a prime"
. . . . .Exit outer if
           End if
           D = D + 2
        End loop
        Output "Is a prime"
   End outer if
   Stop

Exercise 1.4

1. /We use a major part of the algorithm described
       in the answer to Question 3 of Exercise 1.3/
  Input N
  If (2 divides N)
      L = "false"
    else
      D = 3
      Loop while (D $\leq$ N$^{1/2}$)
         If (D divides N)
            L = "false"
. . . . .Exit outer if
         End if
         D = D + 2
      End loop
      L = "true"
  End outer if
  Stop

2. L = "false"
  Loop for i = 1, 2, . . . , n
     If (x = a$_i$)
        L = "true"
. . . . . . .Exit loop
     End if
  End loop
  Stop

3. Loop for i = 1, 2, . . . , n
     Loop for j = 1, 2, . . . , n
        If (a$_{ij}$ = 1)
           b$_{ij}$ = "true"
         (a$_{ij}$ = 0)
           b$_{ij}$ = "false"
        End if
     End loop
  End loop
  Stop

/The elements of the corresponding boolean
            matrix are b$_{ij}$/
/To convert from the form in Fig. 1.14(b) to 1.14(c),
    assume the edges are given as pairs c$_k$, d$_k$,
    for k = 1, 2, . . . , m/
/First set all the entries in a$_{ij}$ to 0/
Loop for i = 1, 2, . . . , n
    Loop for j = 1, 2, . . . , n
       a$_{ij}$ = 0
    End
End
/Now change to 1 those entries that correspond to
    values of c$_k$, d$_k$. Two entries must be changed
    for each such pair./
Loop for k = 1, 2, . . . , m
    a$_{c_k d_k}$ = 1
    a$_{d_k c_k}$ = 1
End
Stop

The converse is straightforward; the matrix is searched
and the subscripts are output for each nonzero entry.

4.

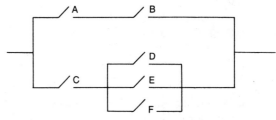

represents the expression A and (B or C)

represents (A and B) or (C and (D or E or F))

    The first is open, but the second is closed under the
circumstances stated in the question.

5. /Assume that records are input in order, with an
       end-of-file signal following the last record/
  Count = 0   /This is to be the required number/
  Loop
       Read next record, or end-of-file signal
       If (end-of-file signal)
. . . . .Exit loop
       (male, and in 30's, with income between
             $20,000 and $30,000)
          Count = Count +1
       End if
  End loop
  Output Count
  Stop

Alternatively, we could use

```
Count = 0
Read next record, or end-of-file signal
Loop while (not end-of-file signal)
        If (male, in 30's, etc.) Count = Count + 1
        Read next record, or end-of-file signal
End of loop
Output Count
Stop
```

Note that this form avoids the use of an "exit," but it is necessary to have two "Read" statements.

6. /Suppose the array of characters is c_i, $i = 1, 2, \ldots, n$ and the subarray is s_i, $i = 1, 2, \ldots, k$, where $k \le n$. The idea of the algorithm is to search $c_1, c_2, \ldots, c_{n-k+1}$ for a match with s_1 and then compare subsequent values of c_i with s_2, s_3, etc. (if any). If a successful match for the substring is not found, the subsequent values of c_i are searched for the next successful match with s_1, and so on/

```
Loop for i = 1, 2, ..., n - k + 1
        If (c_i = s_1)
                flag = "true"
                If rest of subarray, if any, does not match,
                                set flag = "false"
........Exit loop if (flag = "true")
        End if
End loop
If (flag = "true")
                Output "yes"
        (flag = "false")
                Output "no"
End if
Stop
```

```
Where "If rest of subarray, etc." means
.       Loop for j = i + 1, i + 2, ..., i + k - 1
.       .       If (a_j ≠ s_{j-i+1})
.       .               flag = "false"
.       ..........Exit loop
.       .       End if
.       End loop
End where
```

It would be necessary to save the input values obtained after a match of s_1, in case the subsequent comparisons fail to produce a successful match of s_2, s_3, etc., and it is necessary to look for a new match of s_1.

7. /Plan is to have a counter that is initially set to zero, and that is increased by 1 for every left parenthesis encountered as the array is read, but decreased by 1 for every right parenthesis. If the counter ever becomes negative, or if it is not zero at the end, the parentheses are not properly balanced. Suppose the characters are $c_1, c_2, \ldots, c_n$/

```
Counter = 0
Loop for i = 1, 2, ..., n
        If (c_i is left parenthesis)
                Counter = Counter + 1
        (c_i is right parenthesis)
                Counter = Counter - 1
        End if
...Exit if (Counter < 0)
End
If (Counter ≠ 0)
        Parentheses not properly balanced
else
        Parentheses are O.K.
End if
Stop
```

8. /Push character onto stack. Suppose stack is s_1, $s_2, \ldots$, and pointer is i/

```
Where "Push object onto stack" means
        i = i + 1
        s_i = "object"
End where
```

/Pop object from stack 3. Suppose stack is $s3_1$, $s3_2, \ldots$, and pointer is i3. Also, suppose we want to have flag f3 set to "false" as indication that stack was empty/

```
Where "Pop object from stack, etc." means
        If (i3 = 0)
                f3 = "false"
        else
                "object" = s3_i
                i = i - 1
        End if
End where
```

9. /We use refinements like those of Question 8/

```
Flag = "true"
Loop for i = 1, 2, ..., n
        Input character
        If (character is left parenthesis)
                Push character onto stack
        (character is right parenthesis)
                Pop top of stack
.........Exit loop if (flag = "false")
        End if
End loop
If (flag = "true" and stack is empty)
        Parentheses are balanced
else
        They are not
End if
Stop
```

10. /Suppose a tridiagonal matrix is represented by three arrays l, d, u as in the following:

$$
\begin{array}{cccccc}
d_1 & u_1 & & & & \\
l_2 & d_2 & u_2 & & & \\
& l_2 & d_3 & & & \\
& & & \cdot & & \\
& & & & \cdot & u_{n-1} \\
& & & & l_{n-1} & d_n
\end{array}
$$

where d is for "diagonal," u for "upper" and *l*
   for "lower"./
/An algorithm for adding the matrices represented
   by *l*1, d1, u1 and *l*2, d2, u2 is as follows/
Loop for i = 1, 2, .., n − 1
   $l3_i = l1_i + l2_i$
   $d3_i = d1_i + d2_i$
   $u3_i = u1_i + u2_i$
End loop
$d3_n = d1_n + d2_n$
Stop
/The matrix represented by *l*3, d3, u3 is the
   required sum/

Another way of representing a tridiagonal matrix is
to use a matrix of columns, say *M*. In this case *M* would
have 3 rows and *n* columns, each column consisting of the
3 nonzero entries of the corresponding column of the tridiagonal matrix, except that the first and last columns
would of course have only 2 nonzero entries.

The product of two tridiagonal matrices is a penta-
diagonal matrix, i.e., a matrix with (i, j)th entries that are
nonzero only when $j = i$, $i \pm 1$, $i \pm 2$. An algorithm for
finding the product of two tridiagonal matrices would be
quite difficult to read if special ways of representing the
matrices are used, such as the two mentioned above. The
only advantage in using such special forms would be in not
having to represent all the zero elements, and this would
be helpful in conserving space in the memory of a computer.

11. a) The items in a queue can easily be stored in an
      array. The difficulty that arises is that items are re-
      moved from one end and added at the other, so
      that the queue could "move along" the array, and
      perhaps require an enormously long array unless
      some corrective action is taken. One way around
      the difficulty is to limit the length of the array, but
      have the queue start reusing the elements at the
      beginning of the array once they have reached the
      end. We can think of the array as "circular," the
      last element being followed by the first.
    b) A linked list can quite easily represent a queue. It
      would be helpful if there were two pointers, one for
      the head of the queue and another for its tail.

Algorithms for both (a) and (b) are discussed in some
detail in Section 10.3.

12. One way to represent a deque would be with a "doubly
linked" list, i.e., a linked list in which each element has
two pointers, one to point forward to the next item in the
list, and a second one to point back to the preceding item
in the list. As with a queue, it would also be convenient to
have two other special pointers, separate from the linked
list itself, one to mark the head and another to mark the
tail of the deque.

13. f = "true"
   Loop for i = 1, 2, . . . , n
      If (x = a_i)
         f = "false"
   . . . . Exit loop
      End if
   End loop
   If (f = "true") a_{n+1} = x
   Stop

If the a's are already sorted it is possible to speed up
the search when n is reasonably large. (See Section 12.2)

To delete x it would be much simpler to have the a's
represented by a linked list. Otherwise, the a's beyond the
one that is deleted would all have to be shifted back one
place.

14. As an example, suppose that we are provided with a
file of records organized as a linked list, as shown in Fig.
1.18, and that another linked list of available components
is also provided. For insertion, we can suppose that a new
record has been copied into the first location in the available list. To insert this new record into the file, we have to
first find the appropriate place in the file and then change
the values of a number of pointers. This is outlined as
follows:

   Find location in file where record is to be inserted,
      and suppose it follows record x
   Change pointers

   Where by "change pointers" we mean
      Assign to temporary-location value of pointer-
         to-available-list
      Assign to pointer-to-available-list value of
         pointer-in-new-record
      Assign to pointer-in-new-record value of
         pointer-in-record-x
      Assign to pointer-in-record-x value of
         temporary-location
   End where

Note that we must be careful about the order in which the
values of the pointers are updated. The situation is analogous to what is required when we refine the statement "interchange *A* and *B*, if necessary . . ." except that, in this
situation, there are three values to be changed.

In practice it is important to include some additional
tests to ensure that the algorithm does something sensible
when special situations arise. For example, it is necessary
to consider what is required when the new record is to be
inserted at the beginning of the file. It is also necessary to
decide what should be done when an appropriate place to
insert the new record cannot be found.

An algorithm for deletion, using the assumptions noted
above, can be described in an analogous way. Again, it is
important to consider special situations, such as being un-
able to find the record to be deleted.

It would be altogether inconvenient to have an unambiguous language, and, therefore, mercifully, we have not got one.
Bertrand Russell

CHAPTER 2

Programming in Basic

In Chapter 1, we introduced several ways in which algorithms could be described. We also indicated our choice of a notation in the form of a pseudo-code. In order that an algorithm be carried out by a computer, it is necessary to describe the algorithm in a particular programming language for the machine being used. The purpose of this chapter is to provide an overview of programming in Basic. Some of the main rules of Basic programming are also introduced.

The Basic programming language was originally designed for use on a computer system that supports *interactive* computing, although there are a few versions of Basic that do not require interactive facilities. There is no standard Basic language and the reader must therefore expect to find differences among various versions of the language. We will usually restrict our attention to the original Basic that was developed at Dartmouth College and, when appropriate, mention extensions that may be useful if such features are available in the particular version being used by the reader.

Programs written in the Basic language may be executed by a computer in two main ways. One common way is for the Basic program to be handled by an *interpreter,* which is a program that causes the computer to imitate a computer that "understands" the Basic language. Interpreters are considered in Chapter 14. An alternative way is for the Basic program to be handled by a *compiler*. With this alternative method, the Basic program is translated into a machine language program by a Basic compiler. If the statements in the program satisfy the rules of Basic, the interpreter or compiler is able to carry out its task successfully. Usually, the computer will then be directed to execute the program, although the computer can be directed to perform other tasks, such as entering the program into a library of programs for use at some later point in time. If the statements in the program do not satisfy the rules of Basic, the interpreter or compiler will cause error messages to be printed. These *diagnostics* are intended to help the programmer locate and correct the errors. The portions of the program containing the errors can be corrected and the corrections entered into the computer. This process is repeated until the desired results are obtained.

2.1 EXAMPLES OF BASIC PROGRAMS

In this section, we provide a few simple examples of programs written in Basic to introduce some features of the language and also give an overview of programming in Basic. More details of how algorithms, once they have been described in the pseudo-code of Chapter 1, can be rendered in Basic are provided later. A summary of Basic is also provided following Chapter 7; it should be referred to as necessary for additional details.

Each Basic statement is usually typed on a special typewriter or display device called a *terminal* that is connected to the computer. If input to the computer is by some other means, the change in terminology is easy to make. For example, the first position of a line being typed on a typewriter becomes the first column of a punched card, and so on.

An example of a Basic program is shown in Fig. 2.1. This simple program, which finds the sum of two numbers, is used to illustrate some features of the Basic language. Each line of the program consists of a statement number followed by a statement. The first statement indicates that two numbers are to be input and their values assigned to the variables A and B. The second statement provides some sample data values to be input. The third statement indicates that the sum of the values of A and B is to be computed and the result assigned to the variable C. The fourth statement indicates that the values of A, B, and C are to be output. The last statement indicates that this program is completed and the computer can therefore go on with some other task.

Each statement number must be a positive integer. The statements are executed one at a time in order of increasing statement number. Because we may wish to insert additional statements into a program at some later point in time, we will usually number the statements in increments of 10; this allows flexibility for subsequent modification in our programs.

With the input and output statements illustrated in Fig. 2.1, a list of variable names, separated by commas, is provided following READ or PRINT. In Basic, each variable name must consist of a letter, as in this example, or a letter followed by a digit, such as A1, A2, etc. Note in this example that we have caused the values that were input, as well as the sum, to be output. This will be convenient when we are checking the results to determine whether or not our program is correct. Other examples of input and output statements are

```
10 READ A4
15 PRINT X, Y2, 2
20 PRINT "THE RESULT IS", Z
```

The second example above shows how a numerical value can be output (2, in this case), along with values of variables. The third example shows how alphabetic

```
10 READ A, B
15 DATA 12345, −222
20 LET C = A + B
30 PRINT A, B, C
40 END
```

FIG. 2.1 A Basic program for finding the sum of two numbers. The numbers 12345 and −222 are used only for illustration; any two numbers could have been used.

information can be output, as well as the value of a variable; such information is enclosed within quotation marks. It is often convenient to include some such identifying information with the values that are output. It may also be that the desired output consists entirely of a printed message without any accompanying numerical values, as in

```
40 PRINT "THE LINES ARE PARALLEL"
```

With the program in Fig. 2.1, the data values to be used when the program is executed are provided by a DATA statement, which contains a list of values, separated by commas. In this example, the value 12345 will be read and assigned to the variable A and the value −222 will be read and assigned to the variable B when the program is executed. This illustrates that, when a READ statement is executed, data values are taken from the list provided in a DATA statement and assigned to the specified variables in the specified order.

Two or more DATA statements following one another may be used to provide a single list of values. Thus,

```
15 DATA 12345
16 DATA −222
```

would have the same effect as the single statement given in Fig. 2.1. The statement

```
15 DATA 12345, −222, 17, 45
```

would also have the same effect, at least in this example, since the superfluous data items would simply be ignored by most systems.

Other examples of DATA statements are

```
25 DATA 1, 2, 3., 4.6
30 DATA 6.7, −4.5, −1236
```

The numbers may be written as integers (with or without a decimal point), or decimal fractions; the last data value in each statement is not followed by a comma. DATA statements may appear anywhere in a Basic program; for convenience, they may be placed immediately following the READ statement, or they may be placed near the end of the program, just prior to the END statement.

It is also possible to have the data values for a program provided by the user from the terminal device, by using an INPUT statement. We will illustrate this later; such statements are also discussed in Chapter 7. In most of our examples, we will use READ and DATA statements to supply the input to programs.

The assignment statement used in Fig. 2.1 indicates that the sum of two values is to be assigned to a variable. The variable to which the value is assigned is given following LET and preceding the equals sign. For statements involving other arithmetic operations, the three symbols **–**, *****, and **/** are used to represent subtraction, multiplication, and division, respectively. The results obtained with these four arithmetic operators are, generally speaking, what we expect, although the results may be only approximations, because of roundoff error. (See Section A.5.) Parentheses may also be used in the usual mathematical way. Other examples of assignment statements are

```
15 LET A = 3*B - K2
20 LET M = (N-M)/3 + 2.5
25 LET X = X + 1
```

The third statement indicates that the value of X is to be increased by 1.

To run the program given in Fig. 2.1 on a computer, we first have to LOGON to the computer system. The way in which this is done depends on the computing facility being used and the reader must become familiar with the requirements at his or her particular installation. A sample interactive session is given in Fig. 2.2, where items printed by the computer have been identified with dagger symbols in the left-hand column. The other lines are typed into the computer by the user. The end of each such line is determined by pressing the RETURN key on the keyboard.

After a LOGON sequence, which usually requires a name (in this example, we have used STUDENT) and a password (the latter is typed in, but is usually not printed for security reasons), the computer replies READY. At this point NEW, SAMPLE is typed, indicating that a new

program is about to be entered and that its name is SAMPLE. Now the program can be typed, as shown. At any point, we can type LIST to obtain a listing of the program as it is currently stored in the computer. When RUN is typed, the computer proceeds to execute the program, and the output specified by the PRINT statement is printed. Finally, we terminate the session by logging off (LOGOFF).

In an interactive terminal session the program is stored inside the computer as it is typed so it can be listed or run at any time, using *system commands* such as those illustrated in Fig. 2.2. It can be saved as well (using a SAVE command) for use during a subsequent session, if so desired.

It is also possible to make changes to the program whenever we wish. Suppose, for example, that prior to logging off we decide to change the program of Fig. 2.2 so that it finds and outputs the product of the numbers as well as the sum. This may be accomplished by typing the two lines

```
25 LET D = A*B
30 PRINT A, B, C, D
```

The additional statement, numbered 25, will be inserted between statements 20 and 30, and the new statement 30 replaces the old one with that statement number. (An existing statement can be deleted by simply typing the statement number.) Thus, it is seen that programs can be modified easily when an interactive system is being used. The result of listing and running the program at this point is illustrated in Fig. 2.3.

```
†   BASIC ONLINE
    LOGON STUDENT                          ⎫
†   ENTER PASSWORD:                         ⎬  Logon procedure
†   READY                                  ⎭

    NEW, SAMPLE                            ⎰ User announces new
    10 READ A, B                           ⎱ program named SAMPLE
    15 DATA 12345, -222                    ⎫
    20 LET C = A + B                       ⎬  User types in the
    30 PRINT A, B, C                       ⎪  program
    40 END                                 ⎭
    LIST                                      User requests a listing

†   SAMPLE                                 ⎫
†   10 READ A, B                           ⎪
†   15 DATA 12345, -222                    ⎬  Computer provides a
†   20 LET C = A + B                       ⎪  listing of the program,
†   30 PRINT A, B, C                       ⎪  as requested
†   40 END                                 ⎭

†   READY
    RUN                                       User requests a run
†     12345        -222        12123         Results specified by
                                              PRINT statement
†   READY
    LOGOFF                                    Logoff procedure
```

FIG. 2.2 A sample interactive Basic session. The lines preceded by † were printed by the computer. The † has been used in the figure only to identify these lines; it does not appear in practice.

```
10 READ A, B
15 DATA 12345, -222
20 LET C = A + B
25 LET D = A*B
30 PRINT A, B, C, D
40 END


READY
RUN
  12345         -222          12123         -2740590
```

FIG. 2.3 The program in Fig. 2.2 has been changed to find the sum and product of two numbers.

```
10 READ A, B
15 DATA 23, 18
20 PRINT A, B
30 IF A>B THEN 60
40      PRINT "THE LARGEST IS", B
50      GO TO 80
60   REM
70      PRINT "THE LARGEST IS", A
80   REM
90 END
```

FIG. 2.4 A Basic program that finds and outputs the larger of two numbers. We use the numbers 23 and 18 for illustration.

One additional feature that could be considered for our programs at this stage is the possibility of inserting comments into a Basic program to help identify the purpose of the program. In other instances, it is useful to use comments to make more complicated portions of a program easier to understand for anyone who is reading it. Comments are written in the form

s REM *comment*

where *s* is a statement number. Except for listing such lines, the computer ignores them. Comments should not be overused in a program, as in

```
35 REM ADD 1 TO K
40 LET K = K + 1
```

since such a comment is clearly redundant and only lengthens the program listing.

A third example of a Basic program is given in Fig. 2.4. This example is a program that finds the maximum of two numbers. For checking purposes, we have once again caused the input values to be output. Several new features are illustrated in this example. The third statement in the program indicates that if the value of A is greater than the value of B, the next statement to be executed is the one with statement number 60; otherwise, the statement following the IF statement, 40 in this example, is to be executed. This is illustrative of how the usual sequential flow of control in a Basic program can be altered. A second control statement

```
50      GO TO 80
```

is used in the program in Fig. 2.4. This statement unconditionally directs that the next statement to be executed is the one with statement number 80. As noted earlier, the REM statements are comments. As illustrated here, they can also be used to mark places in the program to which the flow of control may be directed.

Finally, it should be noted that, in two instances, a group of one or more statements has been indented. In this example, the alternative statements to be executed are displayed more clearly by being indented, as was the case with our pseudo-code notation in Chapter 1. The

spaces preceding the indented statements are ignored. Unfortunately, with some systems, these spaces do not appear when we LIST the program.

The IF statement that was used in the example above indicates that control is to be transferred to statement 60 if the value of A is greater than the value of B. The relational operators that may be used in such statements are given in the summary. Other examples of IF statements that may be used to direct the flow of control are:

```
35 IF I = 5 THEN 20
47 IF A*C - B*D = X THEN 10
90 IF 3*(I+J)<N THEN 110
```

The program in Fig. 2.4 requires some data values to be input. These are supplied using the statement

```
15 DATA 23, 18
```

As indicated earlier, such statements can appear at any point in a program.

We mentioned earlier that it is also possible to have the data values for a program provided by the user from a terminal device. This is illustrated in Fig. 2.5. The program for finding the maximum of two numbers has been changed to illustrate this alternative way of supplying input to programs. In the program in Fig. 2.5, the first statement causes a message to be output. The second statement causes a question mark to be output, and the computer waits for the user to type in two numbers. When an INPUT statement is used, a DATA statement is not required, since the input is supplied directly from the terminal device. We have shown the program being run twice in Fig. 2.5.

In Figs. 2.4 and 2.5 we have illustrated two methods that can be used to supply input to our programs. The READ input statement requires data to be supplied in a DATA statement, whereas the INPUT input statement requires the data to be typed on a terminal when the program is being executed. We will usually use the former method, although either method can be used. Further details are given in Chapter 7.

In the many different versions of Basic, some of the rules about the language depend on special circum-

```
            LIST

            MAX
            10 PRINT "GIVE TWO NUMBERS"
            20 INPUT A, B
            30 IF A>B THEN 60
            40      PRINT "THE LARGEST IS", B
            50      GO TO 80
            60   REM
            70      PRINT "THE LARGEST IS", A
            80 REM
            90 END

            READY
            RUN
            GIVE TWO NUMBERS
            ? 23, 18
            THE LARGEST IS   23

            READY
            RUN
            GIVE TWO NUMBERS
            ? 9, 13
            THE LARGEST IS   13

            READY
```

FIG. 2.5 Finding the maximum of two numbers with input from a terminal device.

stances, and may vary from one installation to another. One example is the maximum value of statement numbers. Often, the largest value that can appear is 9999, but some versions require that statement numbers be less than some other value, which may be larger or smaller than this number. The reader must be familiar with the particulars of the version of Basic to be used.

EXERCISE 2.1

1. Each of the following is not a correct statement in the Basic language. Give a reason in each case.

a)   10 READ I, J.
b)   20 LET A + 1 = A
c)   30 PRINT, X1, Y2, Z3
d)   40 LET B = 2(X + Y)
e)   50 GO TO TEN
f)   60 IF X>=Y THEN Y < X
g)   70 LET I = J * (6.2 + L*(K + M − 4.5)
h)   80 PRINT "THE ANSWER IS, A
i)   90 IF A6 > B3 THEN 60.5
j)   100 DATA 12.62, −17, 3/4, 10.
k)   110 THE END

2. Suppose that the statement

10 READ A, B, C

is to be executed. Give a table of values that are read and assigned to the variables for each of the following.

a)   15 DATA 6, 3, 7
b)   20 DATA 8, −7, −6, −5
c)   25 DATA −1
     27 DATA 3, −8

3. How would you modify the program in Fig. 2.1 to find the product of three numbers?

4. Refer to the Basic program given in Fig. 2.4. Follow through the program to determine what happens when the input is 6, 3. Do the same for the input 3, 6. What happens when the two input numbers are equal? Does the program work when the input numbers are negative? What would happen if the statement

50   GO TO 80

were inadvertently omitted from the program?

5. Study the portion of an interactive session given in Fig. 2.6.

a)   Give a listing of the program that would be obtained if LIST were typed in following the entry of the last line given in Fig. 2.6.
b)   What does the program do?
c)   Compare the answer to (a) with the program given in Fig. 2.4. Is one program better than the other? Why?

Determine the exact nature of the LOGON *procedure that is required at the computer installation that you are planning to use. Then, after attempting some of Questions 6–12, select one program and have the program run on the computer you are using.*

6. Write a program that will input four numbers and that will find and output their sum and the sum of their squares.

7. Give a program that will input one number and assign it to the variable *m*, and that will then find and output the value of the polynomial

$$3m^4 + 7m^3 − m^2 − 5m + 13.$$

8. Give programs for finding each of the following:

a)   the absolute value of a number,
b)   the largest of three numbers,
c)   the smallest of three numbers.

9. Write a program that will input the values of four numbers *a*, *b*, *c*, and *d*, and output YES or NO depending on whether $a/b = c/d$, or not. Make sure that your program does something sensible if either *b* or *d* is zero.

10. Construct a program for adding two fractions. It should input the values of four integers *a*, *b*, *c*, and *d*, and find and output the values of two integers *x* and *y* such that $a/b + c/d = x/y$.

```
            10 READ A, B, M
            20 LET M = A
            30 IF M>B THEN 60
            40      LET M = B
            60 REM
            70 PRINT M
            80 END
            15 PRINT A, B
            10 READ A, B
            12 DATA 6, 10
```

FIG. 2.6 A portion of an interactive session. See Question 5 in Exercise 2.2.

11. Construct a program that will input three numbers and then output YES or NO, depending on whether or not the three numbers can be the lengths of the sides of a triangle. Be sure that your algorithm works for any three numbers, even if some of the numbers are negative.

12. Construct a program that will input six numbers, assign their values to *a*, *b*, *c*, *d*, and *e*, and then output one of the statements

LINES INTERSECT
LINES ARE PARALLEL
LINES ARE COINCIDENT

given that the equations of the lines are

$$ax + by = c,$$
$$dx + ey = f.$$

2.2 REPETITIVE CALCULATIONS

One of the most important aspects of any notation used for describing algorithms is that the flow of control for the algorithm be displayed in an understandable way. The pseudo-code notation introduced in Chapter 1 is intended to serve this purpose. When a programming language is used, we must use the constructs of the particular programming language to describe the flow of control. As we will see, it is fairly straightforward to render repetitive algorithms in Basic once they have been described in the pseudo-code notation of Chapter 1.

To illustrate this idea, we return to our first example of a Basic program. The program for finding the sum of two numbers can be extended easily to find the sum of three numbers, or four numbers. A similar program for finding the sum of 200 numbers is also possible, but a simpler way of solving this problem certainly would be preferable. It would also be better if the algorithm for summing numbers were not restricted to a particular number of numbers, such as 200. An outline of an algorithm, using the notation described in Chapter 1, for finding the sum of any number of numbers is given in Fig. 2.7. It is assumed that the numbers are all nonnegative. Since this is the case, we can use a negative number to signal the end of the data.

In Fig. 2.7, the variable S has been used to represent the sum of the input numbers. Note that S is assigned the value zero at the beginning, after which the

first data value is input and assigned to N. If this number is positive or zero, it is added to the value of S, and control returns to the input statement. This means that the next data value is then input. The value of the second number is assigned to N, and the process is repeated. Eventually the value assigned to N is negative. This signals the end of the input, and control is transferred out of the loop to the statement that outputs the value of S, together with some identifying information.

It is a good idea to test the program on some carefully chosen examples to be sure that it will work properly. A worthwhile procedure is to work through a simple example by hand, using some input that is easy to work out, but that will nevertheless use all parts of the algorithm. For the algorithm described in Fig. 2.7, a sequence of numbers such as 4, 5, 7, and −2 can be used to follow through the procedure. A table of values of all the variables immediately after the input has occurred would appear as shown below.

After input of	Value of N is	Value of S is
4	4	0
5	5	4
7	7	9
−2	−2	16

Since N is negative,
the value 16 is output.

This type of table is called a *checking table,* or a *program trace.* Such tables can often be used to help determine whether or not an algorithm will work properly. Also, when it is known that an algorithm is not working properly, a checking table can often help locate the difficulty, if it contains the values of all the variables at some strategic point in the algorithm.

A Basic program that corresponds to the algorithm outlined in Fig. 2.7 is given in Fig. 2.8. Some comments

```
 10   REM INITIALIZE THE SUM S
 20   LET S = 0
 30   REM LOOP
 40      REM INPUT NEXT NUMBER OF SEQUENCE
 50      READ N
 60   REM...IF(N < 0)EXIT LOOP
 70      IF N < 0 THEN 110
 80      REM OTHERWISE ADD INPUT TO SUM
 90      LET S = S + N
100   GO TO 30
110   REM END LOOP
120   PRINT "THE SUM IS", S
130   DATA 4, 5, 7, −2
140   END
```

FIG 2.8 The algorithm in Fig. 2.7 rendered in Basic. Sample data has been introduced in the statement numbered 130 to make the program complete; it is the data used for the checking table discussed in the text.

```
S = 0
Loop
   Input N
... If(N<0) exit loop
   S = S + N
End loop
Output 'The sum is', S
Stop
```

FIG. 2.7 An outline of an algorithm for finding the sum of any number of nonnegative numbers.

have been used to identify portions of the program. Note how the loop and the exit from the loop have been rendered using statements of the form introduced in the previous section, and that the statements within the loop have been indented to help show the flow of control. Note also that while the Basic program in Fig. 2.8 is described in a way that is suitable for processing on a computer, the details required when the algorithm is rendered in Basic make the algorithm somewhat more difficult to read and to understand.

With the program given in Fig. 2.8, the data values are contained in one DATA statement. Since we are using a negative number to signal the end of the data, we follow the data values whose sum is required with one additional value, a negative number. With the data we have given, the output will appear as follows when the program is run:

```
THE SUM IS      16
```

The use of a checking table and a careful examination of the program will not eliminate the possibility of error. A common way in which further errors may occur is for some rather trivial errors to be present in the details of the Basic statements. For example, a zero may be transcribed as the letter O. Similarly, 1 and I, or 2 and Z, or 5 and S, may be confused. Sometimes a comma is misplaced. To help uncover errors of the kind just described, it is essential that the program be run on a machine with some test data. The data used in the checking table will often be sufficient.

The program just described has an important feature that is characteristic of many useful computer programs. It is repetitive, in that a part of the program is repeated over and over, perhaps hundreds of times. For a relatively small amount of programming we are able to accomplish a large amount of work. The reason computers are so useful is that they can do large amounts of repetitive work very rapidly and very cheaply. On some machines, doing a complicated calculation might require less than one hundredth of a second and cost less than one cent. Using a nonprogrammable hand or desk calculator, a person might require an hour to do the same calculation—several thousand times as long—and the calculation would cost hundreds of times as much. Moreover, the person is much more likely to make mistakes.

We turn now to a second example of a repetitive calculation. Euclid's algorithm was described in Chapter 1. A Basic program that corresponds to the pseudocode description given in Fig. 1.9 is given in Fig. 2.9. As was the case with our earlier example, the exit from the loop has been highlighted by the use of a comment that is consistent with our higher-level notation. Again, comments have been used to help explain other portions

```
5   READ A, B
7   DATA 210, 154
10  REM IF(A>B) INTERCHANGE A, B
15  IF B >= A THEN 35
20      LET T = A
25      LET A = B
30      LET B = T
35  REM
40  REM LOOP
45      REM FIND REMAINDER R IN B/A
50      LET R = B - INT(B/A)*A
55  REM...IF(R=0) EXIT LOOP
60      IF R = 0 THEN 85
65      REM REPLACE B,A BY A,R RESPECTIVELY
70      LET B = A
75      LET A = R
80  GO TO 40
85  REM END LOOP
90  PRINT A
95  END
```

FIG. 2.9 Euclid's algorithm, described earlier in Fig. 1.9, rendered in Basic. The numbers 210 and 154 are used only for illustration; any two positive integers would do as well.

of the program. Note also how the Basic program causes the values of A and B to be interchanged. It was necessary to introduce another variable to store the value of one of the variables temporarily in order to accomplish the desired result.

Euclid's algorithm requires that the remainder be computed each time around the loop. This has been accomplished with the assignment statement

```
50      LET R = B - INT(B/A)*A
```

We mentioned earlier that the result obtained with division is the (perhaps approximate) quotient. The built-in function INT causes the value of INT(B/A) to be the greatest integer less than or equal to B/A. For example, the value of INT(3.6) is 3, while the value of INT(−3.6) would be −4. A few examples will convince the reader that the statement given above will produce the desired result.

In order to ensure that the program is correct, it should be run on a machine. The program should be run with a variety of data values. (See Question 3, Exercise 2.2.) We should also consider the fact that it is unusual for a program to work the first time it is run on a computer; we are usually overly optimistic. A useful idea is to obtain extra output when our programs are run initially. The information obtained can help to uncover errors that we have made. For example, an extra output statement within the loop of the program in Fig. 2.9 could produce information similar to that provided by a checking table. When we know that the program works properly, the extra output statement can be removed. Finally, it is left as an exercise (Question 3) to improve the robustness of the program given in Fig. 2.9.

EXERCISE 2.2

1. What is the effect of replacing the statement

```
70      IF N < 0 THEN 110
```

with the statement

```
70      IF N <= 0 THEN 110
```

in the program of Fig. 2.8?

2. How would you change the program in Fig 2.8 so that both the sum of the numbers and the sum of the squares of the numbers will be found?

3. The program given in Fig. 2.9 for Euclid's algorithm does not contain provision to output the data values that are being input. How can this be accomplished? The program assumes that the two input numbers are positive integers. What changes would you make to the program to ensure that it does something sensible when the data values are negative or zero? What if the values are not integers? What additional changes would you make so that the program will process a sequence of pairs of data values?

In each of the following questions a program is required to solve a certain problem. For at least one of these questions a brief report should be prepared. The report should contain the following information:

a)   Title of report.
b)   Name of author.
c)   Date.
d)   Purpose of program.
e)   Statement of how to use the program, or a statement of what the program has already done, whichever is appropriate.
f)   A description of the algorithm, using the notation of Chapter 1, or perhaps a flowchart.
g)   Description of tests made on the program.
h)   Other comments about the program's limitations, efficiency, accuracy, and so on, if appropriate.
i)   A listing of the program, together with the output. Comments can make the program easier to follow.

(An example of the kind of report that is required is given with the solution to Question 4 in the Answer Section.)

4. Write a Basic program that will find the largest number in a sequence of any number of positive numbers.

5. Repeat Question 4 and find also the position of the largest in the sequence. For example, if the largest number is 59 and it occurs twelfth in the sequence of numbers, the output should be 59 and 12.

6. A hydroelectric company charges 8 cents per kilowatt-hour up to the first 100 kilowatt-hours, and 5 cents thereafter. The number of kilowatt-hours for each customer is given in a sequence of data values. Write a program that will cause the computer to input a data value and then calculate and output the cost in cents, along with the number of kilowatt-hours. It is then to repeat this process with succeeding data values until a negative number is input.

7. Employees of the ABC Company are paid $4.50 per hour up to 40 hours each week and $6.75 per hour for overtime. A program is required to input a sequence of numbers, each one giving the number of hours worked by a particular employee in one week. After each number is input, the computer is to output the number of hours and the amount to be paid. (Assume that the last data value is a negative number.)

8. All transactions in a certain stock have been recorded. There are two numbers for each transaction. The first of the numbers is the number of shares traded in a particular transaction, and the second is the price per share. Write a program that will input such pairs of data values and then output the total number of shares that have been traded, followed by high, low, and closing (or final) prices. Use (0, 0) to mark the end of the sequence.

9. A program is required that will input a sequence of natural numbers and that, for each number, will output the message ODD or EVEN. Assume that the last number in the sequence is followed by a negative integer.

10. A program that will input a natural number and find and output its natural number divisors is required. For example, if the input is 12, the output is 1, 2, 3, 4, 6, 12.

11. Write a program for Question 15, Exercise 1.3.

2.3 FURTHER REMARKS

The name Basic is an acronym for Beginner's All-purpose Symbolic Instruction Code and the Basic language was developed and implemented with two purposes in mind. It was intended to be easy to learn and at the same time relatively inexpensive (compared to other programming languages) to support in an interactive mode. Many different computer installations have the facilities to process programs written in Basic and, as a result, there are many variants of the Basic language. Major differences arise because some versions of Basic contain features that other versions do not have. Some of the minor differences arise because of the peculiarities of the machines being used. The system commands for saving programs and performing other tasks, such as renumbering all statement numbers in a program, also vary from one installation to another, and the reader must determine the particulars for the computing facility being used.

When we use a computer to do something worthwhile, it is important to describe in a convenient way what has been done. The results should be recorded in such a way as to make them easily available to others, or to ourselves at some later date. We need to document what we have done. We have indicated in Exercise 2.2 what we consider the essential information to be included in a report of this type. While no one way of documenting the results of a program is necessarily best in all cases, we should keep in mind that the documentation should be as convenient as possible for other people —or for ourselves at some later date.

To some extent, we have also indicated in this chapter how attention should be paid to the idea of robustness when our algorithms are transcribed into a programming language such as Basic. It is often necessary to include additional tests to ensure that our programs provide meaningful results under all possible conditions.

A number of important aspects of programming, including documentation and robustness, were mentioned in Section 1.5. As indicated there, all of these ideas are important in practice, and perhaps should be reviewed at this time by the reader.

CHAPTER 3

Arithmetic Expressions

An overview of programming in Basic was provided in Chapter 2. We also indicated the steps that must be taken in order to have our programs run on a machine. Some of the details, such as the system commands and the input medium to be used, depend on the installation. Other details, such as how statements are written in Basic, depend mainly on the rules of the Basic language. We now begin a systematic study of the details of the Basic language: how statements in Basic are written, as well as the meaning of the statements.

As we mentioned in Chapter 2, a summary of the rules is given following Chapter 7. The summary should be used for reference purposes whenever necessary.

This chapter is devoted to a discussion of arithmetic expressions in Basic that appear in assignment statements and with IF statements, as we have already seen. Such expressions can appear in other places as well (with output statements, and as function arguments), as we will see later. Besides constants, variables, and simple expressions, we will also introduce the ideas of subscripted variables and functions, in order to complete our discussion of arithmetic expressions.

3.1 SIMPLE ARITHMETIC EXPRESSIONS

In all of the programs considered so far, the data involved has been numerical. For example, in Fig. 2.8 we used the constant 0, the variables S and N to represent numerical values, and the arithmetic expression S + N.

The Basic interpreter or compiler must provide memory locations for constants and variables. The memory locations that are used store numerical values in a way that corresponds to the way in which numbers are written in scientific notation, as in 0.637×10^{17}. The numbers are stored in memory locations in two parts. One part corresponds to the significant digits and the other part represents the position of the decimal point. In this example, the 637 would be stored, as well as the 17. This method of storing numbers is often referred to as *floating-point*. Using this form, it is possible to deal with a wide range of numbers, including fractions. (See Section A.5.)

Constants may appear in a Basic program as numbers with or without decimal points. For example, the following are allowed:

$$0 \qquad 0. \qquad 3.14 \qquad -6.2$$

Besides numbers in these forms, it is also possible to include a decimal exponent, as in

$$.637E\ 17 \qquad 2.5E-7 \qquad -4E6$$

as explained in more detail in the summary.

As we indicated in Chapter 2, a variable name in Basic consists of a letter or a letter followed by a digit. This restriction often makes Basic programs difficult to read, since it is usually more convenient for the reader if more descriptive variable names are used. For example, if the names SUM and NUMBER could be used in the program of Fig. 2.8, it might be easier to interpret the meaning of some of the statements in the program.

One technique that can often be used to help the reader to understand a program is to provide, using a number of comments, a table of the variable names and a description of what each variable represents. For example, we might add the following to Fig. 2.8:

```
5 REM  S REPRESENTS THE SUM
7 REM  N REPRESENTS A NUMBER IN THE SEQUENCE
```

We turn now to a description of *arithmetic expressions*. The simplest examples of arithmetic expressions are constants and variables, examples of which are the following:

$$3 \quad 4.56 \quad -17 \quad 2.1E3 \quad A \quad A2 \quad N6$$

Expressions like these can be combined with arithmetic operators to make more complicated expressions such as

$$A + 3 \quad K6 - N6 \quad 4.56*A2 \quad L/4.56$$

The first two examples illustrate how blanks, or spaces, may be inserted in an expression wherever we wish, without changing its validity. We may use blanks in this way to make the expressions easier to read.

Besides the four operations already introduced, Basic also allows exponentiation; it is usually denoted by ↑, as in the following:

$$J↑3 \quad 2↑17 \quad 9↑16$$

With some versions of Basic, the ↑ must be written as **. This operator is read as "raised to the power of." Thus J↑3 means J raised to the power of 3. In ordinary mathematics we would write this as j^3, but the notation must be changed if our programs are to be typed on one line at a terminal device, or punched on a card.

We can also form more complicated expressions. Combining simpler expressions with any of the five operators and using parentheses in the way they are used in ordinary mathematics produces valid expressions, such as the following:

$$A + 3 + K - N \quad (A + 3)*(K - N)$$
$$A2 - (I + 3) \quad A/(A + 3) \quad J6↑(K - N)$$

This process of combining expressions to give more complicated expressions may be repeated many times. For example, the following is a valid expression in Basic:

$$(I + J + 5)/(23 - 17 * K6) + M*(K5↑(I - J))$$

Two other operators that we can use in forming expressions are the unary operators + and −. They differ from the binary operators + and − in that the unary

operators have only one operand. For example, a unary + appears in each of the following:

$$+(J + 5) \quad +I5 \quad L↑(+I)$$

Similarly, a unary − appears in each of

$$-(J + 5) \quad -K \quad 37*(-J)$$

The only remaining point to explain about combining expressions concerns the use of parentheses. There are two rules to remember. The first is that the order of precedence for the binary operators is as follows:

Top priority: ↑
Next priority: *, **/**
Lowest priority: +, −

This order is the same as it is in mathematics.

In the expression I + J*K the precedence of * is higher than +; as a result, the * operation is performed first. The result is the same as with I + (J*K). The use of parentheses is therefore optional in this case. On the other hand, to have the + operation performed first, we must use parentheses so that the expression appears as (I + J)*K. Similarly, in the expression L/M − N the division is performed first, whereas in the expression L/(M − N) the subtraction is performed first.

The second rule about using parentheses is that they should be used to avoid ambiguities. The exact meaning of this rule depends on the particular interpreter or compiler you are using. For example, some systems do not allow an expression such as I↑J↑K to appear in a Basic program, since this expression can be interpreted as I↑(J↑K) or as (I↑J)↑K. The use of parentheses in this expression is mandatory with such systems.

In many situations, it is possible that an expression will not contain any ambiguity so far as the interpreter or compiler is concerned, but the expression may nevertheless be ambiguous to the human reader. It is therefore a good idea to use parentheses whenever there is any possible doubt. Thus, we should write I↑(J↑K) or (I↑J)↑K, depending on what we want, even if the system does allow I↑J↑K.

Another example in which there may be some ambiguity for the reader is −3↑2, which might be interpreted as (−3)↑2, which is 9, or as −(3↑2), which is −9. If the unary − had top priority, the first interpretation would hold. But it is best to use parentheses to indicate which one of the expressions we want.

One exceptional situation should be avoided. With some systems, two operators should not appear next to each other in an expression. For example, according to the previous rules we could have 3*−5, and this would have to mean the same as 3*(−5), but with other systems we are not allowed to have the two operators beside each other. Only the form 3*(−5) is permissible.

Once again, it is best to use parentheses to avoid any possible difficulties with interpretation.

In addition to knowing the rules concerning how expressions can be written, it is also important to know how these expressions are evaluated on the particular machine being used or with a particular version of Basic. The magnitude of a number is restricted by the machine, as is the number of significant digits that can be stored. Moreover, while the meaning of an arithmetic expression is what we generally expect, there are a few exceptions. One of the most important considerations in the evaluation of expressions concerns roundoff error. The effect of roundoff can often be neglected, but there are many situations in which it is important to know what kinds of errors can occur. First of all, it is important to realize that, when a number is converted to obtain the significant digits, a small error may be introduced in the conversion process. Another possibility is that, in evaluating an expression, the result of a particular calculation may be rounded, or, as is usually the case, the digits that cannot be stored in a storage location are simply discarded, without proper rounding. In this case, the result is said to be chopped. Overflow and underflow, which arise when the result is too large or too small to be stored, may also occur; what happens in such circumstances depends very much on the system and on the machine being used.

More details are given in Section A.5, where we use the SIMON computer as an illustration. In addition, Appendix C contains material on number representations that may be helpful. We postpone a more detailed discussion of roundoff error to Chapter 9. The only circumstance that we have not considered is that which arises when the divisor of a calculation is zero. The result in such a situation depends once again on the particular installation and it is important to know what happens with the particular system being used. One common situation is that division by zero causes an error message to be produced and execution to be terminated.

EXERCISE 3.1

1. Which of the following expressions could be interpreted differently by different interpreters or compilers?

a) I + J + K   b) I + J − K
c) I + J*K   d) I − J/K
e) I*J*K   f) I/J/K
g) I*J/K   h) I/J*K
i) I↑J↑K

2. None of the following expressions is allowed in most versions of Basic. Give the reason in each case.

a) 3(5 + I)   b) KILL/(−3)
c) ((K2 + K3)*K4) − K5)   d) I + J + 3K
e) L6↑−2

3. What are the two basic rules concerning the use of parentheses in Basic expressions? What exceptional situation should be avoided?

4. What is the value of each of the following Basic expressions?

a) 5 − 9 + 4.   b) 5. − (9 + 4)
c) 6*(4/3)   d) (6*4)/3
e) (2↑3)↑2   f) 2↑(3↑2)
g) 1/9.0E0
h) (13 + (2*3) − 4)/(2 + 3) − 1.4E1
i) 17↑0   j) 3↑(−2)

5. Assume that neither overflow nor underflow takes place in any of the following. State which of the following sets of expressions have equal values.

a) A + B   B + A
b) A*B   B*A
c) (A + B) + C   A + (B + C)   A + B + C
d) (A*B)*C   A*(B*C)   A*B*C
e) A*(B + C)   A*B + A*C

6. Which answers in Question 5 are affected if overflow can occur? Illustrate with examples.

7. The value of 13↑2 is 169, which is a constant. Nevertheless, the expression 13↑2 is not a constant. Explain.

8. Write expressions that correspond to each of the following mathematical expressions.

a) $\frac{1}{2} bh$ b) $a^2 + b^2$

c) $\frac{ax^2 + bx + c}{dx + f}$ d) πr^2

9. In the answer to an earlier exercise it was suggested that an expression such as

$$a + bx + cx^2 + dx^3 + ex^4$$

can be written as

$$(((ex + d)x + c)x + b)x + a.$$

a) Write expressions in Basic that correspond to these mathematical expressions.
b) Compare the number and type of operations required to evaluate each expression and comment on the efficiency involved in evaluating these expressions.

10. For the machine that you are using, give values of A for which

a) A + 1 = A
b) A + 1 = 1

11. Write a Basic program that inputs a sequence of pairs of numbers and that, for each pair, finds and outputs their sum, difference, product, and quotient. Use the pair 0,0 to signal the end of the input. What does your program do if the pair 3,0 appears in the sequence of inputs?

3.2 SUBSCRIPTED VARIABLES

Until now each of our variables has been the name of a single quantity. At any one time during a calculation it can have only a single value. Its value might be 3 at one stage and may be changed later to 4, but at any particular time it can have only one value. In many problems it is extremely useful to have variables that can represent not a single value but a list of values. In Basic such variables are called *subscripted variables*. For example, if A is a subscripted variable, the first item in the list is denoted by A(1), the second item by A(2), and so on. (In ordinary mathematics we would write a_1, a_2, and so on.) The entire list is called an *array* and the individual items in the list are called the *components* of the array. In this example, the name of the array is A, and the name of the first component is A(1), the name of the second component is A(2), and so on.

The components of an array are treated just like ordinary variables. They are expressions, and they can be combined with other expressions to form more complicated expressions, such as

$$(A(1) + B(3)\uparrow 2)/13.4 \qquad P(13) - 7*Y$$

The names of arrays must be denoted by a letter; a letter followed by a digit may not be used to denote an array.

The subscripts need not be constants. Thus, we may write A(I) and this refers to the *I*th component of the array A. In Basic, any arithmetic expression can be used as a subscript. Thus, we can refer to components of the array X such as

$$X(I + 6) \qquad X(J + 2*I)$$

The value of an expression that denotes a subscript must be converted to an integer value, and the value must be positive. If a noninteger value is encountered, it is rounded down. Thus, X(6.7) refers to the same component as X(6).

An example of a portion of a Basic program that finds the sum S of the 50 components of the array A is given in Fig. 3.1. The sum is initialized in statement 40, and the sum is added to each time statement 70 is executed. Also, each time the statements within the loop are executed, the value of I is increased by 1 and a test is used to decide whether or not the loop is to be executed again. Additional examples are considered in Exercise 3.2 and in Chapter 4.

The ideas outlined above are easily extended to include subscripted variables having more than one subscript. All versions of Basic allow arrays with up to at least two subscripts. In such cases, the individual subscripts are separated by commas, as in

$$T(I, 3) \qquad B(K - 1, L + 3)$$

The same variable name may not be used to represent a singly subscripted array and, at the same time, a doubly subscripted array. The same variable name may represent both a nonsubscripted variable and an array with most systems, but this could be confusing to the reader and should be avoided. In any event, we see that Basic contains features that allow vectors and matrices to be represented directly, in a reasonably convenient way, by using subscripted variables.

An interpreter or a compiler must allocate memory locations for all variables. Single memory locations are required for nonsubscripted variables, but a number of locations, one for each component, is required for subscripted variables. In Basic, singly subscripted variables of up to 10 components and doubly subscripted variables of up to 10 rows and 10 columns may be used, and the system will allocate a sufficient number of memory locations for each such variable automatically. For arrays with subscripts of less than 10, dimensioning information may be supplied by DIM statements in order to conserve memory locations. For arrays in which the value of a subscript exceeds the value 10, dimensioning information *must* be supplied using a DIM statement. The use of such a statement is illustrated by the following example:

```
10 DIM X(100), Y(6,12)
```

This statement declares that the variable X represents a singly subscripted array, or vector, with 100 components, and the variable Y represents a doubly subscripted array, or matrix, with 6 rows and 12 columns. The system reserves 100 locations for X and 72 locations for Y. The values of the expression that denote subscripts must be less than 101 for X and less than 7 or 13 for Y, respectively.

If a subscript is a constant, the system must determine the correct location. When the subscript is a variable, the system must produce instructions that determine the correct location each time. Some systems also produce instructions that check to ensure that a subscript is within the range of allowed values for the particular array being referenced, before the value of the subscript is used. For example, if X(I) appears in a program that contains the dimensioning information given earlier, instructions to ensure that the value of I is greater than zero and less than 101 are produced, to prevent errors that would otherwise arise.

```
 40  LET S = 0
 50  LET I = 1
 60  REM LOOP
 70     LET S = S + A(I)
 80     LET I = I + 1
 90  IF I <= 50  THEN 60
100  REM END LOOP
```

FIG. 3.1 A portion of a Basic program that finds the sum of the 50 components of the array A.

Some systems allow dimensioning to be changed in the course of a program so long as it is decreased, but this feature can lead to confusion and should not be used.

EXERCISE 3.2

1. Which of the following expressions are allowed in Basic? Give a reason for each one that is not allowed.

a) P + Q(5)*7.6 − A(I)
b) L(0) + M(J + I) + 17E6
c) A(I−6)*3 + A(7,J)
d) T(2) + U(3 − J) + T(T(2))
e) (B3(3)↑3)/(3.5*F(2)
f) (I + J)/(16 − 4↑2)

2. The portion of a Basic program given in Fig. 3.2 illustrates how we could find the sum of the numbers x_1, x_2, x_3, ..., x_n. How many times is statement 130 executed? What would happen if N = 0? Construct another sequence of statements that finds the sum of the numbers x_1, x_2, x_3, ..., x_n by using a loop containing statements that

a) test the value of I to decide whether or not the loop should be executed;
b) then add the next component of x to the sum;
c) then increment the value of I.

Which alternative is preferable?

3. Suppose the following appears in a Basic program:

```
10 DIM X(200), Y(200), Z(200)
```

Give statements that will assign the value of X(1) + Y(1) to Z(1), the value of X(2) + Y(2) to Z(2), and so on.

4. Write a portion of a Basic program that finds and outputs the inner product of two vectors.

5. A Basic program begins with

```
10 LET C(1) = 3.
20 LET C(2) = 46.
30 LET C(3) = −18.
40 LET C(4) = 7.6
50 LET C(5) = −3.
```

Complete the program so that it will input a value X and find and output the value of the polynomial

$$3X^4 + 46X^3 − 18X^2 + 7\tfrac{3}{5}X − 3.$$

6. A large number of examination results is to be input to a program that determines the frequency distribution of the marks. The program is to find and output the number of tests for which the scores were 0, 1, 2, ..., 99, 100. One

```
100 LET S = 0
110 LET I = 1
120 REM LOOP
130     LET S = S + X(I)
140     LET I = I + 1
150 IF I <= N  THEN 120
160 REM END LOOP
```

FIG. 3.2 A portion of a Basic program that finds the sum of the numbers $x_1, x_2, x_3, ..., x_n$. See Question 2 in Exercise 3.2.

way to organize the program is to initialize each component of a vector with the value 0, and to construct a loop that processes each score. As each score is input, the appropriate component of the vector is incremented by one. Use a negative score to signal the end of the data. A loop such as the following can be used to output the frequency distribution:

```
200 LET I = 1
210 REM LOOP
220     PRINT I, N(I)
230     LET I = I + 1
240 IF I <= 101 THEN 210
```

where it is assumed that the name of the vector is N. Note that the vector will contain 101 components, where the ith component represents the number of scores that had the value $i − 1$. Ensure that your program does something sensible if a mark greater than 100 is input.

3.3 BUILT-IN FUNCTIONS

In building up expressions in Basic we begin with constants and variables, including subscripted variables, and combine these with operators, according to certain rules. In this chapter we have considered two unary operators (the unary + and unary −) and five binary operators (the exponential operator ↑, and the operators for addition, subtraction, multiplication, and division). There is one other kind of operator to be considered, namely, *function* operators. We consider *built-in* functions in this section; user-defined functions will be considered in Chapter 5.

There is a variety of built-in functions in all versions of Basic. A partial list is included in the summary. The first function in the list is ABS. Whenever ABS appears in a Basic expression it must be followed by parentheses containing an expression, as in ABS(2*I + J). The result is a new expression, which can then be combined in the usual way with other expressions to form still more complicated expressions, such as

$$25 + J/*ABS(2*I + J)$$

ABS causes the system to find the absolute value of the expression in parentheses. Whatever appears in parentheses after the name of the function is called the *argument* of the function.

The second function listed in the summary is INT, which causes the system to find the greatest integer less than or equal to the value of the argument. This function can be used in a number of ways. It was used in Fig. 2.9 in the implementation of Euclid's algorithm. As another example, it can be used to round financial calculations to the nearest cent, so that at each stage of a calculation the intermediate results are calculated to the nearest cent. (See Question 7 below.) It can also be used to determine whether a given expression has an integer value. (See Question 2 below, and Question 3 of Exercise 2.2.)

Other function operators are needed to enable us to use certain mathematical functions such as square roots, logarithms, and trigonometric functions. These are given in the summary. For example, we can write SQR(X) and the result will be an approximation to the square root of X. More analysis of such approximations is considered in Chapter 9.

One other function should be mentioned, since it can be used in a number of ways. The RND function provides a "random" value in the interval (0, 1). It can be used to have our programs supply their own data. This is often useful when we are testing our programs, and we require some data to use for testing purposes. Usually, however, it is necessary for us to test our programs with test data that is carefully selected, so that different portions of the program are tested.

The RND function can also be used to write programs that imitate, or simulate, various random processes. An example of such a program is given in Fig. 3.3, where we have given a program that simulates the rolling of a die 100 times, and that finds and outputs the number of times a 1 or a 2 turns up. Note that the variable X in statement 40 will be assigned a random integer 1, 2, 3, 4, 5, or 6, since the value of RND(0) is a value in (0, 1), 6*RND(0) is a value in (0, 6), and INT(6*RND(0)) is one of the integers 0, 1, 2, 3, 4, 5. The remainder of the program is straightforward; the variable C is used to count the number of times a 1 or a 2 appears, and the variable N controls the number of times the loop is executed. (In many versions of Basic, RND can be used in place of RND(0).)

Additional examples of simulations are considered in Chapter 11; with some of these, the use of the Basic function RND can be extremely useful.

```
10   LET C = 0
20   LET N = 1
30   REM LOOP
40       LET X = INT(6*RND(0)) + 1
50       IF X > 2  THEN 70
60           LET C = C + 1
70       REM
80       LET N = N + 1
90 ' IF N <= 100 THEN 30
100 REM END LOOP
110 PRINT "NUMBER OF 1'S OR 2'S =", C
120 END

READY
RUN
NUMBER OF 1'S OR 2'S =          35
```

FIG. 3.3 A Basic program that simulates the rolling of a die 100 times, and that counts the number of times a 1 or a 2 turns up. We obtained the output indicated when the program was run on one particular system; other systems may produce slightly different results.

EXERCISE 3.3

1. What is the value of each of the following?

a) ABS(7 − INT(35/3)) + SQR(36*9)

b) SQR(17 + SQR(ABS((−4)↑3)))

2. What does X − INT(X) represent? If A is a singly subscripted variable, what is the difference, if any, between writing A(X) and A(INT(X))?

3. Check the accuracy of some of the built-in functions in Basic. Write programs that input a sequence of values of X and that compute and output the value of the following expressions:

a) $\sin^2(x) + \cos^2(x)$

b) $e^{\log_e x} - x$

You may wish to use the RND function instead of supplying the input yourself.

4. Construct a program that simulates the roll of a die 100 times and that finds and outputs separately the number of 1's, the number of 2's, etc., that appear.

5. Construct a program that simulates the roll of a pair of dice 500 times and that finds and outputs the number of 7's that appear.

6. Construct a program that will output a table of values of the function

$$\frac{1}{x} + \frac{1}{x+5} + \sqrt{\frac{x-1}{x+1}}$$

for $x = 1, 2, \ldots, 25$.

7. Write programs for the following problem. At the beginning of each year for 25 years someone invests $100 in a fund that earns 6% interest per year on the accumulated value. Thus, at the end of the first year, the fund is worth $100 × 1.06 = $106, and at the end of the second year it is worth $(106 + 100) × 1.06 = $218.36, and so on.

a) Find the value of the fund at the end of the 25th year, doing the calculations in the arithmetic provided by your machine.

b) Find the corresponding value if interest is calculated to the nearest cent, and added to the value of the fund at the end of each year. Determine the value of the fund to the nearest cent at the end of the 25th year.

c) Comment on the difference between the results of (a) and (b).

8. Hero's formula for finding the area of a triangle in terms of the lengths of the sides is

$$A = \sqrt{s(s-a)(s-b)(s-c)},$$

where $2s = a + b + c$. Write a program that inputs three numbers and finds and outputs the area of the triangle whose sides are represented by these three numbers. Your program should do something sensible if the three numbers cannot represent the sides of a triangle.

9. Give a program that will input the coordinates of three points (x_1, y_1), (x_2, y_2), (x_3, y_3) and output a message regarding their collinearity. (Three points are collinear if they all lie on the same straight line.) Assume that round-off can be neglected.

10. How would you modify the program in Question 9 so that roundoff errors can be taken into account in a reasonable way?

11. The quadratic equation $ax^2 + bx + c = 0$ has roots

$$r_1 = \frac{-b + \sqrt{b^2 - 4ac}}{2a}, \qquad r_2 = \frac{-b - \sqrt{b^2 - 4ac}}{2a}.$$

Write a program that inputs values of a, b, and c, and outputs the roots of the corresponding equation. The procedure should be designed carefully to allow for such possibilities as $b^2 < 4ac$.

3.4 FURTHER REMARKS

We have been emphasizing the rules for forming correct arithmetic expressions in the Basic language. These rules, together with other rules for forming correct statements, form the rules of grammar for the Basic language, defining what is called the *syntax* of the language. Statements that satisfy the rules are said to be *syntactically* correct. For example, a statement containing $J = 3*(4+5)$ is a syntactically correct Basic statement. On the other hand, a statement containing $J = 3(4+5)$ is not correct, although the latter would be correct in ordinary mathematical language. The syntax of Basic is more rigid than the syntax of ordinary mathematics. If this were not the case, interpreters and compilers would have to be quite a lot more complicated than they are at present.

The Basic statements we use must not only be syntactically correct, they must be logically correct as well. For example, if we want to add 3 to the value of the variable A, we must use LET $A = A + 3$, whereas LET $A = A + 4$ is not correct. Both of these are syntactically correct, but only the first has the meaning we want.

The meaning of a Basic statement is often called the *semantics* of the statement and is usually obvious, once we know something about the language. An asterisk means multiplication, words like READ, IF, and GO TO have obvious meanings, and so on. Some details of the meaning, such as roundoff and overflow, depend on the system, but most of the meaning of a program is implied by the Basic notation.

An interpreter or a compiler accepts all statements, whether or not they are syntactically correct or semantically correct. Whenever a statement is syntactically incorrect, the system should output a diagnostic message to help the programmer find the error in syntax.

If a Basic statement is semantically incorrect, the system cannot be expected to find the error. Suppose you have used GO TO 301 in your program, when you should have used GO TO 15. If there is a statement numbered 301, the system usually cannot find this error. It is up to you to see that your program has no such logical errors.

As another example of an error in semantics, suppose that the value of I is 2 when the statement

60 LET J = 24/(I - 2)

is executed. This statement is syntactically correct and will therefore not cause any diagnostic message before it is executed. What happens then depends on the system being used. Usually, execution is terminated and an appropriate message is printed.

There are many other situations that are usually noticed only at execution time, such as:

a) evaluation of A/B or A↑B when both A and B are zero,
b) evaluation of A↑B when A is negative and the value of B is not an integer,
c) evaluation of A*B when overflow or underflow occurs,
d) evaluation of SQR(Q) when Q is negative,
e) reference to A(I) when I is zero or negative.

In each of these examples, the syntax is correct, but the meaning is not what the programmer intended. To understand how the meaning in such cases can depend on the installation, consider A(I) when I has the value 0. At some installations this would refer to the storage location immediately before the location for A(1), which might contain the value of another variable, or a constant. At other installations the interpreter or compiler produces instructions that check the subscript before it is used. These instructions would find that the subscript was not allowed and execution would be terminated, along with an appropriate diagnostic message.

CHAPTER **4**

Control Constructs

In Chapter 1, we introduced two basically different constructs (looping and selection) to describe the flow of control in an algorithm. We have already illustrated in Chapter 2 how these constructs can be rendered in Basic in a few simple situations. In this chapter, we provide a more detailed study of this topic.

We have already shown how indentation of lines of code can improve the readability of a program and how comments can help explain portions of a Basic program. These ideas will be further illustrated in the material of this chapter as well.

4.1 LOOPING

In Chapter 1 we introduced the idea of loops and illustrated how they can be described using our higher-level pseudo-code. A variety of loop constructs can arise when an algorithm is being composed. It is sometimes not known, in advance, how many times a repetitive process is to be carried out; in other situations, the number of times may be known. In any event, we require a mechanism to terminate a repetitive process. In some situations, an exit may appear at the beginning of a loop; in other situations, an exit may appear at the end of a loop; still other situations arise in which we allow exits from anywhere within a loop, although, as noted in Chapter 1, such exits can add to the complexity of an algorithm.

In Chapter 2, we introduced the IF statement. This statement allows control to be transferred to another statement depending on a logical condition, as in

```
60    IF R = 0 THEN 85
```

which was used in Fig. 2.9, when we rendered Euclid's algorithm in Basic. IF statements can be used to construct exits from a loop wherever we wish. It is important that the exit be easily identified, especially when the exit does not appear at the beginning or the end of a loop, as was the case with Euclid's algorithm. A comment, or REM statement, consistent with the notation of Chapter 1, may be used to help the reader identify the exit, as was done in statement 55 of Fig. 2.9. And it is also important that the exit be constructed in such a way that control is transferred to a statement immediately following the construct that is being exited. We have already seen how to use REM statements to mark places in a program to which the flow of control may be transferred.

A portion of a Basic program that causes a process to be repeated 100 times is given in Fig. 4.1, together with the corresponding "Loop for" construct introduced in Chapter 1. In this example, a counter has been used to determine when the repetitions should be discontinued. The counter is denoted by I and is set equal to 1 before the repeated part is begun. Each time that part is carried out, the counter is increased by 1 and tested

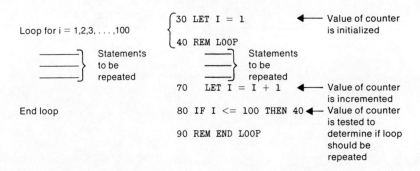

FIG. 4.1 A portion of a Basic program that causes a process to be repeated 100 times, which corresponds to the pseudocode "Loop for . . ." construct discussed in Chapter 1.

to see whether it has exceeded 100, so that a decision to repeat or go on to the next step can be made.

The exit from the "Loop for" construct is given at the end of the loop in Fig. 4.1. We could also have rendered the "Loop for" construct in such a way that the exit appears at the beginning of the loop. In this way, the "Loop for" construct may be rendered in a way that is similar to a "Loop while" construct, which is considered later in this section.

In the examples that we have considered thus far, the condition being tested is quite simple, as in $i \leq 100$. In some situations, more complicated conditions must be rendered in Basic. For example, to handle a condition such as $0 < x < 1$ we might write

```
250 IF 0<X AND X<1 THEN 375
```

if the version of Basic we are using allows the use of logical operators. Such operators are mentioned in the summary, and are available with some versions of Basic. With many versions of Basic, two statements must be used, as in

```
250 IF X <= 0 THEN 260
255 IF X<1 THEN 375
260 REM
```

Note how in this example the first logical condition had to be changed to achieve the desired result.

A FOR statement may often be used to control the number of times a part of a program is repeated. For example, the portion of a program given in Fig. 4.2 is equivalent to that given in Fig. 4.1.

```
30 FOR I = 1 TO 100
```
⎤ Statements to be
⎦ repeated
```
80 NEXT I
```
Next statement following loop

FIG. 4.2 A portion of a program that is equivalent to that given in Fig. 4.1.

FOR statements are always of the form

s FOR $v = i$ TO f

or of the form

s FOR $v = i$ TO f STEP d

where s is a statement number, v is a nonsubscripted variable name, and i, f, and d are arithmetic expressions. FOR statements are always used in conjunction with a corresponding NEXT statement, to form a FOR-NEXT loop. A FOR statement is interpreted as follows: Execute all Basic statements down to the corresponding NEXT statement, first using the value of $v = i$, then with $v = i + d$, then with $v = i + 2d$, and so on, but stopping before v becomes larger than f if d is positive, or less than f if d is negative. If the STEP d is missing, it is assumed that $d = 1$.

The use of FOR statements with subscripted variables is illustrated by finding the dot product of two vectors X and Y, where it is assumed that each vector contains 100 components. The following statements will produce the desired result:

```
40 LET D = 0
50 FOR I = 1 TO 100
60    LET D = D + X(I)*Y(I)
70 NEXT I
```

Note that the value of I is used to control the number of times the loop will be carried out and also as the subscript for X and Y. The first time the part to be repeated is carried out, the value of x_1y_1 is added to D. The second time, x_2y_2 is added, then x_3y_3, and so on.

In some situations one FOR-NEXT loop may contain another, as in, for example, finding the sum of two matrices. If the two matrices are denoted by U and V, and the sum by S, the following will achieve the required result:

```
140 FOR I = 1 TO 100
150    FOR J = 1 TO 100
160       LET S(I,J) = U(I,J) + V(I,J)
170    NEXT J
180 NEXT I
```

where it is assumed that each matrix consists of 100 rows and 100 columns. Note that the innermost loop is contained within the outer; the loops must not "overlap."

Another type of loop construct that may arise in some applications was described in Chapter 1. It was suggested as an alternative to the constructs that have been described thus far, where we may wish to cause a sequence of statements to be executed while some given condition is true. Figure 4.3 contains an example of such a situation, where we have once again described an algorithm that finds the dot product of two vectors. We have changed the logical relationship that must be tested, since an `IF` statement will cause control to be transferred to some other point in the program when the relationship is true. When using this approach, care must be exercised, especially when the condition to be tested is more complicated than in the example given in Fig. 4.3. Alternatively, with some versions of Basic we may use the `NOT` operator and translate the logical expression directly, as in

```
40     IF NOT (I <= 100) THEN 60
```

Using this statement in place of the `IF` statement in Fig. 4.3 will produce the same result. This latter approach has the advantage of allowing the same logical expression that is used in our higher-level description to be used when the translation to Basic is being produced.

As mentioned earlier in this section, the "Loop for" construct may be rendered in a form that is similar to that used in Fig. 4.3 for the "Loop while" construct. The exit from the loop would then be given at the beginning of the loop and, it should be noted, this alternative rendering produces the correct result in the special situation that sometimes arises when the statements within the loop should not be executed at all. Except for this special situation, the two methods of rendering the "Loop for" construct are equivalent.

As a final example, suppose that there are two arrays named x and y and a single variable a. The problem is to find which component of x is equal to a and then to set b equal to the corresponding component of y. For example, if a is equal to x_{14}, the value of y_{14} is to be assigned to b. This procedure is an example of a

```
d = 0                      10  LET D = 0
i = 1                      20  LET I = 1
Loop while (i ≤ 100)     ⎧30  REM LOOP
                          ⎨40      IF I > 100 THEN 80
    d = x + xᵢyᵢ           50      LET D = D + X(I)*Y(I)
    i = i + 1              60      LET I = I + 1
End loop                  ⎧70  GO TO 30
                          ⎨80  REM END LOOP
```

FIG. 4.3 An example of a "Loop while" construct rendered in Basic.

```
Loop for i = 1,2, ... 500     50  FOR I = 1 TO 500
   ... If (a = xᵢ) exit loop   60      IF A = X(I) THEN 80
                               ⎧70      NEXT I
End loop                       ⎨80  REM
b = yᵢ                         90  LET  B = Y(I)
```

FIG. 4.4 An example of a table lookup, where it is assumed that an item to be looked up is contained in the table. Thus, an exit from the loop will always occur at some point, via the `IF` statement.

table look-up, since we are searching a table of values to find a given entry. The Basic statements that are given in Fig. 4.4 will accomplish this task, where it is assumed that each array has 500 components, and also that there is an entry that corresponds to a. The statements in Fig. 4.4 do *not* solve this problem if none of the components of the array x is equal to a.

It may be unwise to assume that one of the components of x is equal to a. Provision should then be made in case this assumption fails. For example, if such a situation means that there is an error, and computation should be stopped, the following could be added to the program in Fig. 4.4:

```
72 PRINT "THE VALUE OF A IS", A
74 PRINT "NO COMPONENT OF X HAS THIS VALUE"
76 PRINT "EXECUTION IS THEREFORE TERMINATED"
78 STOP
```

The `STOP` statement causes execution of the program to terminate.

Adding this to the program makes it more "robust," in the sense that the program is now more dependable. Without this protection, an incorrect value of a could cause the program to simply assign y_{500} to b (or perhaps attempt to assign y_{501} to b) and then proceed as if nothing had gone wrong!

EXERCISE 4.1

1. Identify the errors in each of the following.

a) `10 FOR I=1 STEP 5 TO 20,`
b) `30 IF A=7 PRINT "YES"`
c) `50 FOR A(1) = 1 TO 10`
d) `40 FOR 1=I TO 10`

2. Give renderings for each of the following portions of pseudo-code.

a) Loop for j = 1, 3, 5, 7, . . . , 49

   ———
   ———
   ———

   End loop

b) Loop while x > 0 and y > 0

   ———
   ———
   ———

   End loop

c)   Loop while x > 0 or y > 0

———

———

———

End loop

d)   Loop for i = 2, 4, 6, 8, . . . , 1000 while |a| < 25

———

———

———

End loop

e)   Loop for k = 10, 9, 8, . . . , −10

Loop for j = 0, 5, 10, 15, . . . , 45

Loop while x < 10

———

———

End loop

End loop

End loop

3. Write a portion of a program that finds the sum *s* of two vectors *x* and *y*. Assume that each vector contains *n* components, where *n* cannot exceed 200.

4. Suppose that *v* is a vector with *n* components, and that *a* is a matrix with *m* rows and *n* columns. Construct a portion of a program that produces *u*, which is to be the product of *a* and *v*. Assume that the subscripts cannot exceed 100.

5. Suppose *a* and *b* are two matrices, where the dimension of *a* is $n \times m$ and of *b*, $m \times k$. Write a portion of a program that finds *p*, the product of *a* and *b*, assuming that the subscripts cannot exceed 50.

6. Write a program that will input a number *N* and find and output the sum of the first *N* terms of the sequence

1, 3, 5, 7, ...

7. Give a program that will calculate and output a table of numbers and their squares for all numbers between 50 and 100, inclusive.

8. Consider the table look-up described in this section and assume that

$$x_1 < x_2 < \cdots < x_{500}.$$

Give a sequence of Basic statements that will find the component of *x* nearest to *a* and then set *b* equal to the corresponding component of *y*. In the case where *a* is midway between two components, choose the smaller component of *x*.

In each of the following questions, a program is required to solve a certain problem. For at least one of these questions, a brief report should be prepared, as outlined in Exercise 2.2.

9. A program is required that will find all three digit integers with the property that each integer is equal to the sum of the cubes of its digits. One method that can be used is to test each number, in turn, to determine if the property is satisfied. In order to minimize the amount of arithmetic that is required, the cubes of the digits 0–9

can be stored in an array, making it unnecessary to compute the cubes of the digits each time.

10. Write a program for Question 6 of Exercise 1.3, assuming that the matrix is of order 10. The matrix can be input using the following:

```
30 MAT READ M
```

where we have assumed that the data values for the matrix M are given in a sequence of DATA statements in the following order: M(1,1), M(1,2), M(1,3),..., M(1,10), M(2,1), M(2,2),..., M(10,10).

11. Write a program for Question 7 of Exercise 1.3, using the assumption of Question 10.

4.2 SELECTION

The selection construct is used in an algorithm to select one of a sequence of possible actions that is to be carried out. In some situations, the number of alternate actions may be small, whereas in a few situations, one of a large number of alternatives must be carried out during the course of a calculation.

The simplest situation that could arise will occur when there is only one action that may be carried out, as in

If(x<0) increment y by 1

Such a statement must be rendered in Basic by using more than one statement, as in

```
50 IF X>=0 THEN 70
60    LET Y=Y+1
70 REM
```

Because the IF statement directs the flow of control to be transferred if a given condition is true, we have had to change the logical relationship that must be tested and use the IF statement to "skip over" the Basic statement that increments *y*.

As a second example, consider

If(A>B) interchange A and B

which was used in Euclid's algorithm in Chapter 2. Again in this situation, more than one statement must be written to obtain the desired result, as in the following:

```
15 IF A <= B THEN 35
20    LET T = A
25    LET A = B
30    LET B = T
35 REM
```

Once again we have changed the logical relationship to be tested in order to "skip over" the statements when the condition A > B is false. We could also use IF NOT A > B THEN 35 in this example if the version of Basic being used allows the use of logical operators.

The example given above is a special case of an `IF-THEN-ELSE` construct, in which the flow of control within an algorithm is directed to one of two possible courses of action, depending on a stated condition. Three descriptions of such a control construct are given in Fig. 4.5, where it is assumed that the condition being tested is $i > n$. We have aligned the boxes in the flowchart with portions of the other descriptions. As shown in Fig. 4.5, one way of achieving the desired result with Basic is to change the logical expression that represents the condition being tested. Care must be exercised if this approach is adopted, especially when the condition being tested is more complicated than in this example. An alternative that may be used in some versions of Basic is

```
s IF NOT ——————— THEN —————
```

which we mentioned earlier.

The most general type of selection construct is often referred to as a *case* construct. In this situation, a number of courses of action are provided, as well as a condition for causing each to be carried out. The pseudo-code example introduced in Chapter 1 is given in Fig. 4.6, together with some statements that can be used to render the construct in Basic. Once again, we have changed the conditions that must be tested in each situation, in order to render this construct in Basic. Note also that in this example we used two Basic statements to render the condition $0 < x < 1$.

It is also important to realize that, in this example, the logical expressions

$$x < 0, \qquad 0 < x < 1, \qquad x = 1$$

are mutually exclusive. The order in which the various conditions are tested is therefore arbitrary, although the else clause appears at the end of the list of conditions.

Before we conclude this section, it should be pointed out that an alternative approach may be used when we are translating the case construct into Basic. We may use the `IF` statement to cause control to be sent directly to a sequence of statements that are to be carried out,

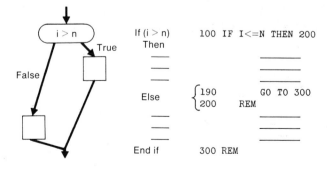

FIG. 4.5 Three descriptions of an `IF-THEN-ELSE` control construct.

```
If (x < 0)            100 IF X>=0 THEN 200
————
————                    190       GO TO 500
————                   ⎧200       REM
(0 < x < 1)            ⎨210       IF X<=0 THEN 300
                       ⎩220       IF X>=1 THEN 300
————
————
                        290       GO TO 500
(x = 1)                ⎧300       REM
                       ⎩310       IF X<>1 THEN 400
————
————
                        390       GO TO 500
else                    400       REM
————
————
End if                  500 REM
```

FIG. 4.6 An example of how a case construct may be rendered in Basic.

and use a `GO TO` statement to "skip over" that code when the condition is not satisfied, as in

```
100 IF X<0 THEN 110
105       GO TO 200
110     REM
        ————
        ————
        ————
        GO TO 500
200     REM
```

where we have translated the first portion of Fig. 4.6. It can be seen that this approach leads to the use of a greater number of statements.

As was the situation with the various loop constructs, it may be that an exit appears within a case construct. The translation into Basic can be accomplished by the use of an appropriate `GO TO` statement. As was mentioned earlier, it is important that such exits be clearly identified; a comment that is consistent with our higher-level pseudo-code of Chapter 1 might also be helpful.

Some versions of Basic provide a limited case construct. See the `ON` statement described in the summary.

EXERCISE 4.2

1. Rewrite the following in the notation of Chapter 1. Then write a portion of a Basic program that corresponds to this new description.

If the square of $x - y$ is greater than 25, increase the value of N by 1, find the sum of the N components of Y and assign its value to Z; otherwise, decrease the value of N by 1 and find the sum of the squares of the components of V, except when the values of x and y are equal. In this latter case output an error message and set the value of E to 1.

A report as outlined in Exercise 2.2 should be prepared for one of the following questions.

2. The program should input six values (a, b, c, d, e, f) and should calculate and output the values of x and y that satisfy the equations

$$ax + by = c,$$
$$dx + ey = f.$$

(Be sure to consider the exceptional cases, such as $ae - db = 0$.) What happens if $ae - db$ is nearly zero?

3. The first number to be input is the number of students who wrote a certain aptitude test. The remaining data items contain the scores obtained, each data value giving the score for one student. A program is required that will input these data items and count the number of scores below 50, the number between 50 and 65 inclusive, the number between 66 and 74 inclusive, and the number above 74. The program is to output the final counts and the total number of students.

4, 5, 6. Write programs for Questions 8, 9, and 10 of Exercise 1.3. For Question 9 of Exercise 1.3, if the sequence of numbers is denoted by A, the statement

```
100 MAT READ A
```

may be used to input all numbers at one time.

7. A gas company has a billing rate based on consumption by its customers. The rate structure is given in the following table:

First 50 m³	$1.00 minimum cost
Next 100 m³	$0.015 per m³
Next 300 m³	$0.008 per m³
Remainder	$0.005 per m³

Write a program that will input the customer's account number, and two meter readings (four digit numbers) representing 100's of cubic meters, and output these together with the amount of the bill. Care should be exercised in computing the consumption to allow for situations in which the new reading is less than the old reading; for example, the old reading might be 9946, while the new one is 0023. After all the data has been input, the program should output the total consumption and the total billing for the period. A negative account number can be used to indicate the end of the input.

8. A perfect number is a number that is equal to the sum of all its divisors other than itself. Thus, 6 is a perfect number since 1, 2, and 3 are its divisors and $6 = 1 + 2 + 3$. Write a program that will find and output the next largest perfect number.

9. Diophantine problems are problems in which we are required to find integer solutions of equations. For example, it can be shown that all integer solutions of $2x + 3y = 5$ are given by $x = 1 + 3t$ and $y = 1 - 2t$, where t is any integer. Write a program that will input I, J, and K and then find and output L1, L2, M1, and M2 with the property that all integer solutions of $Ix + Jy = K$ are given by $x = $ L1 $+$ L2t and $y = $ M1 $+$ M2t, where t is any integer, provided such solutions exist.

4.3 FURTHER REMARKS

We have seen in this chapter how the pseudo-code control constructs that were used in Chapter 1 can be rendered in Basic. It is clear that, from our point of view, the language does not contain appropriate constructs for all situations. For example, only some versions of Basic allow the logical operators AND, OR, and NOT to be used in conjunction with IF statements. It is also clear that, from our point of view, a construct such as

```
100 IF expression
110 THEN
      _____
      _____

150 ELSE
      _____
      _____

200 END IF
```

would be useful, as would a DO WHILE construct, as part of the Basic language. A few processors do support extensions to the Basic language that allow such constructs to be used. Because such extensions are not generally available, the techniques described in this chapter will usually be required when we render our algorithms in Basic. In any event, as illustrated in this chapter, the translation into Basic can be accomplished in a reasonably straightforward way, using only those features of Basic that are generally available.

CHAPTER 5

Refinement

We introduced the idea of *refinement* in Section 1.3. It was intended that one way of using the term was to refer to the process of developing an algorithm in stages, beginning at a very high level, and then filling in the details, or refining, to reach successively lower levels, until we finally reach the level of a program that will run on a computer. At least part of this "top-down" structure of a program will usually be reflected in a description of the program in the pseudo-code notation of Section 1.3. Using this notation, a second use of the term "refinement" is to refer to a portion of a program that explains how to carry out, or refine, another part of the program that is stated only briefly.

An example of this second use of the term was given in Fig. 1.13. The "Where-End" portion of the program given there explains in detail how the "Search" statement used earlier in the program is to be carried out.

The purpose of the following three sections is to discuss a number of ways in which refinements described in the "Where-End" notation of Section 1.3 can be rendered in Basic. One result is that we are led to a discussion of an important feature of Basic known as subprograms.

In the final section of this chapter, we return to a general discussion of refinement. It is an extremely important idea, and deserves further discussion, particularly at this stage. There are several ramifications of the idea for the development of good programs, and they should be emphasized.

5.1 SUBSTITUTION, TRANSFER OF CONTROL

One straightforward way in which the description given in Fig. 1.13 can be rendered in Basic is to insert, at the appropriate place in the program, the Basic statements that correspond to what appears between "Where by . . ." and "End where." (See Fig. 5.1.) The appropriate place in this instance is, of course, the location of the "Search . . ." statement. It will be necessary to select appropriate statement numbers to ensure that the statements are inserted in the correct place. A comment can also be placed in the program to explain the purpose of the substituted part.

The straightforward method illustrated in Fig. 5.1 will always work. All that is required is a replacement of the higher-level statement by the more detailed description that is outlined later in the "Where-End" notation of Section 1.3. When this method is used, it will be necessary to duplicate the same portion of code if the same higher-level statement appears in more than one place in the top level description of the algorithm. This is not always convenient, and we will return to this difficulty in the next two sections.

An alternative to straightforward insertion is to transfer control to the Basic statements that correspond

Search $a_i, a_{i+1}, \ldots$ etc.

Where by "Search $a_i, a_{i+1}, \ldots$ etc." we mean
    smallest $= a_i$
    $k = i$
    Loop for $j = i + 1, i + 2, \ldots, n$
        If ($a_j <$ smallest)
            smallest $= a_j$
            $k = j$
        End if
    End loop
End where

```
200  LET S = A(I)
210  LET K = I
220  FOR J = I+1 TO N
230    IF A(J)>=S THEN 260
240      LET S = A(J)
250      LET K = J
260    REM END IF
270  NEXT J
```

FIG. 5.1 The "Search" statement and the "Where-End" part of Fig. 1.13, followed by part of a program. The Basic statements can replace the "Where-End" part, which in turn can be substituted for the "Search" statement.

to the refinement and to follow the refinement with a statement that transfers control back to the statement following the original transfer. This can be accomplished in Basic with GO TO statements. (See Fig. 5.2.) Once again, an appropriate comment would be helpful.

The alternative method illustrated in Fig. 5.2 cannot be used in all circumstances. For example, if the same higher-level statement appears in more than one place in the top level description, the method cannot be used without modification, since the GO TO statement corresponding to the end of the "Where-End" construct will always return control to the same point in the program.

Finally, it must be pointed out that situations will arise in which we wish to have the same process carried out but with different variables. Neither of the methods

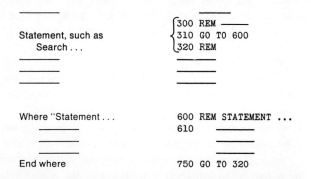

FIG. 5.2 An alternative way of handling "Where-End" in Basic. The statements on the right illustrate how the flow of control is transferred to statements corresponding to the refinement. The flow of control is later directed back to the appropriate place.

discussed so far can cope with such situations, at least not without further modifications. However, in the next two sections, we will show how this can be accomplished in Basic with the help of subprograms. The use of subprograms also avoids the other difficulties mentioned above.

EXERCISE 5.1

1. Write Basic statements that correspond to refinements for Question 3 of Exercise 1.3.

2. Write an outline of a program, using the notation of Section 1.3, that finds the minimum of three integers and that uses a statement of the form

    i = smaller of j and k

twice. Give a refinement for such a statement. Using the straightforward method of insertion for implementing refinement described in this section, construct the corresponding Basic program. Discuss the possible use of the alternative method involving transfer of control.

3. Repeat Question 2, but have the program sort the three numbers, rather than finding their minimum. In the top level description, make use of statements of the form

    interchange a and b, if necessary, so that a $\leq$ b.

4. Outline a few programs that involve refinements that are used one or more times in the course of the program, and discuss ways of rendering these programs in Basic. The refinements can, for example, be used to explain how to carry out statements involving matrix-vector calculations, or finding greatest common divisors, or primes, and so on.

5. Discuss the use of comments as an aid in rendering refinements in Basic.

5.2 FUNCTION SUBPROGRAMS

There are two different kinds of subprograms in Basic. We shall see that subprograms are very much like programs, except that they can be used by other programs or subprograms.

Function subprograms, or *functions,* can be used when the result to be obtained by the subprogram is a single value. We have already introduced, in Section 3.3, a number of built-in functions that are part of the Basic language. These include functions such as ABS(X), SQR(X), and so on.

It is also possible to define our own functions, using statements of the form

s DEF FN$n(p) = e$

where s is a statement number, n is a single letter, p is a list of parameters, and e is an expression that may contain the variable names appearing in p. For example, the function definition

```
100 DEF FNY(X) = SQR(1 - X↑2)
```

defines a function, named FNY, which requires one argument. The value of the function is

$$\sqrt{1 - \text{argument}^2}.$$

The argument X is a "dummy" variable, or *parameter,* and can be replaced by any expression when the function is actually used.

As a second example, consider

```
120 DEF FND(A,B,C) = B↑2 - 4*A*C
```

This definition describes a function named FND that requires three arguments.

In most versions of Basic, it is necessary to define functions in a single line, with the definitions appearing at the beginning of the program. Subsequent statements in the program may use these functions in any arithmetic expressions. For example, the program given in Fig. 5.3 illustrates the use of the function FNY to provide a table of values of $y = \sqrt{1 - x^2}$ for values of x in the interval $(0, 1)$.

An important advantage of functions is that they can be used more than once in the same program, with the same or different arguments each time. FNY is used only once in Fig. 5.3, with the argument Z. But it could have been used any number of times, just as ABS or SQR could be, with any arithmetic expression as its argument for each use.

Some versions of Basic allow function definitions that require more than a single line. With such versions, the refinement described in Fig. 1.13 can be rendered in Basic using a function subprogram, since the top level description of the algorithm has to be supplied only with the value of k. (It does not need to be provided with the value of a_k as well, since it can easily obtain a_k if it has the value of k.)

```
100 DEF FNY(X) = SQR(1-X↑2)
110 PRINT "X", "SQR(1-X↑2)"
120 FOR Z = 0 TO 1  STEP .1
130     LET F = FNY(Z)
140     PRINT Z, F
150 NEXT Z
160 END

RUN
X                 SQR(1-X↑2)
0                 1
0.1               0.994987437
0.2               0.979795897
0.3               0.953939201
0.4               0.916515139
0.5               0.866025404
0.6               0.8
0.7               0.714142843
0.8               0.6
0.9               0.435889894
1                 0
```

FIG. 5.3 An example of a program using a function definition, together with the output produced when it is executed.

```
10   DIM A(100)
100  DEF FNS(A, I, N)
110     LET S1 = A(I)
120     LET K = I
130     FOR J = I+1 TO N
140        IF A(J) <= S1 THEN 170
150           LET S1 = A(J)
160           LET K = J
170        REM
180     NEXT J
190     LET FNS = K
200  FNEND
300  REM ASSUME A(1), A(2),...,A(N) ARE AVAILABLE
310  FOR I = 1 TO N-1
320     REM    FNS PROVIDES THE SUBSCRIPT OF THE
330     REM    SMALLEST COMPONENT OF A(I), A(I+1),...,A(N)
340     LET K = FNS(A, I, N)
350     LET T = A(K)
360     LET A(K) = A(I)
370     LET A(I) = T
380  NEXT I
390  REM A(1), A(2),...,A(N) ARE NOW SORTED
```

FIG. 5.4 The algorithm in Fig. 1.13 for sorting n numbers rendered in Basic. A multiple-line function has been used to help render the refinement.

To illustrate how such function subprograms are written and used, consider Fig. 5.4, which shows how the algorithm of Fig. 1.13 can be rendered in Basic with the help of a function subprogram called FNS. The first statement in a multiple line function definition does not contain an arithmetic expression giving the value of the function, but at some point in the definition the value of the function must be assigned to the function name, as illustrated in this example. The end of the function definition is marked by an FNEND statement.

Note how the calling program uses the function subprogram FNS. The translation of the top level description of the "Search" statement of Fig. 1.13 has been done with the help of the assignment statement

```
340    LET K = FNS(A, I, N)
```

A function subprogram may be used in an expression in exactly the same way that other functions such as SQR and ABS are used. As mentioned earlier, the variables A, I, and N given in the assignment statement are called arguments of the function and they correspond to the parameters in the definition of the function. In this example, the same names have been used in the argument list and the parameter list, but this is not necessary.

EXERCISE 5.2

1. How would you change the program given in Fig. 5.3 so that it outputs a table of values of $y = x^2 - 4$ in the interval $(-10, 10)$ in increments of 0.5?

2. Improve the robustness of the function subprogram given in Fig. 5.4.

If the version of Basic that you are using does not allow multiple line function definitions, it will be necessary to use the subroutine technique given in Section 5.3 to answer the following questions.

3. Give a function that will produce the smallest of three given numbers, say I, J, and K.

4. Give a function that will find the smallest of ten given numbers, where the numbers are the components of a subscripted variable L.

5. Repeat Question 4, but have the function find the smallest of N given numbers.

6. Construct a function to use with one argument whose value is a prime number. The function is to produce the value of the next prime.

7. Write a function that will find the lowest common multiple of two given positive integers.

8. A function is required that will find the second largest in a list of numbers, assuming the numbers are all different.

9. Construct your own function for finding the square root of a given number, based on the following ideas.

There are several procedures that one might use to develop a suitable algorithm. The usual one is based on a method commonly known as Newton's method, which may be described as follows:

1. Start with the number whose square root is required; call it *a*.
2. Make a guess at the square root of *a*; call it *g*.
3. The next approximation to $\sqrt{a}$ is derived by substitution in the formula $\frac{1}{2}[g + a/g]$.
4. Rename this new approximation *g*.
5. Repeat steps (3) and (4) until the value of *g* is a good approximation to $\sqrt{a}$.

This description is not yet complete because we still have to decide how to make the first guess and decide when the value of *g* is close enough. It does not matter very much how the first guess is made. A simple way to make the first guess is to choose *g* = *a*. The method of determining when to stop could use a counter to control the number of times steps (3) and (4) are repeated. This may not be satisfactory, however, because the number of iterations required to obtain a close approximation depends on the magnitude of the number. A second possibility is to stop when the new approximation is fairly close to the previous one, for example, within some small number ϵ. A new difficulty arises here since the value we choose for ϵ might suffice for some numbers and not for others. For example, $\epsilon = 0.00001$ might do for finding $\sqrt{410}$, but not for $\sqrt{0.000000410}$.

There is a way out of this last difficulty. If *g* represents a particular approximation and *x* represents the next approximation, the value of *g/x* is very close to 1 whenever *x* and *g* are close to each other. Thus, we can test the condition

$$\left| \frac{g}{x} - 1 \right| \leq \epsilon$$

and we can choose a value of ϵ that will be suitable for finding square roots of a wide range of numbers.

Document your subprogram carefully. Compare the results obtained by your subprogram with the SQR function.

5.3 SUBROUTINE SUBPROGRAMS

In addition to built-in functions and user-defined functions, another type of subprogram, called a subroutine subprogram, or *subroutine,* is available in Basic. Functions are convenient to use when only one value is to be returned, but subroutines can be used to return any number of values. Moreover, only some versions of Basic allow multiple line function definitions, whereas all versions allow multiple line subroutines to be used. Thus, subroutines can be used to render any refinement that we wish. On the other hand, subroutines are less convenient than functions in one respect. Their parameters are not handled in the same convenient way.

An example of a subroutine is given in Fig. 5.5, where we give one for finding the greatest common divisor of two given parameters. (The Basic statements in Fig. 5.5 should be compared to those given in Fig. 2.9.) Note that, in statement number 970, the value of the greatest common divisor is assigned to the variable G. Following this action, a RETURN statement is encountered.

Subroutines are used in Basic by executing a GOSUB statement, which gives the statement number of the first statement in the subprogram. To use the subroutine in Fig. 5.5, a statement such as

260 GOSUB 800

is required. This causes the flow of control to be directed to statement 800. When the RETURN statement is encountered, the flow of control is directed back to the statement following the GOSUB statement.

```
800 REM SUBROUTINE FOR GCD(I,J)
810 REM IF(I>J) INTERCHANGE I,J
820 IF J >= I THEN 860
830     LET T = I
840     LET I = J
850     LET J = T
860 REM
870 REM LOOP
880     REM FIND REMAINDER R IN J/I
890     LET R = J - INT(J/I)*I
900 REM...IF(R=0)EXIT LOOP
910     IF R = 0 THEN 960
920     REM REPLACE J,I BY I,R
930     LET J = I
940     LET I = R
950 GO TO 870
960 REM END LOOP
970 LET G = I
980 RETURN
```

FIG. 5.5 A subroutine that uses Euclid's algorithm to find the greatest common divisor of two integers.

It is important to realize that the variable names that are used in a subroutine should not conflict with variable names used elsewhere, either in the calling program or within another subroutine. Such problems could be avoided by using "obscure" variable names, such as G1, G2, G3 in the subroutine of Fig. 5.5. On the other hand, this technique usually makes the subroutine more difficult for the reader to understand.

As well as illustrating how subroutines are used, we also return now to the questions raised at the end of Section 5.1 regarding certain difficulties about implementing refinements with the help of straightforward insertions of code, or transfers of control. We want to show how subroutines can be used to get around these difficulties very easily.

As an illustration, let us suppose that we already have a subroutine for finding the greatest common divisor of two integers. Suppose also that we have a program in which a pair of integers is obtained, either from input or by a calculation. This program can call on the subroutine to find the greatest common divisor of the two integers. If another pair of integers is obtained later in the same program, the same subroutine can be used again to find the greatest common divisor of this new pair.

To be specific, let us suppose that the top level description of our algorithm contains a statement such as

M = the greatest common divisor of L1, L2

and that, later on, another statement such as

N = the greatest common divisor of L3, L4

appears in the description of the algorithm, as illustrated in Fig. 5.6.

When the main program of Fig. 5.6 uses the subroutine for the first time, the parameters I and J correspond to the arguments L1 and L2. Note that it was necessary to assign these values to I and J in statements 200 and 210. The second time it is used, the parameters I and J correspond to the arguments L3 and L4. In this way, it is seen how a subroutine that represents a refinement can be used with different arguments at different points. (By contrast, with functions we would merely have to substitute the different arguments each time the function is referenced.)

Using the GOSUB and RETURN statements provides a technique to implement whatever refinement we wish. With the Basic language, we are required to assign the values of the arguments to the parameters, prior to the transfer of control to the subroutine.

With subroutines, it is often useful to include among the parameters an output parameter that provides some indication to the calling program as to whether or not the subroutine has encountered an unusual situation, as would arise when an error condition is detected. The calling program can then test the value of the corresponding argument to determine whether or not the results that have been produced by the subroutine (or the results that were supposed to be produced) should be used in further computations.

It should be noted that one subprogram can make use of another subprogram simply by using the appropriate GOSUB statement or function reference. However, one subprogram is not allowed to call itself or to call another subprogram that calls the original subprogram, and so on. This is one of the important restrictions in Basic that does not apply in some other programming languages. In some applications it turns out to be very convenient to have subprograms that are able to call

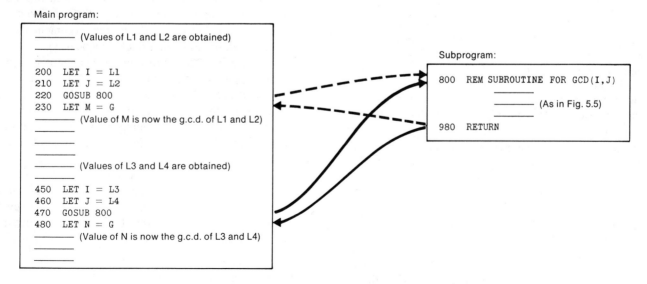

FIG. 5.6 A main program uses the subprogram of Fig. 5.5 on two different occasions.

themselves. Subprograms with this property are said to be *recursive*.

One of the main advantages of subprograms is that they can be designed to carry out specific tasks, such as finding the greatest common divisor of two integers, and then used whenever they are required by other programs or subprograms. Every computer installation will have a library of programs or subprograms available for specific tasks such as sorting, searching, solving certain kinds of equations, finding areas, doing statistical calculations, and so on. The user does not need to write programs for these tasks; he or she merely uses whatever programs or subprograms are needed.

EXERCISE 5.3

1. How does the description of a subroutine subprogram differ from that of a function subprogram? How does the reference to a subroutine subprogram differ from that of a function subprogram?

2. Explain how to change a function subprogram into a subroutine subprogram. Under what circumstances can a subroutine subprogram be changed into a function subprogram?

3. Write a subroutine subprogram that is equivalent to the function subprogram given in Fig. 5.4.

4. Improve the robustness of the subprogram given in Fig. 5.5.

5. Write a subroutine with two parameters, N and K, that will assign the value 1 to K if N is a prime, and the value 0 if N is not a prime.

6. Write a subroutine that will search a list of numbers L(1), L(2), ..., L(100) for the first one to match a given number, say J. Then, if the first match is with L(I), the value of I is to be returned. If there is no match at all, I is to be assigned the value 0.

7. Write a subroutine that will find the median of a given list of *n* numbers. The median is the number in the list whose size is in the "middle." Thus, if *n* is odd and the numbers are all different, half of the remaining numbers are larger than the median and half are smaller. This definition must be modified slightly if *n* is even or if more than one number is in the middle. What modifications would you make?

8. Develop subroutines for doing addition and subtraction in any given base. The subroutine for addition could be designed to manipulate the values of the vectors L and M to produce a vector N, using the value of K as the base. Assume that the values of L(2), L(3), ..., L(30) and M(2), M(3), ..., M(30) are the digits of the two given numbers in base K. The values of L(1) and M(1) are used to indicate the signs of the numbers. The values of N(2), N(3), ..., N(30) are the digits of the sum (or difference) in the same base and N(1) indicates the sign of the sum (or difference). The values of N are to be found by the

subroutines. The least significant digits have the highest subscripts. Write a report on the two subprograms.

9. Write a subroutine for multiplication in any given base.

10. Write a subroutine for finding the quotient and remainder in any given base.

5.4 FURTHER REMARKS

In this chapter, we have indicated how refinement can be expressed in Basic in a number of ways. The most important technique is the use of subprograms, and, with Basic, subroutine subprograms provide a fairly direct method that can be used in all situations.

We have restricted our attention to refinements involving numerical values. But similar techniques can be used to implement refinements involving other kinds of data, particularly the character string values described in Section 6.1.

Attention should be drawn to one particular characteristic of subprograms, called *side-effects*. One example of a side-effect is the way in which a subprogram can change the values of various variables which, perhaps inadvertently, also appear in other parts of the program. The user of a subprogram must know that such side-effects are possible and must be able to modify his or her programs to avoid any difficulties that might arise because of them.

Some programming languages, such as Algol and PL/I, allow subprograms to be recursive. In order to implement this feature in machine language, the return address must be placed in a stack when the subprogram is entered. When the computations within the subprogram have been completed, control must then be returned to the address given at the top of the stack, and the top item in the stack must be removed. (The use of a stack was introduced in Section 1.4.) In this way, it is possible to have a subprogram call itself. Provision must also be made to have the correct argument values available, and, once again, a stack may be used.

We have been concentrating in this chapter on explaining various ways in which "Where-End" constructs can be rendered in Basic. But, before closing, we should emphasize the importance of the idea of refinement in the overall process of developing programs, as opposed to the use of "Where-Ends" in the description of a particular program.

From this somewhat broader point of view we are led to considering the development of a program as a sequence of refinements, starting at a very high level, with perhaps, for the purpose of illustration, an outline of the following general form:

Input data
Do the necessary calculations
Output results

This is then refined in several ways; we make more specific statements about the input data, we break the "calculations" stage into a succession of smaller stages, and we specify the output more precisely.

As this process is continued, we become more precise about each part. We may, of course, have to back up frequently and redefine higher levels of the specifications, possibly even to redefine the original problem. Eventually, we may wish to express some parts of the program as a sequence of subroutine "calls," which, with the Basic language, would be expressed using a sequence of GOSUB statements, where we are able to

state quite precisely what each subroutine is required to do. At this point, we are in a position to isolate parts of what has to be done; we could then consider these tasks separately, for their development, testing, and documentation.

In any event, this general view of refinement, and the resulting top-down development of programs, is helpful in producing programs in a sound, systematic way. And it is clear that the subprogram facility, especially the subroutine subprogram facility, plays a very important role in this process.

CHAPTER **6**

Data Structures

In earlier chapters we gave considerable attention to features of Basic programming, such as control structures, subprograms, and so on, that were used only in conjunction with relatively simple data items. We have mainly used only simple numerical variables and subscripted variables. It is the purpose of this chapter to show how other data types that were introduced in Section 1.4 can be represented in Basic. We also show how linked lists can be represented in Basic, and we introduce some ideas that may be useful for representing and manipulating other data structures that were mentioned in Section 1.4.

6.1 OTHER TYPES

In all the programs considered so far, we have concentrated on manipulating numerical values. It is also desirable to be able to manipulate *alphanumeric* or *character* information, which includes alphabetic, numeric, and special characters. We have already indicated how such information can be output, as in the statement

```
120 PRINT "THE SUM IS", S
```

which was used in Fig. 2.8. This illustrates how constant alphanumeric information may appear in a PRINT statement to be output.

In Basic, it is also possible to use variable names that represent alphanumeric or character information. Such variable names are identified by the use of a dollar sign at the end of the variable name. Thus, while the names A, X, and Y2 can represent numerical values, the variables A$, X$, and Y2$ may be used to represent alphanumeric or character information. (Some versions of Basic allow only a letter followed by a dollar sign; with such versions the variable name Y2$ is not allowed). The information consists of a string of one or more characters and the variable names are sometimes called string variables. The maximum number of characters that can be contained in a string depends on the particular version of Basic being used, and is usually 72 or more, but can be less, especially with versions that are available with smaller machines.

An example of a program that uses string variables is given in Fig. 6.1. This simple program inputs a character string and outputs it. It then inputs the next character string and outputs it. When the character string END OF INPUT is encountered, the program stops. The data for the program of Fig. 6.1 is provided by the statements numbered 100 and 110. With these statements, the program in Fig. 6.1 will output four lines; the first is

```
FIRST STRING
```

the second is

```
XYZ
```

and so on.

```
10   REM A PROGRAM TO LIST STRINGS OF SYMBOLS UNTIL
20   REM AN "END OF INPUT" STRING IS REACHED
30   REM LOOP
40      READ A$
50   REM ... IF("END OF INPUT" REACHED) EXIT LOOP
60      IF A$ = "END OF INPUT" THEN 90
70      PRINT A$
80   GO TO 30
90   REM END LOOP
100  DATA FIRST STRING, XYZ, NOW IS THE TIME
110  DATA 12345, END OF INPUT
120  END
```

FIG. 6.1 A program that uses a string variable A$.

Note how we have used a constant string, "END OF INPUT", in statement 60 of the program in Fig. 6.1. This shows how, at least with some versions of Basic, character strings can appear in IF statements. Character strings can also appear in assignment statements, as in

```
300 LET A$ = "YES"
```

The string is enclosed in quotation marks in such cases.

When character strings are given in DATA statements, they need not be enclosed in quotation marks; the strings may simply be separated by commas. It should also be pointed out that when the string 12345 is input and assigned to the variable A$, the representation is not the same as the value that would be assigned to a numerical variable X in such a situation. A$ would be a string consisting of the five characters 1, 2, 3, 4, and 5, whereas X would have the numerical value 12345. (Further details are given in Section B.2, where we use a hypothetical machine to illustrate.)

Some versions of Basic provide a number of built-in functions and special operations for character strings. For example, built-in functions for determining the length of a string, or the position of a particular character in a string, may be included; an operation for concatenation, that is, for joining two strings together, may also be available. However, we will not make use of any such special functions or operators in our examples and they are not required in the exercises that follow.

Character variables may be subscripted according to the same rules that applied to numerical variables. Y(3) is the third component of an array and has a numerical value, such as 3.456; Y$(3) is also the third component of an array, but its value would be a character string, such as THE 3 PIGS.

String variables may also be compared with the help of the relational operators. In Fig. 6.1 we have already seen an example using =, but the other relational operators, such as < and >, can be used as well. The "order" used is the usual alphabetical order. Thus,

```
500  REM SUBROUTINE THAT COUNTS THE
510  REM NUMBER OF BLANKS AMONG THE
520  REM CHARACTERS STORED IN
530  REM THE ARRAY L$
540  REM
550  LET C = 0
560  LET I = 1
570  REM LOOP
580  REM ... IF (SPECIAL SYMBOL FOUND) EXIT LOOP
590     IF L$(I) = "↑" THEN 660
600     REM IF (BLANK FOUND) INCREMENT C
610     IF L$(I) <> " " THEN 630
620        LET C = C + 1
630     REM
640     LET I = I + 1
650  GO TO 570
660  REM END LOOP
670  RETURN
```

FIG. 6.2 A subroutine that determines the number of blanks in an array of characters.

if A$ is JOHN and B$ is MARY then A$ < B$ is true, and

```
100 IF A$ < B$ THEN 200
```

would cause transfer of control to statement 200.

User-defined character string functions are permitted in some versions of Basic. Again, the name used is the same as a name for a numerical function, except that it is followed by a dollar sign. Thus, FNA is the name of a numerical function, whereas FNA$ is allowed as the name of a character string function.

To further illustrate how character strings can be manipulated in Basic, we give a subroutine in Fig. 6.2 that counts the number of blank characters, or spaces, in a given array of characters. It is assumed that each character is stored in a separate component of the singly subscripted array L$ and that a special symbol such as ↑ has been used to mark the end of the array. (Thus, the symbol ↑ cannot appear as a character within the array being examined.) Note how the subroutine examines each character, one at a time, until the special symbol is encountered.

Another data type that was introduced in Section 1.4 was the logical type. The Basic language has no logical data type, and we must use numerical values, such as 0 and 1, to represent such values. As noted earlier, some versions of Basic allow the three logical operators AND, OR, and NOT to be used in IF statements.

EXERCISE 6.1

1. Give a Basic program that makes use of the subroutine given in Fig. 6.2 to determine the number of blanks in each of a sequence of character string arrays. Your program should try out a variety of inputs, until the end of the data is encountered.

2.–6. Give subprograms corresponding to Questions 1, 2, 5, 6, and 7 of Exercise 1.4.

7. Write a subroutine that is able to begin with an array similar to that provided to the subroutine in Fig. 6.2, and then remove all blanks from the array. Describe carefully what your subroutine will do, and document any side-effects of which the user must be made aware.

8. Write a subroutine that will sort an array of names.

6.2 LINKED LISTS

The idea of linked lists was introduced in Section 1.4. In the present section, we develop some additional motivation for their use, and show how they can be represented in Basic. In the discussion that follows, we illustrate the use of linked lists to represent lists of symbols.

There are many situations in which we are required to handle lists of symbols. For example, we might wish to handle the symbols used to construct a section of this book. We might wish to search them for certain words, or we might wish to "right justify" the material and divide it into pages so that it can be printed. Another example in which lists of symbols appear is in mathematical expressions, such as $(A + B)*C/3.14 + D$. There are several reasons for wanting to handle lists of this kind. One of the most important for our purposes is to analyze such a list in order to produce machine language instructions for evaluating the expression. (We consider this question in Chapter 14.)

A subscripted variable is a satisfactory way in which to represent a list for some applications, as indicated in the previous section. If the variable is $V\$$, then the value of $V\$(1)$ can represent the first symbol in the list, the value of $V\$(2)$ the second, and so on. If we want to search a list for some particular symbol, or to substitute one symbol for another, it is convenient to represent the list in this way, as we saw in the preceding section.

There are many applications for which the representation just mentioned is extremely inconvenient. For example, this would be true of any application in which we want to insert extra symbols, or to delete unwanted symbols. As a specific example, let us suppose that the text of a particular programming manual is available. Let us also suppose that we have programs that do the right justification, the paging, and so on, needed for

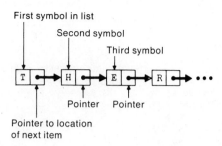

FIG. 6.3 A linked list representing a list beginning with THER.

printing the manual. Then, before producing a new edition of the manual, we need programs that will help us to edit the material. Programs for *text editing* enable us to delete and correct parts that are in error, to add new material, and so on. Manipulations of this kind will be much too slow if the list of symbols is represented by a subscripted variable in the same way that we ordinarily represent a list of numbers. For example, to insert a sublist within a given list, all the symbols beginning at the point at which the insertion is to be made must first be shifted.

The difficulty just mentioned can be overcome if we represent lists by means of *linked lists*. We consider only *one-way* linked lists in this section. These are lists in which each item consists of a symbol and a pointer to the next item in the list. A linked list that represents a list beginning with THER is shown in Fig. 6.3.

To show how this idea can be used, let us suppose that some text material beginning with THER ARE is represented by such a list and that all the unused locations are joined together in another linked list called the *available list*. (See Fig. 6.4.) There is an error in the text and THER ARE must obviously be replaced by THERE ARE. A solution to this problem is shown in Fig. 6.5. The problem has been solved without having to shift any of the original text in order to make room for the inserted symbol.

One way of representing linked lists in Basic is to use a doubly subscripted array, but this can be used only when the symbols are numbers. Another way, and the one we use in this section, is to begin with two subscripted variables that have the same number of components. In practice the number of components might be quite large. Let us denote the first variable by $S\$$ (for

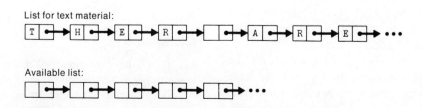

FIG. 6.4 Text material and available locations are organized into two linked lists.

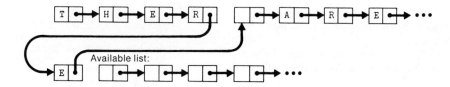

FIG. 6.5 The error in the text in Fig. 6.4 has been corrected without having to shift any of the original text material.

list of Symbols) and the second by P (for list of Pointers). Then the first item is the pair of values of S$(1) and P(1). The value of S$(1) is the symbol in the first item; it is T in Fig. 6.6. The value of P(1) is the pointer in the first item; it is 2 in Fig. 6.6. The values of S$(2) and P(2) constitute the second item in the list, and so on. For the purposes of illustration in Fig. 6.6, the symbol E that was inserted in the list THERE ARE is the value of S$(366).

A convenient way to refer to a list that is represented in the way just described is to refer to the subscript of its first element. We can give the list a name and the value of that name can be the subscript of the first item in the list. We have referred to such a name as the header. We can give such a name to the list beginning with THERE ARE; the value of this name is 1. We can give another name to the list represented by the available list. Its value was originally 366, but after the error was corrected its value was changed to 367. The end of a list can be marked with a special symbol that is not used for any other purpose, but a common practice is to simply make the final pointer equal to 0.

Let us now consider operations that can be performed on lists. We need subprograms for searching lists in various ways and for making insertions and deletions. We also need subprograms for input and output of lists. In particular, we would like to right justify and page material, as was mentioned earlier. Developing the required subprograms will be left as problems in the following exercise, and to Section 13.3, where these ideas are further developed.

It should be pointed out that we can easily handle several lists in addition to the available list, rather than just one as was done in the illustration. It would be useful to have a subprogram for splitting one list into two separate lists and another for joining two lists to form one large one. When we join two lists in this way, we say we *concatenate* the two lists. (As we mentioned earlier, some versions of Basic have built-in functions or special operators for some of these tasks.)

One final point should be mentioned. In the discussion so far we have considered lists to be lists of single symbols. However, the ideas can be extended so that the individual symbols can be replaced by more complicated things, for example, by pairs of symbols, by triples, or even by other strings of various lengths. We will not pursue this idea any further at this stage.

EXERCISE 6.2

1. Assume that we have two subscripted variables of equal length and develop a subprogram for organizing these two variables into a single linked list. This list is intended to be the available list at the beginning of an application, and an appropriate name should be given to this list. The value of the name of the list should be the first subscript in the list.

2. Two subprograms are required: one that will input a vector of numerical values containing n components and that will then store the values in a linked list L(H), L(H+1),..., whose pointers are P(H), P(H+1),..., and one that will output the components of such a linked list in the order specified by the pointers.

3. Modify the subprograms that were required in Question 2 so that they will handle character values.

4. Write subprograms for carrying out each of the following:

a) search a specified list, from a specified location, for the first occurrence of a particular symbol, and determine the location of that symbol as well as the location of its immediate predecessor (if it has one);

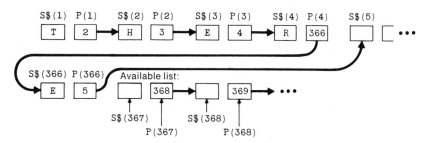

FIG. 6.6 Two subscripted variables, S$ and P, are used to represent the linked lists shown in Fig. 6.5.

b) count the number of occurrences of a particular symbol in a specified list;

c) search a specified list for the first occurrence of a particular sublist and determine the location of the beginning of that sublist as well as the location of its immediate predecessor (if it has one).

5. Write a program that will input a vector of n positive components in nondecreasing order into a linked list. The program is to then input additional positive numbers, and insert these numbers into the linked list so that the numerical order is preserved. When the end of the input is reached, the components of the linked list are to be output in numerical order.

6. Construct a program that will input a vector of n components that are in increasing order into a linked list. The numbers are unique; no duplicates are to be contained in the list. The program is to then input a sequence of ordered pairs that represent transactions to be performed on the linked list. The first item represents the type of the transaction, and the second provides the data for the transaction. The transactions to be processed are modifications and additions to, and deletions from, the numbers in the linked list. When the end of the transactions is reached, the components of the linked list are to be output in increasing order.

Ensure that your program does something sensible when invalid transactions are encountered. For example, consider the insertion of a number that is already contained in the list, and the deletion of a number that is not contained in the list. Document your program carefully.

7. Write a subprogram that will replace the portion of a list beginning at a specified location with a given sublist. Assume (a) that the portion being replaced and the given sublist are of the same length, and (b) that the location of the immediate predecessor is known whenever necessary.

8. Develop subprograms for deleting portions of lists and for inserting given sublists at specified locations.

9. Write a subprogram for concatenation. This subprogram should begin with two distinct lists and join them, so that the second follows on from the end of the first to make one long list. Provide another subprogram that will split one list into smaller ones.

6.3 OTHER DATA STRUCTURES

As indicated in Section 1.4, there are many forms in which we might want to work with data. We have seen how single values of various types are represented in Basic and how arrays are represented in a direct way. In Section 6.2, we showed how linked lists can be constructed using arrays in Basic. We consider now some of the other data structures that were mentioned in Chapter 1.

The use of a *stack* in evaluating arithmetic expressions was introduced in Section 1.4. We also mentioned stacks briefly in connection with recursive subprograms.

```
1000 REM SUBROUTINE TO PERFORM ADDITION
1010 REM ON THE TOP TWO NUMBERS ON THE STACK
1020 REM S REPRESENTS THE STACK
1030 REM T POINTS TO THE TOP OF THE STACK
1040 REM
1050 LET S(T-1) = S(T-1) + S(T)
1060 LET T = T-1
1070 RETURN
```

FIG. 6.7 A Basic subroutine that corresponds to the ADD operation in Fig. 1.16. The subroutine replaces the top two numbers on the stack with their sum.

To represent a stack in Basic, an array is all that is required. The operations that are to be performed with the stack can then be carried out by various subprograms. For example, if we consider the application illustrated in Fig. 1.16, we would require subprograms for placing an item on the stack, adding, multiplying, and so on. An example of a subprogram for addition of two numbers on the top of a stack is given in Fig. 6.7. Note how the result is obtained and assigned to the component that becomes the new top item on the stack. It is left as an exercise to improve the robustness of the subprogram in Fig. 6.7.

A *queue* can be rendered in Basic using an array, or a linked list. With the latter representation, we require a pointer to point to the head of the queue, and possibly another pointer to point to the end of the queue, as well as a header for the available list.

With queues, we require subprograms that will add items to the end of the queue and remove items from the head of the queue. (With queues, the "first-in, first-out" rule governs how items are added and removed.) In Fig. 6.8, we give a subroutine that adds an item to the end of a queue. In this example, we have used a singly subscripted array to represent the queue. Note that, when the end of the array is reached, we start back at the beginning. It is left as an exercise to improve the robustness of this program, since we have not made any provision for the case in which the queue "overflows."

In Section 1.4, we illustrated a number of ways in which *graphs* can be represented. With Basic, a list of

```
1200 REM SUBROUTINE TO ENTER AN ITEM INTO A QUEUE
1210 REM
1220 REM I - ITEM TO BE ADDED TO QUEUE
1230 REM Q - VECTOR OF N COMPONENTS REPRESENTS QUEUE
1240 REM H - THE HEAD OF THE QUEUE
1250 REM T - THE END OF THE QUEUE
1260 REM
1270 LET T = T + 1
1280 IF T <= N THEN 1300
1290       LET T = 1
1300 REM
1310 LET Q(T) = I
1320 RETURN
```

FIG. 6.8 A subroutine that adds an item to a queue. The queue is represented by a singly subscripted array.

edges can be represented directly using an array. An adjacency matrix can also be represented directly using a doubly subscripted array of numerical values. In Section 13.1, we suggest additional methods for representing such structures; these can be handled using what is available in Basic.

In Fig. 6.9, we have illustrated a *tree* consisting of numerical values. The set of integers 3, 16, 19, 21, 22, 25, 29, 36, 45, 69 is shown as a tree. This tree has a special property. For each node in the tree, all numbers contained in the left subtree are less than the number at the node being considered. As well, all numbers contained in the right subtree of a node are greater than the number at that node. A tree with this property is said to be *ordered*. The property is useful, especially for searching. To carry out a search, we start at the root. If the number being searched is smaller, we follow the left branch; otherwise, we follow the right branch (unless we have found the number). The process terminates when we find the item, or when we reach a leaf, or when there is no branch to follow.

It is natural to represent the tree in Fig. 6.9 using a linked list. As well as storing the number at each node, we require two pointers for each node, one for each of the two branches at each node. We also require a pointer to the root of the tree. The tree can be represented using a doubly subscripted array. In Fig. 6.10 we have given a representation of the tree of Fig. 6.9. The first column of the array contains the data values for each node; the second column contains the pointers to the left subtree for each node; the third column gives the pointers to the right subtree for each node. The values of the pointers are row numbers in the array. At each leaf, the pointers are zero. The root of the tree is 6.

In Fig. 6.11, we give a subroutine that determines whether or not an item is contained in a tree. We have assumed that the tree consists of numerical values and is ordered in the same manner as the tree illustrated in Fig. 6.9. The representation of the tree is assumed to be as given in Fig. 6.10.

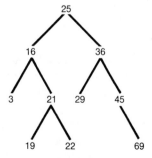

FIG. 6.9 A tree of numerical values, organized in such a way that the tree has a special property. It is said to be *ordered*.

Component of array	Node data	Left subtree	Right subtree	
1	3	0	0	
2	16	1	4	
3	19	0	0	
4	21	3	5	
5	22	0	0	Root
6	25	2	8	is 6
7	29	0	0	
8	36	7	9	
9	45	0	10	
10	69	0	0	

FIG. 6.10 The tree in Fig. 6.9 is represented by an array containing the data for each node and pointers to each subtree of each node.

In the subroutine we have provided comments that describe the process in terms of the tree; these should help the reader to understand portions of the program. The value of K is used to denote the node currently being considered; we should not use R for this purpose throughout the subprogram since the subroutine should not change the value of this variable.

```
2000 REM    SUBROUTINE TO DETERMINE WHETHER OR NOT
2010 REM    AN ITEM IS CONTAINED IN AN ORDERED TREE
2020 REM
2030 REM    T(N,3)    REPRESENTS THE TREE
2040 REM    R         REPRESENTS THE ROOT
2050 REM    I         ITEM TO BE FOUND
2060 REM    K         LOCAL VARIABLE POINTS TO A NODE
2070 REM    A         ANSWER = 1 IF FOUND, = 0 IF NOT
2080 REM
2090 LET K = R
2100 REM LOOP
2110 REM
2120     REM ... IF(NODE FOUND) SET ANSWER AND EXIT
2130     IF T(K,1)< >I THEN 2160
2140        LET A = 1
2150        GO TO 2380
2160     REM
2170     REM  CAN THE SEARCH CONTINUE DOWN A BRANCH
2180     REM  TRY THE LEFT BRANCH
2190     IF T(K,1)<I THEN 2270
2200 REM ... IF(NO BRANCH TO FOLLOW)SET ANSWER AND EXIT
2210        IF T(K,2)< >0 THEN 2240
2220           LET A = 0
2230           GO TO 2380
2240        REM
2250        LET K = T(K,2)
2260        GO TO 2350
2270     REM
2280     REM  TRY THE RIGHT BRANCH
2290 REM ... IF(NO BRANCH TO FOLLOW)SET ANSWER AND EXIT
2300        IF T(K,3)< >0 THEN 2330
2310           LET A = 0
2320           GO TO 2380
2330        REM
2340        LET K = T(K,3)
2350     REM
2360 GO TO 2110
2370 REM  END LOOP
2380 REM
2390 RETURN
```

FIG. 6.11 A subprogram that searches an ordered tree of numerical values to determine whether or not a given item is contained in the tree.

So far, we have considered a tree in which the nodes are single numerical values. In some applications, the nodes may consist of other data types, or the nodes may be records or arrays or linked lists. Also, we have considered trees with the property that each node contains at most two branches. Such trees are called *binary trees*. In the more general situation, a node of a tree may have many branches.

As a final example, we have given in Fig. 6.12 an extension of the representation for a tree that is given in Fig. 6.10. An additional column has been added to the representation of the tree given in Fig. 1.15; this column provides a link from each node to its *parent*. (The nomenclature is derived from an obvious analogy.) This additional information provides a more complete description for each node, and has the advantage that we can trace a path very quickly from a leaf to the root, as well as from the root to a leaf.

What we have done in Fig. 6.12 is to represent the tree using a three-way linked list. At any node we can immediately determine whether or not we are at a leaf, where to find the parent for this node, if any, where to find the root of the left subtree for this node, and so on. There are a number of types of operations that we may wish to perform on a tree, and the representation that we have used makes it convenient to do such things as traverse the tree from the root to a leaf, traverse the tree visiting each leaf once, add new leaves, and "prune" leaves and branches.

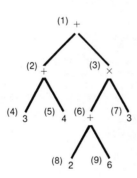

Number of node	Node data	Link to left leaf	Link to right leaf	Link to parent node
1	+	2	3	0
2	+	4	5	1
3	×	6	7	1
4	3	0	0	2
5	4	0	0	2
6	+	8	9	3
7	3	0	0	3
8	2	0	0	6
9	6	0	0	6

FIG. 6.12 A representation of the tree in Fig. 1.15 is provided by a three-way linked list.

When deciding on an appropriate data structure one must remember the operations that must be performed on the data. Often, the operations that must be carried out will dictate the type of data structure to be used to represent the data. Also, it is sometimes convenient to change the representation from one type of structure to another, in order to perform a process that can be described more easily, or carried out more efficiently in terms of the new structure.

EXERCISE 6.3

1. How can the robustness of the subroutine given in Fig. 6.7 be improved? What change would be required to the subroutine in order that it correspond to the Multiply operation of Fig. 1.16?

2. Write subroutines that place items on a stack, and remove items from a stack. Assume that the stack is represented by a singly subscripted array. What steps should be taken to ensure that your subroutines handle unusual situations?

3. Assume that a stack is represented by a linked list. What difficulty will be encountered in constructing subroutines that place items on a stack and remove items from a stack? How can this difficulty be overcome? Write the two subroutines.

4. How can the robustness of the subroutine given in Fig. 6.8 be improved? Write a subroutine that removes an item from a queue, using the representation assumed in Fig. 6.8.

5. Write subroutines that add and remove items from a queue, if the queue is represented by a linked list.

6. Write a subroutine for Question 3, Exercise 1.4.

7. Write a program that inputs a set of numbers in numerically increasing order, and that organizes the data into a tree similar to the representation suggested in this section.

8.–10. Write subroutines for Questions 9, 12, and 13 of Exercise 1.4.

6.4 FURTHER REMARKS

We have illustrated in this chapter how character information can be handled in many versions of Basic. The data structures that we also considered will be sufficient for all the problems that are encountered in Part III of this book. The choice of data structure depends to a large extent on the application being considered; we have shown how various structures can be implemented with the features of Basic that are generally available.

Because there is no standard version of Basic, some versions contain features that other versions do not contain. This is especially the case with character strings.

For example, we indicated that some versions contain built-in functions for dealing with character strings. It is often difficult to assess the trade-offs when this situation arises. On the one hand, using an available feature often produces a concise, understandable program that runs well on the machine being used. On the other hand, the program may not run on other machines! This further illustrates why so few computer programs are completely *portable*. Even when standards exist for a programming language, it is usually the case that compilers or interpreters are developed that support extensions beyond the standard features.

CHAPTER 7

Input and Output

So far, we have mostly used only one type of input statement, namely, the READ statement. We have also not directed much attention to the problem of arranging the output from our programs in the most appropriate way for the user. We have, until now, concentrated on how other aspects of algorithms can be translated from the notation of Chapter 1 into Basic.

In some applications we would like to be able to handle many numbers at one time, and know how to arrange them in any way we like. For example, we would like to be able to output numbers in the form of tables, with proper spacing between the numbers and suitable headings for each column of the table. Unfortunately, the flexibility that is needed to do all this can make input and output statements quite complicated. It is also the case that some versions of Basic do not have a sufficient number of features to allow us to achieve all of the results we might desire. The purpose of this chapter is to explain in more detail the use of input and output statements in Basic.

7.1 READ AND INPUT STATEMENTS

In almost all the examples considered so far, we used READ and DATA statements to input values to our programs. The DATA statements must appear within the program and, as noted earlier, provide a list of values to be used each time a READ statement is executed.

Whenever a READ statement is encountered, a sufficient number of values from the list is used to supply the data values.

The order in which the data is given in DATA statements, and the statement numbers of the DATA statements themselves, are important. For example, if a program is to input pairs of numbers, the order in which the numbers are written in the DATA statements determines which numbers will be the "first" and which will be the "second" for each pair. With the statements

```
35 DATA 6, 3, 8.1, 9, 4
36 DATA −6, 9, 7
```

the pairs will be (6, 3), (8.1, 9), (4, −6), and (9, 7). On the other hand, with the statements

```
35 DATA −6, 9, 7
36 DATA 6, 3, 8.1, 9, 4
```

the pairs will be (−6, 9), (7, 6), (3, 8.1), and (9, 4).

Sometimes we do not know in advance what values are going to be input. Instead, the data values are known only when the program is being executed. Also, it is sometimes convenient to be able to supply the data interactively for a program as it is being executed, rather than when the program is being written. In such cases, an INPUT statement is useful. In Fig. 2.5, we illustrated how such a statement can be used. When such statements are used, the data must be supplied from the

```
 5 INPUT A, B
10 REM IF(A > B) INTERCHANGE A, B

   ──────
   ──────  (as in Fig. 2.8)
   ──────

90 PRINT "THE GCD IS", A
92 GO TO 5
95 END

RUN
? 210, 154
THE GCD IS        14
? 3, 5
THE GCD IS        1
? 27, 9
THE GCD IS        9
? 101, 101
THE GCD IS        101
?
```

FIG. 7.1 An example of an INPUT statement being used to supply data to Euclid's algorithm.

terminal device being used, and the computer waits for the user to type in the data values. For example, with the Basic statement

```
10 READ A, B
```

the computer is directed to use the list of values that are supplied in DATA statements to obtain values for the variables A and B. But with the statement

```
10 INPUT A, B
```

the computer is directed to obtain values for the variables A and B from the terminal device. The computer prompts the user with a question mark, and waits for the user to type in the two values to be used. The numerical values must be separated by a comma when the user types them, but no statement number or other identifying information is required.

An example of an interactive session is shown in Fig. 7.1, where we have used Euclid's algorithm to determine the greatest common divisor of two numbers. The READ statement was changed to an INPUT statement, and we inserted a GO TO statement just before the END statement; otherwise, the program is identical to that given in Fig. 2.8.

Note that each time some data is required, a question mark is typed by the computer and the user then types in the data to be used. Then the program determines and outputs the result, as specified by the PRINT statement. This feature of Basic for supplying data at execution time can be very useful, especially when programs are being tested.

Before leaving this example, we should point out that one improvement would be to have the program output a message to indicate to the user the action that is required. For example, the following illustrates what might be used:

```
5 PRINT "TYPE TWO POSITIVE INTEGERS"
6 PRINT "SEPARATED BY A COMMA"
7 INPUT A, B
```

It should also be pointed out that the program given in Fig. 7.1 does not contain any provision for stopping. One possibility that works with most systems is for the user to type STOP; another possibility is to modify the program, as suggested in Question 3, Exercise 2.2.

One further point about the use of INPUT statements should be explained at this point. Suppose that a program contains the two statements

```
35 INPUT X
40 INPUT Y
```

In this case, the computer will type a question mark and wait for the user to provide a value for X. Then it will type a question mark and wait for the user to provide a value for Y. This should be compared to what happens if the program contains the single statement

```
37 INPUT X, Y
```

since, as indicated earlier, a different response is required from the user. In the latter case, two numbers are required, separated by a comma.

The input of arrays of values can become more complicated. For example, suppose the array B has three components and we wish to input all three values. We might use

```
50 INPUT B(1), B(2), B(3)
```

or we might use

```
50 FOR I = 1 TO 3
55     INPUT B(I)
60 NEXT I
```

A third alternative is to use

```
50 MAT INPUT B
```

which causes all values of B (the number of values depending on the information given in a DIM statement) to be input. With the first example, the user is expected to type one line containing three numerical values, with commas separating the numbers. In the second example, the user will type one number on each of three lines, being prompted by a question mark on each line. With the third example, the same action as with the first example is required, as long as a statement such as

```
5 DIM B(3)
```

is given in the program.

When arrays of two dimensions are used, it is also important to note the order in which values are to be input. For example, the statements

```
40  FOR I = 1 TO N
50    FOR J = 1 TO M
60      INPUT X(I,J)
70    NEXT J
80  NEXT I
```

indicate that the array is being input in row order, and the numerical values must be organized so that the value of X(1,1) is followed by the value for X(1,2), and so on.

Finally, it should be remembered that when a program is to input both numerical and character string data, the organization of the data is once again very important. Whether the input is being accomplished by READ or INPUT statements (or both!), it is necessary to be extremely careful to ensure that the program does not attempt to assign the character information to variables that represent numerical values, or assign numerical information to variables that represent character values. In the first instance, an error message will be produced. However, in the second instance, no error message is produced, since a character string might consist of a string of digits.

EXERCISE 7.1

1. DATA statements have been prepared for a program that makes a payroll calculation. Each statement contains the following information:

(1) the name of the employee;
(2) the employee's number;
(3) the number of dependents;
(4) the number of hours worked;
(5) the hourly rate of pay (in cents);
(6) whether or not the employee is a union member.

Give an appropriate READ statement that will input these items.

2. Three arrays, A, B, and C, have 100 components each. Their values are given in DATA statements, the three first components in the first DATA statement, the three second components in the second DATA statement, and so on. Give Basic statements that will input all these values.

3. Suppose that a large number of positive numbers has been collected and is to be input to a program that will find and output the smallest and the largest of these numbers. How would you organize the data for the program? Write the required program.

4. A common problem in statistics is to find the mean and the standard deviation of a large number of numbers. If the numbers are denoted by $x_1, x_2, x_3, \ldots, x_n$, the mean is

$$\frac{x_1 + x_2 + \cdots + x_n}{n}$$

and the standard deviation may be written as

$$\sqrt{\frac{n(x_1^2 + x_2^2 + \cdots + x_n^2) - (x_1 + x_2 + \cdots + x_n)^2}{n^2}}.$$

Write a program that will find the mean and the standard deviation for the input described in Question 3. A report should be provided, as outlined in Exercise 2.2.

7.2 PRINT STATEMENTS

We have already indicated that values to be output, together with identifying information, can appear in PRINT statements, as in

```
80 PRINT "THE ANSWER IS", A
```

With PRINT statements, a list of items to be output is given, separated by commas. The items may be character strings enclosed in quotation marks, or variables, as in this example. They may also be expressions. For example, we could write

```
50 PRINT "THE SUM IS", A + B
```

In this case, the value of the numerical expression $A + B$ will be output. The printing occurs in columns across the page, usually in five columns, and each column usually uses 15 positions. If too many items appear in a PRINT statement to be printed in one line, additional lines will be used to output the required values. For example, if seven values are output, the first five will appear on one line and the next two will appear on the next line of output. A single item—for example, a long message—may require more than one column.

It is also possible for a program to contain a statement such as

```
50 PRINT
```

in which no items are specified to be printed. This results in a blank line being printed.

It is also possible to use a semicolon to separate the items in a PRINT statement. When this is done, the extra spaces between the output values are not used. For example, with

```
10 PRINT 1, 2
```

the output would appear as

```
1          2
```

whereas with

```
10 PRINT 1; 2
```

the output would be

```
1    2
```

In the first case, each number occupies 15 positions (the first position is for the sign); in the second case, space is provided only for the maximum number of significant digits allowed by the system.

If a comma or semicolon is given at the end of a PRINT statement, the next item to be printed will appear on the same line, so long as the line is not "filled up." This feature of Basic is often useful in conjunction with INPUT statements to help identify to the user of a program the action that is required. For example, we might use the following:

```
50 PRINT "WHAT ARE THE TWO NUMBERS";
60 INPUT A, B
```

When the program is executed, the next line would appear as follows:

```
WHAT ARE THE TWO NUMBERS? 6, 3
```

The question mark is printed by the computer, as noted in the previous section, as a result of executing the INPUT statement. The user then types in the 6, 3.

We indicated earlier that it is often useful to include identifying information when a program produces some output, to help the user identify the result. This can be done in various ways. For example, it is sometimes useful to have column headings printed above the numerical values in a table of output. Figure 7.2 illustrates this with a very simple program. Note that the column headings are printed before the loop is executed, as the PRINT statement appears prior to the statements that make up the loop.

As was the case with READ and INPUT statements, it is also possible to use the qualifier MAT to output arrays. For example, the statement

```
50 MAT PRINT X
```

will cause all values of the array X to be output.

Most versions of Basic do not provide for format control of the output, but a few do have such a feature. However, the details are too specific to each of these versions to be considered in this book.

```
10 PRINT "NUMBER", "SQUARE", "SQUARE ROOT"
20 FOR I = 1 TO 10
30    PRINT I, I*I, SQR(I)
40 NEXT I
50 END

RUN
NUMBER          SQUARE          SQUARE ROOT
1               1               1
2               4               1.414213562
3               9               1.732050808
4               16              2
5               25              2.236067977
6               36              2.449489743
7               49              2.645751311
8               64              2.828427125
9               81              3
10              100             3.16227766
```

FIG. 7.2 A simple program that generates the squares and square roots of the integers from 1 to 10.

```
10 FOR I=0 TO 4 STEP .2
20    PRINT TAB(10*SIN(I) + 15.5); "*"
30 NEXT I
40 END

RUN
```

FIG. 7.3 A program that uses the TAB function to produce a graph.

The use of one function that is standard with almost all versions of Basic does provide some facility for organizing the output of our program. The function TAB can be used to position the output of a line in a particular column. The argument of the TAB function gives the column number. We can use this feature to construct simple graphs, as illustrated by the program in Fig. 7.3, where we give a program that generates a graph of the sine function. Note how the TAB function has been used to cause an asterisk to be printed in an appropriate column for each line that is printed by the program in Fig. 7.3. If X is not an integer, TAB(X) is evaluated as TAB(INT(X)).

EXERCISE 7.2

1. Give a PRINT statement that will output the values of x and y in the form

⎵⎵X⎵IS⎵⎵$xxxxxx$⎵⎵⎵AND⎵Y⎵IS⎵⎵$yyyyyy$

where ⎵ stands for a blank, while $xxxxxx$ and $yyyyyy$ are the values of x and y.

2. Suppose that all 25 components of two arrays X and Y have been evaluated. Give Basic statements that will output 5 blank lines, followed by the heading

⎵THE⎵COMPUTED⎵VALUES⎵OF⎵THE⎵TWO⎵ARRAYS
⎵⎵⎵⎵⎵ARE⎵GIVEN⎵IN⎵THIS⎵TABLE

followed by two blank lines, and then the column headings for I, X(I), and Y(I), followed by one blank line, and then the 25 lines of values.

3. The arrangement of the numbers given below is referred to as Pascal's triangle. The first five rows of the triangle are shown below.

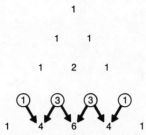

```
            1

         1     1

      1     2     1

   ①    ③    ③    ①
   1    4    6    4    1
```

The number of entries in each row is the same as the number of the row. If we start with any given row, we may calculate the entries in the next row as follows: The first and last entries are 1; each of the other entries is the sum of the two numbers directly above, as shown in the diagram.

a) What are the sixth and seventh rows of the triangle?
b) Suppose that the entries of the Nth row are the components of an array R? Write a sequence of Basic statements that will produce the values of a second array, whose components are the elements of the $(N + 1)$st row.
c) If the suggestion in (b) is followed, what procedure would be required before the same sequence of statements could be used to generate the $(N + 2)$nd row?

4. In generating the rows of the Pascal triangle, a second array is not required for the entries of the next row, provided we are careful about the order in which we produce the new entries. Describe such a procedure.

5. Write a program that will generate and output the first 15 rows of the Pascal triangle. Print the results as in the diagram below.

```
1
1   1
1   2   1
1   3   3   1
```

6. Write a sequence of Basic statements that will input a natural number N, a special character (such as an asterisk), and the blank character, and then print a line consisting of all blanks, except that the special character is printed in the Nth position.

7. Write a sequence of Basic statements that will convert a ten-digit positive integer into its equivalent ten one-digit representation, and then print the number by printing each digit.

For at least one of the following, a report should be prepared, as outlined in Section 2.2.

8. Write a program that counts and outputs the number of occurrences of a sublist in a given list of characters. For example, if the sublist is ** and the list is 1**3(*)*AB**C*, the output should be 2.

9. Write a program that inputs several sentences. The output is to be the number of five-letter words that appear in the sentences.

10. Write a program that will input a value of N ($0 < N \leq$ 50), and will then input the N pairs of values of I and Y(I) that are given in subsequent DATA statements. Assume that the values of I and Y(I) are natural numbers between 1 and 50 inclusive, and that the values of I are distinct. The program is to plot a graph of the ordered pairs (I,Y(I)). The simplest way to arrange the output is to have the Y-axis across the page and the I-axis down the page.

11. Develop a program that will print the calendar for a one-year period. Input to the program should specify the day of the week on which January 1 falls and it should indicate whether the year is a leap year.

12. Suppose that pairs of positive integers are to be provided to a program. The first integer represents a student registration number and the second is his or her mark in a certain course. Prepare a program that will input all these pairs of numbers, and, after completing the input, will find and output the pairs of numbers for the top three students in the class. (More than three may have to be output in case of a tie.)

7.3 CONCLUDING REMARKS

We have seen in this chapter that some flexibility is provided by the available features of Basic to perform the input and output associated with our programs, and have indicated that some versions provide additional features to format the output in more specific ways. It is worth noting that a considerable amount of time is often required to execute the portion of a program corresponding to INPUT and PRINT statements. Much time can be spent converting data from one code to another; numbers being input must be transformed to floating-point form and numbers being output must be transformed to a printer code, and so on.

Other types of input and output statements are available with some versions of Basic. Some of these pertain to *files,* which were mentioned in Section 1.4 and are also considered in the material of Chapter 12. The input and output of data associated with such files is accomplished in a way similar to the input and output statements we have considered, but they vary from one installation to another and we will not consider them any further. The reader must determine the particulars for his or her own installation.

Answers to
Selected Questions in Part II

CHAPTER 2

Exercise 2.1

1. a) Period following J must be omitted.
   b) With an sssignment statement, an expression such as A+1 may not precede the equals sign.
   c) The comma following PRINT must be omitted.
   d) An asterisk is required following the 2; multiplication cannot be implied by juxtaposition.
   e) GO TO must be followed by a statement number; TEN must be replaced by 10.
   f) The THEN must be followed by a statement number.
   g) The parentheses are not properly matched.
   h) Another pair of quotation marks is required (probably following IS).
   i) The 60.5 is not a valid statement number; statement numbers must be positive integers.
   j) The 3/4 is not a valid constant; it must be written as .75.
   k) The word THE must be omitted.

2.
	A	B	C
a)	6	3	7
b)	8	−7	−6
c)	−1	3	−8

3. A solution, using 18, −2, and 26 as sample data, is as follows:

```
10 READ A, B, D
20 DATA 18, −2, 26
30 LET C = A * B * D
40 PRINT A, B, D, C
50 END
```

4. When the two input numbers are equal, the value of the second number is output. The program does work properly when the input numbers are negative. If the GO TO statement is omitted, the correct result is obtained when the first of the two input numbers is the larger; otherwise, both numbers are output.

5. a) The listing would be as follows:

```
10 READ A, B
12 DATA 6, 10
15 PRINT A, B
20 LET M = A
30 IF M > B THEN 60
40    LET M = B
60 REM
70 PRINT M
80 END
```

   b) The program inputs two numbers, outputs them, and then finds and outputs their maximum. It is equivalent to the program given in Fig. 2.4.

c) The program given in Fig. 2.6 is probably slightly easier to understand. Also, the program given in Fig. 2.6 can be extended easily to handle more than two numbers. In the more general case, it leads to the following group of statements being executed repeatedly, once for each number being considered:

- IF maximum > next number THEN n
-     LET maximum = next number

n REM

We will exploit this idea in Question 4, Exercise 2.2.

6. A program, including some sample data, is given below.

```
10 READ A, B, C, D
20 DATA 6, 37, −6, 12
30 LET X = A + B + C + D
40 LET Y = A*B*C*D
50 PRINT A, B, C, D
60 PRINT "SUM IS", X
70 PRINT "PRODUCT IS", Y
80 END
```

7. In the program below, the input value for M is 2.

```
10 READ M
20 DATA 2
30 LET P = 3*M*M*M*M + 7*M*M*M − M*M − 5*M + 13
40 PRINT M, P
50 END
```

The following assignment statement could also be used; it requires fewer arithmetic operations to be carried out.

```
30 LET P = (((3*M + 7)*M − 1)*M − 5)*M + 13
```

8. a) A program with some sample data is as follows:

```
10   READ N
20   DATA −7
30   IF N < 0 THEN 60
40      LET A = N
50      GO TO 80
60   REM
70      LET A = −N
80   REM
90   PRINT N, A
100  END
```

Alternatively, we could have the following:

```
10 READ N
20 DATA −7
30 LET A = N
40 IF A > 0 THEN 60
50    LET A = −A
60 REM
70 PRINT N, A
80 END
```

This solution is simpler, since it is shorter; it is also easier to read and to understand. The output, when either program is RUN, would be

-7   7

Can you provide a modification to the programs given above so that the output will be identified?

b) A program, with some representative data, is as follows:

```
10   READ A, B, C
20   DATA 4, 8, -6
30   PRINT A, B, C
40   LET M = A
50   IF M > B THEN 70
60      LET M = B
70   REM
80   IF M > C THEN 100
90      LET M = C
100  REM
110  PRINT "LARGEST IS", M
120  END
```

c) Change the two IF statements in the answer to Question 8(b) to read

```
50 IF M < B THEN 70
80 IF M < C THEN 100
```

It is also necessary to change "LARGEST IS" to "SMALLEST IS" in the output statement.

9. With the program given below, the output will be YES.

```
10   READ A, B, C, D
20   DATA 6, 18, 1, 3
30   PRINT A, B, C, D
40   IF B*D = 0 THEN 110
50   IF A*D = B*C THEN 80
60      PRINT "NO"
70      GO TO 130
80   REM
90      PRINT "YES"
100     GO TO 130
110  REM
120     PRINT "UNDEFINED"
130  REM
140  END
```

10.

```
10   READ A, B, C, D
20   DATA -3, 5, 2, 7
30   PRINT A, B, C, D
40   IF B*D <> 0 THEN 70
50      PRINT "UNDEFINED"
60      GO TO 110
70   REM
80      LET X = A*D + B*C
90      LET Y = B*D
100     PRINT X, Y
110  REM
120  END
```

Modify the program given above so that the input, as well as the output, will be identified.

11. A program, including some sample data, is as follows:

```
10   READ A, B, C
20   DATA 4, 7, 10
30   PRINT A, B, C
40   REM ENSURE EACH NUMBER IS POSITIVE
50   IF A <= 0 THEN 170
60   IF B <= 0 THEN 170
70   IF C <= 0 THEN 170
80   REM THE LENGTH OF EACH SIDE MUST
90   REM BE LESS THAN THE SUM OF
100  REM THE LENGTHS OF THE OTHER TWO
110  IF A >= B + C THEN 170
120  IF B >= A + C THEN 170
130  IF C >= A + B THEN 170
140  REM
150     PRINT "YES"
160     GO TO 190
170  REM
180     PRINT "NO"
190  REM
200  END
```

Special cases, such as 5, 5, 0 and 5, 3, 2, are not considered to be triangles by this program. How would you change the program if you wanted to consider these cases to be triangles?

12. A solution follows. What is the output with the data we have used?

```
10   READ A, B, C, D, E, F
20   DATA 1, 2, -3, 2, 0, -4
30   PRINT A, B, C, D, E, F
40   LET I = A*E - B*D
50   LET J = A*F - C*D
60   IF I <> 0 THEN 130
70      IF J <> 0 THEN 100
80         PRINT "LINES ARE COINCIDENT"
90         GO TO 150
100     REM
110        PRINT "LINES ARE PARALLEL"
120        GO TO 150
130  REM
140     PRINT "LINES INTERSECT"
150  REM
160  END
```

Exercise 2.2

1. The domain of the algorithm would now consist of sequences of positive integers, each followed by a negative integer or zero. A negative integer or zero is used to signal the end of the input.

2. Use an additional variable, such as M, to represent the sum of the squares of the numbers. Initialize the value of M using the following:

```
25 LET M = 0
```

Insert the following statement within the loop:

```
95      LET M = M + N*N
```

and, finally, include the following to identify and output the value of M:

```
125 PRINT "SUM OF SQUARES IS", M
```

3. The program given below contains a number of improvements as suggested by this question. Note how the input, as well as the output, has been identified. (See statements 90 and 350.) It is important to realize that the input must be printed before the loop consisting of statements 250–330, since the values of A and B are changed within this loop.

Statements 110–180 ensure that the two input numbers are positive integers. The INT function has been used to determine whether or not each number is an integer, and the program outputs a message if either data value is zero, a negative number, or not an integer.

Finally, the program has been designed to process a sequence of pairs of data values, until the pair 0, 0 is input.

It is worthwhile noting that the number of statements in the program is considerably larger when all these features are incorporated in the program. In the listing given below, we have placed the DATA statements at the end of the program. We have included data pairs that test a wide variety of possible inputs. Are there any possibilities that we have not tested?

```
10    REM EUCLID'S ALGORITHM
20    REM LOOP UNTIL 0, 0 IS INPUT
30       READ A, B
40       IF A <> 0 THEN 80
50          IF B <> 0 THEN 80
60    REM......EXIT LOOP
70             GO TO 370
80       REM
90       PRINT "INPUT NUMBERS ARE", A, B
100      REM ENSURE NUMBERS ARE POSITIVE INTEGERS
110      IF A <= 0 THEN 160
120      IF A <> INT(A) THEN 160
130      IF B <= 0 THEN 160
140      IF B <> INT(B) THEN 160
150      GO TO 190
160      REM
170         PRINT "INVALID INPUT"
180         GO TO 360
190      REM IF(A > B) INTERCHANGE A, B
200      IF B >= A THEN 240
210         LET T = A
220         LET A = B
230         LET B = T
240      REM
250      REM LOOP
260         REM FIND REMAINDER IN B/A
270         LET R = B - INT(B/A)*A
280      REM...IF(R = 0) EXIT INNER LOOP
290         IF R = 0 THEN 340
300         REM REPLACE B, A BY A, R RESPECTIVELY
```

```
310         LET B = A
320         LET A = R
330      GO TO 250
340      REM END INNER LOOP
350      PRINT "THE G. C. D. IS", A
360 GO TO 20
370 REM END OUTER LOOP
380 DATA 210, 154, 17, 1, 70, 6, 4, 0, 2.5, 5
390 DATA 1, 1, 7.1, 7.1, 25, 5, 13, 78
400 DATA 0, 1, 9, 4.5, 29, 29, 0, 0
410 END
```

4.   *A Program for Finding the Largest*
Number in a Sequence of Positive Numbers
by D.D.F. Day and T.E. Hull
October 1978

Purpose. The purpose of this program is to find the largest number in a sequence of positive numbers. The program is designed to work for sequences with any number of terms.

Use. Each term of the sequence must be a positive number. The last term of the sequence must be followed by a negative number, or zero. The data for the program is given in one or more DATA statements, and the program reads the data and finds and outputs the largest number in the sequence. The purpose of the extra data item is to signal the end of the input.

Description of the algorithm.

```
Largest = 0
Loop
    Input number
... If(number ≤ 0) exit loop
    If(number > largest) largest = number
End loop
Output 'The largest is', largest
Stop
```

Tests. The following sets of input have been used to test the program:

16, 3, 19, 256, −4
−10
5, 5, 4, −6
12345, 12346, −12346
12346, 12345, −12346
17, 296, 32, 295, 100, 6, 14, 1, 301, 87, 0

In each case, the program worked properly. It should be noted that the output for a sequence with no terms is the following:

```
THE LARGEST IS        0
```

Miscellaneous. The program was run on an IBM 370 computer, using the VS Basic processor.

Program listing.

```
10    LET L = 0
20    REM LOOP
30       READ N
40    REM...IF(NUMBER <= 0) EXIT LOOP
```

```
50      IF N <= 0 THEN 100
60      IF N <= L THEN 80
70         LET L = N
80      REM
90   GO TO 20
100  REM END LOOP
110  PRINT "THE LARGEST IS", L
120  DATA 16, 3, 19, 256, -4
130  END
```

5. The program would be very similar to that given with the answer to Question 4. The program must keep track of the number of numbers that have been input. When a larger number is input, it will then be possible to determine its position in the sequence. What does your program do if the sequence 2, 16, 8, 16, 3 is input?

6. One approach to determining the cost is outlined in the following:

```
If(kilowatt-hours ≤ 100)
    cost = 8 × kilowatt-hours
  else
    cost = 800 + 5 × (kilowatt-hours −100)
End if
```

Another is as follows:

```
cost = 8 × kilowatt-hours
If(kilowatt-hours > 100)
   cost = cost − 3 × (kilowatt-hours − 100)
End if
```

You should test such inputs as 99, 100, 101, as well as a few others. What checks of the data might you include in the program to ensure that the data is reasonable?

7. Ensure that you test your program using values such as 39, 40, and 41. Does your program do something sensible if the number of hours is less than zero? What other checks should be included to test the data for reasonableness?

CHAPTER 3

Exercise 3.1

1. The expressions in (f), (h), and (i) could be interpreted differently by different systems. The expressions in (a), (b), (e), and (g) could be as well, but in these cases the order of carrying out the operations would not matter, except in the case of overflow, or in the case of slight differences caused by different roundoff errors. (See Chapter 9.)

2. a) Multiplication cannot be implied by juxtaposition.
 b) A variable name must be a letter or a letter followed by a digit; KILL is invalid.
 c) Parentheses are not matched.
 d) The 3K is invalid; it must be written as 3*K (or it may be that it should be K3 if this was what the programmer intended).

e) Two operators should not be adjacent.

4. a) 0 b) −8 c) approximately 7.9
 d) 8 e) 64 f) 512
 g) approximately .1 h) −11 i) 1.
 j) approximately .1

5. Only (a) and (b) have equal values. In (c), (d), and (e), the values may differ by small amounts because the associative and distributive rules of arithmetic do not hold exactly with floating-point arithmetic. This topic is discussed in more detail in Chapter 9 and briefly in Section A.5.

6. The values in (c), (d), and (e) may differ drastically. See Chapter 9, as well as Sections A.5 and C.3.

8. a) .5*B*H
 b) A*A + B*B or A↑2 + B↑2
 c) (A*X*X + B*X + C)/(D*X + F)
 d) 3.1416*R*R

Exercise 3.2

1. The expressions in (a), (c), (d), and (f) are allowed. In (b), the L(0) is invalid, since a subscript cannot be zero (although L could possibly be a function, as discussed in Chapter 5). In (e), the parentheses are not matched; moreover, B3 cannot be the name of an array. Finally, although (f) is a valid expression, when the expression is evaluated, a division by zero condition arises.

2. Statement 130 is executed N times. If N = 0, then the loop is still executed once. An alternative sequence is

```
100 LET S = 0
110 LET I = 1
120 REM
130    IF I > N THEN 170
140    LET S = S + X(I)
150    LET I = I + 1
160 GO TO 120
170 REM
```

This alternative is preferable, since it is correct in the situation when N = 0.

3. The following portion of a program will do the task.

```
100 LET I = 1
110 REM LOOP
120    LET Z(I) = X(I) + Y(I)
130    LET I = I + 1
140 IF I <= 200 THEN 110
```

4. The following pseudo-code outlines what is required:

```
PRODUCT = 0
Loop for i = 1, 2, 3, . . . , N
    PRODUCT = PRODUCT + FIRST(I)*SECOND(I)
End loop
```

In the above, we have used FIRST and SECOND to represent the names of the vectors and we have assumed that they each have N components. The loop constructs considered in Question 2 will be helpful.

5. The polynomial can be evaluated by constructing a program that contains a loop such as

```
70   LET V = C(1)
80   LET I = 2
90   REM
100      LET V = V*X + C(I)
110      LET I = I + 1
120  IF I <= 5 THEN 90
```

or the following could be assigned to V

$$C(1)*X\uparrow4 + C(2)*X\uparrow3 + C(3)*X\uparrow2 + C(4)*X + C(5)$$

or, alternatively, we could use the expression

$$(((C(1)*X + C(2))*X + C(3))*X + C(4))*X + C(5)$$

which is, in fact, exactly what the loop given above would calculate.

Exercise 3.3

1. a) approximately 22.
b) approximately 5.

2. The expression $X - INT(X)$ represents the fractional part of the number X if $X > 0$ and it represents $(1 -$ the fractional part of X) if $X < 0$. There is no difference between writing $A(X)$ and $A(INT(X))$ if A is a singly subscripted variable.

3. a) The following solution uses the RND function to generate 25 values.

```
10 LET I = 1
20 REM LOOP
30    LET X = RND(0)
40    LET Y = SIN(X)↑2 + COS(X)↑2
50    PRINT X, Y
60    LET I = I + 1
70 IF I <= 25 THEN 20
80 END
```

4. A solution is as follows:

```
10   LET I = 1
20   REM LOOP TO INITIALIZE COUNTERS
30      LET N(I) = 0
40      LET I = I + 1
50   IF I <= 6 THEN 20
60   REM END LOOP
70   LET I = 1
80   REM LOOP TO ROLL DIE 100 TIMES
90      LET X = INT(6*RND(0)) + 1
100     LET N(X) = N(X) + 1
110     LET I = I + 1
120  IF I <= 100 THEN 80
130  REM END LOOP
140  LET I = 1
150  REM LOOP TO PRINT RESULTS
160     PRINT I, N(I)
170     LET I = I + 1
180  IF I <= 6 THEN 150
190  REM END LOOP
200  END
```

6. The following program will suffice.

```
10 LET X = 1
20 REM LOOP
30    LET F = 1/X + 1/(X+5) + SQR((X-1)/(X+1))
40    PRINT X, F
50    LET X = X + 1
60 IF X <= 25 THEN 20
70 REM END LOOP
80 END
```

7. Hint for (b): the value of

$$INT((exp)*100 + .5)/100$$

is the value of the expression *exp* rounded to two decimal places (provided *exp* is nonnegative).

10. To allow for roundoff errors, we could test the condition

$$\frac{y_2 - y_1}{x_2 - x_1} \doteq \frac{y_3 - y_2}{x_3 - x_2}$$

to determine if the points are collinear. One way of doing this is to carry out a test to make sure that

```
ABS((Y2-Y1)*(X3-X2)-(Y3-Y2)*(X2-X1))
```

is very small, less than 0.0001, say. Another test for collinearity is to determine if the area of the triangle formed by the three points is almost zero. (See Question 5.)

CHAPTER 4

Exercise 4.1

1. a) The comma following 20 must be omitted, and TO 20 and STEP 5 must be interchanged.
b) An IF statement cannot contain a PRINT statement.
c) The variable in a FOR loop must be nonsubscripted.
d) The FOR must be followed by a variable; the 1=I should probably be I=1.

2. a) One possible solution is as follows:

```
50   FOR J=1 TO 49 STEP 2
60      ―――――――
.       ―――――――
.       ―――――――
90   NEXT J
```

b) One possibility is as follows:

```
100 REM LOOP
110     IF X <= 0 THEN 210
120     IF Y <= 0 THEN 210
130     ―――――――
.       ―――――――
.       ―――――――
200 GO TO 100
210 REM END LOOP
```

c) A solution is given below; there are other possibilities.

```
300 REM LOOP
310     IF X > 0 THEN 350
320     IF Y > 0 THEN 350
330 REM ... EXIT LOOP
```

```
340      GO TO 410
350      REM
.        _____
.        _____
.        _____
400 GO TO 300
410 REM END LOOP
```

3. A solution is given below.

```
10 DIM X(200), Y(200), S(200)
.    _____
.    _____
60 FOR I=1 TO N
70     LET S(I) = X(I) + Y(I)
80 NEXT I
.    _____
```

4. A portion of a program is given below.

```
10  DIM V(100), A(100, 100), U(100)
.    _____
.    _____
80  FOR I=1 TO M
90      LET U(I) = 0
100     FOR J=1 TO N
110         LET U(I) = U(I) + A(I,J)*V(J)
120     NEXT J
130 NEXT I
.    _____
```

6. The program given below contains some sample data. What is the output?

```
10 READ N
15 DATA 7
20 PRINT "INPUT =", N
30 LET S = 0
40 FOR I=1 to 2*N−1 STEP 2
50     LET S = S+I
60 NEXT I
70 PRINT "SUM =", S
80 END
```

Can you achieve the same result with a much simpler program? (*Hint:* The sum of the series is N^2, if $N > 0$.)

8. A sequence of statements could be as follows:

```
10  DIM X(500), Y(500), ...
.    _____
.    _____
100 IF A > X(1) THEN 130
110     LET B = Y(1)
120     GO TO 270
130 REM
140 IF A < X(500) THEN 170
150     LET B = Y(500)
160     GO TO 270
170 REM
180 FOR I=2 TO 500
190     IF A < X(I) THEN 210
200 NEXT I
210 LET D1 = A − X(I−1)
220 LET D2 = X(I) − A
```

```
230 IF D1 > D2 THEN 250
240     LET I = I−1
250 REM
260 LET B = Y(I)
270 REM
```

Exercise 4.2

1. If$((x−y)^2 > 25)$

$$N = N + 1$$

$$z = \sum_{i=1}^{N} V_i$$

$(x \neq y)$

$$N = N − 1$$

$$z = \sum_{i=1}^{N} V_i^2$$

else

Output error message

$$E = 1$$

End if

The corresponding Basic program follows:

```
100 IF (X−Y)↑2 <= 25 THEN 170
110     LET N = N+1
120     LET Z = 0
130     FOR I=1 TO N
140         LET Z = Z + V(I)
150     NEXT I
160     GO TO 280
170     REM
180     IF X = Y THEN 250
190         LET N = N−1
200         LET Z = 0
210         FOR I=1 TO N
220             LET Z = Z + V(I)*V(I)
230         NEXT I
240         GO TO 280
250     REM
260         PRINT "ERROR MESSAGE"
270         LET E = 1
280 REM END IF
```

2. See the answer given for Question 12, Exercise 2.1.

3. Be sure to include tests that determine whether or not each score is nonnegative and less than 101.

4, 5, 6. The answers given for Questions 8, 9, and 10 of Exercise 1.3 will be helpful.

CHAPTER 5

Exercise 5.1

1. a) The following interchanges A and B, if required, so that A is less than or equal to B.

```
50 IF A <= B THEN 90
60     LET T = B
```

```
70     LET B = A
80     LET A = T
90 REM
```

b) The following sets D = max (A,B).

```
50  IF A >= B THEN 80
60        LET D = A
70        GO TO 100
80     REM
90        LET D = B
100 REM
```

2. Input A, B, C
M = smaller of A, B
M = smaller of M, C
Output M
Stop

A refinement was given with the answer to Question 3(b) of Exercise 1.3. The program below contains some representative data.

```
10   READ A, B, C
20   DATA 6, 12, 7
30   PRINT "INPUT =", A, B, C
40   REM I = SMALLER OF A, B
50   IF A >= B THEN 80
60        LET I = A
70        GO TO 100
80     REM
90        LET I = B
100 REM
110 REM J = SMALLER OF I, C
120 IF I >= C THEN 150
130        LET J = I
140        GO TO 170
150     REM
160        LET J = C
170 REM
180 PRINT "THE SMALLEST IS", J
190 END
```

3. Input A, B, C
Interchange A and B, if necessary, so that A ≤ B
Interchange A and C, if necessary, so that A ≤ C
Interchange B and C, if necessary, so that B ≤ C
Output A, B, C
Stop

A refinement was given with the answer to Question 3(a) of Exercise 1.3.

```
100 READ A, B, C
110 DATA 4, 8, 5
120 PRINT "INPUT IS", A, B, C
130 REM INTERCHANGE A AND B IF NECESSARY
140 IF A <= B THEN 180
150    LET T = B
160    LET B = A
170    LET A = T
180 REM INTERCHANGE A AND C IF NECESSARY
190 IF A <= C THEN 230
200    LET T = C
210    LET C = A
```

```
220    LET A = T
230 REM INTERCHANGE B AND C IF NECESSARY
240 IF B <= C THEN 280
250    LET T = C
260    LET C = B
270    LET B = T
280 REM
290 PRINT "SORTED LIST IS", A, B, C
300 END
```

Exercise 5.2

1. Change the function definition, as follows:

```
100 DEF FNY(X) = X*X − 4
```

and change the loop construct by using

```
120 FOR Z = −10 TO 10 STEP .5
```

2. Include a test following line 100 to ensure that I is a positive integer; include another test to ensure that I <= N. If either test fails, output an appropriate error massage and set FNS equal to some (arbitrary) value so the program can continue (since additional errors may be found if the program is allowed to continue).

3. See Question 3, Exercise 2.2 and the answer.

4. A solution is as follows:

```
100 DEF FNT(L)
110    LET T9 = L(1)
120    FOR T8 = 2 TO 10
130       IF T9 < L(T8) THEN 150
140          LET T9 = L(T8)
150    NEXT T8
160    LET FNT = T9
170 FNEND
```

The name of this function is FNT and we have used the variable names T9 and T8 within this function.

Exercise 5.3

1. A subroutine in Basic does not have a name or a parameter list, while a function has both. A subroutine is a sequence of Basic statements in which the logical end of the sequence is a RETURN statement. A function is described in one line (using a DEF statement) or using multiple lines (using DEF and FNEND statements); a function does not contain a RETURN statement and the value of the function must be assigned to the name of the function.

Subroutines are referenced using a GOSUB statement; a function is referenced simply by using its name, followed by the argument list that is enclosed in parentheses.

3. A solution is as follows:

```
500 REM  SUBROUTINE TO FIND THE SUBSCRIPT K
510 REM  OF THE SMALLEST COMPONENT OF A(I),
515 REM  A(I+1),...,A(N)
520 LET S1 = A(I)
530 LET K = I
540 FOR J = I+1 TO N
550    IF A(J) <= S1 THEN
```

```
560        LET S1 = A(J)
570        LET K = J
580    REM
590 NEXT J
600 RETURN
```

The input parameters are A, I, and N; the output parameter is K.

4. Use some of the suggestions given in Question 3 of Exercise 2.2, as well as the answer to that question.

5. The subprogram can be patterned on the solution given for Question 15, Exercise 1.3.

7. One approach is to sort the numbers and then determine the median. Of course, the sorting process can be stopped after half the numbers have been sorted.

8. The subroutine for addition must first determine whether or not the numbers have the same sign. If the signs are the same, the addition is straightforward. On the other hand, if the signs are not the same, the number of largest magnitude must be found. The subroutine for addition could then use a subroutine for finding the difference between the two numbers. The subroutine for subtraction could simply use the subroutine for addition, after making an appropriate change to the value of L(1).

9. This problem is more complicated. One approach is to use repeated addition. A more efficient approach is to use the "adding and shifting" technique of ordinary long multiplication.

10. One method that could be used is repeated subtraction. For example, to find the quotient and remainder for 100 ÷ 17 in base 10, the string 017 is subtracted from 100 repeatedly, until a number less than 017 is obtained. The quotient is then the number of subtractions, in this example 005, and the remainder is the last value, in this example 015. (It is intended that the individual digits in this calculation be assigned to separate components of the subscripted variables. Base ten has been used only as an illustration. The point of the question is that any base, including very large ones like 1000000, could be used just as well.) The subroutines of Question 8 can be useful. For large numbers this method could be extremely inefficient. Can you develop an efficient subroutine?

CHAPTER 6

Exercise 6.1

1. The following reads arrays of characters in a form that is suitable for the subroutine in Fig. 6.2. It outputs each array and then reports on the number of blanks it contains. It continues this process until a special string, namely, EOF (for End-Of-File), is reached.

```
10   DIM L$(100)
20   REM LOOP
30       READ L$(1)
40   REM...IF(EOF) EXIT LOOP
50       IF L$(1) = "EOF" THEN 200
60       LET N = 1
```

```
70       REM LOOP UNTIL ↑ ENCOUNTERED
80           IF L$(N) = "↑" THEN 120
90           LET N = N+1
100          READ L$(N)
110      GO TO 70
120      REM END LOOP
130      GOSUB 500
140      PRINT "INPUT ARRAY WAS "
150      FOR J=1 TO N
160          PRINT L$(J)
170      NEXT J
180      PRINT "NUMBER OF BLANKS IS", C
190  GO TO 20
200  REM END LOOP
210  STOP
500  ⎫
  ·  ⎪
  ·  ⎬  as in Fig. 6.2
  ·  ⎪
670  ⎭
700  DATA F, I, R, S, T, , S, T, R, I, N, G, ↑
710  DATA ↑
720  DATA A, , A, , A, , ↑
730  DATA 1, , 2, , 3, , 4, , 5, ↑
740  DATA EOF
750  END
```

In the above program, we have given some sample data. The form of the output would be improved if statements 140 and 160 are terminated with semicolons. As explained in Chapter 7, this has the effect of causing the output characters to be placed on a line without intervening spaces, instead of on separate lines, as would be the case with the program as it appears above.

Exercise 6.2

1. A subroutine is given below; it initializes the values in the list of pointers, P, as described in this section.

```
300 REM   SUBROUTINE TO INITIALIZE THE
310 REM   LINKED LIST WITH POINTERS
320 REM   P(1), P(2),..., P(M), AND HEADER H
330 FOR I = 2 TO M
340     LET P(I-1) = I
350 NEXT I
360 LET P(M) = 0
370 LET H = 1
380 RETURN
```

2. A subroutine for carrying out the required input is given below. How would you improve this subroutine to ensure that the available space does not overflow?

```
500 REM   INPUT SUBROUTINE
510 LET S = H
520 FOR I = 1 TO N
530     READ L(H)
540     LET H1 = H
550     LET H = P(H)
560 NEXT I
570 LET P(H1) = 0
580 RETURN
```

The corresponding output subroutine can be constructed in an obvious way, although there are opportunities to vary the format of the output to suit the particular application one has in mind, as explained in more detail in Chapter 7.

4. a) The subroutine should search the linked list starting at the specified location. If the location L is found, the value of its predecessor R should also be determined. What values should be returned for L and R if the symbol is not found? What value should be returned for R if the first symbol that is examined turns out to be the one sought?

b) Ensure that your program works with special cases, such as those that arise when the specified list contains no symbols. How could such a "null string" be represented?

c) Assume that the "particular sublist," as well as the "specified list," are both represented by linked lists.

5. Let us assume that the first number to be input is the value of n. This is followed by the n positive numbers in nondecreasing order. These in turn are followed by a sequence of numbers to be inserted; let us assume that this sequence is terminated in a special way, such as the input of a negative number.

Then here is an outline of a program that will accomplish the required task:

Dimension the arrays L and P, say to 100.
Set M = 100
Use the subroutine in Question 1 to initialize the list
Input the value of N
Use the subroutine in Question 2 to input the first N numbers
Initialize B to 1 and E to N; those mark the beginning and end of the list.
Now input numbers repeatedly until a negative number is reached; insert each positive number properly in the list.
Finally, output the list.

Three cases will have to be considered separately for the insertion of a number in the list, depending on whether the number is inserted at the beginning, at the end, or somewhere in between.

For example if the number, say V, is to be inserted at the beginning, the following sequence of statements will do what is required:

```
100 LET L(H) = V     (V is placed at head of available list)
110 LET T = H        (Location of V is saved)
120 LET H = P(H)     (New head of available list)
130 LET P(T) = B ⎫
140 LET B = T    ⎬   (V is placed at beginning)
                 ⎭
```

Exactly the same sequence of statements is required to insert V immediately after L(J) in the list, except that B is replaced by P(J). Something similar is required if V is to be inserted at the end.

6. A complete program for this question would make a good project.

Exercise 6.3

1. The value of T should be tested to ensure that $T \geq 2$ and $T \leq$ the dimension of S. In the first situation, the call-

ing program is attempting to add numbers that are not available; in the second situation, stack overflow will occur. To have the subroutine correspond to the Multiply operation, we use the following:

```
1050 LET S(T-1) = S(T-1)*S(T)
```

2. A subroutine to place an item I onto the stack S is given below. It is assumed that the dimension of S is N.

```
1100 REM  SUBROUTINE TO PUSH I ONTO
1110 REM  TOP T OF STACK S OF LENGTH N
1120 IF T >= N THEN 1160
1130     LET T = T+1
1140     LET S(T) = I
1150     RETURN
1160 REM ERROR
1170     PRINT "ERROR IN PUSH ROUTINE"
1180     PRINT "STACK OVERFLOW - ITEM IGNORED"
1190     RETURN
1199 REM END SUBROUTINE
```

3. The difficulty is that if a "one-way" linked list is used, the subroutine will have to search through the linked list to determine the predecessor of the top item every time the subroutine is called. This difficulty can be overcome by using a "two-way" linked list consisting of

(1) a list of symbols,
(2) a list of pointers to the next item for each symbol,
(3) a list of pointers to the preceding item for each symbol.

4. A test to ensure that the value of H is "greater than" the value of T so that H does not "catch up" to T would improve the robustness. The subroutine for removing an item is straightforward, similar to the subroutine given in Fig. 6.8.

5. The difficulty suggested with Question 3 will be encountered; see the answer to Question 3. Otherwise, the programs are straightforward.

CHAPTER 7

Exercise 7.1

1. A suitable statement might be

```
20 READ E$, N, D, H, R, U
```

where we have assumed that all data items with the exception of the employee's name are provided as numerical values.

2. The following could be used:

```
10 FOR I=1 TO 100
20     READ A(I), B(I), C(I)
30 NEXT I
```

3. The question does not specify how the end of the input is to be recognized. Since only positive numbers have been collected, we can use a negative number to signal the end of the input. What special situations should be tested to ensure that your program works properly?

Exercise 7.2

1. The following could be used:
```
50 PRINT "␣␣X␣IS␣␣"; X; "␣␣␣AND␣Y␣IS␣␣"; Y
```

2. The following could be used:
```
50  FOR I=1 TO 5
60     PRINT
70  NEXT I
80  PRINT "␣THE␣COMPUTED␣VALUE␣OF␣THE␣TWO␣ARRAYS"
90  PRINT "␣␣␣␣␣ARE␣GIVEN␣IN␣THIS␣TABLE"
100 PRINT
110 PRINT
120 PRINT "I", "X(I)", "Y(I)"
130 PRINT
140 FOR I=1 TO 25
150    PRINT I, X(I), Y(I)
160 NEXT I
```

3. a)
```
    1    5    10    10    5    1
  1    6    15    20    15    6    1
```

b) A suitable sequence is as follows:
```
50 LET S(1) = 1
55 LET S(N+1) = 1
60 FOR I=2 TO N
65    LET S(I) = R(I−1) + R(I)
70 NEXT I
```

c) The N+1 components of the array S must be copied into the array R using a sequence of statements such as
```
100 FOR I=1 TO N+1
110    LET R(I) = S(I)
120 NEXT I
130 LET N = N+1
```

4. Suppose that the elements of the Nth row are stored in the first N components of the subscripted variable R. The following statements will produce the entries for the (N+1)st row, for $N \geq 2$.
```
200 LET R(N+1) = 1
210 LET J = N
220 REM LOOP WHILE J > 1
230     IF J <= 1 THEN 270
240        LET R(J) = R(J) + R(J−1)
250        LET J = J−1
260 GO TO 220
270 REM END LOOP
```

The entries are produced in reverse order so that values that are required are not destroyed. It should also be mentioned that since the components of each row are symmetric about the middle entry, only half of the values need be generated. This could result in some saving for large values of N.

8. The question does not specify whether or not the list of characters is contained in a linked list or simply in a singly subscripted variable. See also Question 6, Exercise 1.4, and the solution given in the Answers to Part I.

9. As with Question 7, the representation used to store the sentences is not specified. Assume that a word consists of the blank character (unless it is the first word), followed by a string of nonblank characters, followed by a space, or a comma, or a period. What other circumstances might one want to include in a practical application?

Summary of Basic

The main purpose of this summary is to present the rules for Basic that have been discussed or referred to in the preceding chapters. Almost all the rules given are common to most versions of Basic, and, except where specifically noted, they are consistent with the original version of Basic developed at Dartmouth College. We also refer to a few of the useful extensions that are available in some versions of Basic.

The rules in the summary are primarily concerned with specifying the syntax of the language, especially where the meaning has been discussed in the preceding chapters or where the meaning is easily determined from the notation itself. In other cases, the meaning is also discussed along with the syntax.

Unfortunately, the details of the rules can vary from one version of Basic to another, even between different versions on the same machine. It is therefore not always possible to be absolutely precise; we try instead to avoid such situations if possible, or we at least draw attention to places where such variations can arise. The user must determine the particulars for the specific version of Basic he or she is using.

GENERAL REQUIREMENTS

A **Basic program** is a sequence of statements that are formed according to the rules of the language. Each statement starts with a statement number, which must be a positive integer less than some specified value (9999 in many cases). The statements are executed in increasing order of the statement numbers, unless this sequential order is specifically altered, as it can be by some statements. The last statement of a program must be an END statement.

The **character set** includes

a) the letters A B C D E F G H I J K L M N O P Q R S T U V W X Y Z

b) the digits 0 1 2 3 4 5 6 7 8 9

c) the special characters $+ - * / \uparrow = < > ( ) . ,$; " $ and the blank character. (We denote the latter by ⎵ whenever it is necessary to draw special attention to it.)

Some versions of Basic allow additional special characters, such as &, ', #, |, ¬, which can be used in comment statements and in character strings that appear between quotation marks. Some versions allow lower-case characters.

Blanks or spaces in a statement are generally ignored. However, they are not ignored in strings of characters that appear between quotation marks.

CONSTANTS, VARIABLES, EXPRESSIONS

Constants in a program may be of the following two types:

1. A **numerical constant** is a string of one or more digits, optionally preceded by a sign, with or with-

out a decimal point, and optionally followed by a decimal exponent written in the form $E \pm n$, where the $+$ is optional, and n is a string of one or more digits. The maximum permissible magnitude, as well as the number of significant digits, depends on the particular implementation.

Examples:

```
   6.              -3               0
+1234.5            .00001        -1000.01
   3.141E5        -6.2E-10        123.4E 21
```

2. A **literal constant** is a string of zero or more characters (excluding the character `"`) enclosed in quotation marks. The maximum numbers of characters depends on the implementation being used.

Examples:

```
"THE ANSWER IS"      "  A ="
"THIS IS A LITERAL CONSTANT"
```

A **simple variable name** is a letter, or a letter followed by a digit.

Examples:

```
A    B    X6
```

A **string variable name** or **character variable name** is a letter followed by a `$`. (Some versions also allow a letter followed by a digit before the `$`.)

Examples:

```
C$    X$
```

A **subscripted variable** or **array name** consists of a letter. Dimensioning information may be given in a dimension statement, as explained later; if dimensioning information is not given, it is assumed that the maximum value of each subscript is 10.

Examples:

```
K    J    X
```

A particular **component** of an array is denoted by the name of the array, followed by a list of subscripts enclosed within parentheses and separated by commas. The subscripts can be any arithmetic expressions, where the values of the expressions are positive. The maximum number of subscripts depends on the implementation; the maximum is usually two.

Examples:

```
K(1)          J(6,3)
K((I1+6)*3)   J(M,N+1)
```

Arithmetic expressions may be defined in stages in the following way:

a) Any constant is an expression. Thus,

```
123    -12.06
```

are expressions.

b) Nonsubscripted variable names and components of subscripted variables are expressions. For example,

```
I    J    K2    L(3)    X(I,3)    A(I+2)
```

are expressions. Note that an array name by itself is not an expression; only individual components of arrays can appear in arithmetic expressions.

c) Simple expressions may be combined to make more complicated expressions. For example, `123` and `I` can be combined to give the arithmetic expressions

```
I+123    123*I    123/I    I/123    123↑I
```

This process can be repeated to produce still more complicated expressions, such as

```
24*(I+123)      A+V(S)*(X-Y)
-(R+S+T)        (A+B)↑(I-7)
```

Five arithmetic operators are available, namely $+$, $-$, $*$, $/$, and $\uparrow$, along with parentheses (in some versions, `**` is used in place of $\uparrow$). Parentheses are used in the usual mathematical way, and also to avoid ambiguity. No two operators should appear side by side in an expression. For example, we should not replace $3.1\uparrow(-2)$ with $3.1\uparrow-2$ in most versions of Basic, even though we may feel the meaning of the latter is perfectly obvious.

d) The final stage in defining arithmetic expressions is to state that any function of an expression is also an expression. The functions can be built-in functions, like `ABS` and `SQR`, or user-defined functions specified using `DEF` statements, as described later in this summary. Thus the following is an expression:

```
X + 4*SQR(Y + Z)
```

Logical expressions can be formed by combining two arithmetic expressions with a relational operator, as in

```
I + 123 < X
```

The relational operators are as follows:

$<$	less than
$<=$	less than or equal to
$>$	greater than
$>=$	greater than or equal to
$=$	equal to
$<>$	not equal to

Relational operators have a lower precedence than arithmetic operators. Some versions of Basic use the character `#` in place of $<>$ to denote "not equal to." Logical expressions involving character variables, such as $A\$ < B\$$ are also allowed (order is then alphabetic).

Parentheses may be used as one would expect, and should be used whenever necessary to avoid ambiguity. No two operators should appear side by side.

Some versions of Basic also allow the operators `AND`, `OR`, and `NOT` to be used in logical expressions, as in the following examples:

```
A > 0 AND (B = 6 OR X <>Y(3))
I > J OR (NOT(B >= 4*A*C))
```

Some versions also allow operators for manipulating character strings.

EXECUTABLE STATEMENTS

In each of the following general forms, *s* represents a statement number.

An **assignment statement** is of the form

s LET *v* = *e*

where *v* is a nonsubscripted variable name or a component of an array, and *e* is an arithmetic expression.

Examples:

```
10 LET I = 0
25 LET A2 = A↑3 + B − 7*(−X)
50 LET X = ABS(B+C)
75 LET N(J) = (A−X3)/1.0E6
```

A **GO TO statement** is of the form

s GO TO *si*

where *si* is the statement number of some other statement.

Example:

```
10 GO TO 75
```

An **IF statement** is of the form

s IF *l* THEN *si*

where *l* is a logical expression and *si* is the statement number of some other statement.

Examples:

```
10 IF I > J THEN 25
20 IF B*B < 4*A*C2 THEN 75
56 IF A(N) <= A(N+1) THEN 35
```

A **FOR-NEXT loop** is of the form

```
si FOR v = i TO f STEP k
.    ————
.    ————
.    ————
sj NEXT v
```

where *v* is a simple variable, and *i, f,* and *k* are arithmetic expressions. The statements between the FOR and NEXT statements must not redefine the value of the variable *v*. If STEP *k* is omitted, it is assumed that the increment is 1.

Examples:

```
10 FOR I = 1 TO 10
.    ————
.    ————
.    ————
30 NEXT I
```

```
40 FOR J = K2+6 TO (A+B)*C STEP X9
.    ————
.    ————
.    ————
100 NEXT J
```

A **READ statement** is of the form

s READ *l*

where *l* is a list of variable names or components of arrays, separated by commas. The data values are obtained from the list provided in DATA statements.

Examples:

```
10 READ A1
25 READ I, J2, L(3)
50 READ A$, B$
75 READ A(N), B(N + J)
```

An **INPUT statement** is of the form

s INPUT *l*

where *l* is defined as with READ statements. The data values are obtained from the terminal device being used.

Examples:

```
10 INPUT R$
20 INPUT I, J(I)
```

A **PRINT statement** is of the form

s PRINT *l*

where *l* is a list of expressions, separated by commas and/or semicolons, optionally followed by a comma or semicolon.

Examples:

```
10 PRINT I, J, K
20 PRINT "THE ANSWER IS"; A
37 PRINT
40 PRINT A; H, 30*(H−40), A↑B(6)
50 PRINT N$;
```

A **GOSUB statement** is of the form

s GOSUB *si*

where *si* is the statement number of the first statement in a subroutine.

Example:

```
50 GOSUB 1000
```

A **STOP statement** is of the form

s STOP

Example:

```
162 STOP
```

NONEXECUTABLE STATEMENTS

A **comment statement** is of the form

s REM *c*

where *c* is any character string. (Although nonexecutable itself, control can be transferred to a REM statement.)

Examples:

```
10 REM THIS IS A COMMENT
62 REMARK — AT THIS POINT A<=D↑2
```

A **DATA statement** is of the form

```
s DATA l
```

where *l* is a list containing numerical constants, and/or literal constants, and/or literal constants without their quotes.

Examples:

```
30 DATA 6, −7, 14.3, 8.
50 DATA TORONTO, NEW YORK, BOSTON
40 DATA 37, "UNITED STATES", 14, "CANADA"
```

A **dimension statement** is of the form

```
s DIM l
```

where *l* is a list of array names, each followed by a list of unsigned, nonzero integer constants, enclosed in parentheses and separated by commas. In most implementations, the maximum number of subscripts is 2.

Examples:

```
10 DIM X(100)
15 DIM A(16), B(26)
20 DIM Y(100), Z(16,4)
```

SUBPROGRAMS

A **subroutine** is a sequence of Basic statements, in which the execution sequence must terminate with a **RETURN** statement of the form

```
s RETURN
```

More than one such RETURN statement may appear in one subroutine.

Example:

```
600 REM SUBROUTINE
  .    ————
  .    ————
670    RETURN
  .    ————
690 RETURN
```

A **user-defined function** may be written in the form

```
s DEF FNa(p) = e
```

where *a* is any letter, *p* is a list of parameters, and *e* is any arithmetic expression (which may contain the parameters, or other functions). For a function whose value is a string, *a* is a letter followed by $ and *e* is a string expression.

Example:

```
20 DEFL(X,Y,Z) = SQR(X↑2 + Y↑2 + Z↑2)
```

Multiple line functions are available in some versions of Basic. They are of the form

```
si  DEF FNa(p)
 .     ————
 .     ————
 .     ————
sj     LET FNa = e
sk  FNEND
```

where *a*, *p*, and *e* are as with single line functions, and *si*, *sj*, and *sk* are statement numbers.

Example:

```
30 DEF FNM(A,B)
35    REM — MAX OF A AND B
40    LET M = A
50    IF B > A THEN 70
60       LET M = B
70    REM
80    LET FNM = M
90 FNEND
```

Table S.1 shows the commonly available **built-in functions.**

TABLE S.1

Function	Definition
ABS(x)	$|x|$
INT(x)	Greatest integer $\leqq x$
SQR(x)	$\sqrt{x}$
EXP(x)	e^x
LOG(x)	$\log_e x$
SIN(x)	sine (x)
COS(x)	cosine (x) } x in radians
TAN(x)	tangent (x)
ATN(x)	arctangent (x)
RND(x)	Random number, uniformly distributed in (0, 1); the interpretation of x depends on the installation (in some versions it may be omitted)
SGN(x)	$\begin{cases} -1 \text{ if } x < 0 \\ 0 \text{ if } x = 0 \\ 1 \text{ if } x > 0 \end{cases}$
TAB(x)	Used in PRINT statements to start printing in column INT(x)

Array operations may be provided using statements of the form illustrated below.

s MAT A = B	Assigns array B to array A
s MAT A = B + C	Sum of arrays B and C assigned to A
s MAT A = B − C	Difference of arrays B and C assigned to A
s MAT A = (a)*B	Multiplies B by scalar expression a, assigns to A
s MAT A = B*C	† Product of array B and C assigned to A
s MAT A = ZER	Each element of A set to zero
s MAT A = CON	Each element of A set to one
s MAT A = IDN	Identify matrix assigned to A
s MAT A = INV(B)	† Inverse of matrix B assigned to A

s MAT A $=$ TRN(B)	† Transpose of matrix B assigned to A
s MAT INPUT A	Inputs array (from terminal)
s MAT READ A	Inputs array (from data in DATA statement)
s MAT PRINT A	Outputs array

In the explanations labeled with a dagger †, the arrays must be distinct. For example, MAT A $=$ INV(A) is not allowed.

Dimensioning information can sometimes be supplied along with array operations, and the need to supply such information in separate dimension statements can then be avoided. For example, if A and B have already been dimensioned (they must have the same dimensions if they are to be added), then

110 MAT C $=$ A + B

will automatically provide C with the same dimensioning as A and B, as well as assigning the sum to C.

The dimensioning can also be included explictly in assignment and input statements. For example,

120 MAT I $=$ IDN(4,4)
130 MAT INPUT P(15)

automatically provides the appropriate dimensioning for I and P.

Finally, the dimensions of an array can be changed in the course of a calculation, provided they are not increased. Thus,

200 MAT READ I(L,M)

would provide the appropriate dimensioning for I, following statement 120 above, so long as the values of L and M are known, and do not exceed 4.

SYSTEM COMMANDS

The system commands are highly installation dependent, and it is necessary for the user to determine the particulars for the computer system being used. The following is a list of some "typical" commands:

NEW	Indicates a new program is about to be introduced
OLD	Find a program previously saved
LIST	List the program
RUN	Run the program
SAVE	Save the program
UNSAVE	Delete a program previously saved
LOGON	Part of the sign-on procedure
LOGOFF	Part of the sign-off procedure

INSTALLATION DEPENDENT FEATURES

The following is a list of some of the more important features that might be available at a particular installation:

1. logical operators AND, OR, and NOT,
2. string constants in other than PRINT statements,
3. input to and output from files,
4. multiple-line function definitions,
5. built-in functions operating on character strings,
6. subroutine and program libraries.

Mention has been made of most of these already, with more detail about some than others. The list is included here only to provide some of the more important examples of what a user might want to inquire about at a particular installation.

SUMMARY **2**

Rendering Constructs

In the material below, we summarize the constructs introduced in Section 1.3 and provide examples of how these constructs can be rendered in Basic.

EXITS

We allow **exits** from within any construct. An exit must be such that the flow of control leaves the construct being exited. The following are examples of how such exits may be rendered:

exit	s1	GO TO si
exit outer	s2	GO TO sj
If(———) exit	s3	IF ——— THEN sk

In these examples, s1, s2, s3 are statement numbers, and si, sj, sk are statement numbers of REM statements that appear immediately following the constructs being exited.

REPETITION

The **LOOP FOR** construct requires the execution of a sequence of statements a certain number of times. The sequence of statements within the loop is executed according to the values of a parameter. In the first example, it is assumed that $k > 0$ and also that $j \leq n$.

Loop for i = j,j+k, . . . ,n
$\begin{cases} s1 & \text{LET I = J} \\ s2 & \text{REM LOOP} \end{cases}$

```
——— ⎫ Statements          .        ——— ⎫ Statements
——— ⎬ to be               .        ——— ⎬ to be
——— ⎭ repeated            .        ——— ⎭ repeated
```

End loop
$\begin{cases} si & \text{LET I = I + K} \\ sj & \text{IF I <= N THEN s2} \end{cases}$

(An alternative rendering, with the exit at the beginning of the loop, is given later.) If the increment were to be negative in the above example, <= would have to be changed to >=. In either case, this construct can also be rendered using a FOR statement as follows:

Loop for i = j,j+k, . . . ,n   s1 FOR I = J TO N STEP K

```
——— ⎫ Statements          .        ——— ⎫ Statements
——— ⎬ to be               .        ——— ⎬ to be
——— ⎭ repeated            .        ——— ⎭ repeated
```

End loop   sn NEXT I

The initial value (j), increment (k), and the maximum value (n) may be any arithmetic expressions; if the increment is omitted, it is assumed to be 1.

Loops may be **nested,** as in the following:

Loop for i = 1,2, . . . ,n   s1 FOR I = 1 TO N

Loop for j = 1,2, . . . ,m   si   FOR J = 1 TO M

```
———                                  .        ———
———                                  .        ———
———                                  .        ———
```

End loop   *sj*   NEXT J

——————   .   ——————

——————

End loop   *sk* NEXT I

The **LOOP WHILE** construct requires the execution of a sequence of statements repeatedly, so long as a given condition is satisfied. An example is

Loop while (*l*) $\begin{cases} s1 & \text{REM} \\ s2 & \quad \text{IF } l' \text{ THEN } sj \end{cases}$

——————   .   ——————

——————   .

End loop   *si*   GO TO *s1*
                 sj   REM

where *l* and *l'* are logical expressions, and *l'* is the negation of *l*. For example, if *l* is I > J the translation of *l'* can be I <= J. In some versions of Basic the translation can also be written as NOT (I > J). As another alternative, the IF statement in the translation can be replaced by the three statements

```
s2 IF l THEN s4
s3      GO TO sj
s4 REM
```

These alternatives are also applicable with other constructs described later in this summary.

An alternative way of expressing the **LOOP FOR** construct given earlier uses a "while" construct, as illustrated in the following:

i = j   *s1* LET I = J
Loop while (i ≤ n) $\begin{cases} s2 & \text{REM} \\ s3 & \quad \text{IF I > N THEN } sk \end{cases}$

——————   .   ——————

——————   .

i = i + k   *si*   LET I = I + K
End loop   *sj* GO TO *s2*
                   sk REM

This has almost the same effect as the first example given earlier, the difference being that, with this alternative way, the exit appears at the beginning of the loop rather than the end. In the special case where the loop should not be executed at all, as when J > N, the earlier method does not work properly, whereas this alternative method (as well as the method using a FOR statement) always produces the correct result.

The **LOOP UNTIL EVENT** construct requires the execution of statements within a loop until an event occurs that causes an exit from the loop. In the following example, the events are *i < j* and *k = 0*.

Loop until i < j or k = 0   *s1* REM LOOP UNTIL I < J
                            s2 REM LOOP K = 0

——————   .   ——————

——————

... If(i < j) exit loop $\begin{cases} si & \text{REM...IF(I < J) EXIT} \\ sj & \quad \text{IF I < J THEN } sn \end{cases}$

——————   .   ——————

——————

... If(k = 0) exit loop $\begin{cases} sk & \text{REM...IF(K = 0) EXIT} \\ sl & \quad \text{IF K = 0 THEN } sn \end{cases}$

——————   .   ——————

End loop   *sm* GO TO *s1*
                          sn REM

We may also wish to use a **loop** consisting simply of a sequence of statements to be repeated; usually at least one exit will appear within the loop, as in the following example:

Loop   *s1* REM LOOP

——————   .   ——————

——————   .

——————   .

... If (———) exit $\begin{cases} si & \text{REM...IF(———) EXIT} \\ sj & \quad \text{IF ——— THEN } sn \end{cases}$

——————   .   ——————

——————   .

End loop   *sm* GO TO *s1*
                      sn REM

Of course, in some circumstances it may be convenient to terminate execution of a loop with a RETURN statement, or with a STOP statement.

In some situations, an exit from a loop may appear within an If-then construct contained within the loop, as in the following example:

Loop   *s1* REM LOOP

——————   .   ——————

——————   .

If (*l*) then   .   IF *l'* THEN *sk*

——————   .   ——————

——————   .

...... exit loop $\begin{cases} si & \text{REM...EXIT LOOP} \\ sj & \quad\quad \text{GO TO } sn \end{cases}$

End if   *sk*   REM

——————   .   ——————

——————   .

End loop   *sm* GO TO *s1*
                     sn REM

Selection constructs, such as the If-then construct used here, are described in more detail in the next section.

A nested loop may be exited, as in the following example:

Loop for i = 1,2,...,n   *s1* FOR I = 1 TO N

——————   .   ——————

——————   .

Loop for j = 1,2,...,m   *si*   FOR J = 1 TO M

——————   .   ——————

——————   .

```
......If(l) exit outer    { sj  REM...IF (l) EXIT OUTER
                          { sk      IF l THEN sn
                          .
End loop                  sl    NEXT J
                          .
End outer                 sm  NEXT I
                          sn  REM
```

SELECTION

The **IF THEN** construct requires the execution of a sequence of one or more statements if a given condition is satisfied. This was illustrated as part of the next to the last example, but is repeated here by itself for the sake of completeness:

```
If(l)            s1 IF l' THEN sk
                 .
                 .
End if           sk REM
```

where l and l' are logical expressions, and l' is the negation of l. Alternative renderings, as described with **LOOP WHILE,** may also be used.

The **IF THEN ELSE** construct requires the execution of one sequence of statements if a condition is satisfied; otherwise, another sequence of statements is executed, as in the following example:

```
If(l)            s1 IF l' THEN sj
   then          .
                 .
                 si     GO TO sk
   else          sj  REM ELSE
                 .
                 .
End if           sk REM END IF
```

where l and l' are logical expressions, and l' is the negation of l. Alternative methods may be used to render this construct, as was the case earlier with repetition constructs.

The **CASE** construct requires the execution of one of a number of sequences of statements, depending on various conditions. This is the most general type of selection construct.

```
If(l1)               s1 IF l1' THEN se
                     .
                     .
```

```
                     sd     GO TO sq
(l2)             { se  REM
                 { sf  IF l2' THEN si
                     .
                 sh     GO TO sq
                 si  REM
                     .
                     .
                     .
(li)             { sk  REM
                 { sl  IF li' THEN sp
                     .
                     .
                 sn     GO TO sq
   else          sp  REM
                     .
                     .
End if           sq REM
```

where $l1, l1', l2, l2', \ldots,$ are logical expressions, and li' is the negation of li. Alternative methods may be used here as well.

REFINEMENT

```
                         .
                     { sd  REM PERFORM TASK
Perform task that ── { se  REM THAT ────
                     { sf  GOSUB sj
                         .
Where by "perform    sj  REM SUBROUTINE
   task ──" we mean  sk  REM TO────
                         .
                         .
End where            sm  RETURN
```

The example above uses a GOSUB statement to transfer control to a sequence of Basic statements that correspond to the statements between the "Where by..." and the "End where." A RETURN statement is used to cause the flow of control to be returned to the statement following the GOSUB statement when the subroutine has been executed. Other methods of rendering a **refinement** in Basic are possible. For example, the sequence of Basic statements between sj and sm may be inserted in place of the statement numbered sf.

The Only Solution

We shall have to evolve
problem-solvers galore—
since each problem they solve
creates ten problems more.

From *Grooks II* by Piet Hein.

CHAPTER 8

Numerical Calculations and Truncation Errors

One of the principal motivations behind the early development of computers was the need to carry out long numerical calculations quickly and reliably. Computers were soon adapted to other kinds of applications as well, particularly in data processing. However, numerical applications continue to be important, not only in the physical sciences and engineering, but also in such areas as biology, economics, and management science.

The distinguishing feature of what we call "numerical" calculations is the presence of numerical errors that can have an important effect on the final result of a calculation. We distinguish two kinds of error, *truncation* and *roundoff*. Our main purpose in this chapter is to study numerical processes that are affected primarily by truncation error. We postpone a detailed study of roundoff error until the following chapter.

It should also be acknowledged that there are some kinds of calculations involving numbers, even with errors, that we do not classify as "numerical" calculations, because the errors do not have an important effect on the final result. A payroll calculation is one example. In this case truncation errors do not appear at all. And while roundoff errors can occur when the results of calculations are rounded to the nearest cent, such errors do not usually accumulate through lengthy calculations to affect the final results, as they might for example in solving a large system of equations.

Some practical problems lead to finding sums or integrals, and we need numerical techniques for finding these values, or at least for finding good approximations to these values. Other practical problems have to do with solving equations, or with finding maxima and minima, and again we need techniques for producing approximations to their solutions. Examples of each of these problems will be considered in this chapter. (Some other numerical problems which lead to differential equations will be introduced in Section 11.1.)

An important purpose of this chapter is to determine something about the truncation errors in the final results of a numerical calculation. One objective is to determine a bound for the final error in a particular calculation. Although this can usually be done, the bounds we obtain in practice are usually too pessimistic, or the effort involved in deriving the bounds may be prohibitive. In either case, we may try other techniques for finding *approximations* to the error (rather than bounds), usually with the help of further calculations on the computer.

The mathematical analysis of numerical methods, and in particular of the errors associated with these methods, is usually called *numerical analysis* or *numerical mathematics*. Using the mathematical results as a basis for developing reliable, efficient, and otherwise generally useful computer programs is often referred to as the development of *numerical software*. When it seems appropriate, we will follow up the analysis of a method with some discussion of the corresponding software.

8.1 FINDING SUMS

One of the simplest situations in which truncation error arises is in finding an approximation to the sum of an infinite series. We consider two examples in this section: the first is intended only to illustrate the basic idea and how it can be used, but the second, although a bit more complicated, is of considerable practical importance.

For the first example, consider the infinite series

$$1 + 1 + 1/2! + 1/3! + \cdots + 1/(n-1)! + 1/n! + \cdots.$$

The sum of this series is usually denoted by e and this value appears in many different applications of mathematics. Suppose we use the sum of the first n terms of this series, i.e.,

$$1 + 1 + 1/2! + 1/3! + \cdots + 1/(n-1)!,$$

as an approximation to e. Then the error in the approximation is a *truncation* error, because we have cut off, or truncated, the infinite series to get the approximation.

It is fairly easy to obtain an upper bound on the truncation error in this example. Let us denote the error by T. Then we have

$$T = 1/n! + 1/(n+1)! + 1/(n+2)! + \cdots$$
$$= (1/n!) \, (1 + 1/(n+1) + 1/(n+1)(n+2) + \cdots)$$
$$< (1/n!) \, (1 + 1/(n+1) + 1/(n+1)^2 + 1/(n+1)^3 + \cdots)$$
$$= (1/n!) \, ((n+1)/n).$$

The last step results from the fact that the sum of the infinite geometric series

$$1 + 1/a + 1/a^2 + \cdots$$

is $a/(a-1)$, provided $a > 1$.

For a given value of n, we can use this bound to guarantee the accuracy of the corresponding approximation. For example, suppose we take $n = 10$. Then the partial sum

$$1 + 1 + 1/2! + \cdots + 1/9!$$

can be guaranteed to approximate e with an error of less than $(1/10!) \, (11/10)$, which is easily shown to be less than 4×10^{-7}. (Of course, the evaluation of the partial sum will ordinarily involve roundoff errors. Our analysis will not be complete until we have taken this source of error into account as well, but we post-

pone consideration of roundoff errors until the next chapter.)

Another way in which we can use the bound $(1/n!) \, ((n+1)/n)$ is to determine how many terms in the partial sum will guarantee a prescribed accuracy. For example, suppose we wish to calculate e to within an error of no more than 10^{-5}. How many terms should we use? We want to find a value of n such that

$$(1/n!) \, ((n+1)/n) \le 10^{-5};$$

in fact, we would like to find the smallest value of n that satisfies this inequality. The required value is 9, as is easily found by testing a few values, such as $n = 6$, 7, 8, and 9. Thus, the sum of 9 terms, i.e.,

$$1 + 1 + 1/2! + \cdots + 1/8!,$$

approximates e with an error of no more than 10^{-5}. Because we are using an upper bound for the error, we are sure only that 9 terms are sufficient to guarantee the required accuracy. The argument does not prove that 9 terms are necessary, although in this case they probably are.

We turn now to the second example, and consider the infinite series for $\cos(x)$, i.e. (where x is in radians),

$$1 - x^2/2! + x^4/4! - x^6/6! + \cdots.$$

This is a Taylor series, and we can use the theory of such series to determine the error, or "remainder" as it is often called, in truncating the series. In this particular case, it turns out that the error is bounded by the magnitude of the first term neglected. This means, for example, that the error in using

$$1 - x^2/2! + x^4/4! - x^6/6! + x^8/8!$$

as an approximation for $\cos(x)$ is bounded by $x^{10}/10!$. Thus, with small values of x, the bound on the error will be sufficiently small. For example, with x in the interval $[-\pi/4, \pi/4]$, a short calculation will show that $x^{10}/10! < 3 \times 10^{-8}$, which suggests that the polynomial approximation given above will be quite adequate for most purposes, for values of x in that interval.

Similar remarks can be made about the corresponding series for $\sin(x)$. In fact, the error bound in

$$x - x^3/3! + x^5/5! - x^7/7! + x^9/9!$$

as an approximation for $\sin(x)$ in the interval $[-\pi/4, \pi/4]$ is somewhat smaller.

We now want to show how the two polynomials can be used together, to approximate $\cos(x)$ or $\sin(x)$ with an error of no more than 3×10^{-8}, for *all* values of x, including values of x that are outside the interval $[-\pi/4, \pi/4]$. (We are of course continuing to neglect the effect of roundoff error.) Our plan is to show that, beginning with any value of x, along with a request for an approximation to either the cosine or the sine, we can reduce the problem to that of evaluating one of the two series for a related value of x that is in the interval $[0, \pi/4]$.

The reduction of x from its original value to the related value in the interval $[0, \pi/4]$ is done in stages, which are illustrated in Fig. 8.1. First, we make use of the fact that both $\sin(x)$ and $\cos(x)$ have the period 2π, i.e., that

$$\sin(x + 2\pi) = \sin(x) \text{ and } \cos(x + 2\pi) = \cos(x).$$

This enables us to replace x with x', such that $x = 2n\pi + x'$, where n is an integer and x' is in the interval $[0, 2\pi]$.

To reduce the interval still further to $[0, \pi]$, we use the identities

$$\sin(2\pi - x) = -\sin(x) \text{ and } \cos(2\pi - x) = \cos(x).$$

Thus, if $x' > \pi$ we can replace x' with $x'' = 2\pi - x'$, but we would also have to note the change of sign needed when the sine function is required.

To reduce the interval to $[0, \pi/2]$, we use

$$\sin(\pi - x) = \sin(x) \text{ and } \cos(\pi - x) = -\cos(x),$$

so that, if $x'' > \pi/2$ we can replace x'' with $x''' = \pi - x''$, noting at the same time the need to change sign when the cosine function is required.

Finally, to reduce the interval to what had been our original objective, namely $[0, \pi/4]$, we use

$$\sin(\pi/2 - x) = \cos(x) \text{ and } \cos(\pi/2 - x) = \sin(x).$$

This leads to the rule: if $x''' > \pi/4$, replace x''' with $x^{iv} = \pi/2 - x'''$ and use the sine series for cosine (or vice versa).

An outline of a program for finding an approximation to $\sin(x)$ or $\cos(x)$, based on these ideas, is presented in Fig. 8.2. Something at least in the spirit of what is indicated in Fig. 8.2 is used in practice to produce values for sine and cosine functions in the standard scientific programming languages. In Question 4 of Exercise 8.1 it is suggested that a program along these lines be developed and the results compared with those produced by the functions already available in the programming language employed by the user. (See also Questions 5 and 6 of Exercise 8.1.)

In practice the supplied function programs differ in a number of ways from what is outlined in Fig. 8.2. For example, they probably carry out the range reduction more quickly. Also, if well designed, the effect of round-off will have been analyzed carefully and kept to a minimum, especially with regard to making use of an accurate approximation to π (see Question 6). They also use better polynomial approximations, known as Chebyshev polynomials, which enable them to obtain the same accuracy with fewer terms; moreover, Horner's rule

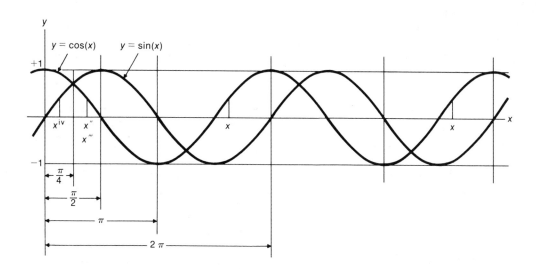

FIG. 8.1 Illustration of range reduction for cos (x). The reduction proceeds in stages from x to x', x'', x''' and finally to x^{iv}, according to the following formulas:

$x' = x - 2\pi$ (n is only 1 in this example)
$x'' = 2\pi - x'$ (x' is greater than π in this case)
$x''' = x''$ (x'' is not greater than $\pi/2$ in this case)
$x^{iv} = \pi/2 - x'''$ (x''' is greater than $\pi/4$ in this case)

Note that with the change from x''' to x^{iv} it is necessary to switch from the cosine curve to the sine curve in this example.

```
/Start with a value of x, and a request for an approximation to
    either sin(x) or cos(x)/
Designate which series is to be used, and initialize sign flag
Replace x by an equivalent value in [0,2π]
If new x > π, replace it with 2π − x and note need to change
    sign if function is sine
If new x > π/2, replace it with π − x and change sign flag if
    function is cosine
If new x > π/4, replace it with π/2 − x and change designation
    of which series is to be used
Find sum of designated series (see below)
Change sign of result if required
/Final result is now the required approximation/


Where "Find sum of designated series" means
    If sine series set term = x, k = 2, but if cosine set
        term = 1, k = 1
    Set sum = term
    For i = k, k + 2, k + 4, k + 6
        term = − term × x²/i(i + 1)
        sum = sum + term
    End for
End where
```

FIG. 8.2 Outline of a program for calculating approximations to sin (x) or cos (x), for any x, with a truncation error of no more than 3×10^{-8}.

would be used in the evaluation of the polynomials in order to minimize the number of arithmetic operations needed. (See Question 5.)

EXERCISE 8.1

1. How much accuracy can you guarantee in the approximation to e provided by the sum of the first 12 terms of the series for e? How many terms would be needed to guarantee an error of no more than 10^{-10}?

2. It can be shown that

$$\frac{\pi}{4} = 1 - \frac{1}{3} + \frac{1}{5} - \frac{1}{7} + \cdots.$$

This is an alternating series whose terms are decreasing in magnitude. It can be shown that the truncation error in such a series is bounded by the first neglected term. This means, for example, that $\pi/4$ is approximated by

$$1 - \frac{1}{3} + \frac{1}{5} - \frac{1}{7} + \frac{1}{9}$$

with an error of no more than $1/11$. (The series obviously converges very slowly!) How many terms are sufficient if you wish to guarantee an error of no more than 10^{-3}?

3. It can be shown that

$$\frac{\pi^2}{6} = 1 + \frac{1}{2^2} + \frac{1}{3^2} + \frac{1}{4^2} + \cdots.$$

This series converges more rapidly than the one in Question 2. Show that, if $n > 1$,

$$\frac{1}{n} < \frac{1}{n^2} + \frac{1}{(n+1)^2} + \frac{1}{(n+2)^2} + \cdots < \frac{1}{n-1},$$

from which it can be concluded that

$$1 + \frac{1}{2^2} + \frac{1}{3^2} + \cdots + \frac{1}{(n-1)^2} + \frac{1}{n}$$

approximates $\pi^2/6$ with an error of no more than

$$\frac{1}{n-1} - \frac{1}{n} = \frac{1}{n(n-1)}.$$

How large should n be if $\pi^2/6$ is to be approximated to within 10^{-3}?

4. Write a subprogram based on the outline in Fig. 8.2 and compare the results obtained by this subprogram to those obtained by the corresponding functions in the language you are using.

5. There are two ways in which you might consider increasing the speed of the subprogram developed in Question 4. One is to make the number of terms in the polynomials depend on x, since fewer terms would be required for smaller values of x. Another is to precompute the coefficients in the polynomials and use Horner's rule for the evaluations of the polynomials. Discuss the advantages and disadvantages of these two suggestions. (Horner's rule for evaluating $a_n x^n + a_{n-1} x^{n-1} + \cdots + a_0$ is obtained by rewriting this polynomial in the form

$$(\ldots ((a_n x + a_{n-1})x + a_{n-2})x + \cdots)x + a_0,$$

and carrying out the steps of the calculation in the order implied by the parentheses.)

6. A program for calculating approximations to $\sin(x)$ and $\cos(x)$ needs to have a reasonably accurate approximation to π, particularly for range reduction when x is large in magnitude. How serious is this problem in terms of the inaccuracy of the x used in the polynomials, and the resulting inaccuracy in the calculated approximation?

7. The truncated Taylor series for e^{-x} is

$$1 - x + x^2/2! - \cdots + (-x)^{n-1}/(n-1)!$$

and the corresponding truncation error, or "remainder term," can be written in the form

$$(-1)^n e^{-\xi} x^n/n!,$$

where ξ is some value in the interval $[0, x]$. How many terms in the series are enough to guarantee an approximation that is in error by no more than .0005 for any x in the interval $[0, 2]$?

8. Write a subprogram that will deliver an approximation to e^{-x} to within a prescribed accuracy, for any given value of x in the interval $[0, 2]$. Assume that roundoff can be neglected. The number of terms used in the series should be made to depend on the value of x, as well as the accuracy required, since fewer terms are needed when x is small.

9. Outline a strategy that makes use of a polynomial to compute approximations to e^{-x} or e^x over a wide range of values of x. What is required is something analogous to the range reduction used with $\cos(x)$ and $\sin(x)$.

10. The Taylor series for $\log(1 + x)$, where the base of the logarithm is e, is

$$x - x^2/2 + x^3/3 - x^4/4 + \cdots.$$

Discuss the development of a program for evaluating approximations to $\log(y)$ for $y > 0$. Note that the series converges very slowly for $|x| < 1$ if x is close to 1 in magnitude, and does not converge at all for $x > 1$. Another series, related to the above, is as follows:

$$\log (1 + x) = 2 \left(\frac{x}{x + 2} + \frac{x^3}{3(x + 2)^3} + \frac{x^5}{5(x + 2)^5} + \cdots \right),$$

which converges for $x > 0$. How could this series be used to advantage over the one given above?

11. Design a subprogram for finding approximations to the Bessel function $J_0(x)$, which is defined by the series

$$1 - x^2/(2!)^2 + x^4/(4!)^2 - x^6/(6!)^2 + \cdots.$$

The subprogram should produce an approximation to within a prescribed accuracy for any given x in the interval $[0, 4]$, assuming roundoff can be neglected.

8.2 FINDING AREAS, QUADRATURE

In this section we consider techniques for what is sometimes known as *numerical integration,* or *approximate* quadrature. Geometrically, if $f(x) > 0$ and $b > a$, the evaluation of a single integral

$$I = \int_a^b f(x)\,dx$$

is equivalent to *finding the area* under the curve $y = f(x)$ between the ordinates $x = a$ and $x = b$, and our purpose is to find a good approximation to this area. (See Fig. 8.3.)

The problem of evaluating integrals occurs in several branches of mathematics. For example, many important functions can be defined in terms of integrals. Integrals occur in other subjects as well. An example arises in physics if the function f represents a force. If

$f(x)$ is the force acting at a distance x against the direction of motion, then the integral is the work involved in moving from a to b. Another example arises in statistics, where $f(x)$ is the probability density for a particular random variable, in which case the integral is the probability that the observed value of the variable lies between a and b.

One commonly used method for finding approximations to integrals is known as the *trapezoidal method* or the *trapezoidal rule*. To derive this method we divide the area into vertical strips of equal width. If we choose n strips of width h, we will have $nh = b - a$. The top of each strip is replaced by a straight line to make the shape of the strip a trapezoid. (The first two trapezoids are shown in Fig. 8.4.)

The trapezoidal method uses the areas of the trapezoids as approximations to the areas of the original strips. The sum of the areas of the trapezoids is the approximation to the area under the curve. This leads to the following expression

$$S = h(f(a)/2 + f(a + h) + f(a + 2h) \\ + \cdots + f(a + (n - 1)h) + f(b)/2)$$

being used as the approximation to the integral I.

Once again the theory provides an expression for the error in the approximation. The best known expression for this error is as follows:

$$I - S = -h^2(b - a)f''(\xi)/12,$$

where ξ is a "mean-value" in the interval $[a,b]$. (This result is applicable only if the second derivative f'' exists and is continuous in $[a,b]$; the result must be modified if this requirement is not met.) The error approaches 0

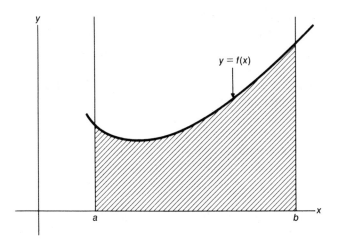

FIG. 8.3 The function f is given, along with the values of a and b. A good approximation to the area of the shaded portion is required.

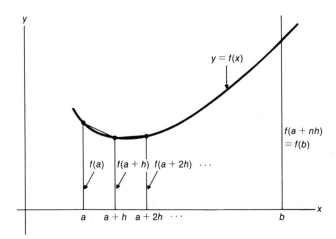

FIG. 8.4 In the trapezoidal method, strips shaped like trapezoids are used to approximate the area under the curve. Only the first two trapezoids are shown.

as h approaches 0. We can think of the error as a truncation error because it arises when we truncate this limit process, by choosing some value of h which, although usually small, will not be 0.

Even though we do not know the value of ξ, the expression for the error can be used to derive an error bound. As an illustration, consider the integral

$$I = \int_1^{10} \frac{dx}{x}.$$

Here $f''(x) = 2/x^3$, and $|f''(\xi)| \leq 2$ for ξ in the interval $[1,10]$, so that, from the above expression for the error, we can obtain $|I - S| \leq 1.5h^2$. This bound can be used to guarantee accuracy for a given h, or, alternatively, to determine a suitable h for a prescribed accuracy. For example, to determine I with an error of no more than .01, it is sufficient to take $h \leq (0.1/1.5)^{1/2}$. A convenient choice for h that is well below this bound is $1/2^4$. In fact, with this value of h the bound becomes $1.5(1/2^4)^2$, which is $<.006$. (Of course, we will have to take account of the roundoff error as well, but this will be postponed until later.)

The expression for the error in the trapezoidal approximation can be used in quite a different way, and one which illustrates a commonly used technique. The idea is to calculate approximations with two different values of h, and then use the difference between these approximations in order to determine an approximation to the error. For example, suppose one approximation, $S(h)$, is obtained with the interval h, so that

$$I - S(h) = -h^2(b - a)f''(\xi(h))/12,$$

and that another, $S(h/2)$, is obtained with the interval $h/2$, so that

$$I - S(h/2) = -(h/2)^2(b - a)f''(\xi(h/2))/12.$$

If we subtract these two equations, and assume for the moment that $\xi(h) = \xi(h/2)$, we obtain

$$S(h/2) - S(h) = -3(h/2)^2(b - a)f''(\xi)/12.$$

Thus, one third of the difference between the two approximations is equal to the error in the approximation with $h/2$.

The weakness in this argument is of course the assumption that $\xi(h) = \xi(h/2)$. The assumption is not valid in general, but, with relatively small values of h, the values of $\xi(h)$ and $\xi(h/2)$ may in practice be very nearly equal. This means that $(S(h/2) - S(h))/3$ may be a good approximation to the error in $S(h/2)$.

Let us return to the earlier integral,

$$I = \int_1^{10} \frac{dx}{x}.$$

Calculations with a program based on the trapezoidal rule, using $h = 1/2^3$, yielded

with the interval h, $S = 2.30385$,
with the interval $h/2$, $S = 2.30286$.

An approximation to the error in 2.30286 is therefore $(2.30286 - 2.30385)/3 = -.00033$, which is considerably smaller than the bound, .006, found earlier. (If the error estimate $-.00033$ is applied to 2.30286, we obtain 2.30253. This result happens to be extremely close to the true value of I; in fact, by determining bounds for both the truncation and roundoff errors with still smaller intervals, it can be shown that it is actually within .00002 of the true value.)

The difference just observed between a relatively large but guaranteed error bound and a smaller but only approximate error estimate is typical of what happens in practical numerical computations. It is sometimes possible to carry the theoretical analysis a bit further, but in practice it is more common to accept the error estimate, although with reservations of course. One's reservations should be based on a good understanding of the theoretical limitations (such as the fact that we have assumed the existence of f''), and on experience. More confidence in error estimates can often be obtained in practice by carrying out the calculations for several different values of the interval, instead of just two as in the above example.

The analysis so far has been based on the assumption that f'' exists. This does not mean that the trapezoidal rule cannot be used in other cases as well. In fact, it obviously can be applied as long as the values of f exist, but, as mentioned earlier, the analysis would have to be modified when f'' does not exist. We will not discuss any such modification in detail but only suggest that it might still be worthwhile experimenting with the trapezoidal rule in such circumstances. (See Questions 4(d) and (e) in Exercise 8.2, where $f(x)$ behaves near one of the limits of integration the way $\sqrt{x}$ behaves near the origin.) It should also be acknowledged that there are cases where f may not exist at all points, even though the integral has a value, and the trapezoidal rule cannot be applied at all. One example is $\int_0^1 x^{-1/2}dx$. Such cases will ordinarily need some special treatment, including some preliminary mathematical analysis, before numerical methods can be applied.

Let us now consider using the theoretical ideas discussed so far as a basis for the development of programs. To begin with, it is a straightforward matter to develop a subprogram for applying the trapezoidal rule, given a,b, and h, along with another subprogram for evaluating the integrand. (See Questions 1 and 2 in Exercise 8.2.) It is convenient to keep the subprogram for evaluating the integrand a separate entity, so that the trapezoidal subprogram can be applied to different integrands.

A more sophisticated subprogram, and one that would likely be of more interest to users of a program library, is one that would use the trapezoidal subprogram repeatedly, with smaller and smaller values of h, while making estimates of the error at each stage. Such a program could be made to stop when its error estimate finally becomes smaller than a tolerance supplied by the user, or when it does more work than some upper limit that is also set by the user.

An outline for such a program is shown in Fig. 8.5, where it is assumed that the user provides the limits of integration and the integrand, the latter being in the form of a subprogram (whose name could be supplied to the quadrature subprogram by the user). The user also provides a tolerance, which is intended to be an upper bound for the error (or at least the error estimate), and a limit on the amount of work to be done (such as a limit on the number of times the integrand is to be evaluated). It may also be desirable to allow the user to specify a minimum number of intervals to be used, for example, by specifying the initial interval size. Besides returning the value of the approximation it obtains, the subprogram would have to give an indication of why it stopped, and perhaps also its estimate of the error when it did stop. (See Question 4 in Exercise 8.2.)

There are several ways in which we might try to improve the quadrature program that has just been described. One way is to avoid repeating evaluations of the integrand after the interval size has been changed; if the interval size is halved, only every second value of the integrand in the new trapezoidal formula needs to be evaluated, since the others have already been used in the previous approximation. Another possibility for improvement is to use the error estimate to adjust the approximation in the hope that the adjusted value will be an even better approximation. A third is to consider using formulas other than the trapezoidal rule. (See Question 6 in Exercise 8.2.) A fourth way is to experiment with interval sequences other than those provided by halving.

We will not discuss these possibilities in any further detail. But there is one quite important alternative approach that should be mentioned, and perhaps proposed as a project for further exploration. (See Question 10 in Exercise 8.2.) The idea is to reorganize the approach in order to make it *adaptive,* in the sense that the subprogram distributes the work it does over the interval of integration in order to *adapt* its efforts to the nature of the integrand. Since this is a rather vague statement we will now be more specific.

The approach considered earlier and outlined in Fig. 8.5 envisaged the use of subintervals of uniform size. However, in practice an integrand may behave quite differently in different parts of the interval of integration, and it is likely that different subinterval sizes would be more appropriate in different parts of the integration interval. We would like to mention two basically different ways of trying to cope with this problem. Both ways involve saving information about the integration over individual subintervals, and this raises questions about how this storage of information is to be managed as the number of subintervals grows, as well as questions about the trade-off between the cost of such storage and any improvement in efficiency that results from it.

First of all, we should notice that the formulas we have developed for $S(h)$ and $S(h/2)$ can be applied to individual subintervals. We can compute $S(h)$ for an individual subinterval of length h, which merely means that we use only one trapezoid for that subinterval. We can also compute $S(h/2)$ for the same subinterval, using two trapezoids. The difference between the two approximations, divided by 3, is an approximation to the error in $S(h/2)$. For our adaptive quadrature programs we will keep a record of the information we have for each individual subinterval in the following form:

> Left endpoint of subinterval,
> Length of subinterval,

```
Given:        Limits of integration A and B
              Integrand (in the form of a subprogram for its
                 evaluation)
              TOLERANCE
              Measure of work not to be exceeded
              Perhaps an initial H, or initial number of subin-
                 tervals

Required:     Approximation to integral
              Value of INDICATOR to indicate whether suc-
                 cessful or not
              Perhaps an estimate of the error as well

Subprogram:   Determine initial H
              Calculate initial approximation
              Loop until tolerance achieved or workload too
                 great
                 Save value of most recent approximation
                 Determine new H
                 Calculate corresponding approximation
                 Make estimate of error
              ....If this estimate ≤ TOLERANCE set INDI-
                    CATOR accordingly and exit
              ....If workload too great set INDICATOR ac-
                    cordingly and exit
              End loop
              Return to calling program
```

FIG. 8.5 Outline of quadrature subprogram.

Three function values (at endpoints and midpoint),
Approximation to integral over the subinterval,
Estimate of error in approximation.

We begin by calculating this information for some initial number of equally spaced subintervals; the initial number may be provided by the user as before.

One way of then proceeding with an adaptive quadrature program is as follows: The list of subintervals is first searched for the one with the largest error estimate. This subinterval is then divided in half and replaced by two smaller ones. (This subinterval is chosen on the grounds that work on this subinterval is where the most good will be done.) The process is repeated until the total error estimate is small enough, or until the work limit is exceeded, as before.

A second way is similar in that the same records are kept, but differs in that each subinterval is divided if it has more than its share of the total error allowed. Thus, for example, if a subinterval is one sixteenth of the total interval of integration but has an error estimate that is more than one sixteenth of the tolerance, it will be divided. If the list of subintervals is handled systematically from left to right, the information can be kept in a stack. This method of storage management would be simpler or more efficient than with the first way suggested above, but the resulting subprogram may not be quite as efficient, because it does not appear to concentrate the work "where it will do the most good" to quite the same extent. In any event, as already indicated, these two adaptive strategies can be explored further (as suggested in Question 10), and this could lead to a number of interesting and worthwhile projects.

EXERCISE 8.2

1. Write a subprogram for applying the trapezoidal rule, given the limits of integration a and b, the interval size h or the number of subintervals, and another subprogram for evaluating the integrand. Verify the results quoted in the text for the integral $\int_1^{10} (dx/x)$ with subintervals of length $1/2^3$ and $1/2^4$.

2. A second method can be based on approximating the area of a strip with the area of a certain rectangle, instead of the trapezoid used in this section. The width of the rectangle is h, while the height is taken to be the value of the function at the midpoint of the interval. (Thus, the height of the first rectangle is $f(a + h/2)$.) Develop a program based on this idea and calculate results corresponding to the results obtained in Question 1. (Note: the truncation error for this method can be written in the form

$$h^2(b - a)f''(\xi)/24$$

where ξ is in $[a, b]$, and will in general not be the same as the ξ associated with the trapezoidal method.)

3. Show that, if the effect of roundoff can be neglected, the results obtained by the trapezoidal method in the example of this section with $f(x) = 1/x$ are too large, while the results obtained by the midpoint method suggested in Question 2 are too small.

4. Develop a subprogram along the lines outlined in Fig. 8.5 and use it with a tolerance of 10^{-3} on each of the following examples:

a) The area under the curve $y = 1 + x^2 + x^3$ between $x = 0$ and $x = 1$.

b) The area under the graph of $y = 1/(1 + x^2)$ between $x = -2$ and $x = 2$.

c) The area below the graph of $y = 2^{-x}$ between $x = 0$ and $x = 5$.

d) The area of the quarter circle that is cut off from the first quadrant by the graph of $y = \sqrt{1 - x^2}$. (The area in this case is $\pi/4$, so the result will give an approximation to $\pi/4$.)

e) The area between the two parabolas $y = \sqrt{3x}$ and $y = x^2 - 2x$.

Comment on the validity of applying the trapezoidal rule to the last two examples.

5. Compute a table of natural logarithms, $\log(x)$, for $x = 1, 2, \ldots, 20$, in which you can guarantee that the error in each entry does not exceed .00005.

6. The trapezoidal rule is based on approximating a curve over a subinterval of length h by a straight line through the endpoints. Another rule, known as Simpson's rule, is based on approximating a curve over a subinterval of length $2h$ by a parabola through the endpoints and the midpoint. Show that the resulting approximation to the area over this subinterval is

$$(h/3)(f(x_1) + 4f(x_2) + f(x_3))$$

where x_1 and x_3 are the endpoints and x_2 is the midpoint. Show also that the result of applying Simpson's rule to a subinterval of length $2h$ is the same as applying the trapezoidal rule to an interval of length $2h$, and then to two intervals of length h, and then using the error estimate to improve the second of the two approximations. (The trapezoidal rule and Simpson's rule are just two of many different formulas that have been proposed for numerical quadrature.)

7. Modify the subprogram developed in Question 4 by using Simpson's rule in place of the trapezoidal rule and compare the results obtained. It should be noted that, with Simpson's rule,

$$I - S(h) = -h^4(b - a)f^{(iv)}(\xi)/90$$

where ξ is some value in the interval $[a, b]$. From this result it can be concluded that $S(h/2) - S(h)$ is approximately 15 times the error in the approximation $S(h/2)$.

8. Find approximately the amount of work required to lift a 2000-kilogram body to a height of 500 kilometers from the earth's surface. Take the force to be proportional to $1/x^2$, where x is the distance from the center of the earth, and take the earth's surface to be 6500 kilometers from the center.

9. We wish to know the amount of work done in a certain process. However, instead of knowing the force as a function of the distance, we know only some measurements of the force that have been made at certain distances. The points at which measurements have been made are fairly close together but not necessarily equally spaced. How would you estimate the total amount of work? How much can you say about the accuracy of the result?

10. Write a subprogram to carry out one of the adaptive quadrature ideas described at the end of Section 8.2. How do the results for this subprogram compare over a few test examples with those obtained by the subprogram in Question 4? Comparisons can be made in terms of accuracy and efficiency; most users would probably prefer a comparison based on differences in cost or efficiency (if any) for the same accuracy.

8.3 SOLVING NONLINEAR EQUATIONS

The following are three examples of nonlinear equations:

$$x^2 = 3,$$
$$x^4 - 2x^3 - x^2 - 7x - 4 = 0,$$
$$x = \cos(x).$$

We also consider *systems* of nonlinear equations, such as

$$x^2 + 4y^2 = 10,$$
$$xy = 1.$$

Nonlinear equations are generally much more difficult to solve than linear equations (which are discussed in Chapter 9). Unfortunately, the method you should use will usually depend to a considerable extent on the particular problem being considered.

Most methods for solving nonlinear equations require one or two initial approximations to the solution. Sometimes the approximations need not even be particularly good ones, but quite often the difficulty in a problem is to find suitable initial approximations. The methods then provide a sequence of improved approximations, each approximation being, it is hoped, better than the preceding one. One way to find the initial approximations is to draw a graph and make guesses. The computer might be useful in doing the necessary calculations and in helping with the search for good starting points. In discussing different methods below we will usually assume that reasonably good starting points have already been obtained.

The method of *bisection* is often quite useful. It can be employed whenever we are trying to solve an equation of the form

$$f(x) = 0$$

and we have already found two values of x, say a and b, at which f has opposite signs, and where f is continu-

ous between a and b. For example, consider the first problem mentioned above, for which we can take $f(x) = x^2 - 3$. We can choose $a = 1$ and $b = 2$ since $f(1) < 0$ and $f(2) > 0$. The situation is illustrated in Fig. 8.6 where a graph of the function is shown. The function is continuous, so we can guarantee that the graph must cross the x-axis somewhere between $x = 1$ and $x = 2$.

The method of bisection requires us to bisect the interval between a and b and evaluate the function at the midpoint. This point may be the zero we want. If not, we know that the sign of the function at the midpoint will differ from the sign at a or the sign at b. We therefore have a new situation in which the function has opposite signs at two points, except that the distance between the points has been halved. Obviously the process can be repeated until the zero has been found or until the interval is so small that we have determined the zero to sufficient accuracy. Some rule is needed to determine when the process is to be terminated.

The only difficulty that can arise in practice with the method of bisection is caused by possible errors in the evaluation of $f(x)$. If the value of $f(x)$ is small and roundoff errors are relatively important, we may not be able to determine its sign. However, in most cases there should be no practical difficulty. For example, in Fig. 8.6 the accuracy with which we can determine the zero is no worse than the accuracy with which we can determine the values of the function.

A second method, known as the *secant* method, is illustrated in Fig. 8.7. Two values of x, say a and b, are needed at the start. Then a chord, or secant, is drawn through the two points $(a,f(a))$ and $(b,f(b))$. In Fig. 8.7 the points are $(2,1)$ and $(3,6)$. The place where the secant crosses the x-axis provides a new value of x, which replaces one of the two values of a and b. The new value and the remaining one of the other two values

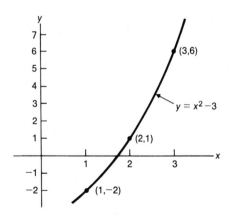

FIG. 8.6 Graph of the function $x^2 - 3$ showing that it has a zero between $x = 1$ and $x = 2$.

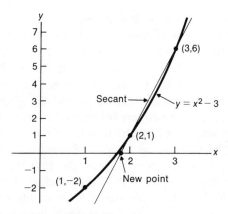

FIG. 8.7 The secant method begins with two points on the graph and finds a new point where the secant cuts the x-axis.

are then used to repeat the step with the new secant. The process can be repeated as often as we wish. The method is not completely described until we have a rule for deciding which of the two points to keep each time. The simplest rule is to keep a.

A formula for calculating the new point is required and can be obtained from the equation of the secant, which is

$$y - f(a) = \frac{f(a) - f(b)}{a - b} (x - a).$$

To find where this straight line crosses the x-axis, we set y equal to zero and solve for x. The resulting value of x turns out to be

$$a - \frac{a - b}{f(a) - f(b)} f(a).$$

There are two main difficulties that can occur with the secant method. The method obviously fails if $f(a) = f(b)$, and in fact we can expect trouble if $f(a)$ and $f(b)$ are nearly equal. The second difficulty that can arise is at the end of the procedure. If we program the procedure to stop when the value of the function at the new point is small enough, say smaller than some value we choose, such as 10^{-5}, the difficulty is that we still do not know how close the new point is to the desired zero. Some further analysis of the problem will be needed. Despite these two difficulties the method, when it works properly, is much faster than the method of bisection; moreover, it does not require such special starting values as are required by the method of bisection.

A third method, known as *Newton's* method, is what we would obtain from the secant method in the limit as we allow b to approach a. Thus, if a is taken

to be an approximation to the root, the new approximation is

$$a - f(a)/f'(a).$$

This process can obviously be repeated, and a sequence of approximations, say $x_2, x_3, x_4, \ldots$, can be calculated, once a starting value x_1 has been chosen.

Newton's method has difficulties that arise with small values of the denominator ($f'(a)$ in this case) and knowing when to stop the iteration, like those of the secant method. It has an additional one in that it usually requires more work per step than with the secant method, since both f and f' must be evaluated with each step. Nevertheless, Newton's method is widely used, and variants of Newton's method form the basis of many very useful computer programs.

Before considering programs based on Newton's method, we would like to discuss one more approach. It is a very general one known as the method of *functional iteration*. This method requires the original equation to be rewritten in the form

$$x = g(x).$$

Then a starting value for x is chosen, say x_1. New values of x, which we denote by $x_2, x_3, \ldots$, are obtained by iterating on the above equation, which means that these new values are defined by

$$x_{i+1} = g(x_i), \quad i = 1, 2, \ldots.$$

The procedure should stop when the difference between some value of x, say x_n, and the corresponding value of $g(x_n)$ is small enough. When $x_n - g(x_n)$ is small it is assumed that x_n is close to the required zero, although some further analysis would be needed to determine how close.

The major difficulty with the method of functional iteration is to make an appropriate choice for the function g. For example, if $f(x) = x^2 - 3$, we might choose $g(x)$ to be

$$x^2 + x - 3 \qquad \text{or} \qquad \frac{1}{2}\left(x + \frac{3}{x}\right).$$

It turns out that the first choice will always lead to failure, no matter what value we choose for x_1 (unless, of course, we choose x_1 to be almost exactly equal to $\sqrt{3}$). On the other hand, the second choice is a good one. It turns out to be a special case of Newton's method, which, if applied to $f(x) = x^2 - a$, leads to the iteration

$$x_{i+1} = \frac{1}{2}\left(x_i + \frac{a}{x_i}\right)$$

for calculating the square root of a. It can be shown that this iteration will converge, that is, the values $x_1, x_2, \ldots,$

will approach the required value $\sqrt{a}$, regardless of what value is chosen for x_1, as long as $x_1 > 0$. (See Question 6 in Exercise 8.3.)

Another difficulty with functional interation is in choosing the starting value x_1. Usually, the choice will depend very much on the particular problem being considered. As with the secant method and Newton's method, it also may be difficult to know when to stop the iterations or to determine how accurate the final result is. On the other hand, an advantage of the method of functional iteration is that it can be applied with only trivial modification to systems of equations. For example, suppose that

$$x = h(x, y),$$
$$y = k(x, y),$$

are two equations for the two unknowns, x and y.

Once we have chosen some starting values, x_1 and y_1, we can carry out an iterative procedure based on

$$x_{i+1} = h(x_i, y_i),$$
$$y_{i+1} = k(x_i, y_i),$$

to produce a sequence of new values, first x_2 and y_2, then x_3 and y_3, and so on. Again, the main difficulty is to know what to use for h and k.

The method of bisection cannot be applied to systems of equations, but the secant method and Newton's method can be adapted. In fact, the appropriate generalization of Newton's method, or some modification thereof, is the most common technique used in practice. As with single equations, it turns out to be a special case of functional iteration.

The four methods we have considered are typical examples of methods used to solve nonlinear equations. There are other ways, more complicated than either the secant method or Newton's method, of calculating a new point at each step. There are also some reasonably good ways of choosing the function g, or the functions h and k, for the method of functional iteration. However, all general methods for solving nonlinear equations are similar to the four considered here, at least in broad outline. Each requires starting values, and it is often the case that finding these values is the most difficult part of the problem. Sometimes good starting values can be obtained from a graph, as was done from Figs. 8.6 and 8.7, or from a systematic search of possible values. On other occasions we may have some physical experience or some measurements that provide good starting values. Once starting values have been chosen, some kind of iterative procedure is followed. We have seen four examples. This part of the method is obviously well suited to computer programming. The final stage of each method involves the use of a stopping criterion which requires the program to test some quantity and stop if it

is small enough. What can be considered small enough will depend on circumstances, on the problem, and on the machine being used. Some analysis is needed to determine whether or not the final approximation to the solution is satisfactory. We have not considered any such analysis because it is often fairly obvious that the approximation is good enough and because a more sophisticated analysis would lead to the need for more advanced mathematical techniques. In any event, a major factor to be taken into account is the truncation of the iterative process, although it often turns out that other factors (including roundoff error, the appropriateness of the starting value, and the stopping criterion itself) play equally important roles with this class of methods.

One more point should be mentioned. Our discussion thus far has been restricted to real numbers, but the solutions to nonlinear equations can in general be complex numbers. Many of the methods developed for nonlinear equations can be applied even when the numbers are complex. The bisection method cannot, but the other three we have considered can be used.

One important special problem is that of finding all the zeros of a polynomial, including both real and complex zeros. There are formulas for the zeros of polynomials up to and including degree 4 but, except for the formulas for quadratic equations, they are never used in practice. However, computer programs are available that can find all the zeros of almost any polynomial that can arise in practical applications. These programs usually involve a fairly systematic way of choosing starting values, followed by several iterations of a formula. Usually the polynomials are reduced after each zero is found, by dividing out the factor associated with that zero. Thus if x_1 is found to be a zero, the polynomial is divided by $x - x_1$ before an attempt is made to find another zero. Care is also needed to restart the procedure with new values whenever difficulties arise. An example of such a difficulty occurs with Newton's method when $f'(a)$ is zero, or nearly equal to zero.

Let us now consider the main features of a program for solving nonlinear equations. We restrict our attention to single equations, but the basic ideas can be generalized in a natural way to systems of equations. We also assume that Newton's method is the basis.

An outline of a program is given in Fig. 8.8. It begins by obtaining a starting value; this might be provided by the user, or it might be generated in a somewhat arbitrary manner by the program. Inside the loop the program needs values of f and f'. The values of f must be provided by the user, most likely in the form of a subprogram for evaluating f (the name of which could be provided by the user). The values of f' could also be provided by the user, or it might be that the

Get a starting value of x, either provided or generated
Initialize INDICATOR
Loop for number of iterations, or until success achieved
    Calculate f
    Calculate f'
    Determine new value of x, possibly constrained
. . . . If acceptable, change INDICATOR and exit
End loop
Return to calling program

FIG. 8.8 Outline of a program for using Newton's method to solve a nonlinear equation. The program returns with a solution (if it has found one) and an indication of whether it has found one or given up after trying a certain number of iterations. The idea is used again as part of Fig. 8.9.

program is able, at least optionally, to compute numerical approximations to f'.

Some provision should be made to avoid the problem that arises when f' is zero or very small. This is the reason for including the phrase "possibly constrained," since it is envisioned that some sort of constraint will be placed on the size of the Newton "step" f/f'. For example, if a bound for the root is known, the program could make sure that no iterations went beyond this bound, perhaps reducing f/f' accordingly when this fraction becomes too large.

The iteration must eventually stop, either by finding a sufficiently good approximation or by giving up because too many iterations have been tried without success. An upper bound on the number of iterations allowed could be provided by the user, or it could be built into the program.

In the program of Fig. 8.8 it is understood that when the iteration does stop there will be a return to a calling program along with the solution (if there is one) and an indication to the user as to whether or not a solution has been found.

Initialize INDICATOR
Loop for number of starting values, or until success is achieved
.   Determine trial starting value (the first of these may be
.   prescribed by the user)
.   Loop for number of iterations (but exit outer loop if suc-
.   cess achieved)
.   Calculate f
.   Calculate f'
.   Determine new value of x, possibly constrained
. . . . If acceptable, change INDICATOR and exit outer loop
.   End loop
End outer loop
Return to calling program

FIG. 8.9 Newton's method is used as it was in Fig. 8.8 except that this time it does not give up until it has tried a number of different starting values.

The idea of the program is used again in Fig. 8.9, where a somewhat more complicated program is outlined. The new point about the program in Fig. 8.9 is that it does not give up immediately if it has exceeded the limit on the number of iterations. It tries another starting value and iterates again, and it repeats this process until a limit on the number of starting values has been exceeded before it finally gives up completely. The initial starting value could be prescribed by the user, but some mechanism would be needed for generating alternatives. (The latter could even involve generating random starting values near to the original one, using a random number generator, such as is described in Section 11.3.)

EXERCISE 8.3

1. Write a program or subprogram based on the method of bisection and use it to find an approximation to the positive root of each of the following equations:

a) $x^2 = 3$
b) $x^4 - 2x^3 - x^2 - 7x - 4 = 0$
c) $x = \cos(x)$

One of the parameters of your program should be used to determine when the procedure is to be stopped. How much can you guarantee about the accuracy of the result in each case?

2. Repeat Question 1 with the secant method.

3. Repeat Question 1 with the method of functional iteration. For (a) use Newton's formula, for (b) use $g(x) = 2/x + 1/x^2 + 7/x^3 + 4/x^4$, and for (c) use $g(x) = \cos(x)$.

4. On the basis of the material in this section and your experience with the methods in Questions 1–3, write a report on the relative advantages and disadvantages of the various methods.

5. Write a general subprogram based on the outline in Fig. 8.8 or Fig. 8.9 and use it to solve the equations in Question 1. A write-up on how to use the program that will be clearly understood by a potential user should be included.

6. Show that the Newton iteration given in the text for finding $\sqrt{a}$ can be rewritten in the form

$$x_{i+1}^2 = (x_{i+1} - x_i)^2 + a$$

from which we can conclude that $x_2, x_3, \ldots$ are all $\geq \sqrt{a}$, regardless of the value chosen for $x_1 > 0$. Then show that the iteration can also be rewritten in the form

$$x_{i+1} - \sqrt{a} = (x_i - \sqrt{a})^2/2x_i$$

and thus conclude that $x_1, x_2, x_3, \ldots$, must converge to $\sqrt{a}$, regardless of the choice of $x_1 > 0$.

7. Develop a subprogram for finding the nth root of a number based on the functional iteration formula derived from Newton's method. Show that the required formula is as follows:

$$x = \frac{1}{n}\left((n-1)x + \frac{a}{x^{n-1}}\right).$$

8. Find all solutions of the following two equations:

$$x^2 + x + 4y^2 = 10,$$
$$xy = 1.$$

9. Two walls face each other across an alley. A ladder 10 meters long slopes across the alley from the base of one wall to lean against the other wall. A second ladder 13 meters long slopes from the base of the second wall to lean against the first. As shown in Fig. 8.10, the two ladders cross at a height of 3 meters above the alley. Use a drawing that has lengths approximately in the right proportion to obtain a rough approximation to the width of the alley. Then use the computer to calculate a more accurate approximation, for example, to the nearest centimeter.

10. Find the root of $x = e^{-x}$ to three decimal places.

11. How many roots of the equation $x = \tan x$ are there? Find approximations to some of the smaller ones and indicate what you know about the larger ones.

12. Find a solution of

$$x = 1 + \frac{1}{10}\sqrt{x^2 + y^2}\cos y,$$
$$y = 2 + \frac{1}{20}(\sin x + \sin y - x)$$

that is accurate to approximately three decimal places.

13. If the rate of interest is i, then one dollar invested now will become $(1 + i)^n$ dollars at the end of n years. If one dollar is invested at the beginning of each year and left to collect interest, how much will have accumulated by the end of 10 years? What rate of interest will cause the total amount to have become exactly double the amount invested, that is, twenty dollars?

8.4 MAXIMA AND MINIMA

A problem that quite often arises in practical applications is that of finding the maximum or minimum value of a function. For example, the function might represent the volume of a tin can and we want to know what shape of can will have the maximum volume for a given amount of tin. Or the function might represent the cost of manufacturing a tin can and we want to know which shape of can will have the minimum cost for a given volume.

Sometimes the calculus can be used to convert maximum and minimum problems into problems of solving equations. This occurs because the calculus enables us to find slopes of graphs and the slope of a graph is often zero at a point where the graph has a maximum or minimum value. When the problem can be changed to one of solving equations, we can use the methods of the preceding section or of Section 9.3 on solving linear equations. However, it often happens that the calculus cannot be used or that the resulting equations are very complicated. It is therefore useful to be able to solve maximum and minimum problems directly.

We will emphasize only one approach to this general problem. The idea is not very sophisticated. It is to search different values of the function until we find the desired maximum or minimum. In extreme cases we may have to compute a rather large number of values of the function but, whenever possible, we will attempt to limit our search in a reasonably economical way.

To illustrate this approach, we consider the problem of determining the path of light as it travels from one medium into another, as shown in Fig. 8.11. We

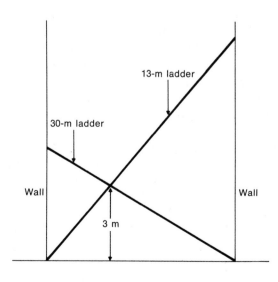

FIG. 8.10 The two ladders cross at a height of 3 meters.

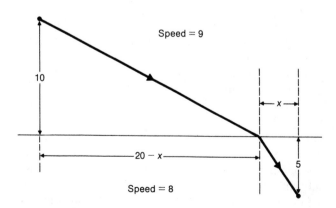

FIG. 8.11 Light is traveling from a point in the upper medium to a point in the lower one. The time of travel is a minimum.

suppose that the speed of light in the upper medium is 9, in some convenient unit, and that the speed in the lower medium is 8, in the same unit. The path taken by the light is governed by a law of physics which states that the travel time is a minimum. Since the light travels in straight lines in the two media, the problem is to find the value of x, shown in Fig. 8.11, that is associated with the minimum travel time.

The first step in the solution of this problem is to express the travel time as a function of x. The distance traveled in the upper medium is

$$\sqrt{10^2 + (20 - x)^2}.$$

The travel time in the first medium is this quantity divided by the speed in the first medium, so the travel time is

$$(\sqrt{500 - 40x + x^2})/9.$$

Similarly, the travel time in the second medium is

$$(\sqrt{25 + x^2})/8.$$

Therefore the total travel time is

$$(\sqrt{500 - 40x + x^2})/9 + (\sqrt{25 + x^2})/8,$$

and it is this expression that we wish to minimize. (It often happens that the main difficulty in solving maximum and minimum problems is in finding the function that is to be maximized or minimized.)

We can write a computer program to search for the minimum. It is obvious from the physical situation itself that this function must decrease to a single minimum and then rise again, as x increases from 0 to 20. One way of finding this minimum is to output first the 21 values of the function for $x = 0,1,2,\ldots,20$. By examining these values we can determine an interval of length 2 in which the minimum must lie. Then we can output another 21 values evenly spaced in the new interval. By examining these new values we can select another interval, this time of length .2, in which the minimum must lie. This process can be continued until we have located the minimum with sufficient accuracy. Better yet, we can program the computer to select the intervals for us and to print out only the final result.

Choosing 21 values in each interval was quite arbitrary. There may be more efficient procedures that can be followed, but the machines are so fast that attempts to find faster methods would not be justified, unless our program is likely to be used many times. The only difficulty we might experience with a search procedure of the kind just described is that roundoff and similar errors prevent us from calculating the values of the function exactly. This limits the accuracy with which we can locate the minimum. However, the lim-

itation is usually unimportant in practical problems. The example used to illustrate the problem of finding maxima and minima happens to be one to which the calculus can be applied. The calculus can transform the problem into a problem of solving an equation, but a lot of work could still be required to solve the equation.

Search methods can also be used with functions of more than one variable. However, search methods become quite inefficient as the number of variables increases. Even with functions of only two variables it is usually necessary to develop more sophisticated procedures. The main idea of these procedures, once a certain value of the function has been found, is to move to a new trial value in a direction in which the function appears to be changing most rapidly. For example, suppose that the value of a function of two variables is known at a point (x_1, y_1). We can then compute the value at a few points in the neighborhood of (x_1, y_1), such as $(x_1 + h, y_1)$, $(x_1 - h, y_1)$, $(x, y_1 + h)$, $(x_1, y_1 - h)$, for some not very large value of h. From these values we would have some idea of the direction in which we should move if we want the value of the function to increase or decrease most rapidly. In this way we are led to a new point and we examine the value of the function at this new point. Such methods are usually somewhat arbitrary in the way the new points are chosen.

There are many very interesting maximum and minimum problems in which the number of variables is 5 or 10, or even as many as several hundred. An example of a problem area involving a large number of variables is that of production scheduling. Many factors may enter into the determination of a factory production schedule. Decisions must be made as to which items have to be produced on which machines, as well as the particular times at which the various items are produced. Other factors include amounts of overtime, quantities to be stored temporarily in the warehouse, and so on. The cost of keeping the amount of pollution below acceptable levels must also be included. Each factor will help determine the total cost of the operation. The cost, therefore, is a function of a large number of variables—and of course we would like to minimize the total cost.

Such large-scale problems are very different from those we have been considering with only one or two variables, and they must be solved by entirely different methods. There are two major differences. First of all, the function to be minimized or maximized is usually quite simple; often it is a linear function of the variables. Secondly, the variables are usually restricted in significant ways. For example, the items that are produced must be ones that we want to produce; there is no point in producing the cheapest possible item if it is not what the customers want. The capacities of the machines are limited, as is the amount of overtime that can be required, and so on. Fortunately, these two differences have made it possible to develop techniques for solving such problems. The general technique is called *mathematical programming*. Many important special problems are linear, and the technique is then called *linear programming*. The word "programming" has nothing to do with computer programming. The word is used in the sense of programming or scheduling of activities. However, computer programs are certainly needed to handle the massive amounts of computation that are required to solve linear programming and other kinds of mathematical programming problems. To go further into a discussion of mathematical programming problems would involve more advanced mathematics. The problems are merely mentioned here to help give an overall understanding of the kinds of maximum and minimum problems that can arise.

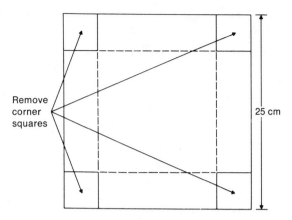

FIG. 8.12 Corner squares are removed from the large square of tin and the sides are folded along the dotted line to make an open box of maximum volume.

EXERCISE 8.4

1. Write a program to follow a procedure like the one outlined in this section and use it to find the path traveled by the ray of light.

2. A man owns a large piece of property that borders on a straight river. He has 100 meters of fencing and he wishes to fence off a rectangular area, using the river as the boundary along one side of the rectangle and the fencing along the other three. Find the shape of the rectangle with maximum area. What is the shape with maximum area if fencing can be installed only in four-meter lengths?

3. A piece of tin is square, with a side of 25 centimeters. A small square is cut from each corner, as shown in Fig. 8.12. The sides are then folded up along the dotted lines to make an open box. What size of small square must be cut from each corner in order to make a box of maximum volume?

4. We wish to manufacture aluminum cans that hold 100 cubic centimeters. Suppose we can buy aluminum at a certain price per square centimeter regardless of the shape of the pieces, so we can order circular pieces for the top and bottom and rectangular pieces for the sides at the same price per square centimeter. What shape of can should we manufacture in order to minimize the cost?

5. What would be the answer for Question 4 if the cost of circular pieces was fifty percent higher per square centimeter than the cost of rectangular pieces?

6. Consider again the problem in Question 4. Suppose that taller cans afford a small selling advantage because taller cans appear to be larger than they really are and people tend to choose such cans in the supermarket in preference to others. Suppose I have discovered that my profit per can increases at the rate of 1/20 cent for every

increase of one centimeter in the height of the can, if I assume the costs remain fixed. My problem now is to take into consideration the costs of manufacturing the can and to determine the most profitable shape. Take the cost per square centimeter of aluminum to be 1/10 cent. (There is one aspect of this problem, as presently stated, that is quite unreasonable. What is it?)

7. A man can row at the rate of three kilometers per hour and walk at the rate of four. If he is 100 meters offshore and wishes to reach a point that is 300 meters inland and 500 meters down the shore, what is the least amount of time he requires to reach his destination?

8. Suppose that in Question 7 the man is rowing in a stream that is moving at the rate of 3 kilometers per hour and that his destination is downstream from where he is now situated. What is the least amount of time needed under these new circumstances?

9. A piece of wire 25 centimeters long is to be cut into two pieces. One piece is to be bent into the shape of a square and the other into a circle. Where should the wire be cut so that the sum of the two areas is a maximum?

10. A businessman keeps supplies of a certain item in his warehouse. He has found that the cost of doing so is $.01x + 10/x$ dollars per month, where x is the number of items he orders every time his supply is low. Part of the cost increases as x increases because he has to provide more space to look after the larger deliveries he receives. On the other hand, part of his cost decreases as x increases because it is less expensive for him to place fewer orders. What is the most economical order for him to place? Is the problem harder or easier if the particular item can be ordered only in quantities which are multiples of 10? What is the most economical size in this case?

11. If two unbiased coins are tossed, the probability of obtaining two heads is 1/4. If this experiment is repeated

10 times, the probability of obtaining two heads exactly k times is

$$\frac{10!}{k!(10-k)!}\,(1/4)^k(3/4)^{10-k}.$$

Compute a table of values of this probability for $k = 0$, $1, \ldots, 10$ and determine which value of k is most likely. What is the corresponding result if the experiment is repeated 30 times?

12. Find the maximum value of z, where

$$z = 6 + 4x + 12y + 2\,|x| - |y| - 8x^2 - 8y^2 - xy$$

and where x and y must both lie in the interval $[-1, 1]$.

13. A businessman is planning to produce x Weejees and y Wumpers and he wants to choose x and y in a way that will maximize his profit. On the basis of past experience he knows that he must invest \$5 for each Weejee and \$12 for each Wumper that he produces. Since his total capital is \$10,000, he knows that $5x + 12y$ cannot exceed 10,000. He also knows that he needs to allocate 20 square meters of warehouse space for each Weejee but only 15 for each Wumper. He has 20,000 square meters available in his warehouse so he must not let $20x + 15y$ exceed 20,000. His rate of profit is the same on each product so he hopes to maximize $x + y$. Find the best choice of x and y, assuming that x and y must be integers. What is the best choice if x and y can be fractions? How much more profit would the businessman have to make per Weejee before he would be justified in producing nothing but Weejees?

8.5 FURTHER REMARKS

The main purpose of this chapter has been to develop numerical methods for the solution of problems in a number of important areas. Where possible we have shown how the errors can be analyzed and in other cases we have tried to indicate what kinds of difficulties would have to be considered by a more sophisticated mathematical analysis. The errors considered so far have been primarily truncation errors, although there have been circumstances in which roundoff errors could not be ignored. (In Chapter 9 the emphasis will be on roundoff errors.)

It should be pointed out, however, that there is another major source of error in practical problems. It has to do with the reliability of the mathematical model. It may be that the most important error in a particular problem has nothing at all to do with the numerical method, but is due to the fact that the original mathematical description of the problem is a poor approximation of the real situation. The mathematical model may be a poor approximation because some of the parameters appearing in it have to be measured and the measurements may not be very reliable. This applies to physical quantities, such as force or mass, and to economic and biological quantities, such as invested capital and growth rate. (Further illustrations of this point will appear in later chapters.) The mathematical model may also be a poor one because we have not included all the important factors, sometimes because we do not even know what these factors are.

In this chapter we have considered problems involving numerical calculations on a relatively small scale as compared to many of the problems that arise in practical applications. Nevertheless, the problems we have considered and the methods we have discussed are good indications of what can happen with more realistic problems. However, there is one aspect of large-scale problems that cannot be properly illustrated with simple examples and yet this aspect is extremely important and should be mentioned.

Large-scale calculations of any kind, whether they occur in scientific work or in business data processing, will usually involve large amounts of data. Merely collecting and organizing large quantities of data can consume a large amount of computer time. There is another factor, however, that must be taken into consideration. Such large quantities of data cannot be expected to be completely reliable. In scientific calculations the data may come from measuring instruments, as would be the case for most of the data connected with space shots, or it may come from the control of engineering processes. In such cases the instruments may break down, or the transmission of the data may be faulty. In business calculations the data is more likely to come from keypunching or from character readers, but neither of these sources can be relied upon completely.

The presence of unreliable data means that the program must test to verify data before it is used, and be able to take suitable action if some of the data appears to be invalid or if some of the data is missing. The point to be emphasized is that these are special problems associated with large-scale calculations. In addition to having a reasonably good numerical procedure, the programmer must concern himself with the problem of collecting and organizing large quantities of data and he must provide for the possibility of invalid or missing data.

CHAPTER 9

Numerical Calculations and Roundoff Errors

In the preceding chapter we considered several different numerical problems in which we emphasized the role played by truncation error. We turn now to a consideration of the other kind of numerical error mentioned in the preceding chapter, namely, roundoff error. Our purpose is to begin by introducing a firm basis for understanding and analyzing roundoff error, then to consider a few problem areas in which these ideas can be applied, and finally to present a brief discussion of further directions in which both the theoretical and the practical aspects might be developed.

It should be acknowledged at the outset that roundoff error is itself a kind of truncation error since it is caused by "truncating" a sequence of digits that represent a particular number. However, as we shall see, the effect of this kind of "truncation" error and its analysis are so different that it is reasonable to refer to it by a different name.

As we explain in more detail later, we use the term "roundoff error" in a general way; we use it to denote the error caused by any method of terminating the series of digits, regardless of what rule is used, whether it be chopping off the trailing digits, rounding to the nearest number (nearest even number in the case of ties), or some modification of these.

Of course, all the methods considered in the preceding chapter suffer from roundoff error as well as truncation error when implemented on a computer, as was mentioned a number of times in connection with our study of those methods. We will reconsider some of those methods in the present chapter, particularly sums and quadratures, with the emphasis this time on the effect of roundoff errors. But we will also consider another kind of problem, in this case the problem of solving linear equations, which is affected only by roundoff errors and not at all by truncation errors, and we continue the discussion of linear equations to the point where a program for solving such equations is outlined. Anyone wishing to concentrate on methods for solving linear equations (and postponing a detailed analysis of roundoff error) will find that Section 9.3 on solving linear equations can be studied independently of the other sections in this chapter. (However, consideration of Section 9.4 is also recommended, in order to provide at least some understanding of the effect of roundoff error in solving linear equations.)

A complete theoretical analysis of roundoff error in solving linear equations will not be covered in this chapter. We present instead, in Section 9.4, only a brief indication of how such an analysis would affect our understanding of the program, and, more generally, of how our approach both theoretically and practically affects our view of roundoff error in related areas as well.

We proceed first with a section which is intended to provide a basis for understanding and analyzing the effects of roundoff error, particularly the effects caused by the manipulation of floating-point numbers on a machine. (Details about the representation of such numbers, and conversion between different number bases are given in Appendix C.)

9.1 THE BASIC RULES FOR ERROR BOUNDS

To illustrate the basic facts that are needed for an analysis of roundoff error we fix our attention on two different representations of floating-point numbers. In each case we consider a machine word that consists of 32 bits: 1 bit for the sign, 7 for the exponent part, and 24 for the fraction part of the number. Examples of the two represensations are shown in Figs. 9.1 and 9.2, one being binary and the other hexadecimal. In each case we assume that the numbers are normalized, and that the number zero is represented by a 0 or 1 (for + or −) followed by thirty-one 0's.

Our first task is to obtain bounds for the individual roundoff errors that can occur in calculations involving these numbers. Such errors can occur with each of the four arithmetic operations of addition, multiplication, subtraction, and division. They can also occur with conversion between decimal and binary, or between decimal and hexadecimal, either on input and output, or during compilation of program constants.

To obtain the required bounds we have to make an assumption about how the arithmetic and the conversions are done. The assumption we make is very close to what actually happens on many machines. Modifications to the assumption that might be required for any particular machine can usually be made quite easily.

We assume, provided overflow or underflow does not occur, that the results of arithmetic operations and conversions are the same as what would be obtained by chopping off the exact results to fit the machine word.

More accurate results would be obtained if "true rounding" were assumed rather than "chopping off," but most machines chop. The resulting error could be called a chopping error rather than a rounding error or roundoff

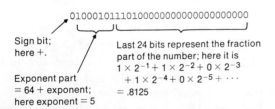

FIG. 9.1 The number represented here in a binary floating-point form is $.8125 \times 2^5$.

Sign bit; here +.

Exponent part = 64 + exponent; here exponent = 5

Last 24 bits represent the fraction part of the number; here it is $1 \times 2^{-1} + 1 \times 2^{-2} + 0 \times 2^{-3} + 1 \times 2^{-4} + 0 \times 2^{-5} + \cdots = .8125$

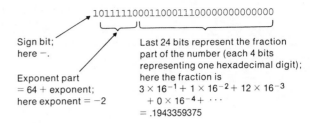

FIG. 9.2 The number represented here in hexadecimal floating-point form is $-.1943359375 \times 16^{-2}$. (The hexadecimal representation for this number is be310000.)

Sign bit; here −.

Exponent part = 64 + exponent; here exponent = −2

Last 24 bits represent the fraction part of the number (each 4 bits representing one hexadecimal digit); here the fraction is $3 \times 16^{-1} + 1 \times 16^{-2} + 12 \times 16^{-3} + 0 \times 16^{-4} + \cdots = .1943359375$

error. But, as indicated earlier, we use the term "roundoff error" to refer to any such error, whether it be due to chopping, true rounding, or something else (there are other possibilities).

We have now made an assumption which determines exactly how the result of any arithmetic operation, or conversion, will appear (unless overflow or underflow occurs). On the basis of this assumption we are able to deduce quite easily a bound for individual roundoff errors. As a first step in this derivation, we know from our assumption that the individual roundoff errors must all be less than 1 in the last place of the fraction part of the result. It turns out that this leads to different bounds for different representations.

With the binary representation described in our first example, the smallest fraction part of a normalized number is

$$10000000000000000000000$$

i.e., a 1 followed by 23 zeros, so that the best relative roundoff error bound is essentially 1 part in 2^{23}, i.e., 2^{-23}, which is just less than 1.2×10^{-7}.

On the other hand, with the hexadecimal representation in our second example, the smallest fraction part is

$$000100000000000000000000$$

i.e., a hexadecimal 1 followed by five hexadecimal zeros, so that the best relative roundoff error bound in this case is only 1 part in 16^5, i.e., 2^{-20}, which is just less than 10^{-6}.

In general, if floating-point numbers are represented in base b, and d digits are used for the normalized fraction parts, the best relative roundoff-error bound for chopping arithmetic is essentially b^{-d+1}. Of course b^{-d+1} is only a bound, and the errors in some individual results are much smaller. In fact, in many cases the errors can even be zero, as, for example, with the sum or product of small integers, or of simple binary fractions such as .5, .25, etc. We will occasionally make use of our special knowledge about these errors.

In case of overflow or underflow, the system usually takes some special action, and may output error messages. These possibilities must be kept in mind, but we will usually not make explicit reference to them.

We now introduce the functions fl to denote "the floating result of" and $conv$ to denote "the result of converting," and we let u be an upper bound for the magnitude of the relative roundoff error. In the general case considered above, $u = b^{-d+1}$. In Fig. 9.3 we summarize the conclusions we have drawn from our basic assumption about machine arithmetic and conversions.

To show how these results can be used, let us suppose we have two machine-representable numbers A and B, and that $|A| < 1$ and $|B| < 10$. Then we can conclude that the error in their floating product is

$$|fl(AB) - AB| < |AB|u$$
$$< 10u,$$

whereas the error in their floating sum is

$$|fl(A + B) - (A + B)| < |A + B|u$$
$$< 11u.$$

If we now introduce a third machine-representable number C, and assume that $|C| < 100$, we can analyze the product and sum of the three numbers A, B, and C. For the product, we obtain

$$fl(fl(AB)C) = fl(AB(1 + \epsilon_1)C)$$
$$= AB(1 + \epsilon_1)C(1 + \epsilon_2)$$

where ϵ_1 and ϵ_2 are each bounded in magnitude by u. The error is

$$|fl(fl(AB)C) - ABC| < |ABC|((1 + u)^2 - 1)$$
$$< 1000(2u + u^2)$$

which simplifies to $2000u$, if we neglect u^2 in comparison to u. For the sum, we have

$$fl(fl(A + B) + C) = fl((A + B)(1 + \epsilon_3) + C)$$
$$= ((A + B)(1 + \epsilon_3) + C)(1 + \epsilon_4),$$

where ϵ_3 and ϵ_4 are bounded by u. The error can then be shown to satisfy

$$|fl(fl(A + B) + C) - (A + B + C)|$$
$$< |A + B|((1 + u)^2 - 1) + |C|u$$
$$< 122u + 11u^2$$

which simplifies to $122u$, if we again neglect u^2 in comparison to u. (We have been assuming A, B, and C are machine representable. Otherwise the error bounds would have been larger. See Question 8 in Exercise 9.1.)

If the machine and compiler do not produce results that are equivalent to the exact results chopped to fit the machine's word length, we may still be able to use the conclusions of Fig. 9.3, except that the value of u may have to be adjusted, but the rest of the analysis will remain valid. With true rounding, for example, the value of u would be only half what it is for chopping.

Most machines and compilers perform in such a way that our conclusions are valid for a reasonably small value of u. The value may not be quite as small as b^{-d+1}, but it will be small enough for practical purposes. We are usually only interested in relatively crude bounds on the effect of roundoff error. If the resulting bounds are not tolerable, then we might try to improve the method, or we might have to resort to higher-precision calculations. Using higher precision means simply that we are able to assume a much smaller value of u.

The only serious way in which our basic assumption is sometimes violated is when a machine has been designed to chop the result of an arithmetic operation *before* normalization, rather than *after* normalization. This can have disastrous consequences when two nearly equal numbers are subtracted. (See Question 11 in Exercise 9.1.)

We need to make provision for one further source of error before we have a proper basis for the analysis of error in numerical computations. This has to do with the accuracy of the built-in elementary functions such as square root, sine, and so on. Fortunately, as far as the user is concerned, we can deal with such errors in much the same way we have dealt with roundoff errors. We should be able to determine the error bound for any particular function, and then use that bound in our analysis in the same way we use the relative roundoff-error bound, u, in our analysis of arithmetic operations.

For a particular function, $f(x)$, we may find from the user's manual that the machine produces a floating-point approximation that satisfies

$$fl(f(x)) = f(x)(1 + \eta)$$

for a given bound on $|\eta|$. As an example, suppose that $f(x)$ is $\sqrt{x}$, and that the bound on $|\eta|$ is $3u$. Then, as

The error bounds for floating point arithmetic and conversion, in the absence of overflow and underflow, are defined by

$$fl(x \circ y) = (x \circ y)(1 + \epsilon)$$
$$conv(z) = z(1 + \epsilon)$$

where each $|\epsilon| < u$, and $\circ$ stands for any one of the four arithmethic operations, and u is the relative roundoff error bound. We also know that $\epsilon = 0$ in some obvious circumstances involving small integers or special fractions.

FIG. 9.3 Summary of required information about roundoff-error bounds, derived from the basic assumption about the results of arithmetic operations and conversions. (Note: Different occurrences of ϵ will normally represent different values).

an illustration consider the expression $x\sqrt{x}$. The value produced by the computer, which can be denoted by $\mathrm{fl}(x\mathrm{fl}(\sqrt{x}))$, is in error by

$$|\mathrm{fl}(x\mathrm{fl}(\sqrt{x})) - x\sqrt{x}| < x\sqrt{x}((1 + 3u)(1 + u) - 1).$$

This bound simplifies to $x\sqrt{x}(4u)$ if we neglect u^2 again.

Finally, we have to consider the possibility that the argument of a function may be in error. For example, we may wish to evaluate $f(x)$, but x itself is in error as a result of earlier calculations. Let us suppose that those earlier calculations have led to y as an approximation to x, but that our analysis of those calculations has led to a guaranteed bound on $|y - x|$.

If f is differentiable, we can apply the mean-value theorem and obtain

$$f(y) = f(x) + f'(\theta)(y - x)$$

where θ is some number in the interval between x and y. Then we have the following error in the final result

$$\begin{aligned}|\mathrm{fl}(f(y)) &- f(x)|\\ &= |(f(x) + f'(\theta)(y - x))(1 + \eta) - f(x)|\\ &= |f(x)\eta + f'(\theta)(y - x) + f'(\theta)(y - x)\eta|\\ &\leqq |f(x)|u + |f'(\theta)||y - x| + |f'(\theta)||y - x|u,\end{aligned}$$

where u is a bound for η. The last term in this expression can probably be neglected in comparison with the others.

As an illustration, suppose that $f(x)$ is again $\sqrt{x}$, and that $u = 10^{-7}$, and suppose that $x = 2$ and $|y - x| < 10^{-6}$. Then $f'(x) = 1/(2\sqrt{x})$, and we obtain

$$\begin{aligned}|\mathrm{fl}(\sqrt{y}) - \sqrt{x}| &< \sqrt{2} \times 3 \times 10^{-7}\\ &\quad + 1/(2\sqrt{2}) \times 10^{-6} + \text{negligible}\\ &< 10^{-6} \qquad\qquad\qquad \text{quantities}\end{aligned}$$

This use of the mean-value theorem is quite typical of what is done in the analysis of computational errors.

EXERCISE 9.1

1. Assuming normalized representations as in the two examples of this section, what is the largest number that can be represented in each case? What is the smallest possible nonzero number in each case?

2. Describe a representation for normalized floating-point numbers like the examples of this section except that the base is 4, rather than 2 or 16. What is the relative roundoff-error bound for this representation? What is the largest number in this case? What is the smallest nonzero number?

3. What is the largest number that can be represented on the machine you are using? What is the smallest nonzero number? What is the value of u for single-precision

arithmetic on this machine? How close is it to the value of b^{-d+1}?

4. What is u for double precision on the machine you are using?

5. What does the system on your machine do in case of overflow or underflow?

6. For the first machine representation considered in this section, and our assumption about chopped arithmetic, give an example of two numbers A and B such that $\mathrm{fl}(A + B) = A$. If $A = 10$, what is the largest such B?

7. Is floating-point arithmetic commutative? Associative? Distributive? Give examples to illustrate which of these properties are not possessed by floating-point arithmetic. (In place of the representations described in this section, it would be easier to use simpler ones; for example, try fraction parts of 2 or 3 decimal digits instead of 24 binary, or 6 hexadecimal digits.) Give an example of A and B such that A and B are both greater than $\mathrm{fl}((A + B)/2)$.

8. Suppose that $|A| < 2$, $|B| < 4$, $|C| < 8$, and $|D| < 16$, but assume that A, B, C, and D are machine representable.

a) What are bounds for the errors in the floating-point values of $A + B$, AB, and $A - B$?

b) Find a bound on the error in evaluating $ABCD$, assuming that u^2 can be neglected.

c) If we also assume that $|B| > 1$, what is an error bound for the evaluation of A/B?

d) What happens in (a) and (b) if A, B, C, and D are not necessarily machine representable?

9. For A, B, C, and D of the preceding question, find an error bound for evaluating the sum in the order A, B, C, D, and another bound if the order is reversed. Which is smaller? Does this suggest anything in general about whether a series should be summed from the smallest to the largest term, or vice versa? (Assume that u^2 can be neglected.)

10. Consider evaluating $a_i = x^{i-1}/(i - 1)!$ for $i > 2$ by starting with x, then multiplying by x and dividing by 2, multiplying by x and dividing by 3, etc., and show that, in this case, $|\mathrm{fl}(a_i) - a_i| < |a_i|((1 + u)^{2i-4} - 1)$. What is the result if the numerator and denominator are evaluated separately and then divided?

11. What is the largest possible magnitude of ϵ that can occur if a machine chops before, rather than after, normalizing?

12. For the system you are currently using, can you find out what guarantees are provided about the accuracy of the mathematical functions such as square root, sine, logarithm, etc? For example, what is the bound for η in $\mathrm{fl}(\sqrt{x}) = \sqrt{x}(1 + \eta)$? (With some functions you may need two bounds, one for η_1 and one for η_2, in $\mathrm{fl}(f(x)) = f(x(1 + \eta_1))(1 + \eta_2)$; the range of possible values of x may also be restricted.)

13. Assuming $u = 10^{-7}$ and $\mathrm{fl}(\sqrt{x}) = \sqrt{x}(1 + \eta)$ where $|\eta| < 3u$, find a bound for the error in the floating-point evaluation of $x\sqrt{1 + x}$, if x is in the interval $[1, 2]$.

14. Suppose that x is not known exactly. Find an error bound for the floating-point evaluation of x^3.

15. Find an error bound for the floating-point approximation to $\log_e(x)$, assuming that x is in the interval $[2, 3]$ but not known exactly. Make some reasonable assumption about the accuracy with which a logarithm can be calculated.

16. How accurately can e^{-x^2} be evaluated? Assume that x is in the interval $[0, 1]$ and known exactly, and make an appropriate assumption about the accuracy with which the exponential function can be calculated.

17. Find a formula for the area of a regular n-gon inscribed in a circle of radius 1 and another for the area of a regular circumscribed n-gon. Compute approximations to these two areas for some fairly large values of n. Give guaranteed bounds on the errors in these results and use them to determine an interval guaranteed to contain π. The length of the interval should not be more than about 10^{-5}.

9.2 EFFECT ON SUMS AND QUADRATURES

In this section we apply the ideas of the preceding section to the analysis of sums. We denote the original mathematical sum by

$$a_1 + a_2 + a_3 + \cdots + a_n + \cdots$$

and proceed to find a bound on the total error that results when we approximate this sum with the floating-point approximation to the partial sum

$$a_1 + a_2 + a_3 + \cdots + a_n.$$

We can divide the analysis into two parts. First, there is the truncation error caused by stopping after only n terms of the series; this was discussed in Section 8.1. Second, there is the error caused by roundoff in the floating-point evaluation of the partial sum.

If the summation is carried out from left to right, we can proceed to analyze the effect of roundoff in the following manner. In the first step of the sum we have

$$\mathrm{fl}(a_1 + a_2) = (a_1 + a_2)(1 + \epsilon_1).$$

Then we obtain

$$
\begin{aligned}
\mathrm{fl}((a_1 + a_2) + a_3) \\
= ((a_1 + a_2)(1 + \epsilon_1) + a_3)(1 + \epsilon_2) \\
= (a_1 + a_2)(1 + \epsilon_1)(1 + \epsilon_2) + a_3(1 + \epsilon_2).
\end{aligned}
$$

As the calculation proceeds we will eventually obtain a number of expressions of the form

$$(1 + \epsilon_1)(1 + \epsilon_2) \cdots (1 + \epsilon_i).$$

Since such an expression is quite common in roundoff-error analysis, it is convenient to abbreviate it simply as

$$(1 + \epsilon)^i,$$

it being understood that the different occurrences of ϵ will in general not have the same value. Each ϵ has a value satisfying $|\epsilon| < u$, but is otherwise not specified.

Later on, in finding error bounds, it then turns out that we often obtain expressions like one of the following:

$$(1 + u)^i - 1, \qquad \frac{1}{(1 - u)^i} - 1,$$

and it will be convenient to introduce a simplification for these expressions as well. If we could neglect small terms involving u^2, u^3, $\ldots$, in comparison to u, we could replace each of these expressions with iu. This kind of reasoning is a bit too imprecise for many of our purposes, but, on the other hand, we don't want to bother with such complicated expressions as the ones shown above in our final results. Fortunately there is a simple way around the difficulty. What is often done is to assume that i is not too large, and that u is small enough, so that

$$(1 + u)^i - 1 < 1.01iu,$$

and

$$\frac{1}{(1 - u)^i} - 1 < 1.01iu.$$

This means that our conclusions will be valid as long as we restrict ourselves to values of i satisfying these inequalities. The number 1.01 may appear to be simply "pulled out of a hat," but we are only interested in obtaining reasonable bounds, and we are just claiming that replacing iu by $1.01iu$ is enough to make the bound a valid one for the values of i and u that we are using.

If $u = 2^{-23}$, the assumption is valid as long as $i < 40{,}000$ (see Question 1(a) in Exercise 9.2), which will be the case in most practical problems. But, even if i is larger than this, we can always replace 1.01 with 1.02, or 1.03, etc., and the rest of the analysis will proceed without further change.

Let us turn now to analyzing the effect of roundoff error on the partial sum, and let us continue with the case where the a_i are known exactly. If the terms in

$$a_1 + a_2 + a_3 + \cdots + a_n$$

are added in order from left to right, we are led to the following:

$$
\begin{aligned}
\mathrm{fl}(a_1 + a_2) &= (a_1 + a_2)(1 + \epsilon), \\
\mathrm{fl}((a_1 + a_2) + a_3) &= ((a_1 + a_2)(1 + \epsilon) + a_3)(1 + \epsilon),
\end{aligned}
$$

$$
\begin{aligned}
\mathrm{fl}(\ldots((a_1 + a_2) + a_3) + \cdots + a_n) \\
= (\ldots((a_1 + a_2)(1 + \epsilon) + a_3)(1 + \epsilon) \\
+ \cdots + a_n)(1 + \epsilon) \\
= (a_1 + a_2)(1 + \epsilon)^{n-1} + a_3(1 + \epsilon)^{n-2} \\
+ \cdots + a_n(1 + \epsilon).
\end{aligned}
$$

This result becomes a bit more symmetrical if we multiply the coefficient of a_1 by another factor of $(1 + \epsilon)$. (The result is still valid, considering what is meant by ϵ, since ϵ can be zero.) Then we obtain

$$
\begin{aligned}
|\mathrm{fl}(\Sigma a_i) &- \Sigma a_i| \\
= |a_1(1 + \epsilon)^n &+ a_2(1 + \epsilon)^{n-1} + \cdots + a_n(1 + \epsilon) \\
&- a_1 - a_2 - \cdots - a_n| \\
< |a_1|((1 + u)^n - 1) &+ |a_2|((1 + u)^{n-1} - 1) \\
&+ \cdots + |a_n|((1 + u) - 1) \\
< 1.01u(|a_1|n + |a_2|(n - 1) &+ \cdots + |a_n|). \qquad (1)
\end{aligned}
$$

This is a basic result showing the way in which roundoff error affects a sum. One of the conclusions that can be drawn immediately from this result is that it will usually be better to sum a series beginning with the smaller terms and ending up with the larger ones, rather than vice versa. Since $|a_1|$ is multiplied by n, and $|a_n|$ only by 1, the bound will certainly be smaller if $|a_1| < |a_n|$ than if $|a_1| > |a_n|$. Of course, this does not guarantee that the error itself will be smaller; however, with more or less random roundoff errors, we expect that the error will usually be smaller.

From (1) we can also derive the somewhat simpler result

$$
|\mathrm{fl}(\Sigma a_i) - \Sigma a_i| < 1.01u \left(\frac{n(n + 1)}{2} \right) \max_i |a_i|. \quad (2)
$$

Although not as small a bound as that given in Eq. (1), for certain special cases, such as when $|a_i|$ increases with i, it should be pointed out that Eq. (2) cannot in general be improved to any substantial extent. An error of very nearly this magnitude can actually be achieved if the circumstances are just right. An examination of our analysis shows that such circumstances can occur only when the a's are all the same sign and approximately the same size. In practice, substantially smaller errors would normally be expected, partly because the a's may be of different signs and magnitudes, but also because it is extremely unlikely that all of the ϵ's will take on the worst possible values simultaneously.

In many practical problems the bound in Eq. (2) is sufficient. It is usually not worthwhile to pursue the analysis of roundoff error in a sum in any more detail. Usually the bound provided by Eq. (2) is small enough to guarantee the accuracy we want. If the bound given by Eq. (2) is not small enough in single-precision arithmetic, then we can consider double-precision arithmetic and thereby take advantage of a much smaller value of u. In rare cases even that will not be good enough and we may have to resort to a more detailed analysis, or perhaps to still higher precision.

So far we have assumed that the a_i's are exact. Very often we know only something like

$$
\mathrm{fl}(a_i) = a_i(1 + \epsilon)^{k_i}.
$$

This is easily incorporated into our earlier analysis and, in this particular case, would lead to

$$
\begin{aligned}
|\mathrm{fl}(\Sigma a_i) - \Sigma a_i| < 1.01u(|a_1|(n + k_1) &+ |a_2|(n - 1 \\
+ k_2) + \cdots &+ |a_n|(1 + k_n)) \quad (3)
\end{aligned}
$$

in place of Eq. (1).

The series for e considered in Section 8.1 can be used as an example. Here $a_i = 1/(i - 1)!$ and, if this is formed by dividing successively by $2, 3, \ldots, i - 1$, we obtain

$$
\mathrm{fl}(a_i) = a_i(1 + \epsilon)^{i-1}
$$

for $i = 1, 2, \ldots, n$. (A sharper result is of course possible for $i > 1$, since there are at most $i - 2$ divisions, and some of them, such as division by 16, are done exactly on most machines. However, it is usually not worthwhile trying to take advantage of such improvements.)

We can now find a bound for the total error in approximating e by evaluating

$$
S = 1 + 1 + \frac{1}{2!} + \frac{1}{3!} + \cdots + \frac{1}{(n - 1)!}
$$

in floating-point arithmetic. The error is

$$
e - \mathrm{fl}(S) = (e - S) + (S - \mathrm{fl}(S)),
$$

the first term on the right being the truncation error (for which a bound was found in Section 8.1), and the second term being the roundoff error (for which a bound can be obtained from Eq. (3) above with $k_i = i - 1$).

We finally obtain

$$
\begin{aligned}
|e - \mathrm{fl}(S)| &\leq |e - S| + |S - \mathrm{fl}(S)| \\
&< \frac{1}{n!} \left(\frac{n + 1}{n} \right) + 1.01un(e) \\
&< \frac{1}{n!} \left(\frac{n + 1}{n} \right) + 2.8un,
\end{aligned}
$$

where we have taken advantage of the fact that $|a_1| + |a_2| + \cdots + |a_n| + \cdots$ is e, and $1.01e$ is less than 2.8.

With $n = 10$, we pointed out in Section 8.1 that the truncation error was bounded by 4×10^{-7}. If u is 10^{-6}, then the roundoff error is bounded by $28 \times 10^{-6} = 280 \times 10^{-7}$, for a total bound of 284×10^{-7}. Perhaps 3×10^{-5} is good enough for whatever purpose we have in mind.

We have analyzed the series for e in considerable detail because the ideas are applicable in other areas as well. For example, with approximate quadrature we have a similar situation, as can be illustrated with the trapezoidal method. The approximation denoted by S in

Section 8.2 is a sum, and can be treated like the partial sum for e, except that separate provision must be made for a common factor (which is h with the trapezoidal method but is usually a bit more complicated with other methods).

In the example

$$I = \int_1^{10} \frac{dx}{x}$$

of Section 8.2, we have $f(a + ih) = 1/(a + ih)$, and we must consider the floating-point evaluation of this expression. This evaluation may be done in a number of ways. One way involves first converting the integer i to floating-point form, then multiplying by h, then adding a, and finally taking the reciprocal. The conversion of i is done exactly, and we can easily choose h so that the multiplication by h is exact, as is the addition of a (which is 1 in this example). Under these circumstances, we would have

$$\text{fl}(f(a + ih)) = f(a + ih) \times (1 + \epsilon),$$

since the only error that occurs is in taking the reciprocal. (However, we will in general have

$$\text{fl}(f(a + ih)) = f(a + ih) \times (1 + \epsilon)^{k_i}.$$

It just happens that $k_i = 1$ in this particular case.)

We therefore have

$$\text{fl}(S) = h \left(\left(\cdots \left(\left(\frac{f(a)}{2} (1 + \epsilon)^2 \right. \right. \right. \right.$$
$$+ f(a + h)(1 + \epsilon) \Big)(1 + \epsilon) $$
$$+ f(a + 2h)(1 + \epsilon) \Big(\ (1 + \epsilon) $$
$$+ \cdots + f(a + (n - 1)h)(1 + \epsilon) \Big)(1 + \epsilon)$$
$$+ \frac{f(b)}{2}(1 + \epsilon)^2 \Big)(1 + \epsilon)(1 + \epsilon)$$

the last $(1 + \epsilon)$ factor being due to the multiplication by the common factor h, while the extra $(1 + \epsilon)$ with each of $f(a)$ and $f(b)$ is due to the division by 2.

We can now apply the same argument used in deriving Eq. (3), except that now we have $n + 1$ terms in place of n. We also know that $k_1 = k_{n+1} = 3$, while all other $k_i = 2$. This leads to

$$|S - \text{fl}(S)| < 1.01u(|a_1|(n + 4) $$
$$+ |a_2|(n + 2) + \cdots + |a_n|4 + |a_{n+1}|4).$$

We can proceed from here in a variety of ways. For example, we can conclude immediately that

$$|S - \text{fl}(S)| < 1.01 \times u \times \frac{(n + 3)(n + 4)}{2} \max |a_i|,$$

and, with $u = 10^{-6}$, $n = 144$ (which corresponds to $h =$

2^{-4}), and noting that $\max |a_i| = 1$, it is easy to show that this is bounded by 1.1×10^{-2}.

The total error can again be divided into two parts,

$$I - \text{fl}(S) = (I - S) + (S - \text{fl}(S)),$$

representing truncation and roundoff, respectively, and the total bound is given by

$$|I - \text{fl}(S)| \le |I - S| + |S - \text{fl}(S)|.$$

In the general case, the right side is bounded by

$$\frac{h^2(b - a) \ \max |f''|}{12}$$
$$+ \frac{1.01u(n + 2 + k)(n + 3 + k)}{2} \ \max |f|,$$

where $k = \max |k_i|$, and, in the special case of

$$I = \int_1^{10} \frac{dx}{x},$$

with $u = 10^{-6}$ and $h = 2^{-4}$, it is bounded by $.006 + .011 < .02$. The calculated result is of course better than this bound suggests, but a more careful analysis would be needed to obtain a better bound. It would be simpler to use smaller values of h and u.

One of the important features of the results derived in this section is the way in which the bound on the total error depends on two separate components. One component is a bound for the truncation error and is generally a decreasing function of some parameter, like n, that is a measure of the amount of computation required. The truncation error may decrease very rapidly with n, as in the case of the exponential series, or less rapidly, as with the trapezoidal rule where the decrease is proportional to $1/n^2$. (One objective of numerical analysis is to develop methods whose truncation errors decrease very rapidly with n.) The other component of the bound on total error is the bound on roundoff error, and it increases with n, perhaps linearly, but it may be proportional to n^2, as in Eq. (2) above, or worse. Both sources of error must be kept in mind in trying to assess the accuracy of numerical results. These ideas are illustrated in Fig. 9.4, which shows the total error bound as the sum of the bounds on the magnitudes of the truncation error and roundoff error.

EXERCISE 9.2

1. a) Show that with $u = 2^{-23}$ and $i < 40{,}000$,

$$(1 + u)^i - 1 < 1.01iu,$$
$$\frac{1}{(1 - u)^i} - 1 < 1.01iu,$$

   b) What is the largest value of i for which these inequalities are valid on the machine you are using?

2. Calculate a floating-point approximation to

$$1 + 1 + 1/2! + 1/3! + \cdots + 1/9!.$$

What can you guarantee about the closeness of your approximation to the true value of this partial sum?

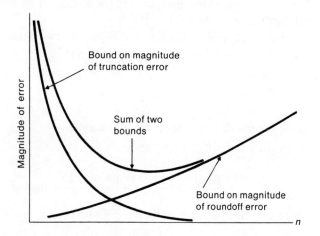

FIG. 9.4 The sum shows how a bound on the total error depends on two components.

3. Find a bound on the error in a floating-point approximation to

$$1 + \frac{1}{2^2} + \frac{1}{3^2} + \cdots + \frac{1}{(n-1)^2} + \frac{1}{n}.$$

4. Suppose that each term in the sum

$$1 - x + \frac{x^2}{2} - \frac{x^3}{3!} + \cdots + \frac{(-x)^{n-1}}{(n-1)!}$$

is evaluated by multiplying the previous term by x and then dividing by the appropriate constant. Determine a bound on the resulting total roundoff error in the sum.

5. Write a subprogram that will produce an approximation to e^{-x} to within a prescribed accuracy, including the effect of roundoff error, for any value of x in the interval [0, 2]. What limitation on the value of the prescribed accuracy must be observed?

6. Write a subprogram for $\sin x$ in the interval $[0, \pi/4]$, along the lines suggested for e^{-x} in Question 5. How far can you extend the interval?

7. Horner's rule for evaluating the polynomial

$$a_0 + a_1 x + a_2 x^2 + \cdots + a_n x^n$$

is suggested by rewriting this polynomial in the form $(\ldots ((a_n x + a_{n-1}) x + a_{n-2}) x \ldots) x + a_0$. Find a bound on the roundoff error associated with this way of evaluating the polynomial, and compare it with what is obtained with a more direct way of evaluating the polynomial. How do the efficiencies of these two approaches compare?

8. Find an approximation to each of the following integrals with an error of no more than 10^{-5}:

a) $\displaystyle\int_0^1 \frac{dx}{1 + x^2}$

b) $\displaystyle\int_0^1 e^{-x^2}\, dx$

9. Discuss the difficulty that arises in trying to treat the integral

$$\int_0^1 \frac{dx}{1 + \sqrt{x}}$$

as you did the ones in Question 8. To what extent can you get around this difficulty?

9.3 SOLVING LINEAR EQUATIONS

Numerical methods are often needed in the solution of linear algebraic equations. The following example is a system of two linear algebraic equations:

$$2x + 3y = 5,$$
$$7x - y = 6.$$

The problem in this case is to find values of the two unknows x and y. An example with three equations is as follows:

$$x + y - z = 7,$$
$$2x - y = 3,$$
$$x + 2y + 3z = 12.$$

Here the problem is to find the values of the three unknowns x, y, and z.

The general case involves n equations and n unknowns. It can be written in the following form:

$$a_{11}x_1 + a_{12}x_2 + \cdots + a_{1n}x_n = b_1,$$
$$a_{21}x_1 + a_{22}x_2 + \cdots + a_{2n}x_n = b_2,$$
$$\vdots \qquad \vdots \qquad \vdots$$
$$a_{n1}x_1 + a_{n2}x_2 + \cdots + a_{nn}x_n = b_n.$$

Our ultimate objective is to develop a computer program that can begin with values of the constants a_{11}, $a_{12}, \ldots$ and b_1, $b_2, \ldots$ and then calculate the solutions $x_1, x_2, \ldots$, or at least reasonably good approximations to these solutions.

The need to solve such systems of equations can arise in many different areas. In engineering, for example, it arises in the design of structures such as bridges and in the study of electrical circuits. It also arises in economic problems and in statistics. Another source of these equations is in the numerical solution of differential equations. The latter are extremely important in engineering and science, but they can be explained only in terms of relatively advanced mathematics. It should be mentioned that some of these sources of linear equations can produce very large systems, possibly involving hundreds or even thousands of equations.

The only source of error in solving linear equations is due to roundoff. In some cases, truncation errors may already have been introduced into the problem before reaching the point where the linear equations are to be solved. For example, the linear equations may be only an approximation to a differential equation. However, once the problem has been reduced to a system of linear equations, the only remaining source of error is due to roundoff, but we will postpone most of our discussion of this difficulty until the next section.

As an example of how a system of linear equations can arise in a practical problem, consider the electrical circuit shown in Fig. 9.5. In this circuit we assume that the resistances $r_1, r_2, \ldots, r_5$ are known and we also assume that the current i flowing into and out of the circuit is known. We are required to find the unknown currents $x_1, x_2, \ldots, x_5$. The five equations needed to determine the five unknown currents are obtained from laws of physics. Kirchhoff's first law states that the sum of all the currents flowing into any point of the circuit must be zero. Examining the leftmost junction of the circuit in Fig. 9.5, we find that

$$i - x_1 - x_4 = 0.$$

We obtain two more equations from the next two junctions. They are

$$x_1 - x_2 - x_3 = 0,$$
$$x_3 + x_4 - x_5 = 0.$$

A fourth equation can be obtained from the fourth junction but it does not provide any new information. In fact, the fourth equation can be obtained easily from the three we already have simply by adding those three equations together. We therefore omit the fourth equation.

Two more equations are needed and they can be obtained by applying Kirchhoff's second law along with another law known as Ohm's law. Kirchhoff's second law states that the sum of the voltage drops around any loop of a circuit must be zero, and Ohm's law states that the voltage drop between two points is equal to the resistance times the current. From the leftmost loop in Fig. 9.5 we therefore obtain

$$r_1 x_1 + r_3 x_3 - r_4 x_4 = 0.$$

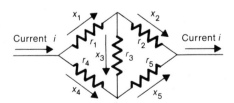

FIG. 9.5 An example of an electrical circuit. The resistances $r_1, r_2, \ldots, r_5$ and the current i are known. The currents $x_1, x_2, \ldots, x_5$ are to be found.

Here, $r_1 x_1$ is (according to Ohm's law) the voltage drop along the top branch of the loop and $r_3 x_3$ is the drop along the vertical branch. The minus sign appears with $r_4 x_4$ because the current in this branch is shown going in the opposite direction to the direction in which we have been going around the loop.

The final equation can be obtained from the rightmost loop of the circuit in Fig. 9.5 and is

$$r_2 x_2 - r_5 x_5 - r_3 x_3 = 0.$$

There is a third loop, the one going around the outside edge of the circuit, but its equation does not provide any new restriction on the unknowns. In fact, it can be derived from the last two equations simply by adding them together.

Rearranging the five equations we finally obtain

$$
\begin{aligned}
x_1 \qquad\qquad + \;\; x_4 \qquad\quad &= i, \\
x_1 - \;\; x_2 - \;\; x_3 \qquad\qquad &= 0, \\
x_3 + \;\; x_4 - \;\; x_5 &= 0, \\
r_1 x_1 \qquad\quad + r_3 x_3 - r_4 x_4 \qquad\quad &= 0, \\
r_2 x_2 - r_3 x_3 \qquad\quad - r_5 x_5 &= 0.
\end{aligned}
$$

These five equations represent a special case of the general problem involving n equations and n unknowns. For particular values of the resistances $r_1, r_2, \ldots, r_5$ and the current i, these five equations can be solved for the five unknown currents $x_1, x_2, \ldots, x_5$. More complicated circuits could obviously lead to much larger systems of equations. Large systems can arise in many other ways as well. It is important that we develop computer programs for solving such large systems of equations.

One small point should be mentioned before leaving this example. The current x_3 is shown going down its branch of the circuit in Fig. 9.5 rather than up. This does not mean that we know in advance that this current goes down rather than up. In fact, the direction of flow depends on the values of the resistances. We have chosen one direction, quite arbitrarily, as the direction in which we *measure* the current flow. It does not matter which we choose as long as we adhere to the same choice in deriving all the equations. If the current happens to flow in the opposite direction, the solution for the current x_3 will be negative.

We turn now to the problem of solving systems of equations. The basic idea can be explained in terms of the system of n equations in n unknowns given earlier. The first stage is to eliminate the term containing x_1 from each equation following the first equation. To eliminate x_1 from the second equation, we subtract the appropriate multiple of the first equation from the second. Assuming for the moment that $a_{11} \neq 0$, the approximate multiple is a_{21}/a_{11}. To eliminate x_1 from the third equation, we subtract a_{31}/a_{11} times the first equation from the third. Similarly, we eliminate x_1 from the fourth, fifth, . . . equations. The final result is a new system of equations of the following form:

$$
\begin{aligned}
a_{11}x_1 + a_{12}x_2 + \cdots + a_{1n}x_n &= b_1 \\
a_{22}^{(1)}x_2 + \cdots + a_{2n}^{(1)}x_n &= b_2^{(1)}, \\
a_{22}^{(1)}x_2 + \cdots + a_{3n}^{(1)}x_n &= b_3^{(1)}, \\
&\vdots \\
a_{n2}^{(1)}x_2 + \cdots + a_{nn}^{(1)}x_n &= b_n^{(1)},
\end{aligned}
$$

where the superscripts are used to indicate that new values of the constants have appeared.

The second stage is to eliminate the term containing x_2 from each equation following the second, assuming that $a_{22}^{(1)} \neq 0$. Appropriate multiples of the second equation are subtracted from the third, fourth, . . . equations. The third stage is then to eliminate the term containing x_3 from each equation after the third, assuming that $a_{33}^{(2)} \neq 0$. This process is continued until we finally obtain a system of equations in the following triangular form:

$$
\begin{aligned}
a_{11}x_1 + a_{12}x_2 + \cdots\cdots\cdots + a_{1n}x_n &= b_1 \\
a_{22}^{(1)}x_2 + \cdots\cdots\cdots + a_{2n}^{(1)}x_n &= b_2^{(1)}, \\
a_{33}^{(2)}x_3 + \cdots + a_{3n}^{(2)}x_n &= b_3^{(2)}, \\
&\vdots \\
a_{nn}^{(n-1)}x_n &= b_n^{(n-1)}.
\end{aligned}
$$

The original equations have now been replaced by a new system that is relatively easy to solve.

The final stage in finding the solutions is to work backwards through the triangular system. The last equation is easily solved for x_n, assuming $a_{nn}^{(n-1)} \neq 0$. Then, knowing x_n, the second last equation,

$$
a_{n-1,n-1}^{(n-2)}x_{n-1} + a_{n-1,n}^{(n-2)}x_n = b_{n-1}^{(n-2)},
$$

is easily solved for x_{n-1}. The third last equation can then be solved for x_{n-2}, and so on until the first equation is solved for x_1.

Modifications must be made to the above procedure before we can use it as a practical method for solving systems of equations. In forming the appropriate multiples, we assumed that the denominators were not zero. For example, each of the multiples to eliminate x_1 had a denominator of a_{11} and we assumed $a_{11} \neq 0$. Similarly, to eliminate x_2 we had to assume $a_{22}^{(1)} \neq 0$, and so on for all other denominators.

If $a_{11} = 0$, we search the other coefficients in the first column, $a_{21}, a_{31}, \ldots$, until we find one that is not zero. We then interchange the equation containing this nonzero coefficient with the first equation. Thus we ob-

tain a new system of equations, which is merely a rearrangement of the original system but which has the new value of a_{11} not equal to zero. Once x_1 has been eliminated from all equations following the first, we examine the value of $a_{22}^{(1)}$. If $a_{22}^{(1)} = 0$ we search the coefficients below this one in the second column, $a_{32}^{(1)}$, $a_{42}^{(1)}, \ldots$, until we find one that is not zero, and interchange its equation with the second. Similarly we can make certain that $a_{33}^{(2)}$ is not zero, and so on.

If we reach a column in which all the coefficients from the diagonal on down are zero, we should stop. This exceptional case is not likely to arise in practical problems; if it does, however, some special action will have to be taken. Consider what can happen even in the special case of two equations and two unknowns:

$$
\begin{aligned}
a_{11}x_1 + a_{12}x_2 &= b_1, \\
a_{21}x_1 + a_{22}x_2 &= b_2.
\end{aligned}
$$

If both a_{11} and a_{21} are zero, we obviously have a situation like

$$
\begin{aligned}
x_2 &= 1, \\
3x_2 &= 2,
\end{aligned}
$$

for which there is no solution, or like

$$
\begin{aligned}
x_2 &= 1, \\
3x_2 &= 3,
\end{aligned}
$$

for which there is an infinite number of solutions, since x_1 can have any value.

The numbers a_{11}, $a_{22}^{(1)}$, $a_{33}^{(2)}, \ldots$ that are used as denominators in forming the multipliers are called the *pivots*. We have made certain that the pivots are not zero (unless, of course, the exceptional case arises). This is all that is required if we are able to do the arithmetic exactly. However, the roundoff errors in the individual arithmetic operations can lead to very large errors in the final result if the pivots are small, even though they are not zero. To avoid such difficulties, it is customary to search a column of coefficients for the coefficient of largest magnitude, rather than for the first nonzero coefficient.

Using the coefficient of largest magnitude as the pivot, in the manner just described, is called *partial pivoting*. (Another approach is known as *complete pivoting;* it involves searching rows as well as columns.) Solving systems of equations by first transforming them to triangular form and then working backwards through the triangular system is known as the method of Gauss. An outline for a program that follows this method, and uses partial pivoting, is shown in Fig. 9.6. Note that provision has also been made for the possibility of a zero pivot, or of the last coefficient of x_n being zero. "Appropriate action" in either of these two cases would

```
Execute the following, except for possible error
        exits in case of zero pivot or zero
        coefficient of xₙ
     /First, do the elimination stage—but only if n > 1/
     Loop for i = 1, 2, . . . , n − 1
          Search ith column, from diagonal down, for largest
               pivot
. . . . . . . .Error exit from "execute" block if pivot is zero
          Interchange ith row and row with largest pivot if
               they're not the same
          Loop for j = i + 1, i+ 2, . . . , n
               Subtract multiple of ith row from jth row to
                  "eliminate" ith unknown from jth equation
          End loop
     End loop
. . . Error exit from "execute" block if coefficient of xₙ is zero
     /Next, do back substitution stage/
     Loop for i = n, n − 1, . . . , 1
          Solve ith equation for xᵢ
     End loop
End execute block
Take appropriate action, depending on whether exit was
     normal, or one of two error exits
```

FIG. 9.6 Outline of program for solving a system of n linear equations using the Gauss method of elimination and back substitution, with partial pivoting.

probably be an error indication of some kind, including an error message if the user ignores the warning. A program developed along these lines could be used as the basis for the sort of numerical software a user would hope to have available in his program library. (See Question 1 in Exercise 9.3.)

In practical problems there is another source of error that arises because the coefficients in the equations are often the result of measurements. For example, the equations associated with Fig. 9.5 depend on the values of the resistances. In specific practical problems, these values must be measured and are therefore known only approximately. Such uncertainty in the coefficients causes uncertainty in the answers.

A considerable amount of analysis is required to assess the effect of roundoff on the calculations involved in solving linear equations. We will not attempt to carry out this analysis completely, but we will give an indication of how this can be done, and the kinds of conclusions we can draw, in the next section. One interesting aspect of the point of view we develop is that the effect of roundoff errors can be considered analogous to the effect of uncertainty in the coefficients. The two sources of error therefore turn out to have similar effects on the accuracy of the final results.

EXERCISE 9.3

1. Write a program or subprogram, based on the method of Gauss with partial pivoting for solving systems of linear equations, as outlined in Fig 9.6. The result should be well documented.

2. Choose nonzero values for the current i and the resistances in Fig. 9.5 and solve the resulting set of five equations for the five unknown currents.

3. It can be shown that the value of a determinant

$$\begin{vmatrix} a_{11} & a_{12} & a_{13} & \cdots & a_{1n} \\ a_{21} & a_{22} & a_{23} & \cdots & a_{2n} \\ a_{31} & a_{32} & a_{33} & \cdots & a_{3n} \\ \cdot & & & & \cdot \\ \cdot & & & & \cdot \\ \cdot & & & & \cdot \\ a_{n1} & a_{n2} & a_{n3} & \cdots & a_{nn} \end{vmatrix}$$

is not changed if a multiple of one row is subtracted from another. It can also be shown that interchanging the ith and kth rows will change the sign, providing of course that $i \neq k$. We conclude that the value of the triangular determinant

$$\begin{vmatrix} a_{11} & a_{12} & a_{13} & \cdots & a_{1n} \\ 0 & a_{22}^{(1)} & a_{23}^{(1)} & \cdots & a_{2n}^{(1)} \\ 0 & 0 & a_{33}^{(2)} & \cdots & a_{3n}^{(2)} \\ \cdot & & & & \cdot \\ \cdot & & & & \cdot \\ \cdot & & & & \cdot \\ 0 & 0 & 0 & \cdots & a_{nn}^{(n-1)} \end{vmatrix}$$

is the same as the original value, except possibly for a change of sign. (We are assuming that $a_{22}^{(1)}, \ldots, a_{2n}^{(1)}$, $a_{33}^{(2)}, \ldots$ are the values produced by the process described in this section for solving equations.) The value of the triangular determinant is simply the product of the diagonal elements, that is, $a_{11} a_{22}^{(1)} a_{33}^{(2)} \cdots a_{nn}^{(n-1)}$. All these facts can now be used to construct a method for evaluating determinants. Write a program or subprogram that will find the value of a determinant. The result should be well documented.

4. There are many methods for solving linear equations but most of them differ from the method of Gauss only in minor ways. One method that differs in a fairly substantial way is known as Jordan's method. In the first stage, x_1 is eliminated from all equations following the first, as in the method of Gauss. However, in the second stage, x_2 is eliminated from all equations except the second, whereas with the method of Gauss x_2 is eliminated from all equations after the second. Thus, in Jordan's method, a multiple of the second row is used to eliminate x_2 from the first equation; this is not done in the method of Gauss. Similarly, with Jordan's method, x_3 is eliminated from all equations except the third, whereas with the method of Gauss x_3 is eliminated from all equations after the third. When the elimination process is finished, Jordan's method produces a diagonal system:

$$\begin{aligned} a_{11}x_1 & & & = b_1, \\ & a_{22}^{(1)} x_2 & & = b_2^{(1)}, \\ & & \cdot & \\ & & a_{nn}^{(n-1)} x_n & = b_n^{(n-1)}, \end{aligned}$$

in place of the triangular system produced by the method of Gauss. (The a's will be the same as with Gauss's method as long as the pivoting is the same; however, the b's will in general be different.) It is obvious that the back substitution process is much easier in Jordan's method than in Gauss's. Develop and document a program or subprogram for solving systems of equations using Jordan's method with partial pivoting.

5. One basis for comparing different methods is to estimate how much work is required with each method. Show that the number of multiplications required with the method of Gauss to solve n equations is approximately $n^3/3$, whereas with Jordan's method the number required is approximately $n^3/2$. Make some reasonable assumption as to how much time is required to perform one multiplication and assume that, when solving equations, the machine requires approximately ten percent of its time for multiplications. How much time would be required to solve ten equations using the method of Gauss? To solve 30 equations? To solve 100 equations? What other factors must be considered when the number of equations becomes extremely large? Approximately how much time do you believe is required by a person to solve ten equations with the help of a desk calculator or a nonprogrammable hand calculator?

6. One way of defining the value of a determinant is by expanding the determinant in one of its rows. For example, if the expansion is in terms of the first row, the definition is as follows:

$$\begin{vmatrix} a_{11} & a_{12} & \ldots & a_{1n} \\ a_{21} & a_{22} & \ldots & a_{2n} \\ & \cdot & & \\ & \cdot & & \\ a_{n1} & a_{n2} & \ldots & a_{nn} \end{vmatrix} \begin{array}{l} = a_{11} \times \text{(original determinant except} \\ \quad \text{first row and first column are} \\ \quad \text{deleted)} \\ - a_{12} \times \text{(original determinant except} \\ \quad \text{first row and second column} \\ \quad \text{are deleted)} \\ + a_{13} \times (\ldots \text{first row and third col-} \\ \quad \text{umn} \ldots) \\ - a_{14} \times (\ldots \text{first row and fourth col-} \\ \quad \text{umn} \ldots) \\ + \ldots \\ \quad \cdot \\ \quad \cdot \\ \quad \cdot \end{array}$$

The problem of evaluating a determinant with n rows and n columns has been reduced to the problem of evaluating determinants with only $n-1$ rows and $n-1$ columns. The process can be repeated to reduce the problem to one of evaluating determinants with only $n-2$ rows and $n-2$ columns, and so on. Eventually, the problem will reduce to one of evaluating determinants with only one row and one column. The original problem is therefore completely solved, at least in principle, if we can evaluate determinants with only one row and one column. The latter are defined simply by taking $|a_{ij}|$ to be a_{ij}. (Note that the vertical bars here do not mean absolute value.) A program based on this way of defining a determinant would be complicated (unless it is recursive). Before you try to write such a program it is worthwhile making an estimate of the amount of time needed to evaluate a determinant by this method

as compared to the time needed for the method described in Question 3. Show that $n!$ multiplications are needed with the method of this question compared to approximately $n^3/3$ for the method of Question 3. Approximately how many years would be required to perform $n!$ multiplications if $n = 25$? How much time is required for $n^3/3$ multiplications if $n = 25$? (Make some reasonable assumptions about the time required for a single multiplication, and for the percent of the machine's time that would be required for the multiplications.)

7. Linear equations are sometimes solved by iterative procedures, which are special cases of the method of functional iteration discussed in Section 8.3. For example, suppose the system of linear equations is rewritten in the following form:

$$x_1 = \frac{1}{a_{11}}(b_1 - a_{12}x_2 - a_{13}x_3 - \cdots - a_{1n}x_n),$$

$$x_2 = \frac{1}{a_{22}}(-a_{21}x_1 + b_2 - a_{23}x_3 - \cdots - a_{2n}x_n),$$

$$\cdot \qquad \cdot \qquad \cdot$$
$$\cdot \qquad \cdot \qquad \cdot$$
$$\cdot \qquad \cdot \qquad \cdot$$

$$x_n = \frac{1}{a_{nn}}(-a_{n1}x_1 - a_{n2}x_2 - a_{n3}x_3 - \cdots + b_n).$$

We can now choose some initial values of $x_1, x_2, \ldots, x_n$ and then substitute these values into the right sides of the rewritten equations. The calculations on the right sides can then be performed to produce new approximations to $x_1, x_2, \ldots, x_n$, and the process can be repeated any number of times. One possibility is to choose the initial values to be zero. The resulting method is known as Jacobi's method. The method will work properly as long as the diagonal elements a_{ii} in the matrix (a_{ij}) are quite large compared to the off-diagonal elements. Write a program to carry out Jacobi's method and test it on some examples of your own choosing.

8. The method of Gauss-Seidel is the same as Jacobi's method (see Question 7) except that the most recent approximation to each unknown is used in the calculations. For example, once the first equation is used to calculate a new approximation to x_1, that value is used in the next equation, along with the old values of $x_3, x_4, \ldots, x_n$, to find a new approximation to x_2. These two new values are then used in the third equation, along with the old values of $x_4, x_5, \ldots, x_n$ to find a new value of x_3, and so on. Prepare a program based on the Gauss-Seidel method. This method is probably better than Jacobi's. However, neither method should be used in preference to elimination methods when the number of equations is not large.

(The only circumstances in which Jacobi or Gauss–Seidel methods should be used are when the matrix is large and most of the matrix elements are zero. By large we mean that n is perhaps 50 or 100 or more. If most of the elements are zero, the amount of computation on the right sides of the equations is reduced to such an extent that many iterations can be performed in less time than it takes to carry out an elimination method. (See Question 5 above.) If most of the elements are zero, the matrix is said to be *sparse,* and it is this kind of matrix that usually arises in the numerical solution of differential equations.)

9. There are various ways in which a person might consider the program in Question 1 to be correct. Can you suggest at least one way? Can you convince yourself that the program is correct in this sense? How?

9.4 MORE ABOUT THE ANALYSIS OF ROUNDOFF ERROR

Having just discussed the problem of solving systems of linear equations, it would be appropriate to attempt an analysis of the effect of roundoff error on the results of the calculations. In particular, it would seem reasonable to attempt the derivation of a bound on the error in the final result that is caused by roundoff.

Unfortunately, the technique we developed in the early part of this chapter and applied successfully to an analysis of roundoff error in sums and quadratures cannot be applied directly to methods for solving linear equations. It turns out that our approach needs to be modified in one rather important way. We have to introduce what we will refer to as a "backward" error analysis, and, as we shall see, this leads to results about the effect of roundoff error that are somewhat less direct than those obtained earlier with sums and quadratures. Nevertheless, the change in approach will appear to be appropriate to the problem being considered and will, in fact, contribute a good deal to our understanding of the role played by roundoff, and ultimately to our being able to control it, or at least make provision for it.

The key idea of a "backward" error analysis can be introduced by referring again to the first example in Section 8.2, which led up to the error bound in Eq. (1). From the basic rule about roundoff error with floating-point arithmetic, we were able to state that

$$fl(a_1 + a_2) = (a_1 + a_2)(1 + \epsilon)$$

where ϵ is some number satisfying $|\epsilon| < u$, and u is the (small) relative roundoff-error bound. Then, applying the rule a second time we obtained

$$fl((a_1 + a_2) + a_3) = ((a_1 + a_2)(1 + \epsilon) + a_3)(1 + \epsilon).$$

Note that we could now write

$$fl((a_1 + a_2) + a_3) = (a_1 + a_2)(1 + \epsilon)^2 + a_3(1 + \epsilon)^2.$$

(The extra factor of $1 + \epsilon$ in the last term can be included if we wish, each ϵ simply standing for some number—zero not being excluded—that satisfies $|\epsilon| < u$.) However, we definitely *cannot* write

$$fl((a_1 + a_2) + a_3) = (a_1 + a_2 + a_3)(1 + \epsilon)^2.$$

(See Question 1 below.) And this means of course that we definitely *cannot* conclude that

$$fl(\ldots ((a_1 + a_2) + a_3) + a_4 \ldots)$$
$$= (a_1 + a_2 + a_3 + a_4 + \cdots)(1 + \epsilon)^{n-1}.$$

In other words, we cannot follow a line of reasoning from getting the sum of 2 numbers to within 1 roundoff error (which is true) to getting the sum of 3 to within 2 roundoff errors (which is in general false), to 4 within 3 errors (also false), and so on.

Fortunately, there is an alternative development which can be followed. Returning to the original result for $fl((a_1 + a_2) + a_3)$, we see that it can be rewritten in the form

$$fl((a_1 + a_2) + a_3)$$
$$= a_1(1 + \epsilon)^3 + a_2(1 + \epsilon)^2 + a_3(1 + \epsilon).$$

From this we can conclude that

$$fl(((a_1 + a_2) + a_3) + a_4)$$
$$= a_1(1 + \epsilon)^4 + a_2(1 + \epsilon)^3$$
$$+ a_3(1 + \epsilon)^2 + a_3(1 + \epsilon)$$

and so on, to obtain finally that

$$fl(\ldots ((a_1 + a_2) + a_3) + \cdots + a_n)$$
$$= a_1(1 + \epsilon)^n + a_2(1 + \epsilon)^{n-1}$$
$$+ a_3(1 + \epsilon)^{n-2} + \cdots + a_n(1 + \epsilon).$$

It was from this form of the floating-point sum of n numbers that we derived the error bound in Eq. (1).

Here, instead of using this form to derive an error bound, we want to view it in another way. We can interpret it as stating that the computed result (the floating-point sum) is the *exact* sum of n numbers, say

$$a_1' + a_2' + a_3' + \cdots + a_n',$$

where the n numbers, a_1', a_2', a_3', ..., a_n', differ only slightly from the original n numbers, $a_1, a_2, a_3, \ldots, a_n$. In fact, we can derive bounds on the differences: a_1' differs by a relative error of no more than $1.01\,nu$ from a_1, a_2' by no more than $1.01(n-1)u$ from a_2, and so on.

From this point of view, we can say that our floating-point computation has produced the exact solution to a problem that is only slightly different from the original. This is a "backward" analysis, because it throws the effect of the roundoff error back on the original problem. We will not consider any details about the derivation, but the backward analysis can also be applied to a method for solving linear equations and, after a fairly long argument, we end up concluding that the floating-point result produced by the method is the *exact* solution to a system of equations that differs only slightly from the original. The "slight differences" depend to some extent on how the details of the calculations are organized. However, a typical result is to find that these differences are no more than $cn^2u \times \max \left|a_{ij}^{(k)}\right|$ in each a_{ij}, where c is a small integer.

Therefore, as already mentioned briefly at the end of the preceding section, the result of a backward error analysis enables us to view the effect of roundoff errors as being analogous to the effect of errors in the data that define the problem. In both cases the errors can be thought of as leading us to computed solutions to problems that are slightly different from what were originally proposed. A typical situation is one in which the effect of roundoff (for example, the "slight differences" referred to in the paragraph above) is smaller than the errors in the data (for example, the measured values of the resistances in an electrical network). In this case, there would not seem to be any point in trying to make the numerical solution any more accurate; it is already as accurate as can be justified on the basis of the errors in the data.

If our purpose is only to satisfy the original equations reasonably well, it may be enough to know that we have solved exactly a slightly different problem. We could then proceed, much as we did in deriving the error bound in Eq. (1), to obtain bounds on the amounts by which the equations are not satisfied. (See Question 3 in Exercise 9.4.) However, we are more likely to be interested instead in the errors in the solutions we have obtained. Knowing that we have solved a problem that differs only slightly from the original is then only a first step. We also want to know what effect this slight difference in the problem might have on the solution. In

particular, we would want to know if such a slight difference in the problem could cause more than a slight difference in the solution.

The two diagrams in Fig. 9.7 show how, even in a relatively simple situation, the outcome can depend a great deal on the problem. In one case a slight change in the problem causes only a slight change in the solution, but in the other case a slight change in the problem causes a large change in the solution. Here is a situation in which two problems appear on the surface to be very similar (each involves two linear equations in two unknowns) but are, in fact, very different in the way they depend on the parameters which define them. One is much more sensitive to small changes in those parameters than the other. We often use the term *condition* to refer to this sensitivity, and we say that a problem whose solution is very sensitive to changes in its parameters (or its data) is *ill conditioned*. When a solution is not sensitive to such changes, the problem is said to be *well conditioned*. (We sometimes have to be more specific, and consider the sensitivity of one particular component of a solution to changes in one particular parameter; for example, one component of a solution can be ill conditioned with respect to one parameter, but not with respect to another.)

Further calculations are needed, as well as more theoretical analysis, in order to determine bounds on the errors in the computed results, but we will not pursue the matter any further. It is relatively easy to do so in the case of sums, but not particularly useful. It is much more complicated in the case of linear equations, and

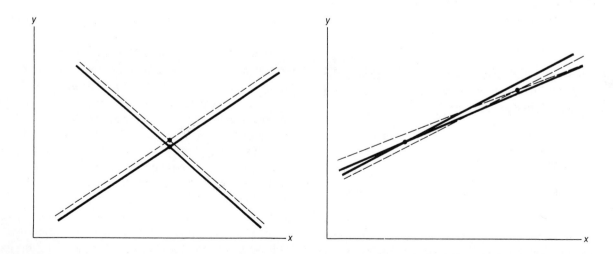

FIG. 9.7 The solid lines are a geometrical representation of the original problem involving two linear equations. The dotted lines represent a slightly different problem in each case. In the diagram on the left the solution to the slightly different problem is only slightly different from the solution to the original. In the diagram on the right the two solutions differ very considerably.

beyond the scope of this book. However, it is hoped that the discussion so far has given a good indication of the general direction in which this kind of error analysis would take us, and has, at the same time, provided a point of view that will be useful in considering the relationship between a backward error analysis (or data errors) on the one hand, and the condition of a problem on the other.

Our general conclusions are more widely applicable than merely to the problem of solving linear equations. For example, there are other problems associated with matrix calculations for which analogous results can be derived. Similar results can be obtained in other areas as well, including the solving of nonlinear equations. The main point that we have introduced is that, with the help of a backward error analysis, we are often able to prove that a numerical procedure produces the exact solution of a problem that differs only slightly from the original. In practice, this is usually quite tolerable, since the data itself is usually not known more accurately, and we can consider the method to be a "good" one. (A method that cannot do this well—such as a method for solving general linear equations which does no pivoting —would be a "bad" one, from this point of view.) Even a "good" method may nevertheless not produce an accurate result, because the problem may be ill conditioned. But that is a difficulty that is inherent in the problem, and can in no way be blamed on the method. (It should be noted that a bad method may actually worsen the condition of a problem. See Question 4 below.)

EXERCISE 9.4

1. Give an example to show that

$$fl((a + b) + c) = (a + b + c)(1 + \epsilon)^2$$

is not necessarily true for $|\epsilon| < u$. What is the worst possible magnitude that ϵ must be allowed to have if we are to be able to guarantee this relationship for all a, b, and c?

2. Prove that the floating-point result obtained in calculating an approximation to the scalar product of two vectors x and y is the exact scalar product of two vectors that differ only slightly from x and y, and give bounds for these slight differences. (The bounds need not be the sharpest possible; it would be more helpful if they were easy to state, even though a bit larger than absolutely necessary.)

3. Suppose that it has been shown that a particular method can solve exactly a system of linear equations whose coefficients do not differ by more than a known small quantity from the a_{ij} of the given problem, and whose b_i are the same as those in the given problem. Find a bound on the amount by which the equations themselves are not satisfied by the computed solution.

4. Doing the calculations by hand, find the exact solution of the following equations:

$$1.0x + 8.0y = 81,$$
$$40x + 40y = 80.$$

Then find the approximate solution produced by the method of Gauss without pivoting, where the result of each arithmetic operation is rounded to two decimal places. What happens if partial pivoting is allowed? Draw graphs of the two equations and explain geometrically the difficulty that arises when pivoting is not allowed.

5. Suppose that the right sides of the equations in Question 4 are known only to two decimal place accuracy. This means that the first right side lies in the interval [80.5, 81.5], while the second is in [79.5, 80.5]. Find the smallest interval within which you can guarantee that x must lie. Find also the smallest interval for y. Will the point whose x-coordinate is the smallest possible value of x and whose y-coordinate is the smallest possible value of y satisfy some pair of equations that is within the known range of possibilities? Do you think you could find bounds for x and y if all the coefficients were known only to two decimal place accuracy?

6. Consider the two quadratic equations

$$x^2 - 4x + 3 = 0,$$
$$x^2 - 4x + 4 = 0.$$

Compare and comment on the sensitivity of the solutions of these two equations to a small change (of, say, .0001) in the constant term of each of them.

7. Suppose that the value of x is known only to within a relative error that might be as large as 10^{-5}. How much effect might this error alone have on the computed approximation to $\sin(x)$ when x is approximately 1? What about when x is approximately 100? What about 10,000?

8. A standard way of solving the quadratic equation

$$ax^2 + bx + c = 0$$

is to use the formulas:

$$x_1 = \frac{-b + \sqrt{b^2 - 4ac}}{2a},$$

$$x_2 = \frac{-b - \sqrt{b^2 - 4ac}}{2a}.$$

Another approach is to first use only one of these two formulas, namely the one in which the two terms in the numerator are of the same sign (so that there is no cancellation of significant digits), and then to obtain the other root from the formula

$$\text{second root} = c/(a \times \text{first root}).$$

Produce an example to illustrate the superiority of the second approach. Write a program to solve quadratic equations that takes advantage of this idea, and that also does something sensible if $a = 0$, or if $a = b = 0$. In what sense would you say your program was correct?

9.5 FURTHER REMARKS

We began this chapter with a description of two floating-point number representations, and we then stated a basic rule for floating-point arithmetic and number conversion. (We assumed a somewhat ideal situation with regard to machine arithmetic, but one that is closely approximated by most machines.) This rule was applied first to the analysis of error in sums and quadratures, where we saw that it was possible to follow through and obtain satisfactory bounds on errors in the final results, at least in some cases. This means that we can do a complete analysis of some important calculations, including, for example, the kind involved in computing approximations to sines and cosines and other elementary functions.

When we considered the more complicated computational methods needed in the solution of linear equations, we were not able to carry the analysis through in detail. However, this example did serve to show how a "backward" error analysis could be introduced, and to illustrate how this approach helped to distinguish between the errors introduced by the method (which turned out to be analogous to errors in the data) and errors in the final results which were inherent in the sensitivity of the problem, or the condition of the problem.

We should mention that there are still a number of aspects that we have not been able to consider. One of the most important of these is associated with the effect of roundoff error on the criteria we use for stopping iterative processes, such as those used for solving nonlinear equations in Section 8.3. What to do in such cases depends very much on individual situations, that is, on the particular methods being used, on the machine details, and so on. It therefore does not seem to lend itself to as general a treatment as we have attempted in the areas already considered.

We believe that a study of roundoff error is important, and have demonstrated a number of ways in which its effect can be usefully analyzed. However, we should also acknowledge the fact that the effect of roundoff error can often be ignored. One of the purposes of a good understanding of the subject is, of course, to know when it can be safely ignored. Alternatively, a good understanding will in many cases enable us to decide when it would be prudent to use higher precision (although most programming languages do not make it particularly easy for the user to change precisions when required). The useful bounds in these circumstances are not usually particularly sharp, but it is also not usually worth the trouble to make them any more precise.

CHAPTER **10**

Statistics

Computers are used to help with statistical calculations in many different situations. It often happens that a large amount of data is available and the purpose of the statistical calculation is to determine certain specific facts that can be derived from the data or to summarize the information in a useful way. For example, from census data the government might want to determine how many people own their homes, or to know the average income of all recent immigrants between the ages of 30 and 35. The government might also wish to have a summary of all incomes according to geographical location. Other examples of statistical calculations arise in trying to fit curves to experimental data and in testing statistical models. Some of the theory about these calculations is too advanced to be considered in this book. However, the general idea can usually be understood fairly easily and we will therefore use whatever formulas are required in the calculations without trying to derive them.

In many statistical applications the most difficult part of the problem is to collect the data. Apart from the fact that this part of the problem may be very time consuming, there are several other difficulties that may arise in collecting the data. Sometimes the data is difficult to obtain because the necessary measurements are difficult to make, or because the information is personal and problems of privacy arise. It is also likely that some of the data we would like to have is either incorrect or missing.

In most of the examples of this chapter we will have to be content to try out the techniques on relatively small amounts of data. This is not a very serious limitation, but we should keep in mind the fact that more realistic problems often involve very large amounts of data. However, in some examples we will be able to avoid this difficulty because the data can be produced by the computer.

Statistical calculations arise in many different areas, including the social and life sciences as well as the physical sciences and engineering. Since the same kinds of calculations can be useful in so many different areas, it is very important that a computing installation have a good collection of programs for carrying out these calculations.

10.1 TABULATIONS

For the purposes of this section we assume that we already have available some items of information about a number of individuals. In a census, for example, items of information might include the name, age, sex, occupation, salary, geographical location, and so on, for each individual person in the population of a country. In another example, the items might come from a poll taken just before an election, and might include the party voted for in the last election, the party favored at the present time, and whether or not the individual believes that a larger share of tax money should be spent on education. In a third example, the days in a year could be the individuals and the items could be maximum and minimum temperatures, rainfall, hours of sunshine, and so on, for each day.

There are several ways in which the information can be made available. For example, it can be on punched cards, or a reel of magnetic tape, or input directly from an automatic recording device. There also are situations in which the data is generated by the computer itself. (One situation where the latter occurs is in generating "random" numbers to be used in certain kinds of simulations, or in order to produce data for the purpose of testing a program.) However, for the sake of convenience in discussing the examples of this chapter, we will usually assume that the information for each individual has been punched onto a card.

Most of our applications, therefore, will require programs that cause the computer to read the cards and obtain whatever information is desired. For example, with census data we might want to determine how many individuals are in certain income ranges. We might want to know how many earn less than $2000, how many earn between $2000 and $4000, and so on. We might also want the same information separately for each sex, or for people living in different geographical regions.

Examples like these require the computer to count and to tabulate but not to do any complicated calculations. The computer may spend a great deal of time on input and so, to make efficient use of the machine, it may be a good idea to have it collect several tables of information at the same time while reading through the cards just once. One table can show how many people are in each income range, as already mentioned. Two other tables can show the corresponding numbers for the separate sexes, while still other tables can show the breakdown of population according to geographical locations, age groups, and so on.

The tables just mentioned show how the population, or part of the population, is distributed according to only one of the items. For example, the first table we mentioned shows the population distributed according to income level. A second table shows the male part of the population distributed according to the same item. Sometimes it is also useful to obtain tables that involve two items. Tables that involve two items are called *bivariate tables*. An example is shown in Fig. 10.1 where the items (or variates) are income and age.

It is often very helpful if the output from the computer is arranged in a convenient format. For example, with bivariate tables it might be helpful if the entries are expressed as percents of the total, rather than as the counts themselves. In place of tables that involve only a single item, it is often convenient to present the output as a graph or a bar chart. (Sometimes it can also be

INCOME	AGE					
	0–20	20–30	30–40	40–50	50–	Totals
$0–2000	90	4	2	1	8	105
$2001–4000	31	25	12	6	12	86
$4001–6000	5	15	16	10	17	63
$6001–8000	1	11	13	14	21	60
$8001–	0	5	8	12	20	45
Totals	127	60	51	43	78	359

FIG. 10.1 Bivariate table showing the distribution of a population according to income and age. (Table entries are in 1000's.)

very helpful to present bivariate information in the form of a "scatter diagram." Examples of this will be given in the next two sections.)

A comment should also be made regarding the input. Obtaining reliable data can often be extremely difficult and sometimes practically impossible, for many different reasons, so that, especially when there are large quantities of data, it is very likely that some of the data items are incorrect or missing. Provision must be made for such possibilities. Usually this is accomplished by *verifying* the data, that is, by testing it to see if it is reasonable, after it has been input and before it is used in any way. For example, we may know that there are no ages in the population greater than 110 and we can test the age item to make certain it does not exceed 110. We should keep in mind that some cards will likely be punched incorrectly. For example, the age may appear to be wrong because it was punched in the wrong columns, or alphabetic information may have been punched in a column reserved for numeric information. If invalid data is detected, the program must do something reasonable. Perhaps the information about that individual should be ignored in the calculation, but at the same time the invalid information can be output so that the user will know what has been ignored. (The action that is appropriate in dealing with invalid data may depend a good deal on the particular circumstances, and could in some cases itself require quite complicated tabulations.) It is impossible to detect all errors in the input, but most of the more serious errors can be caught if the data is carefully verified. Making provision for errors in the input data is sometimes called *data screening*.

The overall organization of a program that would be suitable for most of the examples of this section, as well as for those of later sections in this chapter, is shown in Fig. 10.2.

```
Initialize counters, etc.
Loop until all data has been input
    Input data item
 . . . . If (end-of-file) exit loop
    Attempt to verify data
    If (data is valid)
            update counters, etc.
        else
            take appropriate action
    End if
End loop
Calculate required totals, percentages, etc.
Output required results
Stop
```

FIG. 10.2 Overall organization of a program for processing statistical data. It is assumed that the last "true" data item is followed by another one that is used merely to indicate that the end of the file has been reached.

EXERCISE 10.1

1. The first twenty columns of a punched card are reserved for the name of an individual, column 21 is punched M or F according to the sex of the individual, columns 22–24 contain the person's age, and columns 25–30 contain the person's income in dollars. The last card is followed by a card containing an E in column 21. Write a program that will read these cards and then output a table showing the number of persons in each of the following income groups: 0–2000, 2001–4000, 4001–6000, 6001–8000, 8001–. The total number of individuals should also appear with the table. Give a clear statement of the inputs allowed by your program and the extent to which the input is verified.

2. Modify your program in Question 1 so that it will output an appropriate table for the male individuals only. Have the table entries in percents rather than numbers of individuals.

3. Modify the program in Question 1 so that the output is in the form of a bar chart. This means that the number of individuals in a particular income range is to be represented by a string of symbols, the length of the string being proportional to the number of individuals. For example, if the number 20 is represented by a string of ten asterisks, the number 32 is represented by a string of sixteen asterisks.

4. Write a program that will input the cards described in Question 1 and then output a bivariate table involving income and age similar to the table shown in Fig. 10.1.

5. Suppose that a poll is taken in which each person is asked two questions. In answer to the first question about how they voted in the preceding election, they can reply: Party A, Party B, Can't remember, Didn't vote, or Won't answer. In answer to the second question about how they plan to vote in the next election, they can reply: Party A, Party B, Don't know, Don't plan to vote, or Won't answer. Write a program that will process the results of the poll and produce an appropriate bivariate table. State precisely the format of the input cards required by your program.

6. a) Suppose that a certain item must be an integer between −50 and +50 inclusive and that its value is to be right justified in the first five columns of a punched card. Show how you can input this item and then test it to make certain that it consists of digits, rather than alphabetic or other characters, and that it is within the proper range.

b) Suppose that a second item must have a numerical value that is right justified in the next eight columns of the punched card. A decimal point may or may not appear on the card. Show how the validity of such an item can be tested.

7. Consider a sequence of 1000 numbers generated in the manner described below and determine how many of them lie in the first tenth of their range of values, how many in the second tenth, and so on. The rule for generating the numbers is as follows: take the first number to be 7259; from then on, each number in the sequence is obtained by multiplying its predecessor by 3 and taking, as the next number, the remainder when this product is divided by 10000. Thus, the second number is 1777 since $3 \times 7259 = 21777$ and 1777 is the remainder after dividing by 10000. The third number is 5331 since $3 \times 1777 = 5331$ and 5331 is the remainder. The fourth number is 5993. (The rule is known as a *congruential* rule because, in mathematical terminology, each number in the sequence is congruent to its predecessor, modulo the divisor.)

8. Repeat the experiment described in Question 7 with several different starting numbers in place of 7259 and different multipliers in place of 3. Try to find sequences for which approximately one tenth of the numbers lie in each tenth of the range of values. (Sequences like these will be used to supply "random" numbers for applications in the next chapter. However, they must first be tested more carefully, as will be explained later in this chapter and the next.)

9. Use the sequence of numbers described in Question 7 to construct a table of ten rows and ten columns in which the entry in the jth column of the ith row is the number of those 1000 numbers that fall in the ith interval and are followed by a number in the jth interval. (The first interval is the first tenth of the range, the second interval is the second tenth, and so on.) The 1001st number in the sequence is needed to determine to which entry the 1000th number belongs. Repeat the experiment with different starting values and multipliers. Try to obtain tables in which the entries are not drastically different from each other.

10. Generate 1000 numbers as in Question 7 and count the number of "runups" of different lengths. A "runup" is a sequence of numbers that is steadily increasing but is preceded by a larger number than its first and followed by a smaller number than its last. Thus, in . . . , 12, 4, 13, 45, 39, . . . there is a runup of length 3, namely 4, 13, 45.

11. Generate 1000 numbers according to the rule given below and determine how many lie in the first fifth of their range, the second fifth, and so on. The rule is to start with a number in the interval $(0, 10^4)$, square it to obtain a number in the interval $(0, 10^8)$ and then use the middle four digits of this result as the next number in the sequence. Thus, if the first number is 1234, the second number is 5227 since $1234 \times 1234 = 01522756$. The third number is 3215. Try to find a sequence whose numbers are divided roughly equally between the different parts of the range. (The rule is known as the *midsquare* rule.)

10.2 SAMPLE STATISTICS

A situation that commonly arises in statistics is that a number of observations are available, and we are required to calculate other numbers that are useful measures, or *statistics*, with which to describe the original group of observations. To be more specific, suppose that *n* observations are available and that they are denoted by

$$x_1, x_2, x_3, \ldots, x_n.$$

For example, these observations can be the results of measuring a particular distance on *n* different occasions. As a second example, suppose that twenty coins are tossed *n* times; then x_1 can be the number of heads resulting from the first toss, x_2 the number from the second toss, and so on.

It often happens that most of the observations occur more than once. When this is the case, it may be convenient to present the results graphically in the form of a *frequency diagram*. An example is shown in Fig. 10.3, where it can be seen that the observation 2 has occurred only once, but 3 has occurred 3 times, 4 has occurred 6 times, and so on. The total number of observations in this example is 85.

Assuming that the *n* observations are available, we now consider what kinds of statistics we should compute. The most common statistic is the *mean*, which is defined by

$$m = \frac{x_1 + x_2 + \cdots + x_n}{n}.$$

It turns out to be 8.08 in the example of Fig. 10.3. The mean is a measure of the size or location of the numbers. If the mean is large, the numbers are expected to be large, although of course they need not all be large. The mean is the most commonly used measure of size. The mean is usually what is meant when we speak of an average value, such as the average age in a class or the average mark obtained. However, there are other measures of size.

The next most commonly used measure of size is the *median*. Roughly speaking, the median is the middle number in terms of size in the set of observations; at least half the numbers are less than or equal to the median, and at least half are greater than or equal to it.

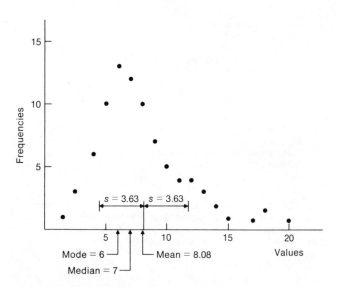

FIG. 10.3 An example of a frequency diagram. The observation 2 has occurred only once, but 3 has occurred 3 times, 4 has occurred 6 times, and so on. The total number of observations in this case is 85. The mean, median, and mode are marked, and *s* is the standard deviation.

The median turns out to be 7 in Fig. 10.3, there being 45 numbers less than or equal to 7 and 52 that are greater than or equal to 7.

The median may not be uniquely defined, as, for example, in the case where the observations are 1, 2, 3, and 6. We could take the median in this case to be any number between 2 and 3, say 2.5. In any event, one important property to notice about the median is that it, unlike the mean, is relatively unaffected by a few extreme data values (which might arise, for example, because of a few large errors in the observations).

A third measure of size is the *mode*. The mode is the number that occurs most frequently. It is 6 in Fig. 10.3. The mode is not defined for a set like

$$2, 3, 3, 4, 4, 4, 5, 5, 5, 8,$$

where no one number occurs most frequently. For many reasons not discussed here the mode is not a particularly useful measure of size.

Thus far, we have discussed only a measure of size. There is one other important measure in statistics, a measure of spread, which is a measure of how much the numbers are spread on either side of the mean. The most common measure of spread is called the *variance* and it is defined to be

$$s^2 = \frac{(x_1 - m)^2 + (x_2 - m)^2 + \cdots + (x_n - m)^2}{n}.$$

The variance is the average value of the squares of the deviations from the mean. The square root of the variance, *s*, is called the *standard deviation*. (For certain rather minor technical reasons, the *n* in the denominator is often replaced by $n - 1$ before calculating the variance and the standard deviation. The result in Fig. 10.3 is 3.63.)

A group of observations is called a *sample*. This is because many observations are possible and we are considering only a sample of them. We have denoted the observations in a sample by $x_1, x_2, \ldots, x_n$, where *n* is the size of the sample. Various measures of a sample, such as the mean and the variance, are called *statistics*. This is one of several uses of the term statistics. Another use of that term is as the name of the subject that we are studying in this chapter. Still a third arises when we are collecting data, since we often say we are collecting statistics.

The two most important statistics are the mean and the variance. Some hand calculators provide function keys for calculating these two statistics automatically after a sequence of observations has been keyed in.

We will briefly mention two other statistics, although they are not used very often. A measure of *skewness* is defined to be

$$a_3 = \frac{(x_1 - m)^3 + (x_2 - m)^3 + \cdots + (x_n - m)^3}{ns^3}.$$

It is called a measure of skewness because it is zero when the observations are symmetrically located on either side of the mean, that is, when they are not skew. (The skewness in Fig. 10.3 is positive.) A measure of what is called *peakedness* is defined to be

$$a_4 = \frac{(x_1 - m)^4 + (x_2 - m)^4 + \cdots + (x_n - m)^4}{ns^4}.$$

(See Fig. 10.4.)

One other statistic that should be mentioned is called the *correlation coefficient*. It can be used when a sample consists of pairs of observations. Suppose the observations in a sample are denoted by

$$(x_1, y_1), (x_2, y_2), \ldots, (x_n, y_n).$$

Suppose also that the mean of the *x*'s is m_x, while their standard deviation is s_x, and the mean of the *y*'s is m_y, while their standard deviation is s_y. Then the correlation coefficient is defined to be

$$r = \frac{\begin{aligned}(x_1 - m_x)(y_1 - m_y) + (x_2 - m_x)(y_2 - m_y) \\ + \cdots + (x_n - m_x)(y_n - m_y)\end{aligned}}{ns_x s_y}.$$

It can be shown that $-1 \le r \le 1$. The value of *r* tends to be close to $+1$ or -1 if the points $(x_1, y_1), (x_2, y_2)$, $\ldots$, tend to lie on a straight line, the value being near to $+1$ if the line slopes up, but near to -1 if the line slopes down. Thus, the magnitude of *r* is a measure of how closely the points tend to lie on a straight line.

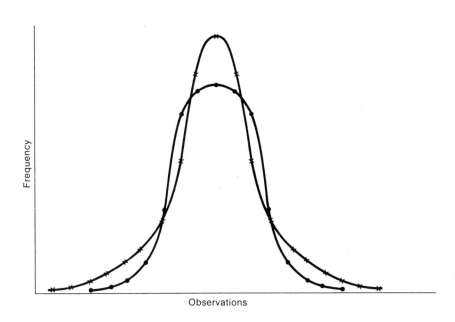

FIG. 10.4 Two frequency diagrams with the same mean, standard deviation, and skewness (the latter is zero), but different peakedness. The frequencies marked with crosses are more peaked than those marked with dots.

An example is shown in Fig. 10.5, where the results of two tests are tabulated and also plotted on a *scatter diagram*. It is seen from the diagram that the results of the two tests are fairly closely related. Students who attained high marks on the language test also tended to attain high marks on the science test. In this case the correlation coefficient is .794.

The interpretation of correlation coefficients is difficult and even somewhat controversial. We will not discuss this aspect of the problem in detail since our main concern is with the computational aspects of statistics. However, it should be pointed out that a high correlation between two variables does not necessarily imply that one is the cause of the other. Being good at languages does not cause one to be good at science. Sometimes we believe there is a definite causal relationship between two variables. For example, if fertilizer is applied to part of a crop, and that part grows more rapidly, we believe that the fertilizer helped cause the extra growth. At other times we believe there is no cause-and-effect relationship. For example, there is a high correlation between income and age, but we do not consider a high income to be a cause of old age or vice versa. In other applications there can be differences of opinion.

For example, there is a fairly high correlation between smoking and lung cancer. Many people believe that smoking can cause lung cancer. On the other hand, some people do not agree with this conclusion; it may be that whatever makes a person susceptible to lung cancer also makes him inclined to smoke. No one suggests that lung cancer is the cause of smoking, so the high correlation by itself is not a proof that one of the characteristics is a cause of the other. We must have additional evidence, such as an experiment in which changes in one variable appear to cause changes in the other, before we can believe in a causal relationship between the two variables.

EXERCISE 10.2

1. a) Prove that

$$s^2 = \frac{x_1^2 + x_2^2 + \cdots + x_n^2}{n} - m^2.$$

What advantage does this formula have over the one given earlier, from the point of view of using a computer to calculate the variance? What disadvantage might it have from a computational point of view?

b) Show also that if m_i and s_i are the mean and standard deviation respectively of the first i numbers,

$$m_{i+1} = m_i + \frac{x_{i+1} - m_i}{i + 1},$$

$$s_{i+1}^2 = \frac{i}{i+1} s_i^2 + \frac{i}{(i+1)^2}(x_{i+1} - m_i)^2.$$

Explain why these formulas might have the computational advantage referred to in (a), without the corresponding disadvantage. What disadvantages do these formulas have?

2. Write a program that will compute the mean and the variance of a sample of data. Assume that the sample is too large for storing in the machine's memory. State precisely how your program is to be used.

3. Suppose that a large number of integers between 1 and 10,000 inclusive has been punched onto cards. Write a program that will find an approximation to the median of these numbers. As the numbers are being input, the program should tabulate how many of them are in the range 1 to 100, the range 101 to 200, and so on. It should determine the range in which the median lies and then make an estimate of where it lies in that range.

4. Suppose that 500 observations are available to a program at one time, rather than having the observations input one at a time with each one being discarded as a new one is input. Write a portion of a program that will find the median of these observations. (The simplest way is to sort the observations first.) Have the program also find the mode, if the mode exists.

5. Suppose that a large number of integers between 1 and 100 inclusive has been punched onto cards. Write a pro-

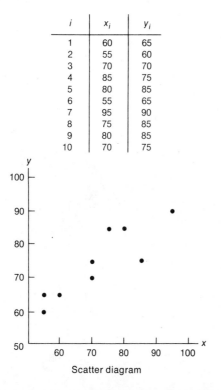

i	x_i	y_i
1	60	65
2	55	60
3	70	70
4	85	75
5	80	85
6	55	65
7	95	90
8	75	85
9	80	85
10	70	75

Scatter diagram

FIG. 10.5 The results from two tests given to a class of ten students. Student i obtained x_i on his language test and y_i on his science test. The correlation coefficient is .794.

gram that will input these values and tabulate the number of 1's, the number of 2's, and so on. Then the program is to calculate and output the mean, the standard deviation, the median, and the mode. Make a clear statement of how your program is to be used and what its limitations are.

6. The following is the average deviation from the mean:

$$\frac{(x_1 - m) + (x_2 - m) + \cdots + (x_n - m)}{n}.$$

Why is this not a suitable measure of the spread of the observations? As an alternative measure of the spread, we can introduce the following average of the magnitudes of the deviations from the mean:

$$d = \frac{|x_1 - m| + |x_2 - m| + \cdots + |x_n - m|}{n}.$$

Write a portion of a program that will compute this value for the observations described in Question 4. Why is this measure computationally less convenient than the variance or the standard deviation?

7. Another measure of spread is the range of the observations, that is, the difference between the largest and smallest observations. Write a program that will find the range of n observations that have been punched onto cards. As usual, state precisely how your program is to be used.

8. a) Show that

$$s^3 a_3 = \frac{x_1^3 + x_2^3 + \cdots + x_n^3}{n} - 3ms^2 - m^3$$

and indicate why this result helps in writing programs to calculate the skewness of some observations. If the sample values are symmetrically located about the mean, the skewness is zero. Construct an example to show that the converse is not true.

b) Show also that, if

$$a_{3,i} = (x_1 - m_i)^3 + (x_2 - m_i)^3 + \cdots + (x_i - m_i)^3$$

then,

$$a_{3,i+1} = a_{3,i} + (x_{i+1} - m_i)^3$$
$$- 3\frac{x_{i+1} - m_i}{i+1} (is_i^2 + (x_{i+1} - m_i)^2)$$
$$+ \frac{2}{(i+1)^2} (x_{i+1} - m_i)^3.$$

9. Find formulas for the peakedness that are analogous to those given in the preceding question for the skewness.

10. Suppose that pairs of observations are punched onto cards. Write a program that will calculate the correlation coefficient for the observations and state how your program is to be used.

11. Suppose that pairs of observations are available to a program, and write a portion of the program that will reorganize the data into a suitable form and output it as a scatter diagram. State precisely what restrictions, if any, must be satisfied by the data, and give a clear description of exactly what your program produces.

12. If y_i is replaced by x_{i+1} in the definition of the correlation coefficient, the result is sometimes called the *serial correlation* or the *autocorrelation* coefficient. (To use n values of y, we need an extra value of x, since $y_n = x_{n+1}$.) Indicate how a program can compute the serial correlation coefficient for $n + 1$ observations that are punched onto cards.

13. Generate 1001 numbers by the method described in Question 7 of Exercise 10.1 and calculate their serial correlation (taking $n = 1000$ in this case).

14. If y_i is replaced by x_{i+k} in the definition of the correlation coefficient, the result is the serial correlation coefficient with lag k. (The autocorrelation coefficient is the serial correlation coefficient with lag 1.) Show how a program can compute the serial correlation coefficient with lag k for $n + k$ numbers that have been punched on cards.

10.3 LEAST SQUARES

Suppose that observations consisting of pairs of numbers have been made. As before, we denote the observations by

$$(x_1, y_1), (x_2, y_2), \ldots, (x_n, y_n).$$

We can imagine that these observations are represented by points, as in Fig. 10.5. A problem that arises very often is to find a function f whose graph is "close" to the points in some sense. The most frequently used sense in which the function is considered to be close is *least squares*. We say that the function is best, in the least-squares sense, if the sum of the squares of the deviations, that is

$$(y_1 - f(x_1))^2 + (y_2 - f(x_2))^2 + \cdots + (y_n - f(x_n))^2,$$

is a minimum.

Many important problems lead to the special case where f must be a linear function. This means that $f(x)$ must be of the form

$$f(x) = ax + b$$

and the problem is to find a and b so that the sum of the squares of the deviations is a minimum. This is an example of *linear regression* and the resulting straight line

$$y = ax + b$$

is called the *regression line*. This special case of a least-squares problem can be handled theoretically in a very satisfactory way. It can be shown that the required values of the regression coefficients a and b are given by

$$a = \frac{n\Sigma xy - \Sigma x\Sigma y}{n\Sigma x^2 - (\Sigma x)^2},$$

$$b = \frac{\Sigma y - a\Sigma x}{n},$$

where

$$\Sigma x = x_1 + x_2 + \cdots + x_n,$$
$$\Sigma y = y_1 + y_2 + \cdots + y_n,$$
$$\Sigma x^2 = x_1^2 + x_2^2 + \cdots + x_n^2,$$
$$\Sigma xy = x_1 y_1 + x_2 y_2 + \cdots + x_n y_n.$$

(See Question 3(b) in Exercise 10.3.)

The scatter diagram of Fig. 10.5 is repeated in Fig. 10.6, along with the straight line which fits this data best, in the least-squares sense just described. (See Question 2 in Exercise 10.3.)

It should be pointed out that it can often be very misleading to apply statistical formulas to data without making some kind of check on what is being done. We have already mentioned automatic "data screening" as one sort of check. Another very useful check of a more "visual" kind is provided by a scatter diagram, and it is particularly appropriate when one is trying to fit straight lines, or other kinds of curves, to data. The two scatter diagrams in Fig. 10.7 are examples where a blind application of the formulas in this section would be quite misleading. In the first, one of the observations appears to be "out-of-line" with the others; it may very well be incorrect (due to an observational error, for example), but it at least deserves further study. In the second, it is obvious that some curve other than a straight line would be more appropriate.

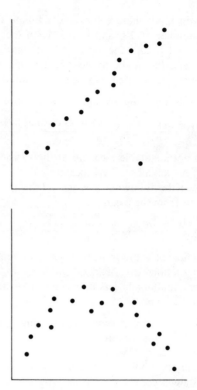

FIG. 10.7 Two examples in which a blind application of the formulas for "best" straight-line fit would be quite inappropriate. The scatter diagrams show the inappropriateness very clearly.

EXERCISE 10.3

1. Develop a program for calculating linear regression coefficients from given observations. Describe how your program is to be used.

2. Use the program developed in Question 1 to find the regression line for the data in Fig. 10.5. What happens if the x and y variables are interchanged? Should you obtain the same line?

3. a) Suppose that several observations on a single variable x are given and denote these observations by $x_1, x_2, \ldots, x_n$. Consider the problem of finding the best approximation to these observations in the sense of least squares. In other words, consider trying to find the value of c that causes

$$(x_1 - c)^2 + (x_2 - c)^2 + \cdots + (x_n - c)^2$$

to be a minimum. Show theoretically that the best value of c is the mean m.

b) Derive the formulas given in this section for the regression coefficients.

4. The following observations were made in a certain experiment:

x	-3	-2	-1	0	1	2	3	4
y	6.5	3.2	2.0	2.9	6.1	11.4	18.1	26.8

Find values of a, b, and c that minimize the sum of the squares of the deviations of these points from the values of the function $f(x) = ax^2 + bx + c$.

5. The mass of a radioactive substance was measured at regular time intervals and the results are shown in the following table:

(Time) t	0	1	2	3	4	5	6
(Mass) m	2.1	1.9	1.7	1.5	1.4	1.2	1.1

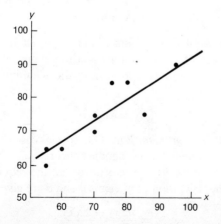

FIG. 10.6 Scatter diagram of Fig. 10.5, along with the straight line that fits this data best, in the least-squares sense described in Section 10.3.

a) Find an equation of the form $m = ab^t$ whose graph is closest to the given points in the sense of least squares. (The problem is nonlinear, and methods such as those described in Section 8.3 must be used.)

b) Take logarithms of both sides of the above equation. The resulting equation is linear in the variables $\log(m)$ and t. Use linear regression to obtain best least-squares values of a and b for this new equation. Why are these values not the same as the ones obtained in (a)?

6. Another radioactive substance yielded the following results:

(Time) t	0	1	2	3	4	5	6
(Mass) m	7.1	5.3	4.0	3.0	2.4	1.9	1.6

Find the best curve, in the least-squares sense, of each of the following forms:

a) $m = A(1.5)^{-t} + B(1.2)^{-t}$,
b) $m = 5a^{-t} + 2b^{-t}$,
c) $m = Aa^{-t} + Bb^{-t}$.

10.4 CHI-SQUARE STATISTIC

One of the most important problems in statistics is to compare the results obtained from a theory with the corresponding results obtained in an experiment. The purpose of the comparison is to determine whether or not the theory and the experiment are consistent. If the experimental results do not agree with what we expect on the basis of the theory, we will probably have to change the theoretical model.

As an example, let us consider tossing a coin 100 times. If we suppose the coin is properly balanced, we are as likely to toss a head as a tail. This means that, on the average, we expect to obtain fifty heads and fifty tails. Of course, we do not expect exactly these numbers each time we toss a coin 100 times. However, we do not expect to obtain results that are very different from these.

We must be more precise about what can be expected. A split of 51 and 49 between heads and tails would not surprise anyone, but what about a split of 55 and 45 or of 60 and 40? If the split we obtain is unreasonable, we conclude that the experimental results do not correspond to the theory. If we decide to reject the theory, we conclude that heads and tails are not equally likely; in other words, the coin is biased. But what should we consider to be unreasonable?

The general problem can be described in the following way. Suppose that k different outcomes are possible in each individual trial. (In tossing a coin only two outcomes are possible.) Suppose that we plan to perform a sequence of n trials, and that, according to the theory we are testing, the first outcome should occur t_1

times on the average, the second outcome t_2 times, and so on. Suppose, finally, that when we do perform the sequence of n trials, we observe that the first outcome occurs e_1 times, the second e_2 times, and so on. We want to determine whether or not the experimental results are consistent with what was expected on the basis of theory.

There are many different approaches to this problem in statistics. One of the best known involves using a statistic called chi-square, which is defined to be

$$\chi^2 = \frac{(t_1 - e_1)^2}{t_1} + \frac{(t_2 - e_2)^2}{t_2} + \cdots + \frac{(t_k - e_k)^2}{t_k}.$$

It derives its name from the fact that the Greek letter χ is used to denote this statistic. Before explaining how this statistic is used, we should point out that it is a measure of the difference between the theoretical and the experimental results. If the differences $t_1 - e_1$, $t_2 - e_2, \ldots,$ are large, the value of χ^2 will be large. Therefore, we might hope to find some values of χ^2 beyond which the results could be considered unreasonable. It turns out that such values can be found. Since the mathematical ideas are advanced, we will try only to give a precise statement of how the values found for χ^2 are to be interpreted.

Figure 10.8 shows part of a table of the required values of χ^2. To understand the meaning of the entries in this table, we consider an experiment with a certain number of degrees of freedom. (The number of degrees of freedom is one less than the number of possible outcomes, provided those outcomes are independent of each other.) We then imagine that this experiment is performed many times. The resulting experimental values will then exceed the table entries ten, five, and one percent of the time, respectively.

Degrees of freedom	Probabilities		
	.10	.05	.01
1	2.7	3.8	6.6
2	4.6	6.0	9.2
3	6.3	7.8	11.3
4	7.8	9.5	13.3
5	9.2	11.1	15.1
6	10.6	12.6	16.8
7	12.0	14.1	18.5
8	13.4	15.5	20.1
9	14.7	16.9	21.7
10	16.0	18.3	23.2

FIG. 10.8 Table of values of χ^2. For a given number of degrees of freedom, an experimental value of χ^2 should exceed the entries in the table ten, five, and one percent of the time, as indicated.

Let us consider a specific example. If the experiment consists of tossing a coin, there are 2 possible outcomes and the number of degrees of freedom is 1. The table entries tell us that χ^2 will be greater than 2.7 ten percent of the time, greater than 3.8 five percent of the time and greater than 6.6 one percent of the time. If we were to obtain a value of 7.1 in our experiment, we would know it was extremely unlikely to have occurred merely by chance. We would therefore have reason to suspect that the coin was biased. (Alternatively, the explanation could be that the data was incorrectly recorded, or that the person tossing the coin was very skilled! Such possibilities must always be kept in mind, although we will not mention them explicitly with each example.) Suppose we obtain 45 heads and 55 tails in tossing a coin 100 times. Then

$$\chi^2 = \frac{(50-55)^2}{50} + \frac{(50-45)^2}{50}$$
$$= 1.0$$

and this is well within the limits we expect by chance alone. We therefore have no reason to consider the coin to be biased.

If we roll a die many times and note whether the result each time is odd or even, we again have an experiment in which the number of possible outcomes is 2. However, if we record the number of 1's, the number of 2's, and so on, we have an experiment in which the number of possible outcomes is 6 and the number of degrees of freedom is 5. If we roll two dice and record the number of 2's, 3's, . . . , 12's, there are eleven possible outcomes for each roll, and the number of degrees of freedom is 10. In this example, it is convenient to denote the theoretical numbers of occurrences by t_2, t_3, . . . , t_{12}, and it should be pointed out that t_2, t_3, . . . , t_{12}, are not all the same. In fact, it can be shown that, in 216 rolls, $t_2 = t_{12} = 6$, $t_3 = t_{11} = 12$, $t_4 = t_{10} = 18$, $t_5 = t_9 = 24$, $t_6 = t_8 = 30$, $t_7 = 36$.

We have not considered any restrictions on how the table in Fig. 10.8 can be used. One restriction that need concern us in most practical applications is that the values of t_1, t_2, . . . , t_k must not be too small. We usually require these values to be greater than at least 5, perhaps 10.

Finally, it should be admitted that we have been restricting our attention to the unlikelihood of obtaining large values of χ^2, which is the usual procedure. However, very small values are also of concern, and can arise, for example, when the theory does not allow for feedback or other regulating mechanisms, or when the data has been "cooked" (which may itself not be an unlikely event!), but we will not pursue this point any further.

EXERCISE 10.4

1. Perform a particular experiment, such as tossing a coin 200 times or rolling a die 300 times, and calculate the resulting chi-square statistic. Have you any grounds for considering that the results do not correspond well with the theory?

2. Suppose that a single die is rolled 315,672 times and a 5 or a 6 appears 106,602 times. If the die is true, the number 5's and 6's in such an experiment would be 105,224, on the average. The observed number is only about 1.3% more than this average number. Have we any cause for suspecting that the die might not be true?

3. Suppose a coin is tossed 500 times. How many more heads than the expected number of 250 would we have to obtain before we should become suspicious if the experimental value of χ^2 is one that can occur by chance less than one percent of the time?

4. One of the properties possessed by a sequence of random numbers from a particular interval is that one tenth of them will lie in the first tenth of the interval on the average, another one tenth in the second tenth, and so on. Consider the sequence described in Question 7 of Exercise 10.1, and use a chi-square test to determine whether or not you have grounds, at least according to this test, for concluding that these numbers do not have the required property. Repeat Question 8 of the same exercise and use chi-square tests to provide more precise answers to that question.

5. Each of the bivariate tables described in Question 9 of Exercise 10.1 has 100 entries. If the numbers in the sequence are random, each of these entries is expected to be 10, on the average. Repeat the experiments described in that question and, for each table, compute the value of

$$\frac{1}{10}[(10-e_{11})^2 + (10-e_{12})^2 + \cdots$$
$$+ (10-e_{ij})^2 + \cdots + (10-e_{10,10})^2]$$

where e_{ij} is the experimental result in the jth column of the ith row. If this statistic is denoted by χ_2^2, and the corresponding one in Question 4 above by χ_1^2, then it can be shown that $\chi_2^2 - \chi_1^2$ is a chi-square statistic with 90 degrees of freedom. The ten, five, and one percent levels are 108, 113, and 124, respectively. What can you conclude about the randomness of the sequences of numbers you are testing?

6. The midsquare method was one of the earliest that was used for the generation of random numbers on a computer, having been proposed by von Neumann and Metropolis in about 1946 for the purpose of producing numbers needed in connection with atomic energy calculations. In practice the method is usually used with numbers having more than twice as many significant digits as the four digits used in Question 11 of Exercise 10.1. What is your opinion of the randomness properties of the sequences described in that question?

7. The first congruential method for generating sequences of numbers with properties resembling randomness was proposed by Lehmer in 1949. He suggested multiplying by 23 and then using the remainder, after dividing the result by $10^8 + 1$, as the next number in the sequence. Thus, if the first number is 11111111, the second is 55555551 since $23 \times 11111111 = 255555553 = 2 \times (10^8 + 1) + 55555551$. What is your opinion of this method as a way of generating numbers that appear to be random?

8. Try to construct a method of your own for generating sequences of numbers that appear to be random numbers in a particular interval. (The purpose of this question is to show that it is not easy to generate "good" random numbers.)

9. In practice we are usually able to avoid the division that appears with each step of a congruential method for generating sequences of numbers. This is because of the way most machines perform integer arithmetic. For example, suppose that a storage location in a particular machine holds ten decimal digits and suppose that overflow with integer (fixed-point) arithmetic is ignored. This means that only the least significant ten decimal digits are retained after a multiplication. This is equivalent to finding the true product and saving only the remainder after dividing this product by 10^{10}. Multiplication alone on this machine is therefore equivalent to true multiplication followed by computation of the remainder that results from division by 10^{10}. The situation is the same on a binary machine, except that the remainder results from division by a power of 2 rather than a power of 10. Not all machines perform arithmetic in this way, however, and not all compilers produce machine-language code that perfroms arithmetic in this way even if the machine itself is able to do so. If you have access to facilities that do operate in this way, you should experiment with generators that make use of this feature. On a binary machine, the starting number should be odd and you should try two different multipliers, one that is an odd power of 5 (such as 5^{11} or 5^{13}) and another that is 3 more than a power of 2 (such as $2^7 + 3$ or $2^{15} + 3$). More details about what methods are most suitable are given in the next chapter, along with suggested multipliers for a decimal machine.

10.5 CONCLUDING REMARKS

Our main purpose in this chapter has been to draw attention to a number of computational procedures that often arise in statistics. It should be noted that the procedures themselves are not particularly complicated. This is not true of all statistical calculations, but it is true of most computational procedures in this area. The difficulties that arise in statistical calculations are therefore not mainly in the basic computational procedures themselves.

We have already mentioned one difficulty that can arise in statistical calculations, which is that we must allow for the possibility of missing or incorrect data. This can make our programs quite a bit more complicated than would otherwise be the case.

The most important difficulty with statistical calculations is in the interpretation of the results. Since our concern has been mainly with the computational procedures themselves, we have not attempted to consider in very much detail either how the formulas are derived or what is the meaning of the results. The mathematical derivations can be quite complicated and the interpretation of the results can be quite difficult. In fact, the interpretation of the results can easily lead to controversy, even between persons who are expert in the field.

These remarks suggest that we should at least be extremely cautious when we draw conclusions from the results of statistical calculations. A large value of a correlation coefficient between two variables does not necessarily mean that these variables are related, and a small one does not prove that they are not related. A large chi-square value is not conclusive proof that the experimental and theoretical results are inconsistent, although it may make us very suspicious about the theoretical model. And a "satisfactory" chi-square statistic certainly does not prove that the theory is an adequate description of the experimental results. In fact, with "satisfactory" chi-square values, we should be very careful to state quite clearly *only* that we have no evidence for disbelieving the theory, rather than saying we have evidence for believing it.

CHAPTER 11

Modeling and Simulations

The use of models is a common technique in solving problems. A road map is an everyday example of a model that is used to solve problems about how to get to a particular destination, how long it will take, where to stop for lunch, and so on. Engineering models are also used in many different situations; an example of such a model is a wind tunnel for experimenting with various aerodynamic shapes.

Many models are more abstract than the two just mentioned and are usually described in terms of mathematical symbols. Examples include models of economic or biological processes, as well as processes in the physical sciences, traffic flow, business activities, and games of various kinds.

In each case the purpose of the model is to imitate the features of interest in a particular situation. A road map imitates a major road system and includes information about such features as road surface and distance, so that we will be able to answer questions about a proposed trip. But the road map does not enable us to answer all questions about the trip; for example, we do not expect a road map to provide information about weather conditions to be expected along the way.

If a model is a good imitation of the features in a situation that we wish to study, we can use the model to obtain answers to our questions, rather than spending what might be prohibitive amounts of time, money, and other resources on getting answers from the situation itself. For example, we may wish to design a computer and we would like to try out several different design possibilities before committing ourselves to the construction of a particular machine.

A model may be the model of a static situation, as in the case of a road map, or it may be the model of a dynamic process, such as automobile traffic. The term *simulation* is used most commonly to mean the modeling of a dynamic process.

The role of the computer in modeling and simulation is simply to store information about a particular model that we specify and to carry out the calculations we prescribe in order to obtain the answers we are seeking. With the help of a computer we can handle very complicated models, but it is essential to realize that we, and not the computer, are responsible for the model. If the answers obtained are not correct or not useful, it is our fault for developing such a model, and not the fault of the computer. A major consideration must therefore be the validity of any model we use, i.e., whether or not the model is a good enough imitation of the situation we wish to study.

11.1 DETERMINISTIC MODELS

A deterministic model is one which does not contain any random components. Such a model can therefore not involve anything, such as rolling dice or traffic arriving at an intersection, that we normally consider to be influenced by chance.

Some of the simplest examples of deterministic processes for which we might use a computer arise in financial calculations. In planning a budget, whether for a family or for a business, it is natural to ask what would happen when various alternatives are tried. For example, if a certain amount of money is invested at a certain rate of interest, what will be its value ten years from now? Alternatively, if the same amount of money is used to purchase equipment that will help produce income, what will the total value become within ten years?

The calculations associated with questions of this kind are relatively straightforward. As an illustration, suppose that an amount of money A is invested at the rate of r percent per annum. At the end of one year the amount will become $A(1 + r/100)$. (We ignore for the moment any minor differences that might result because of different ways in which the calculations can be rounded off.) This process is repeated each year. Although straightforward, the calculations are tedious, and the computer can be very helpful. This is especially true if the calculation is to be done many times with different initial data. In such cases it is worthwhile constructing a general-purpose computer program.

We can view the process of accumulating money at compound interest as producing a sequence of amounts $A_1, A_2, A_3, \ldots$, where

$$A_0 = A$$

and, for $n = 1, 2, \ldots$,

$$A_n = A_{n-1} + (r/100)A_{n-1}$$

(except of course for those "minor differences" caused by different rules for rounding). The equation just given is a *recurrence relation,* which, along with the initial condition, $A_0 = A$, defines the process.

As a second example, we consider a model that involves two dependent variables instead of one. We now require two initial conditions and two recurrence relations. We take the latter to be

$$C_n = a + bP_{n-1},$$
$$P_n = c - dC_{n-1}.$$

Here $a, b, c,$ and d are positive constants. If we are given values of the constants, and initial values C_0 and P_0, it is a straightforward matter to calculate the resulting values of $C_1, P_1; C_2, P_2; \ldots$.

In this model we can imagine C_n to be the amount of a certain commodity that is produced in the nth time period, while P_n is its price. The first recurrence relation indicates that the quantity produced in one time period depends on the price in the previous period. The higher the price, the more that will be produced. The second relation indicates that the price in one period depends

on the production in the previous period. The greater that production, the lower the price.

The result in a special case is shown in Fig. 11.1, where values of P_n and C_n are plotted for a particular choice of $a, b, c,$ and d. Note how, in this particular example, the values of price and commodity fluctuate, while both values gradually settle down to the steady-state values determined by the recurrence relations.

Models of population growth, or the interplay of market forces of the kind just discussed, can be extended very easily to larger numbers of more complicated equations. The tedious calculations associated with such models are easily handled with the help of computers. The difficult tasks are to collect data and to construct models that are consistent with the data. A model that has been successfully tested can then be used in helping us plan for the future.

As a final example of a process that can be treated as a deterministic one, we consider a process from the physical sciences in which the mass of a radioactive substance is gradually decaying. The law governing this process states that the radioactive substance is losing mass at any particular time at a rate proportional to the mass present at that time. The constant of proportionality is a characteristic of the substance, being quite large for some substances but relatively small for others.

The problem we consider is the following. Suppose we know the mass of a certain substance at the beginning of a certain period of time and suppose we also know the proportionality constant. Then the prob-

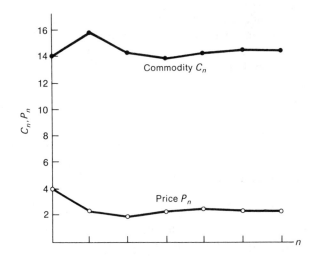

FIG. 11.1 Commodity and price fluctuations according to the model based on $C_n = 12 + P_{n-1}$, $P_n = 6 - .25C_{n-1}$ with $C_0 = 14$ and $P_0 = 4$. The steady-state values are determined by $C = 12 + P$, $P = 6 - .25C$, which give $C = 14.4$ and $P = 2.4$.

lem is to determine how much of the substance is left at the end of the time period.

As a specific example, suppose the period of time is one hour and the mass at the beginning of the period is two grams, while the proportionality constant is .01 per minute. This means that the substance is losing mass at the rate of .01 × 2 grams per minute at the beginning of the period. If it were to continue to lose mass at this rate for the first minute, it would lose .01 × 2 = .02 grams and the mass would be reduced to 1.98 grams at the end of the first minute. This result is only an approximation to the true value at the end of the first minute, since the rate of loss (.02) does not continue throughout the first minute. (This is the important way in which the model we are now considering differs from the earlier one involving the growth of money at a particular rate of interest.) In fact, the rate would decrease slightly as the mass decreases. However, the difference will be small and for the moment at least we will take 1.98 to be a satisfactory approximation for the mass left at the end of the first minute.

Under these circumstances, the rate of loss at the end of the first minute is .01 × 1.98 grams per minute. If this rate were to continue through the second minute, the mass left at the end of two minutes would be 1.98 − .01 × 1.98 = 1.9602 grams. Again, this is only an approximation. The argument can be continued this way through succeeding minutes. At the end of sixty minutes we would have an approximation to the desired result.

The procedure just described is a numerical method known as *Euler's method*. If the physical process is described in precise mathematical terms, we obtain what is called a *differential equation*. Euler's method is therefore a method of finding approximations to solutions of differential equations.

To obtain what we expect to be a better approximation than the one described above, we can use shorter time intervals, for example, half-minute intervals. The mass is decaying at the rate of .01 × (mass) per minute, which is the same as .005 × (mass) per half minute. If we now continue exactly as before, except that we follow the process through 120 half minutes instead of 60 full minutes, we obtain the new approximation. At the end of the first half minute we obtain 2 − .005 × 2 = 1.99 grams. At the end of the second half minute we obtain 1.99 − .005 × 1.99 = 1.98005 grams, which is slightly larger than the previous approximation at the end of the first minute.

A computer program has been written to follow this process with successively smaller values of the time interval and the results are shown in Fig. 11.2. As with the quadrature problem of Chapters 8 and 9, we recognize two sources of error. The truncation error arises

Time interval	Approximation	First difference
1	1.09429	
		.00165
1/2	1.09594	
		.00079
$1/2^2$	1.09673	
		.00033
$1/2^3$	1.09706	
		.00005
$1/2^4$	1.09711	
		−.00019
$1/2^5$	1.09692	
		−.00056
$1/2^6$	1.09636	
		−.00116
$1/2^7$	1.09520	
		−.00238
$1/2^8$	1.09282	
		−.00475
$1/2^9$	1.08807	
		−.01018
$1/2^{10}$	1.07789	

FIG. 11.2 Approximations to the mass remaining after one hour when the mass at the beginning is 2 grams and the proportionality constant is .01 per minute.

because the computational process is not exactly the same as the physical process. This error is expected to approach zero as the size of the time interval approaches zero. However, it can be shown that the truncation error in this example is approximately proportional to the size of the interval, rather than to its square, as was the case with the trapezoidal method.

The effect of roundoff error becomes noticeable with interval sizes less than $1/2^4$. It is more difficult to obtain bounds on the errors for problems of this kind than for quadrature problems. On the basis of the results in Fig. 11.2, we might estimate the mass after one hour to be 1.0971, with an error of no more than about .0001, but this turns out to be too optimistic. (The exact solution can be obtained from the result given in the next paragraph; to four decimal places, it is 1.0976.)

It should be acknowledged that problems of this kind can be solved exactly by means of the calculus. For example, the exact solution of the specific problem considered here is $2e^{-.6}$, which can be evaluated as long as we have values of the exponential function e^x. The importance of numerical methods, such as the one developed for the radioactive decay process, is that they can be used to calculate approximations to the solution of *any* process, including the one used here to illustrate the basic ideas. On the other hand, the calculus can be used to find exact solutions only for a few relatively simple problems.

The preceding remarks are not intended to suggest that the calculus is not very important for a study of the kind of growth and decay processes we have been considering. On the contrary, the calculus is extremely helpful in describing and understanding these processes. It is also needed to analyze the numerical methods used, and to help develop better numerical methods.

The examples of deterministic simulations that we have considered so far have been rather special. A few more complicated examples are considered in Exercise 11.1. Some of the questions point to the possibility of developing quite complicated models for the description of complex economic or ecological systems. It should be easy to see how, on the one hand, the development of the computer program for any particular model is relatively simple, whereas, on the other hand, the determination of suitable equations is quite another matter. And even if suitable equations are obtained, there may still be very severe difficulties in coping with the associated numerical errors that arise with some types of models.

Very often the problem we are confronted with is a kind of "inverse" problem in which we already know the solution and would like to determine the model. For example, we may know the commodity-price values over a period of time and want to determine an appropriate model. In any such case we have to assume the general form of the model, such as the general form of the recurrence relations described earlier, and then determine appropriate values of the parameters (of $a,b,c,$ and d if we assume the general form given earlier). Calculations based on the model will normally not fit the known solution perfectly and we must decide whether the "fit" is good enough or whether we should try another general form. Techniques of the type introduced in Section 10.3 may be used to solve this problem. As a second example, we may have observed the quantity of a substance at different points in time (by measuring its radioactivity at those times) and be required to determine its decay constant, i.e., the rate at which its mass is decreasing. In this case we have assumed a particular form of the model and are required to find only a single parameter.

The examples considered so far are only a small sample of what can be classified as deterministic simulations. In fact, many other calculations can be viewed as simulations of one kind or another. For example, floating-point arithmetic on a computer can be viewed as a simulation of "true" arithmetic. Some of the examples considered later in Chapter 13 can also be viewed as models, and another, very different kind of deterministic simulation is described in Section 14.1, where the simulation of a hypothetical computer is discussed.

EXERCISE 11.1

1. Suppose that $1000 is invested in an enterprise that earns twelve percent per year. Assume that interest is reinvested immediately upon payment.

a) Carry out the calculations in floating-point arithmetic to determine approximately how much the investment

will be worth at the end of ten years, assuming that interest is paid at the end of each year.

b) How much does the answer in (a) change if interest is paid monthly, at the rate of one percent per month?

c) Carry out the calculations in (a) but round intermediate results to the nearest cent. By how much does the result found in (a) differ from this one? Which would you use?

2. Suppose that $100 is invested at the beginning of each year for 10 years and that the money earns interest at the rate of 10 percent per year, payable at the end of each year. If the interest is reinvested, how much money will have accumulated by the end of the tenth year?

3. A man borrows $1000 and agrees to pay back $90 at the end of each month for 12 months. He therefore pays back $1080 altogether, which might appear to represent interest of only 8 percent on the original loan. By making calculations with a few different rates, compounded monthly, determine the true annual interest rate to within .1 percent.

4. A certain 10-year bond has a par value of $100 and pays interest at the rate of 7 percent per year. Find the effective yield to maturity if this bond can be purchased for $93. (The effective yield is the interest rate at which the present value of all returns from this bond—that is, the 9 payments of $7 at the end of the 1st, 2nd, . . . , 9th years and the final payment of $107 at the end of the 10th—is equal to $93.) Find the yield to the nearest .01 percent.

5. There are two alternative ways of investing $100,000 and the problem is to determine which produces the largest sum of money at the end of a given number of years. One way is simply to buy bonds that yield interest at the rate of 7 percent per year, and to reinvest the interest as it becomes payable. The other way is to purchase a certain machine which can be used to produce certain goods making a profit. The initial cost of the machine is $70,000 and this amount must be depreciated at the rate of 20 percent per year. The remaining $30,000 is needed for installation and other initial expenses, the value of which can be assumed to be worth $20,000 at the end of 10 years, and $10,000 at the end of 25 years. A net profit of $12,000 on sales is expected at the end of each year, and this amount is immediately invested in the 7 percent bonds. Which course of action will lead to the largest net worth at the end of 10 years? At the end of 25 years?

6. A man has just reached the age of 65 and is about to purchase an annuity which is to pay $500 at the end of each month, up to and including the month in which he dies. From a table of life contingencies he has obtained the table of values shown in Figure 11.3.

These values are to be interpreted in the following way. The probability of dying in any month of the man's 66th year is .043/12. The probability of dying in any month of his 67th year is .047/12, and so on. What is the present value of such an annuity? What would be its present value if payment were guaranteed for the first 10 years,

Age	65	66	67	68	69	70	71	72
Probability of dying	.043	.047	.051	.055	.059	.064	.069	.075

	73	74	75	76	77	78	79
	.082	.089	.096	.101	.113	.123	.133

	80	81	82	83	.84	85	86
	.144	.156	.170	.184	.199	.215	.233

	87	88	89	90	91	92	93
	.251	.272	.293	.316	.340	.363	.393

	94	95	96	97	98	99	100
	.419	.450	.479	.486	.526	.556	.750

FIG. 11.3 Table showing probability of dying within one year, for each age from 65 up to 100.

even if he did not survive those 10 years? (For the purposes of these calculations, it should be assumed that no one lives beyond the age of 101.)

7. Find solutions of the commodity-price equations with a variety of parameter values. What general conclusions can you draw about the behavior of this model?

8. Develop a program or subprogram for carrying out Euler's method and use it to confirm the first few lines in Fig. 10.1.

9. In an attempt to develop a new method that might improve on Euler's method, we can proceed as follows: Use Euler's method to obtain a first approximation at the end of the interval and then use this result to compute the rate at which mass is being lost at the end of the interval. Then use the average of the two rates, at the beginning and end of the interval, to compute a better approximation to the mass at the end of the interval. Thus, in the example of this section with one-minute intervals, we begin with a rate of .02 grams per minute and obtain 1.98 grams as the first approximation to the mass at the end of the first interval. From this the rate at the end of the interval is .0198. The average of the two rates is .0199, and this average leads to what we hope is a better approximation of 1.9801 grams at the end of the first interval. This procedure is repeated in succeeding intervals. The method is known as the trapezoidal method and has an obvious analogy with the method described in Section 8.2. It can be shown that the truncation error with this new method approaches zero in proportion to the square of the interval size. Develop a program to apply the new method to the problem of this section.

10. It can be shown that Euler's method will always give results for decay processes that are too small, as long as the time intervals are not ridiculously large. Try to prove this

result or at least show that it is plausible. What can happen if time intervals are much too large? Would you guess that the trapezoidal method produces results that are too small? Too large?

11. Use Euler's method for the process described in this section and make an estimate of the time required for the substance to decay to half of its original mass. (This is known as the half-life of the substance.) How much time is required for it to reach one tenth of its original mass? Can you guarantee an upper bound or a lower bound for these times?

12. Suppose a small object at a fairly high temperature is dropped into a liquid at a lower temperature. If the amount of liquid is quite large and is kept well stirred, we can assume that the heat from the object is spread quickly through the liquid without changing the temperature of the liquid appreciably. Under these circumstances we can assume that the object loses heat at a rate proportional to the difference between the temperature of the object and the temperature of the liquid. Suppose that the temperature difference is 100 degrees initially and that the proportionality constant is .03 per second. Calculate a table showing the temperature difference every two seconds. How reliable do you consider your results to be? Why? (It should be noted that a similar problem arises when a cold object is dropped into a relatively hot liquid.)

13. Under certain circumstances the electric charge on a condenser will leave the condenser at a rate proportional to the amount of charge remaining on the condenser. If the proportionality constant is 5 per second, how long will it take before the charge has reached one percent of its initial value? What can you say about the accuracy of your result?

14. Under suitable circumstances the growth of bacteria is governed by a law which states that the number of bacteria increases at a rate proportional to that number. If the constant of proportionality is 1/4 percent per minute, by what factor will the size of the colony have increased in one hour?

15. In some growth processes the rate of increase is proportional to two factors. For example, consider the case of an animal population living in an area that cannot supply food for more than a certain maximum population. In this case the rate of increase can be taken to be $cN(m - N)$, where c is the constant of proportionality and N denotes the number of animals in the population. The constant m is the maximum number that can be supported. The second factor, $m - N$, indicates that the rate of increase becomes smaller as N approaches its maximum value. Using this mathematical model, calculate a table of approximations to the value of N at the end of each year for 20 years. Assume that $c = 10^{-4}$ per year and $m = 10000$, while the initial value of N is 100.

16. Two main forces act on falling objects. The force of gravity tends to increase the rate of fall, while the frictional force of the atmosphere tends to retard the rate of fall. One rule that is sometimes used to describe the situation is that the rate of fall, or the velocity, is changing at a rate equal to $g - kv^2$, where g is the acceleration due to gravity and k is a constant depending on the object that is falling. It is assumed here that the frictional force is proportional to the square of the velocity, a relationship that is not very accurate but that is adequate for the purpose of illustrating the calculation we wish to consider. Suppose that $g = 10$ (meters/sec/sec) and $k = .001$ (per meter), and suppose also that the velocity is zero when the time is zero. Calculate approximations to the velocity at the end of each second, up to the end of 100 seconds. Can you also calculate approximations to the distance fallen by the end of each second? How long would it take to fall to the ground from a height of 5000 meters?

17. In radioactive decay processes, there is often a chain of substances, with the first decaying into the second, the second into the third, and so on. Consider a chain of two substances and suppose that the decay constant for the first substance is .5 per second. If the decay constant for the second substance is .25 per second, the rate of increase of the second substance is $+.5x - .25y$, where x is the mass of the first substance and y is the mass of the second. The reason for the appearance of the term $+.5x$ is that the second substance is increasing by whatever amount the first one decreases. Calculate approximations to the quantity of the second substance at the end of each second for 20 seconds. Assume that the process begins with one gram of the first substance and none of the second.

18. A man starts at the corner of a field and runs north at 5 meters per second, as indicated in Fig. 11.4. His faithful dog starts at another corner, 100 meters east of where the man starts, and runs directly toward his master at the rate of 20 meters per second. Calculate an approximation to the dog's path and to the time taken by the dog to catch his master. How much time would the dog have been able to save if he had had enough sense to take the shortest path?

19. Suppose that W represents the number of wolves in a certain area and R the number of rabbits. Suppose also that W is increasing at a rate equal to $-aW + bR$, where a and b are constants. The term $-aW$ is the rate at which wolves die off if there are no rabbits available as food. The term bR is the rate at which wolves would increase as long as rabbits are available and there is no competition between

different wolves. Suppose that R is increasing at a rate equal to $-cW + dR$, where c and d are constants. Here, $-cW$ is the rate of change caused by the wolves and dR is the natural rate of increase of rabbits if left to themselves. The model obviously does not account for all the factors that occur in a real situation. However, it can be used to give some idea of what more complicated models might be like and of how we can find numerical approximations to the solutions. Take $a = d = 1$, $b = c = 2$ and assume that $W = R = 100$ at the start. Calculate approximations to W and R at regular time intervals and draw graphs to show how W and R change with time. What happens to W and R after a long period of time? How are the solutions affected if constant terms are added to the two rates of increase?

20. Economic processes are extremely complicated and really satisfactory models have not been found. Nevertheless, economists sometimes try to construct models that have at least some of the main features of economic systems. The following is a very much simplified model that can be used to indicate how one might begin a study of economic processes. We let K represent the supply of capital and L the labor force. We suppose that K is changing at a rate given by $aK - wL$. The term aK is intended to account for the growth of capital goods caused by the capital already invested in equipment. The term wL represents the wage payments; it must be subtracted from the capital produced in order to determine how much of that capital is available for reinvestment and a consequent increase in the capital K. We also suppose that L is changing at a rate proportional to $cw - dL$. The labor force is therefore supposed to grow relatively quickly if the wage rate w is high. On the other hand the labor force also decreases at a rate proportional to L because of overcrowding and other factors. The model is not very practical. However, it

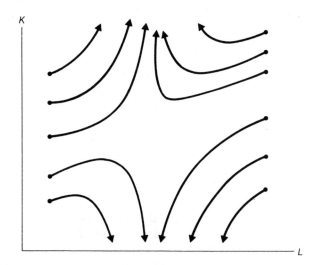

FIG. 11.5 Each curve shows how K and L change with time for particular starting values, according to the simple economic model of Question 20.

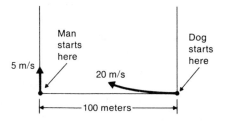

FIG. 11.4 The dog runs directly towards his master, as described in Question 18.

is interesting to study the way in which K and L change with time for different values of a, w, c, d and different starting values. To consider specific examples, take $a = w = c = d = 1$ and calculate approximations to K and L for different starting values. Plot the resulting values of K and L on a graph as indicated in Fig. 11.5. Can you say qualitatively what the different kinds of curves mean? For example, what happens to the size of the labor force according to this model? What is the effect of not having enough capital at the start?

11.2 RANDOM NUMBERS

Many processes that we attempt to simulate involve some randomness. For example, the arrival of cars at an intersection is at least partly random, as are arrivals and departures of goods in a warehouse. Shuffling cards is usually considered to be a random process. (If you are playing a card game in which this is not the case, you would be well advised to try another game!) To simulate randomness we will need to have a method of producing sequences of numbers that are random, or that at least appear to be random. Most program libraries have subprograms available for the production of suitable sequences of numbers so that the programmer need not concern himself with the details. However, it is unfortunately the case that not all library subprograms produce random numbers of good quality. It is sometimes more efficient to produce your own random numbers by means of techniques like those mentioned in the preceding chapter, and we will describe one such technique in more detail later in this section. For the moment we assume that we can produce a sequence of numbers that can be considered to be random and we explain how such a sequence can be used in the simulation of random processes.

Suppose that we have a sequence of numbers between 1 and 1000 inclusive that appear to be random. For example, the sequence might begin with 326, 149, 782, 599, 25, 340, 909, ... Suppose that we are programming the computer to simulate the arrival of cars at an intersection and the process involves one car arriving every four seconds on the average. If the process is divided into one-second intervals, this is almost the same as requiring a car to arrive in each interval with probability 1/4. Then, for each new interval the program obtains the next number in the sequence and, if the number is 250 or less, it is assumed that a car has arrived, otherwise not. As the simulation proceeds, the cars will appear to arrive at the intersection in a random way, at an average rate of one every four seconds.

The same sequence of numbers can also be used to simulate the roll of a die. Any number between 1 and 166 inclusive can be used to represent the roll of a 1, a number between 167 and 333 inclusive can repre-

sent a 2, and so on. If integer arithmetic is performed in a certain way, there is a simpler method than testing each new number in the sequence to determine in which interval it falls. To obtain the value of the roll we evaluate the expression $1 + (\text{number})/167$. If the remainder produced by the division is discarded, the value of this expression is 1 if the number is between 1 and 166 inclusive, 2 if the number is between 167 and 333, and so on. Thus, corresponding to the sequence of numbers

$$326, \ 149, \ 782, \ 599, \ 25, \ 340, \ 909, \ldots$$

the values of the expression are

$$2, \quad 1, \quad 5, \quad 4, \quad 1, \quad 3, \quad 6, \ldots$$

and these values are taken to be the results of successive rolls of a die.

All that remains now is to describe how suitable sequences of random numbers can be produced. One of the most widely used and most effective methods of generating random numbers is the *congruential* method mentioned in the preceding chapter. The so-called *multiplicative congruential* method can be described in the following way. We begin with a multiplier m, a divisor d, and the first number in the sequence, which we denote by n_1. Each succeeding number in the sequence is obtained by multiplying its predecessor by m, and then taking the remainder when the result is divided by d to be the next number. Thus, the second number, n_2, is the remainder obtained on dividing mn_1 by d. (The reason for calling this method a congruential method is that $n_{i+1} \equiv mn_i \pmod{d}$, that is, the $(i+1)$st number is congruent to the ith number, modulo d. Two numbers being congruent modulo d simply means that they have the same remainder after being divided by d.) It is usually convenient to choose d to be a power of 10 or a power of 2 depending on whether we are using a decimal machine or a binary machine. The reason for this is that, with integer arithmetic, ignoring overflow is equivalent to keeping only the remainder after dividing the product by a power of 10 or 2. Thus, if a binary machine has 35 digits in each storage location (apart from the sign) and if overflow is ignored after multiplication, the result is exactly the same as we would get if we had formed the true product and then saved only the remainder after dividing by 2^{35}.

Some fairly difficult mathematical theorems are needed to tell us which numbers to begin with and which to use as multipliers, for any particular choice of d. These two numbers must be chosen so that the sequence does not begin to repeat itself too soon and also so that the resulting sequence appears to be sufficiently random. Starting numbers and multipliers are usually chosen so that the sequence has the maximum possible length. Standard statistical methods can then be used to test portions of the sequence to see if they pass tests for randomness. (See Section 10.4.) But one should be wary of generators that have been subjected only to a few such chi-square tests, without having been scrutinized very carefully in a variety of ways. Some supplementary theoretical support is desirable, and so is a visual examination, as is possible, for example, if pairs are displayed as points scattered over a square.

It turns out that the choices of starting value and multiplier depend a great deal on whether the calculations are to be done in decimal or binary arithmetic. On a decimal machine with more than three digits per word, a sequence of maximum length is obtained as long as the starting number is not divisible by 2 or 5, and provided that, when the multiplier is divided by 200, the remainder is one of the numbers 3, 11, 13, 19, 21, 27, 29, 37, 53, 59, 61, 67, 69, 77, 83, 91, 109, 117, 123, 131, 133, 139, 141, 147, 163, 171, 173, 179, 181, 187, 189, 197. If a word consists of s decimal digits, the sequence length is $5 \times 10^{s-2}$. To make certain that the sequence is sufficiently random, it is important to avoid using simple multipliers like 13 or 10000003. It is also necessary to work with numbers of more than a few decimal digits; at least six or seven are needed to obtain reasonable randomness.

On a binary machine with more than two binary digits per word, a sequence of maximum length is obtained as long as the starting number is odd and provided that the multiplier leaves a remainder of 3 or 5 after being divided by 8. If the word length is s, the sequence length is 2^{s-2}. It is necessary to avoid multipliers with simple binary representations, like 5 or $2^{17} + 3$, and it is also necessary to have s greater than about 20. A common choice is to use the largest odd power of 5 that can be stored in one word. This means 5^{15} if $s = 35$, and 5^{13} if $s = 31$ or 32. (It can be shown that a remainder of 5 is obtained when an odd power of 5 is divided by 8.)

Special mention should be made of computers that use a 2's-complement representation, such as IBM System/370 computers. Because of the way multiplication is performed, and the fact that a 2's-complement representation is used for negative numbers, the result of multiplying two positive quantities may be negative if overflow occurs. A simple way to avoid any difficulties that might arise because of this complication is to take the absolute value of the result before proceeding. The usual theory no longer applies directly to the resulting sequence, but the numbers can still be treated as random numbers in an appropriate interval. In the case of System/370 computers, $s = 31$; the appropriate interval is therefore $(0, 2^{31})$.

It may be difficult to believe that numbers generated in the way we have described are random. In a sense, of course, they are not random at all, since the sequence is completely determined in advance. The point is, however, that they appear to be random, and they appear to be sufficiently random for the purposes of a simulation, which is all that matters. To avoid philosophical discussions about the nature of randomness and related questions, we often call numbers generated in this way *pseudo-random*. However, we will continue to use the word random and hope that this does not lead to any misunderstanding.

Finally, it must be emphasized that the methods described above generate random numbers that are *uniformly distributed* over some interval. The interval depends on the congruence relation that is used by the method. It is sometimes required to have random numbers from a distribution other than the uniform distribution. There is a variety of ways in which random numbers from a uniform distribution can be used to generate numbers from a nonuniform distribution. (For example, see Question 4.)

EXERCISE 11.2

1. Describe a technique for generating random numbers without making special use of how the machine handles integer arithmetic. The random numbers, the multiplier, and the divisor can all be in double precision, if available. The division implied in the congruence must then be carried out explicitly, and the resulting quotient must be rounded down to the next lowest integer value.

2. Write a program for testing random number generators. It should provide the kind of visual results that were asked for in Questions 7 and 9 of Exercise 10.1, and also the corresponding chi-square values required in Questions 4 and 5 of Exercise 10.4. Use the program for testing each of the following:

a) the library subprogram available with the facility you are using,
b) the method you have developed in the preceding question,
c) a method that uses integer arithmetic with 3432 as the multiplier and 9973 as the modulus.

What conclusions can you draw from the results?

3. Write a program to simulate the rolling of two dice 1000 times and output the number of 7's and the number of 11's. Are the results reasonably close to what you expected?

4. Suppose the random values from the uniform distribution on $(0, 1)$ can be generated. Show that the sum of two such values has the following triangular distribution

$$f(x) = \begin{cases} x & \text{, if } 0 \le x \le 1 \\ 2 - x, & \text{if } 1 < x \le 2 \end{cases}$$

on the interval $(0, 2)$. What is the distribution of the sum of three values from the uniform distribution on $(0,1)$? What is the distribution of the average of three such values? The average of 12 such values, minus 6, i.e.,

$$x = \frac{x_1 + x_2 + \cdots + x_{12}}{12} - 6$$

where x_i are uniformly distributed on $(0,1)$, is sometimes taken to be an approximation to the normal distribution with mean 0 and standard deviation 1. Write a program to generate approximations of this kind and compare the results with what you expect from a normal distribution. Under what circumstances do you feel you could rely on such an approximation?

5. a) Develop a program that will generate 500 random points in the square bounded by the coordinate axes and the lines $x = 1$ and $y = 1$. Have the program count how many of these points lie in the quarter circle cut off from the first quadrant by $x^2 + y^2 = 1$.

   b) Of the total number of points in (a), the fraction that lie in the quarter circle is an approximation to the area of that quarter circle and therefore an approximation to $\pi/4$. This way of finding approximations to areas is an example of a Monte Carlo method. Try it with different sets of random numbers and comment on its efficiency as compared to that of other methods of approximating areas. (Note that a random process has been introduced to solve a problem that does not, by itself, have any random properties. This is typical of Monte Carlo methods.)

6. One of the major problems in using simulations is to determine how reliable the results are. However, statistical theory can usually help. In Question 5, for example, we can consider the approximation to $\pi/4$ obtained from one set of random numbers to be a single observation, which we denote by x_1. Other observations, $x_2, x_3, \ldots, x_n$, can be obtained from other sets of random numbers. With the formulas of Section 10.2 we can then calculate the mean and standard deviation of these observations. According to statistical theory, the mean is likely to differ from $\pi/4$ by less than $(2/\sqrt{n})$ times the standard deviation. In fact, the probability that the mean differs from $\pi/4$ by more than this amount can be shown to be only .05. Compute the mean and the standard deviation for 100 different sequences of random points and state whether or not this assertion appears to be reasonable.

7. Modify the program in Question 5 so that only points in the square that are above the line $x + y = 1$ are considered. The approximation to $\pi/4$ is taken to be the area below this line plus the fraction of points above the line that lie inside the quarter circle. In other words, the approximation is taken to be $1/2$ plus the fraction. Can you suggest why this method should be more efficient than the one proposed in Question 5? What further improvements of this kind can you suggest?

8. A stick is broken in two places. Use a computer simulation to determine approximately the probability that the three pieces can form the sides of a triangle. Compute the mean and the standard deviation as indicated in Question 6. Give an interval within which the true value will lie, with probability .95, provided the theory mentioned in Question 6 can be applied.

9. Write a program that will simulate the rolling of three dice and use it to determine approximations to the following two probabilities:

   a) the probability that at least one of the three dice shows a five;
   b) the probability that whenever the three dice show numbers that are all different, at least one of those numbers is a five.

The latter is an example of a *conditional* probability.

10. Mr. B and Mr. C are about to fight a duel in which each takes turns shooting at the other. B hits whatever he shoots at, on the average, once in every two tries. C hits once in every three tries, on the average. Being a gentleman, B naturally allows C to shoot first. Write a program that will simulate the fighting of this duel and try to determine who has the better chance of surviving.

11. Five dice are rolled. Any die that shows a 6 is set aside and the others are rerolled. Any new 6's obtained on the second roll are also set aside and the remaining non-6's are rerolled again. This process is continued until all the dice are showing 6's. Approximately how many rolls are needed on the average?

12. Twelve people are in a room. Use a computer simulation to determine approximately the probability that at least three of them have birthdays in the same month. (Assume that each month of the year is equally likely for any particular birthday.)

13. In one well-known dice game called craps, the player wins on the first roll (of two dice) if he rolls a 7 or 11, but he loses if he rolls a 2, 3, or 12. If he rolls some other number on his first roll, such as a 6, this number is called his point. He then rerolls the dice until he makes his point again, in which case he wins, or until he rolls a 7, in which case he loses. Use a computer simulation to determine approximately the chances of winning at craps if you are the person rolling the dice.

14. Choose one of the many board games, such as Snakes and Ladders, in which the player's progress is determined by rolling a die or two. Write a program to simulate playing the game and use it to determine approximately the average length of a game. What is the main difference between a game like Snakes and Ladders and a game like Monopoly that makes it much more difficult to simulate playing one of the latter kind?

15. In 1773 a French naturalist named Buffon proposed an experiment for finding an approximation to π. He threw a needle of length L onto a large flat piece of paper ruled with parallel lines that were $2L$ units apart. He was able to show that the probability of the needle landing across one of the lines is $1/\pi$. Develop a program that will simulate this experiment and that, by counting the number of crossings in a large number of trials, will produce an approximation to π.

16. Suppose that three points are chosen at random on the circumference of a circle of radius 1 and the three points are joined to form a triangle. Approximately what do you expect the average area of the triangle to be? What area would you expect if the three points are chosen anywhere inside the circle rather than on its circumference?

17. Write a program that will use a random number generator to simulate experiments for determining values of χ^2. Use the program to find approximations to some of the entries in the table given in Fig. 10.8.

11.3 QUEUES

One important application of computers is in the study of queues. The queues can be formed by cars arriving at an intersection, by ships lining up to pass through locks in a canal, by airplanes waiting to land at an airport, by people waiting for service at a counter, and in many other ways as well. One reason for studying queues is to determine better ways of handling them, for example in traffic control. The traffic can be simulated under different conditions, such as different rules for controlling the lights. The computer can keep track of how well the traffic is moving under the different rules in order to determine which method of traffic control is best. Sometimes plans are made to build something that will have to accommodate queues. A new airport is an example. In this case provision would have to be made for queues of people at the check-in counters or taxis at the arrivals ramp, as well as queues of aircraft waiting to land. A careful simulation of different possibilities would be of help in designing an efficient airport.

As our first illustration, we will consider the simulation of a simplified traffic situation. We assume that cars are arriving at an intersection at the rate of one every four seconds on the average, and that the light is green for the first 25 seconds of each minute, then amber and red for the remaining 35 seconds. We also assume that one second must elapse after a car has entered the intersection before another is allowed to do so. The problem is to observe this situation for 10,000 seconds and output the largest queue length that occurs during that period. One approach to a simulation for this problem is described by the program outline given in Fig. 11.6.

It should be pointed out that several minor assumptions and further simplifications have been made in setting up the model described in Fig. 11.6. The length of the queue was set initially at zero and the simulation is started at the beginning of the green phase. However, neither of these assumptions is expected to have any

```
Set length of queue and maximum length of queue to zero, and
    provide whatever initialization is required by the random
    number generator
Loop for time = 1,2,3, . . . , 10000 seconds
    Obtain a random number R in (0,1)
    If (R ≤ .25) add one to length of queue
    If (length of queue > 0 and time = 1,2, . . . , 25 of the cur-
        rent minute) subtract 1 from length of queue
    If (length of queue > maximum observed thus far) record
        new maximum length of queue
End loop
Output maximum length of queue
Stop
```

FIG. 11.6 Simulation of a traffic queue.

significant effect on the final result, provided the period of the simulation is fairly long. Time has been divided into one-second intervals, and it has been assumed that a car arrives at each point in time with probability 1/4. This is not quite the same as one arriving every four seconds on the average, but it is probably a reasonably good approximation, especially since a second or so would have to be allowed between arrivals in any case. We should not worry unduly about the details of our assumptions. The only way to determine exactly what to assume is to observe what happens in actual practice. For example, we could record the arrivals at a particular intersection and then use this information to perform a simulation of different rules for changing the lights in order to determine which rule is best for this pattern of arrivals.

Another assumption has been made about exactly when a car is expected to go through an intersection. We have assumed that a car at the intersection will go through if the time is 1,2, . . . , or 25 seconds after the beginning of the current minute. This means we are assuming that cars can begin to move 1 second after the light turns green and will also move even if the light has just turned amber, but will stop at any time after the light has turned amber. Perhaps it would be more realistic to assume cars will go through even when the time is 26 or 27 seconds after the beginning of the current minute! Once again we would have to observe what happens in actual traffic situations before we could decide on a realistic model.

Many further developments of the model should suggest themselves. More than one lane of traffic could be introduced, left turns could be allowed, and so on, but it is obvious that the situation can rapidly become extremely complicated. Another useful change would be to have the computer collect more statistics. Instead of merely noting the maximum queue length, the computer could be programmed to calculate the average queue length, or the average waiting time. The program could also be modified to try out different rules for changing the lights. For example, what would be the effect on queue lengths and waiting times if the green-amber-red phases were 35-5-40 seconds, instead of 25-5-30?

Another point should be mentioned. In this example, time was divided into one-second intervals. These intervals are probably small enough to provide a sufficiently accurate model in most traffic situations. However, the choice of time interval can be a difficult decision to make. Too large an interval makes the model unreliable. On the other hand, too small an interval causes the computation to be too expensive.

We have considered a particular example of a queue in considerable detail. One purpose in doing so has been to emphasize the extent to which even a rather simple model can depend on a large number of assumptions, most of which are probably not very critical, but which are nevertheless a part of the model, and may affect the outcome of the simulation. It would be important in practice to be aware of the assumptions on which a model is based. It would be particularly important to know as much as possible about how valid those assumptions might be, and also how sensitive the results of the simulation might be to changes in those assumptions.

Another purpose in considering so many details with this one example, and especially in pointing out that we might like to make changes in some of the assumptions, is to suggest one important way in which the program of Fig. 11.6 can be improved. The suggestion is that as many as possible of the properties of the model (length of simulation, rate of arrival, rules for changing lights, etc.) be determined by parameters. Such parameters can be initialized, for example as input near the beginning of the program, and therefore easily changed if we want to run the program under different assumptions about these parameters. It is then not necessary to search through the program to find all places that might be affected by a change in the model.

This last idea leads us to replacing Fig. 11.6 by Fig. 11.7. Of course the outline in Fig. 11.7 can now easily be extended to include the collection of other statistics, such as the average waiting time.

The problem considered so far has been simple enough that we have not had to follow individual cars after they arrived at the intersection. We have had only to keep track of the number in the queue. In many other situations it is necessary to follow the individual items in a queue as separate entities. This occurs, for example, if it is not known until an item reaches the head of a queue just how long is needed to provide the required service. (In the case of cars at an intersection, the time to get through the intersection may depend on how many other cars have already been able to get through

```
Input length of time of simulation, rate of arrival, cycle times
   for lights, and any other parameters needed for the model
Set length of queue and maximum length of queue to zero
Initialize random number generator
Loop for length of time of simulation
   Obtain a random number R in (0,1)
   If (R ≤ appropriate parameter) add one to length of queue
   If (length of queue > 0, and light is green or just started
      the amber phase) subtract 1 from length of queue
   If (length of queue > maximum observed thus far) record
      new maximum length of queue
End loop
Output maximum length of queue
Stop
```

FIG. 11.7 The same simulation of a traffic queue as in Fig. 11.6, except that the parameters are now more easily adjusted between runs.

since the beginning of the current green phase, as well as on other factors.)

This leads to situations in which a data structure representing a queue has to be managed. The data structure (perhaps a linked list) has to be established during the initialization of the program. Provision is made so that each item in the queue contains the necessary information about itself, such as its arrival time in the case of cars coming up to an intersection. Then, during the iterative part of the program, items are added to and removed from the queue as required, and the necessary statistics are accumulated. (See Question 2 in Exercise 11.3.)

The simulation models we have been discussing so far have been examples of *time-driven* models, since the processes have been governed by what happens in a succession of equal time intervals. An alternative approach, which is often referred to as *event-driven,* follows processes from event to event.

As can be seen in Fig. 11.8, the initialization stage for an event-driven simulation requires the initialization

```
Input parameters that determine the model
Initialize the random number generator
Initialize any queues that are required
Initialize the event list, such as the first arrival, and the end
   of the simulation
Initialize the statistics
Loop
   Determine next event to take place
   Take appropriate action, including update of time, queues,
      and statistics, as well as scheduling next future
      events
.... If (end of simulation) exit loop
End loop
Output results
Stop
```

FIG. 11.8 Outline of a program for an event-driven simulation model.

of a list of events, including an event corresponding to the end of the simulation, as well as such events as the first arrival of a car in the traffic queue example of this section. Then, during the iterative stage, the program determines which event is to take place next and takes whatever action is appropriate, including all the necessary updating and scheduling of future events, including the next arrival or departure of a car, for example. The process must eventually terminate since one of the items on the event list provides for termination of the simulation. (See Question 3 in Exercise 11.3.)

An event-driven model can be more efficient than a time-driven model, especially when there may be long time periods between events. The circumstances of a particular problem will determine which approach is the more efficient. Event-driven models also have a potential advantage in that they are not restricted to dealing with events that must occur at particular multiples of a fixed time interval.

EXERCISE 11.3

1. Write a program along the lines suggested by Fig. 11.7 that will find and output the average waiting time as well as the maximum length of queue. Use it with several different arrival rates and show how the waiting times and queue lengths build up as the rate of arrival increases.

2. Redesign the program in Question 1 so that a queue is maintained, and rerun some of the calculations to help confirm the equivalence of this approach. Suggest a change in the rules for getting through an intersection that might force you to adopt this kind of approach to the traffic simulation problem.

3. Redesign the program in Question 1 along the lines suggested by the outline in Fig. 11.8, and rerun some of the calculations again. (One way to determine the next arrival time is to develop a small time-driven subprogram for doing this one task. Otherwise, if you are familiar with the appropriate statistical theory, there are special generators available for such nonuniform random number distributions.) What circumstances might lead you to prefer an event-driven simulation in this case, rather than a time-driven one?

4. Use one of the programs in Questions 1–3, to find the average waiting time (for some particular arrival rate) for several different cycle times, and try to find the cycle time that minimizes the average waiting time. The cycle time is the time for one complete change of the traffic lights; you should assume that the light is red for one half of the cycle and green for the other half, except that five seconds of the other half is needed for the amber phase.

5. a) Suppose that customers are being serviced by a single clerk behind a counter and that three minutes are required to service each customer. Write a program that will simulate the queue and output the average waiting time per customer for several different rates of arrival.

   b) Describe how you would modify the program in part (a) so that it will handle a service time that changes in a random way. Suppose that the service time is two, three, or four minutes, each of these times being equally likely.

6. Develop a program for handling a queue of customers that is waiting to be served at a number of service locations. Only one queue is formed and the customer at the head of the queue goes to the first available service location. The time needed to serve a particular customer is not known until the service location he uses is determined. Describe examples of applications where such a model could be helpful. Determine some results which indicate the effect of changing the number of service locations.

7. A supply of kludges is kept in a warehouse. Orders are filled each day as they come in, if supplies are available. Whenever the supply dips below fifty, a new shipment of 100 is ordered, but it takes one week for the shipment to arrive. The number of orders varies from day to day, but past experience has shown that the number of days in each sixty days on which one can expect orders to total a certain number are as shown in the following table:

Total number of kludges ordered in a single day											
1	2	3	4	5	6	7	8	9	10	11	12
2	5	9	11	11	8	6	3	2	1	1	1
Number of days on which such orders are expected											

Write a program that simulates the situation in the warehouse, and determine whether or not it is likely that any orders will be delayed.

8. The owner of the warehouse described in Question 7 is expecting business to approximately double by this time next year. He is considering building an addition to his warehouse so that he can keep a larger supply on hand, and he is also considering ordering smaller shipments more frequently, but both these steps will cost more money. On the other hand, he must pay a penalty to any customer whose order is delayed. State exactly what cost figures you would like the manager to provide, and explain how you would modify your program so that you could determine the most economical step for him to take.

9. The Instant Bungle Manufacturing Company wants to diversify and has decided to offer a computing service. A market survey has been made and it is expected that the following jobs will have to be processed, on the average, in each 8-hour day:

Execution time							
5 sec	10 sec	30 sec	1 min	2 min	5 min	10 min	30 min
600	180	100	20	25	15	10	2
Number of jobs							

Suppose that the jobs arrive at random times during the day. Write a program that will simulate the process of handling these jobs. Use it to determine the average waiting time for each customer whose work is completed during the 8-hour period, the total amount of work, and the number of jobs left unfinished at the end of the period. Obtain results for each of the following scheduling algorithms:

a) jobs are run on a first-come, first-served basis;

b) shortest jobs are run first but, once started, a job is always run to completion before the next job is started.

10. The company in Question 9 would like to reduce the average waiting time and is willing to change its operating system so that longer jobs are interrupted in order to begin execution of shorter ones. Describe a scheduling algorithm based on this idea. Then simulate the process in order to determine how much you are able to reduce the average waiting time. What other factors would have to be taken into account in real-life situations of this kind?

11.4 RANDOM DRAWS

In the problems considered thus far, the probabilities for individual events have been independent of each other. For example, the probability of rolling a 5 on one particular roll of a die does not depend on what happened on the previous roll. Moreover, in the traffic model we considered, the probability of a car arriving in one particular interval does not depend on whether or not a car arrived in the previous interval. In some situations the probabilities are more complicated. The probabilities in dice games would not change, but we can expect the probabilities in traffic models to depend to some extent on what happens in the preceding short period of time and also on other factors, such as the time of day and the weather.

In practice we will have to depend on observations of existing situations to help determine the required probabilities. However, there is one fairly important situation that can be handled without having to make any observations. It occurs, for example, in card games where the probabilities at one particular stage in the game depend very much on what cards have already been dealt or played. For example, in dealing a card it would obviously be unreasonable to assume a probability of 1/52 that the 3 of spades will appear, unless we are just beginning the deal. Cards are drawn from a deck without replacement and the probabilities are different for each draw.

One good way to handle this situation is first to simulate the shuffling of the deck. Once this is done, the cards can be dealt, beginning with the first card, then the second, and so on. By doing this, the probability that a particular card, such as the three of spades, will appear will change in an appropriate manner as the cards are dealt.

A straightforward method for simulating the shuffle is provided by the following. We begin with a list of the 52 cards in any order, and we generate 52 random numbers. We then sort the 52 random numbers, making the same interchanges of the cards that we make of the random numbers during the sorting of the random numbers. For example, if we interchange the third number and tenth number in the course of sorting the 52 random numbers, we also interchange the third card and the tenth card in the list of 52 cards. When the 52 numbers have been sorted, the 52 cards will be in random order compared to the order in which they started. Once the cards have been shuffled, the deal can begin with the first card, then the second, and so on.

A decision must be made as to how to represent the values of the cards for the purposes of a computer program. One way is to use a subscripted variable having one subscript and 52 components. The components representing Ace, 2, 3, . . . , J, Q, K of spades could have the values $1, 2, 3, \ldots, 11, 12, 13$, the components representing Ace, 2, 3, . . . of hearts could have the values $14, 15, 16, \ldots$, and so on. This is the simplest way of representing the cards as far as the shuffling is concerned. However, a certain amount of computing is required to obtain the usual information about the cards. For example, if the component in the list is $L(I)$ the suit can be determined by calculating the quotient $(L(I) - 1)/13$, without the remainder. If the quotient is 0 the suit is spades, if 1, hearts, and so on. The face value can be determined by $L(I) - 13 \times S$, where S is the suit or quotient. For example, if the value of this expression is 12, the card is a Queen.

EXERCISE 11.4

1. Write a portion of a program that will simulate the shuffling of a deck of cards.

2. Another way of simulating random draws from a deck of cards without replacement is to generate a sequence of integers in the interval $[1, 52]$ and use each in turn to represent the next card, provided it has not already been dealt. This necessitates checking each new number to see if it has already appeared. If it has appeared, that number must be discarded and another number tried. When would this procedure be efficient and when would it be much too inefficient?

3. One relatively simple game of solitaire begins with a deal of nine cards, face up. If any two of these cards have the same face value, they are covered with two new cards, also face up. The last step is repeated until the deck has been exhausted, except for one card, in which case the dealer has won the game, or until there are no more pairs showing, in which case the dealer has lost. Write a program to simulate this game and use it to determine an approximation to the probability of winning. How reliable do you believe the approximation to be?

4. George had five girl·friends and one evening he wrote a letter to each of them. He also addressed five envelopes. George's young sister is always trying to do nice things for George, so she put the letters in the envelopes and mailed them. If she chose the envelope for each letter at random, what are the chances that not one of the letters was put into the correct envelope? Do you think the chances would tend to increase or decrease if George were to have more girl friends?

5. In some games numbered or colored objects are drawn from a container in which the original collection of these objects is first shaken very thoroughly. Suppose there are five white and ten black balls in a bag and three of these balls are to be drawn without replacement. Write a program to simulate these draws on a computer and use it to determine approximately the probability of drawing exactly one white ball and two black balls.

6. In a game of Bingo, 75 tokens numbered 1 to 75 inclusive are placed in a container that can usually be rotated or shaken in order to mix up the tokens. The caller in the game removes one token at a time and calls out its number. If the number is between 1 and 15 inclusive he will usually say "Under the B" and then state the number. Similarly, the numbers between 16 and 30 are under the I, between 31 and 45 under the N, between 46 and 60 under the G, and between 61 and 75 under the O. (See Fig. 11.9.) Write a program to simulate the calls in a game of Bingo. Arrange to have the program stop after the first twenty-five calls.

7. Write a "player" program to play an individual game of Bingo. Modify the program in Question 6 to provide the calls and arrange to have the "player" program stop when it detects a winning situation.

8. A program is to be written to simulate the playing of Blackjack between a dealer and one player. Assume that the deck is shuffled before each game. Two cards are dealt to the player and two to the dealer. The player can see one of the dealer's cards. The player then asks for additional cards, one at a time, until he decides to stand or he goes bust. Face cards count 10, but Aces can be counted 1 or 11. If the player goes bust, that is, if he gets a total of more than 21, he loses. Otherwise he compares his total with that obtained later by the dealer.

The dealer does not play at all if the player has gone bust. If the dealer plays, he must draw another card if his total is 16 or less. (We will assume that he must count an Ace as 11.) He must stand on 17 or more. If he goes bust, he loses to the player. Otherwise he loses, wins, or ties, if his score is, respectively, less than, greater than, or equal to the player's.

One purpose in writing the program is to try different strategies for the player. If the player uses the same strategy as that used by the dealer, approximately how often will he win compared to the dealer? Why does the dealer have such a big advantage?

Another strategy that should be tried is the following:
with soft hands (counting an Ace as 11)
  if dealer shows 9 or 10, stand on 19 or more
  otherwise stand on 18 or more
with hard hands (no Aces or Aces counted as 1)
  if dealer shows 2 or 3, stand on 13 or more
  if dealer shows 4 to 6, stand on 12 or more
  if dealer shows 7 to Ace, stand on 17 or more

An Ace should be counted as 11, if that is possible without going bust. This strategy is a simplified version of the basic strategy proposed by E. O. Thorp in his very interesting book entitled *Beat the Dealer* (Vintage Books, 1966), pages 20 and 21.

9. Ten poker hands of five cards each can be dealt from a deck of 52 cards. Write a program to simulate this process a few hundred times and then find and output the number of poker hands that appeared with four-of-a-kind, a full house (three of one kind and two of another), three-of-a-kind, two pairs, and a single pair.

10. Show how the program in Question 9 can be modified so that it will also count the number of straights (five cards in sequence, as in 7, 8, 9, 10, Jack) and the number of flushes (all five cards of the same suit).

11. Discuss some of the problems that will arise in programming a computer to simulate playing several hands of poker.

12. The game described in Question 3 is relatively simple because the outcome depends entirely on the shuffle, and there are no important decisions to be made by the player. Most games of solitaire require the player to make decisions that affect the final outcome. Consider a game of

BINGO

7	23	42	52	72
9	29	39	46	65
14	17	FREE PLAY	50	69
2	20	32	59	61
10	19	33	57	68

FIG. 11.9 Example of a Bingo card. A marker is placed in the "free play" square. Other markers are placed in the numbered squares if the numbers are called. Five markers in a row is a winning situation. (The rows can be horizontal, vertical, or diagonal.)

this kind and show how a computer can be programmed to play it as long as the computer is not required to play a good game. Discuss the main difficulties involved in trying to program the computer to play well.

13. A section of city street is 150 meters long and it is marked off into parking places of 6 meters each, so that a total of 25 cars can be parked. If the section were not marked off and cars were allowed to park at random, approximately how many could be parked, on the average? (Assume that 6 meters are required to park a car.)

11.5 RANDOM WALKS

Some interesting problems involving randomness can be described in terms of random walks. As an example, suppose a man starts at position 0 on a line as shown in Fig. 11.10. He takes a step of length one, to the right or the left with equal probability. Imagine that he tosses a coin to decide which way to go: heads to the right, tails to the left. After taking his first step, the man takes a second step of the same length, again to the right or the left with equal probability. Then a third step is taken, and so on, until one of the absorbing barriers is reached. At this point the walk is over.

The random walk can be interpreted in a number of ways. The tossing of the coin can be a game and a step of length one to the right can represent winning the toss and being paid $1, whereas a step to the left can represent the loss of $1. At any stage the position of the man would represent his total winnings up to that point, a negative position representing a net loss. The absorbing barriers represent the total initial capital of each player. The barrier at -5 indicates that the man had $5 at the start of the game. If he ever reaches this barrier he has lost all his initial capital and the game is over. Similarly, the barrier at $+10$ indicates that his opponent began with $10 and the game is over if the man wins all $10 from his opponent.

There are many questions to be asked about random walk problems, or about the "gambler's ruin" as it is sometimes called when the alternative interpretation

is being considered. We can ask about the probability of winning, or about the average number of steps that will be taken before termination, and so on. Some of these questions can be answered theoretically, although the theory can be quite complicated. A number of questions, especially with more complicated processes than the one we have considered in this section, can only be answered by means of simulations.

One of the most important applications of random walks is to the study of diffusion, particularly the diffusion of neutrons through shielding materials. In these applications, each neutron is considered to make a random walk, beginning at one side of the shield with a certain velocity. With each step it may continue in the same direction, or it may be deflected into a different direction. At the same time its speed may be reduced by a certain amount. The probabilities of each of the possible events must be known. The kind of problem that is of interest is that of simulating the paths of a large number of neutrons after they move into a shield of a certain thickness, and then determining how many of them are able to penetrate to the other side of the shield.

EXERCISE 11.5

1. Write a program to simulate the random walk indicated in Fig. 11.10. Use it to determine approximations to the probabilities of reaching each of the two barriers.

2. Modify the program in Question 1 so that it will produce an approximation to the average number of steps that will be taken before termination.

3. Suppose that the barriers are removed in Fig. 11.10 so that the walk is not restricted in any way. For each of several values of N, find an approximation to the average distance from the starting point reached after N steps. Find also an approximation to the average number of times the man returns to the origin in N steps.

4. A gambling system sometimes suggested is that of doubling one's bet after each loss. The idea is to start with a small bet, say $1. If we lose, we bet $2 on the next game. If we lose again, we bet $4, then $8, and so on, until we win a game. We will be ahead $1 after our first win. Then we start again with a bet of $1. The system works well, except that we may run out of money! Suppose we try this system in a sequence of games in which the probability of winning each game is 1/2. Suppose also that we have $100 at the start, whereas our opponent has $200, and that we will bet all we have left if we ever reach a point where we do not have enough money to double our previous bet. Write a program to simulate this sequence of games and find an approximation to the probability that we will run out of money before our opponent does.

5. Suppose we begin an experiment with two urns, one containing a hundred Ping-pong balls, the other being empty. Each step in the experiment consists of choosing

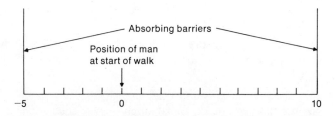

FIG. 11.10 For a random walk, the man takes one step after another, the probability of stepping left or right being equal in each case, until he reaches one of the absorbing barriers.

one of the urns, with a probability proportional to the number of balls in the urn, and transferring a Ping-pong ball from that urn to the other. Simulate this process and determine an approximation to the average number of steps needed to reach the situation, for the first time, where the urns contain an equal number of balls.

6. Suppose that a man sets out at the starting point and walks in a random fashion over the plane. Each step he takes is of length 1, but he takes it in one of the four directions, north, south, east, and west, with equal probability. Find an approximation to his average distance from the origin after N steps.

7. Suppose that a slab of material is to be used as a shield to protect people who are on one side of the shield from the harmful effects of radiation on the other side. The problem is to simulate a particular model of how nuclear particles can move into the shield, and possibly get through it, and hence determine what fraction of the radiation is able to penetrate the shield. Assume that the particles arrive at the side of the shield with a speed of 10 units and move in a direction at right angles to the side. Suppose that each particle follows a kind of random walk, according to the following rule. Time is divided into small intervals, the first interval beginning just as the particle reaches the side. At the beginning of each interval the particle continues one unit of length in its present direction, with probability 3/4, or it moves one unit of length in the opposite direction, with probability 1/4. At the same time, its speed is reduced by one unit, with probability 1/20. If a particle leaves the shield in the direction from which it came, it does not return. If the particle's speed is reduced to zero, it is assumed to be absorbed by the shield. Simulate this process for different widths of shielding and determine approximately what fraction of the particles is able to penetrate the shield for each width. What is the smallest width that will, on the average, allow no more than 1 percent of the radiation to get through?

8. A game consists of tossing a coin twenty times, an equal amount of money being won or lost on each toss. In approximately what fraction of games will one player be ahead after every toss?

9. Suppose that two candidates are hoping to be elected to a certain political office. Suppose also that, of the 1000 voters, exactly 500 are planning to vote for each candidate. Write a program to simulate the returns coming in, assuming that the votes are reported in a random order and one at a time. This means that there will be 1000 reports. At the end of each report one of the candidates will be in the lead or the candidates will be tied. What is the probability that the same candidate will be in the lead after at least 90 percent of the reports?

11.6 FURTHER REMARKS

One of the most important uses of a computer is in the simulation of various processes. There are two basically different situations, one in which the process is deterministic and another in which the process has some random components. The latter kind is often called a *stochastic process*.

The term *simulation* is more likely to be used in connection with stochastic processes. Sometimes the problem to be solved does not have an inherent randomness, whereas the simulation model does have randomness. The classic example is the use of Buffon's needle to find approximations to π. Another example is the approximation of an area by Monte Carlo methods. However, the process being simulated usually has random elements of its own. We have already mentioned examples that involve the formation of queues, the changes in an inventory, the outcome in a game of chance, the motion of nuclear particles, and so on.

Many of the stochastic processes considered in this chapter are quite simple ones and it is possible to answer questions about them with the help of probability theory alone, without going to the trouble of simulating them. It should be pointed out, however, that relatively small changes in a model will often produce a new model that cannot be handled theoretically. On the other hand, small changes in a model are easy to include in the simulation. The main advantage of simulation methods is that they can be used even when the models are too complicated to be handled theoretically, as is the case with realistic problems in areas like traffic control, nuclear physics, and so on.

We have considered relatively simple processes in most cases. The main reason for doing so was that we wanted to illustrate the basic ideas. Whenever the theoretical result is known, we are also able to check the results obtained from the simulation. There is another way of viewing this situation that should be mentioned. A comparison of simulation results with theoretical results can be used as a test of the random number generator. Chi-square tests based on this kind of comparison should be the best possible kinds of test, provided the model used in the test is similar to the model for which the numbers are being tested.

Very large simulation models are now being used by governments and other organizations to help predict future developments in many areas. For example, economic models are receiving a lot of attention. Such models are usually not particularly reliable. Not enough is known about the social and economic relationships they are intended to represent, nor is the basic data required by the models known accurately enough. However, the models will be improved gradually and they will be used increasingly as a basis for planning. There is no doubt that the use of models for social and economic planning will affect the lives of all of us to an increasing extent in the future. The computer has made it possible for us to handle such models but the computer does not construct them. It is extremely important that we realize the assumptions on which such models are based and that we recognize their limitations. We must be very careful about the use of models in such situations, especially when we know so little about the processes being simulated.

There is one serious difficulty in the simulation of stochastic processes. The results obtained are only approximations to what is desired. The approximations can be improved by increasing the number of trials in the simulation. However, it can be shown that the error in the results decreases only at a rate proportional to $1/\sqrt{n}$, where n is the number of trials in the simulation. To appreciate what this means, let us suppose that we wish to obtain one more decimal digit of accuracy in the final result. We therefore want to reduce the error by a factor of ten. To do so, we have to increase n by a factor of 100. To obtain one more decimal digit we must use 100 times as much computer time as has already been used. Two more digits would require 10,000 times as much computer time. It is often possible to modify a simulation model so that it produces approximations to the same desired value but with smaller errors. The error will still be proportional to $1/\sqrt{n}$, but the constant of proportionality will be smaller. (This idea was illustrated in Question 7, Exercise 11.2.)

One area of simulation deserves special mention. Many people are interested in the extent to which machines can be programmed to simulate intelligent behavior. Playing games like checkers and chess is one relatively popular example. Translating languages, composing music, and proving theorems are others. The subject is often referred to as Artificial Intelligence. It is to this area that one is led by questions such as "Can a machine think?" A more meaningful way of formulating this question is to ask "Can we program a machine so that it can imitate intelligent behavior?"

We should bring up the question of correctness, at least briefly. When we say that a simulation program is correct, we usually mean that it carries out the steps in a particular process that we have in mind. This amounts to saying that the program is correct if it, as an algorithm, is identical to another algorithm that we presumably have described in some other language, such as English. (This is in contrast to saying that the program is correct if it evaluates a particular function that we have in mind.) Of course, the process which the program is supposed to follow correctly may itself be in error for a number of reasons: we may have unintentionally forgotten to consider all possibilities, or we may not have had sufficiently accurate data for determining the necessary parameters, and so on. The correctness of a stochastic simulation raises additional questions that are peculiar to this type of simulation. Altogether, we have good reason to temper whatever enthusiasm we might have for simulations with at least some measure of caution.

In conclusion, it should be mentioned that special programming languages have been developed for use in simulations. They are designed to make activities such as managing queues relatively easy to program. After trying to keep track of such activities in a general-purpose programming language, it is easy to see why special languages have been invented.

CHAPTER **12**

Data Processing

Most of the material in Chapters 8 to 11 on numerical calculations, statistics, and simulations can be considered under the general heading of scientific calculations. Data processing is often used as another general heading that includes different kinds of activities such as payroll calculations, billing, and record keeping of various kinds.

The distinction between scientific calculations and data processing is not sharply defined. It is sometimes said that scientific calculations involve small amounts of input and output together with relatively large amounts of numerical calculation, whereas data processing requires large amounts of input and output with only trivial amounts of arithmetic. This distinction is only partly valid. Large-scale scientific calculations can involve input and output of very large quantities of data, as is required in the control of space vehicles for example. Moreover, many problems that arise in data processing can involve quite complicated numerical calculations, as in inventory control or production scheduling, to mention only two examples.

However, one important characteristic of payroll, billing, record keeping, and similar activities is that they do usually involve relatively large files of information, certainly much more so than does the average scientific calculation. For a payroll calculation, the personnel file would contain each employee's name and number along with his rate of pay, number of dependents, birth date, marital status, and so on; a payroll calculation may re-

quire other files as well, such as a file of information about tax rates. Insurance companies need files that contain information on the policies they have in force. Police departments use files containing information on motor vehicle registrations.

Most of this chapter will therefore be concerned with files. We first consider problems that arise in trying to keep a file up-to-date, that is, in maintaining a file. Various methods of sorting files are then discussed, after which we consider a number of special ways in which files are used: to retrieve information, to produce a payroll, to control an inventory, and so on. A section on decision tables is also included, since they provide a convenient way of organizing some data-processing calculations.

The term *data base* is often used to refer to the collection of data that is being handled. The data might of course be organized into files, but the term "data base" is more general and can include collections of data that are organized in more complicated ways, particularly if one body of data is to be used for a variety of purposes.

Data processing is an area of computer applications that is extremely important to all of us. The potential benefits are likely to be very extensive in fields such as medicine, law, and economics, as well as in the more obvious applications to payrolls and accounting. While the potential benefits to society are very great, so are the possible shortcomings and dangers. Serious difficulties can arise if large files, or data bases, are not properly used or controlled. In order to derive the benefits of computers in data-processing applications, while at the same time avoiding the dangers, it is important to acquire a sound understanding of the basic ideas and techniques that arise in this area.

Many of the difficulties in handling files arise only because the files are large, whereas the files considered in this chapter are necessarily quite small. When studying these examples we must keep in mind that the main purpose of our discussion is to understand what is involved in the use of large files. Small files or portions of large files can be stored in the main memory of a computer, but large files are usually stored on disk units or on magnetic tape. We will use only relatively small files and they will usually be kept in the main memory. We will nevertheless be able to illustrate many of the important features of larger files. Moreover, portions of large files must be transferred to main memory for processing and most of our results can be used on the portions that have been transferred.

The advantage of keeping a file in main memory is that we can have very rapid access to any part of such a file. The access time depends on the machine, but is typically a millionth of a second or so if the exact location of the required information is known. It can take a good deal longer to find the required information if it is necessary to search the file for what is required. Essentially the same remarks apply to files stored on disks, except that the access times are likely to be at least 100 times as long. An additional characteristic of files stored on tape is that a long time may be needed to reach the required information, even if its exact location is known. This will be a serious disadvantage unless the file happens to be one we wish to process only in a sequential manner.

12.1 FILE MAINTENANCE

One basic problem in data processing is to *maintain* a file. This means that we must be able to modify records in a file, add new records and delete others, in order to keep the file up-to-date. For example, suppose the file is the personnel file of a large company. The identification item, or *key,* could be the employee number, while other items could include the employee name, rate of pay, and number of dependents. A raise in pay for one of the employees would require a change in his record. As employees are hired, records would have to be added and, as employees leave or retire, records would have to be deleted.

Other interpretations of a file can be imagined quite easily. Each record could contain information about a telephone, such as its number and the name and address of the subscriber. Alternatively, each record could refer to a particular book in a library, to an automobile registration, to a plot of land, and so on. Of course, we expect that files will often be more complicated than the ones we have just mentioned.

Some preliminary ideas about file maintenance have already been introduced in Chapter 1. For example, two different ways of representing files were described in Section 1.4, one based on arrays and the other on linked lists. In the present section and its accompanying exercise, we will consider three basically different approaches to the problem of maintaining a file. One approach is directed toward the maintenance of a *sequential* file stored on some external medium such as magnetic tape, while the second follows up the material introduced in Section 1.4 on handling *random-access* files that are stored as linked lists. The third is an alternative approach to certain kinds of random-access files, and is based on a technique called *hashing.* (See Question 12 in Exercise 12.1.) How best to represent a particular file of information, and how to carry out the operations needed to maintain the file, will depend very much on the circumstances of the particular application itself.

As an illustration, suppose that the file we are interested in must be kept sorted in some particular order. If this file is represented by an array, it will usually be quite a time-consuming task to insert any new records, especially if the file is of a substantial size. In this case, we would probably prefer to have the file represented by a linked list, even though more storage would be required for such a representation. On the other hand, if the file is normally kept on some external medium, such as magnetic tape, it must be read into the computer for updating, and it is relatively easy to insert a record (or to make other changes) as the information is being prepared for output to the new "updated" file. This would be particularly efficient if the changes themselves were sorted beforehand, so that the updating process was one of merging the changes with the file. This is shown schematically in Fig. 12.1.

The outline of a file-maintenance program given earlier in Fig. 1.12 is not suitable for performing the task outlined in Fig. 12.1, since the latter assumes that we do not have access to the complete master file for processing each transaction. An outline of a program to carry out this new task is given in Fig. 12.2. A number of assumptions have been made. First of all, we assume that the records in the master file and the records indicating changes are sorted in increasing order of identification code, or key. Secondly, we have assumed that at most one change record exists for each master file record. (However, see Question 5 in Exercise 12.1.) Finally, we have assumed that the change records contain

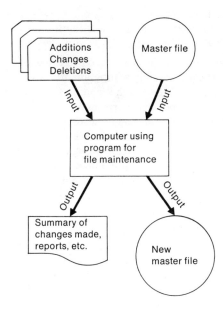

```
Loop until process is completed
.    Input master record
.    Input change record
.    Loop until deletion or modification processed
.    .    If (key of master record = key of change record)
.    .    .        If (record to be deleted)
.    . . . . . . . . . . . . . . . . . . Exit inner loop
.    .    .        . (record needs modification)
.    .    .                Make modification
.    .    .                Output record to new file
.    . . . . . . . . . . . . . . . . . . Exit inner loop
.    .    .        . (end-of-file)
. . . . . . . . . . . . . . . . . . . . . Exit outer loop
.    .    .    End if
.    .    . (key of master record > key of change record)
.    .    .        Output change record (addition) to new file
.    .    .        Input change record
.    .    . (key of master record < key of change record)
.    .    .        Output master record to new file
.    .    .        Input master record
.    .    End if
.    End inner loop
End outer loop
```

FIG. 12.1 Schematic diagram of the general process for file maintenance when the file is stored on an external medium, such as magnetic tape.

FIG. 12.2 Outline of a program to update file as indicated schematically in Fig. 12.1. A number of assumptions must be satisfied if this program is to work properly; in particular, it is assumed that at most one change record exists for each master file record.

transactions that are valid. For example, if a change record indicates that a record is to be deleted, we assume that the master file contains this record. In practice, safety precautions should be taken to test for invalid transactions. (See Question 4 in Exercise 12.1.)

With the program outlined in Fig. 12.2, we require that the input of records indicating changes and the input of records from the master file will eventually provide an indication that the "end-of-file" has been reached. One way of implementing this requirement is to have an "extra" record at the end of each file, indicating that no more records exist. If the key for these records is larger than any other key, then the program will automatically take care of the situation where one or the other input has been exhausted. (See Question 2 in Exercise 12.1.)

There are other safety precautions that must be taken when files are being maintained. Great care must be taken to prevent the introduction of errors into a file. It is a good idea to have the program print out a list of all changes that are made (as indicated in Fig. 12.1), so that they can be checked against the original requests for changes. Other precautions are usually taken as well. For example, data can be checked for reasonableness before it is used. We have already mentioned the need to check data used in statistical calculations. (See Section 10.1.) The need for data verification or data validation is even more important in data-processing applications. Another precaution is to keep

duplicate or backup files so that calculations can be restarted in case trouble should arise because of problems with a program or equipment, or because of accidental damage.

A third precaution is to devise identification codes that can be checked to some extent. To illustrate how this can be done, we begin with a particular code number and extend it with an extra digit equal to the sum of all the original digits, modulo 10. Thus, if the original code is 2345, we note that $2 + 3 + 4 + 5 = 14 \equiv 4$ (mod 10) and we use 23454 as the identification code. If this is done, identification codes can be checked to ensure that the final digit is consistant with the others. This idea can be applied to identification codes for records or to the authorization codes of those who are using the files. Many errors can be detected in this way, especially if a substantial number of errors has been committed, as would be likely if the errors are due to defective equipment such as a faulty keypunch.

EXERCISE 12.1

1. A common error that often arises in transcribing numbers is that of interchanging adjacent digits. For example, if an identification code is 2345, the number 2435 may be recorded by mistake. The extra digit suggested in this section does not detect such an error. However, if we modify that method by multiplying the second, fourth, sixth, etc., digit by two when we compute the extra digit, such transcription errors may be identified. For example, we would use 23452 in place of 2345, and 24353 in place of 2435. The number 24652 would not be a valid identification code using such a rule. Write a program that inputs a sequence of identification codes that are supposed to be constructed using this idea, and that determines whether or not each identification code conforms to this rule. Can you devise other methods that can be used?

2. Develop a program along the lines outlined in Fig. 12.2 for updating a file. For testing purposes it might be helpful to write subprograms which will simulate the files being handled; for example, one subprogram could be used to simulate what happens when "Input master record" is executed, and another could simulate the output of a record to the new file. Assume that the change records contain valid information. Choose a simple example of a record, and state precisely what your program is supposed to do.

3. Develop a program that will edit the change records for the file-maintenance program of Question 2. The program should attempt to validate the data to ensure that errors are not introduced into the file. Do you think it is possible to prevent any errors from being introduced into a file?

4. Expand the program developed in Question 2 so that it will possess the kind of safety features you would expect of a program used in practice. For example, it should handle the situation in which a change record indicates that a new record is to be added to the file, when the record already exists in the file. State precisely what your program does, and discuss briefly what steps it takes to verify data and check for other errors. What does it do if the cards of changes are not in the proper order to begin with?

5. Extend the program developed in Question 2 to allow for the situation in which more than one change record may be provided for an individual record in the master file. Some decision will have to be made concerning the sorting of the change records; for example, it may be decided that the change records for a particular master-file record will be processed in the order: insertion, modifications, deletion. State precisely what your program does, and what safety precautions have been taken.

6. Suppose that a file is represented by a linked list and that there is also a list of "available" records. Write a program that will input the cards of changes envisaged in Figs. 12.1 and 12.2, and will then make the appropriate changes to the file in this alternative form.

7. With the linked list used in Question 6, it is not essential to have the changes appearing in a sorted order, although, if they are not, the list may have to be searched from the beginning for many of the changes that have to be made. Can you suggest a number of ways in which the searching of a linked list might be speeded up?

8. Choose one of the methods you have suggested in Question 7 and, by simulating an example situation, compare the efficiency of what you propose with the straightforward method of searching from the beginning of the list for each record that is required. Are there any other factors to be considered in comparing the effectiveness of your method with the straightforward one?

9. Describe a file that can be represented by a "doubly linked" list, and develop a program for keeping this list up-to-date. Suppose that each record in the file contains the name, address, and telephone number of an individual telephone subscriber, and suppose that one chain of links traces through the file in alphabetical order of subscribers' names, while the other traces through in numerical order of telephone number. The program should be able to modify listings, add new ones, and delete old ones.

10. Write a program for assigning students to classes. Each record in the file corresponds to a class. For example, the seventh record might correspond to Math 3. The identification code is the name of the class or a suitable abbreviation of that name, such as M3. The second item is the number of students already assigned to that class and must be equal to 0 initially. There are 25 more items in each record, one for each student that can be assigned. If it simplifies matters, you can assume that student code numbers, rather than student names, are placed in these items. The program is to maintain this file. Each input card must contain the record number for the class (such as 7 for Math 3), a code to indicate whether or not a student is to be added to or deleted from the class list, and a student code number. The program should output appropriate messages if more than 25 students attempt to register in one class or if a student asks to be dropped from a class in which he has not already been registered. Give a clear statement of exactly how your program can be used and exactly what it is supposed to do.

11. Indicate what changes you would make in the program in Question 10 in order to make it more useful. For example, what would you do so that the input could provide the name of the class instead of having to provide the record number for the class? How would you handle classes with more than one section? How would you handle student names in place of student codes? What steps would you take to verify the data? Do you think it would be reasonable to include the class meeting times in each record so that student timetables can be printed at a later date? How would you prepare class lists when they are required?

12. Until now we have assumed that we knew the position of a record in a file, or that a file had to be searched sequentially in order to find a particular record. If we have direct access to each record in the file, there are more efficient methods for finding a record than a straightforward sequential search. Some methods are appropriate only if the file is being searched for information, without making any additions to the file, and they will be considered in Exercise 12.3. The purpose of the present question is to introduce a method, known as *hash coding*, that can be used to add records to a file and then find them at later times.

The first step in this process is to convert the identification code into the corresponding hash code. The latter must be one of the addresses that can be occupied by the identification code of a record. There are many possible methods of conversion. To illustrate, let us suppose that the hash codes are 1,2, . . . , 100, indicating that the hash table is an array of 100 records. One simple method of conversion is to use the remainder after dividing the identification code by a prime number. In our case the prime number should be slightly less than 100, say 97. Once the identification code has been converted into the corresponding hash code, the location specified by the hash code is examined. If a record is to be added and this location is available, the record is inserted. If this location is already occupied, the next locations are searched until a free one is found. If a record is being sought, it may be at the location specified by the hash code. If not, the next locations can be searched until the required record is found. Write a program that implements the process just outlined. Can you also make provision for the deletion of records?

13. An experiment is to be performed that will determine an approximation to the average number of comparisons needed to find records in a file that has been organized along the lines outlined in Question 12. The average number of comparisons will depend on what fraction of the total file is occupied by records, and results should be obtained for several values of this fraction. Assume that identification codes consist of four-digit numbers and that the possible numbers are equally likely.

14. In Question 12, it was suggested that the locations immediately following the one provided by the hash code be examined in case the one provided by the hash code is not what we are looking for. This method of "collison resolution" is usually referred to as the "linear-search" method. Other methods are worth considering. For example, a sequence of records other than those that are immediately adjacent could be searched. Another possibility would be to follow a link to a linked list of "overflow" records which could be drawn from a pool of records that have been set aside for that purpose. Under what circumstances do you think that either of these approaches might be more efficient than the linear method? Can you suggest any further alternatives?

12.2 SORTING

As we have already seen, a problem that often arises in data processing (and other areas as well) is that of sorting a list of things. We can consider the things to be records in a file, and the problem is that of rearranging the records so that one of the items ends up in some natural order. For example, each record may consist of two items, the name of a telephone subscriber and his number. Even if the file is already sorted according to the name of the subscriber, we may wish to sort it again according to number. However, for the purposes of this discussion it is enough to consider records that consist of only one item.

The choice of method depends a great deal on the nature of the file to be sorted and especially on whether or not the computer has direct access to the entire file. We will assume that the computer does have direct access to the file, but some of the methods we discuss will be applicable to the other case as well. In any event, methods that assume direct access are usually needed even when the computer does not have direct access to the entire file. This is because portions of such files are usually copied into main memory where they can be treated by direct-access methods.

It is quite obvious how two numbers can be compared to determine the order in which they should appear, but to sort alphabetic quantities we must know something about how those quantities are represented in the machine. The usual situation is that they are represented by numerical quantities whose numerical order corresponds to the natural alphabetic order. We assume that this is the case but our illustrations will be in terms of numerical items.

One straightforward method of sorting a list of items into nondecreasing order was described in Chapter 1. It consisted of searching the list for the smallest item, which is then interchanged with the first. The list is searched again, beginning with the second item, for the next smallest, which is interchanged with the second. Then it is searched, beginning at the third item, for the next smallest, and so on. Many other methods have been proposed and we consider a few of them in the following exercise. Our main purpose, apart from their intrinsic interest, is to compare the relative efficiencies of different methods. The process of sorting is required in so many different contexts that it is worthwhile developing particularly efficient sorting programs for various applications, and a great deal of effort has been devoted to this task.

EXERCISE 12.2

1. Write a program that will carry out the straightforward sorting procedure described in this section. Show that it requires approximately $n^2/2$ comparisons to sort n items when n is fairly large.

2. A program is required that will sort n items into nondecreasing order using a method known as the *bubble sort*. In this method the first two items are compared and interchanged if necessary to place them in the desired order. The second and third are treated in the same way, then the third and fourth, and so on. The process is repeated with the first $n - 1$ items, then the first $n - 2$ items, and so on. (The method is called the bubble sort because the largest value "bubbles up" toward the top of the list during each pass through the list.) Approximately how many comparisons are needed with this method? How does its efficiency compare with that of the method described earlier?

3. The program for carrying out the bubble sort can be modified so that it determines whether any interchanges have taken place in each pass through the list. If none has taken place in one particular pass, the list is already in the required order and there is no need to continue. This modification can result in a considerable saving if the list is already partially sorted to begin with. Show what changes are needed in the program. Approximately how much does the modification add to the cost of sorting a list that is not partially sorted to begin with?

4. Another method of sorting which is known as the *insertion sort* can be outlined in the following way. Begin by sorting the first two items. Then place the third item in the proper position relative to the first two. Then place the fourth properly relative to the first three, and so on. Suppose that searching for the proper position in each case is done in a straightforward way by examining each item in the list in order. Then show that, under this assumption, a maximum of approximately $n^2/2$ comparisons are needed with this method. Show also that only $n^2/4$ comparisons are needed on the average. What are the disadvantages of this method compared to those considered in Questions 1 to 3?

5. There are situations in which we may prefer not to move records in a file and in which we therefore do not want to use any of the sorting methods described so far. For example, the records may be very long and too much computer time is required to move them, or it may be that they are already in a convenient order for some other purpose. One way to sort records without having to move them is to construct another file that tells us the order in which the records of the original file would appear if they were sorted. Each record in the new file contains only one item. The first record in the new file contains the record number of the first record that would appear in the old file if it were sorted. The second record in the new file contains the record number of the second record in the old file if it were sorted, and so on. Write a program that will construct the new file.

6. Another way to sort records without having to move them is to redesign the records slightly so that one item in each record is used to give the location of the next record in the new list. This item is a pointer, and the new list is of course just another example of a linked list. Write a program that will begin with an array of records in which one item of each record has not been assigned a value and that will turn the array into a linked list, sorted into the required order with the unassigned items used as pointers.

7. The merge sort is a well-known method that is much more efficient in terms of numbers of comparisons than those considered thus far, at least for large values of n. It it also applicable to files that are available only sequentially. The procedure begins by sorting the first pair, then the next pair, then the next, and so on. After all the pairs have been sorted, the first two pairs are merged to form a

properly sorted sequence of four. Then the next two pairs are merged, then the next, and so on. Eventually the file consists of quadruplets that are in the proper order. The first two quadruplets are then merged to form a properly sorted sequence of eight, and so on, until the entire file has finally been sorted. Write a program that will implement this idea. Can you show that this method requires approximately $n\log_2 n$ comparisons? How much better is this than the more straightforward methods described earlier when $n = 100$? 1000? 10,000? Are there any disadvantages to this method?

8. Can you suggest another method of sorting? Do you think it is possible to devise a method that requires fewer comparisons than the merge sort?

9. Can you prove that one of the programs you have written for sorting will, in fact, always do the job required of it?

12.3 INFORMATION RETRIEVAL

One very obvious reason for maintaining a file is to be able to retrieve information from it whenever required. A bank needs to obtain information about a customer's account. A lawyer must be able to determine who owns a particular piece of land. The police must be able to determine ownership of a particular car or whether or not a particular car has been stolen. In some applications, such as a census, the retrieval of information from a file is separated from the process of putting information into the file. In many cases, for example in airline reservation systems, the two processes are very closely related.

Many factors affect the way in which a file is organized and the way in which it is used. The purpose of the file is the most important consideration. Direct access is required for some files but not for others. Simultaneous access from a large number of input-output locations is required for many files, such as those used for airline reservations.

It is easy to find a record in a file if the location of the record is known. This situation occurs if the identification code is also the address or if it is related to the address in a simple way. To take advantage of this possibility, account codes in a bank or license plates for automobiles would have to be assigned in a very special way. With most files there are usually good reasons why this cannot be done and some kind of searching is required. Hash coding is one possibility that has already been mentioned. Two others are described in the first two questions of Exercise 12.3. The purpose of the file will determine to a large extent the way in which it is organized and used, and efficiency of the search procedure will be an important factor.

Many additional factors must be considered in designing an information retrieval system. One is the difficult problem that arises if the identification codes are not precise. This occurs when the identification codes are words of a language, or people's names, since there may be more than one acceptable spelling for a particular item. Even if a second spelling is not strictly acceptable, it might be the one used by the person who is requesting that the search be made. If you are asking for information about D. R. Schultz and no such name is listed in the file, would you expect the computer to search for D. R. Schulz, D. R. Schulze or D. R. Shultz before giving up?

Another consideration we should mention is that of authorization. Only certain people should be allowed access to files. This is particularly important if a person is to be allowed to change the file in any way. However, even if he merely wishes to obtain information from the file, it may be necessary to require proper authorization for security reasons. One way to check the authorization of a potential user is to require passwords. Each request for information must be accompanied by a password that can be checked by the computer against a list of approved passwords.

One final consideration that has not as yet been given sufficient emphasis is the difficulty of deciding what information should go into a file and then of getting the information into machine-readable form. A library catalogue is a good example of where these difficulties occur. What kind of record should be stored in the library file? Some items, such as author and title, are obviously needed, but what others are needed, especially if the file is to help the user obtain information about topics rather than about specific books? And if we can decide what should appear in such a file, how do we get the information into a form that can be read by a machine?

EXERCISE 12.3

1. Suppose that records are stored in increasing order of their identification codes and that we also have direct access to each record in the file. Then, instead of searching the file sequentially from the first record, we can use what is called a *binary search*. The first step is to examine a record at or near the middle of the file. If this record is not the one being sought, we can determine whether the search should be continued in the lower half or the upper half of the file. A record at or near the middle of the appropriate half is examined next. If this record is not the one being sought, we can determine which quarter should be searched. This process is continued until the desired record is found. A program to carry out a binary search is to be written. (A suggested outline is shown in Fig. 12.3.) It is worthwhile comparing the binary search to a sequential one in terms of efficiency. For example, if a file contains n records the number of comparisons required by

```
/Value of X and table T(1) < T(2) < ··· < T(n) are available/
Set subscripts LOWER = 1 and UPPER = n
Loop until location of X is found
      Set trial value for LOCATION to the middle point between
          LOWER and UPPER
      If (X > T(LOCATION))
          Set LOWER = LOCATION + 1
      (X = T(LOCATION))
········· Exit loop
      (X < T(LOCATION))
          Set UPPER = LOCATION − 1
      End if
End loop
/X is equal to T(LOCATION)/
```

FIG. 12.3 Outline of a program for using a binary search to find X in the table T(1), T(2), ..., T(n). It is assumed that $T(1) < T(2) < ... < T(n)$; it is also assumed that X is one of the entries in the table. (The "middle point" between LOWER and UPPER can be interpreted as rounded up, or down, in case LOWER + UPPER is odd.)

a binary search is approximately $\log_2 n$ when n is large, whereas the number for a sequential search is approximately $n/2$. Can you establish these results? Are there other factors that should be considered in comparing these two methods?

2. When a person looks up a word in a dictionary, he uses a method that is somewhat more efficient than a binary search, at least in the first step or two. His first step is to make a rough estimate as to the location of the word. Thus, if he is looking up the word *program*, he will open the dictionary at a point approximately two thirds of the way through the book. He will then move a few pages ahead or back, depending on the point at which he first opened the dictionary. Write a program that follows a procedure of this kind. Use a random number generator to produce 1000 identification codes consisting of five-digit integers and then sort them. Use the same generator to produce requests for a search and compare experimentally the efficiency of your method with that of the binary search method.

3. The insertion sort described in Question 4 of Exercise 12.2 requires the searching of a sorted list in order to locate the position into which a new item is to be inserted. Write a portion of a program that adapts the idea of a binary search to this situation and then uses it as part of an insertion-sort program. Compare the relative merits of this program to the earlier one.

4. List several items of information that you would consider useful for the records in a file of automobile registrations. Outline two or three programs that would be useful in connection with such a file.

5. Draw up a list of items that you would consider useful in a file of census data. Outline a program that could produce a table showing the distribution of marital status with age. Discuss the construction of a program that would produce tables showing the relationships between particular items specified by the user.

6. Many people are concerned about the potential dangers in the use of files, particularly when they contain information about individual citizens. Such files may be extremely useful, for example, in providing some of the basic information needed by the government for economic planning. However, the files could also be misused. They may contain information about an individual that he considers to be his private concern; such information may be damaging to his credit rating or his reputation generally, aside from the possibility that it may not even be correct. Who should be allowed to have access to such files? Some say that access should only be by permission of the individual concerned. Others say that certain government officials should have access for purposes of the common good, especially, for example, in matters of national security. To protect the individual, it is often argued that he should have the right to challenge its accuracy in the courts. What are your views regarding these questions?

7. What information is an airline likely to keep in its reservation file? What distinct services can be provided with the file you have described?

8. What information do you think an insurance company keeps in its master file? What different kinds of operations can be performed with the help of such a file?

9. Indicate some files that you would deem useful in various areas such as law or medicine. How large would these files have to be? How much do you estimate it would cost to prepare such files? Would it be worthwhile?

12.4 BILLING, PAYROLLS, ETC.

One of the best-known uses of files is in the preparation of regular bills or notices. A store may keep a file of customers' accounts. The records are kept up-to-date with each customer's purchases and the file is used at the end of the month to prepare the bills. Such a file can also be used for many other purposes. It would, of course, have to contain a record of customers' arrears, interest charges, and so on. It can also be used to prepare summaries that might be helpful to the management of the store. Files for similar purposes are maintained by telephone companies, insurance companies, and many other organizations as well.

Another way in which files are used is closely related to the one just described. In the above examples, the file contains all the information needed to prepare the bills. In other examples, the file may contain most of the information required, but additional information is obtained from a different source at the time the bill is prepared. This can occur, for example, with the billing procedure used by a gas company. In this case, each record consists of an account number, the name and address of the customer, the rate charged to that customer, information about usage during previous months, arrears, and so on. The additional information

needed for the bill is the latest meter reading, and this value can be input at the time the bill is prepared. Thus, the computer program effectively merges two files in order to prepare the bills. One file contains the basic information about names, addresses, rates, and so on; the other file contains all the latest meter readings.

Many payroll applications are similar to the billing procedure just described. A record in the master file contains the employee number, name, address, rate of pay, and so on. The number of hours worked is additional information that can be input at the time the payroll is being prepared.

In practice, however, payroll applications can be very complicated. One of the difficulties encountered is that the requirements that must be met will change. For example, labor negotiations ordinarily result in changes to rates of pay, changes are often made to employee benefit plans, and, on occasion, retroactive changes are required for payroll applications. Another possibility is that government legislation often results in a requirement for changes to procedures. These examples illustrate the need to maintain not only the files associated with an application, but also the need to maintain the programs themselves. It is a good idea to organize the programs in such a way that items which may be subject to change are isolated in the form of a table, so that only the items in the table need to be changed. In any event, good documentation is mandatory in all such cases.

EXERCISE 12.4

1. Give a list of items that a store might wish to keep in its records for billing purposes. Assume that the store plans to keep only the current totals of all purchases and not a list of the individual purchases. Describe a computer program for updating this file. Do not forget to allow for the return of unwanted goods. Describe a few other programs for preparing bills, notices of arrears, and so on. For the purposes of this question, the programs should be kept as simple as possible and no attempt should be made to take precautions such as verifying the data.

2. Describe how the programs in the preceding question can be modified so that account numbers are verified, data is checked for reasonableness, lists of changes made are output, and so on. Do you believe that the programs you have designed are reliable enough that the customers would be reasonably happy about the notices they receive?

3. A major difficulty with the programs in the preceding two questions arises if lists of the individual transactions are to be kept in the file. If the file is kept on magnetic tape, it is relatively easy to have records of different lengths. However, if the file is kept in a direct-access memory, a major complication arises. Each record could be made large enough to accommodate a list of the maximum length expected, but then a large amount of storage would be wasted. It is preferable that each record be of only moderate length, but long enough to contain most lists likely to arise, and that some records be set aside to hold the "overflow" caused by a few excessively long lists. One way of linking a particular record to its overflow, if it has one, is to design the records so that they contain a code that indicates whether or not they are continued elsewhere and that also indicates where the continuation, if any, is located. Show how this idea can be implemented.

4. The billing procedures of a telephone company are similar to those discussed in the preceding questions. The lists of individual purchases correspond to lists of long distance calls. Describe some other applications that are similar to those of the store and the telephone company.

5. Describe a file that could be used for the billing procedures of a gas company. Outline a program that will merge the current meter readings with this file and produce the required bills. Without giving all the details, indicate what precautions should be taken to make the program reasonably reliable.

6. One of the difficulties that arises in preparing a gas bill is that it may not be possible to obtain a meter reading each month. One rule that can be used for coping with this difficulty is to assume that the consumption is the same as what was billed for in the preceding month, provided the meter has been read at least once during the past three months. Show what changes can be made in the file and in the program so that this rule can be followed.

7. Payroll files can be similar to those used by a store for billing purposes. This situation occurs when the employees are on salaries or commissions, rather than hourly wages. The updating process then involves adding new records for new employees, changing records when employees receive wage increases, or deleting old records for those who have resigned or retired. If commissions are paid, a record must also be kept of sales made by each employee. Describe a file that could be used for such purposes and outline programs that could be used to keep it up-to-date and to produce the payroll.

8. A slightly different payroll procedure may be needed when employees are paid on an hourly basis. The number of hours worked could be added to the file as part of the updating process, but an alternative approach is to merge the time cards with the master file during the process of producing the payroll. How would the programs in Question 7 have to be modified to follow the latter procedure?

9. Management of a large inventory requires the use of a file. For example, suppose a wholesale hardware company wishes to keep a file on what it has stored in a particular warehouse. On the basis of all orders received and all shipments that have arrived, describe the items of information that should be included in each record if the file is to be kept up-to-date. The file is to be used to issue orders for new shipments whenever the quantity on hand for a particular article falls below a specified reorder point. Give a program that will accomplish these tasks. (It should

be pointed out that the question of issuing orders for new supplies can be quite complicated, especially if an attempt is made to allow for seasonal fluctuations, trends, and so on.)

10. Describe one other situation in which a master file might be merged with current data to produce something analogous to monthly bills, payrolls, or orders for new shipments.

11. Each record of a payroll file will usually contain one item for the total earnings to date. This item is needed for a number of reasons, including the preparation of statements in connection with income tax. Suppose that a company has an agreement with its employees to pay a dividend each year and suppose that the amount paid each employee is proportional to his total earnings for the year, as of the end of December. Assume that the total of all such earnings of all employees is known, as well as the amount to be distributed as dividends. An unscrupulous programmer has been asked to write a program that will produce the dividend checks. He decides to round down the result of each calculation so that a fraction of a cent is lost by each employee. He also arranges to have one extra check made out to himself for the total of all these small amounts. Write programs of the kind the unscrupulous programmer would write. Can you suggest a fair way of calculating dividend payments so that exactly the right total will be distributed? Give the part of the program needed to prepare the checks.

12. The final question in this section is somewhat different from others in this chapter because it does not make use of a file, although its output is a file, and it is appropriate to include it under the general heading of data processing. It is proposed to construct a computer program that will calculate and output a table of mortgage payments. For a change of pace, we will discuss what is required in considerable detail, and suggest that the construction of the program can be an interesting and worthwhile project. It should be accompanied by careful documentation for the user.

We assume that the input for the program consists of the following four items:

1. The name of the person taking out a mortgage, along with a description of the property on which the mortgage is placed. An easy way to handle this information is to have it punched onto one card. For example, it might be

`A.B.WENTWORTH,LOT83,PLAN14,TOWNSHIP OF AJAX`

2. The amount of the mortgage.
3. The annual interest rate.
4. The monthly payment.

We illustrate the sort of output that is required with an example in which the amount is $15,000, the interest rate is 6 percent, and the monthly payment is $95.14. The monthly interest rate is ½ percent, which is obtained by dividing the annual rate by 12.

In the first month the interest is ½ percent of $15,000 which is $.005 \times \$15,000 = \$75.00$. Of the payment of

$95.14, $75.00 is for interest in the first month, leaving $95.14 − $75.00 = $20.14 as the principal payment. The new principal balance therefore becomes $15,000 − $20.14 = $14,979.86.

In the second month the interest is .005 × $14,979.86 = $74.89930. If this is rounded to the nearest cent we obtained $74.90. This leaves $95.14 − $74.90 = $20.24 as the principal payment, leaving a new principal balance of $14,979.86 − $20.24 = $14,959.62 at the end of the second month.

The computer program should produce output which starts out as shown in Fig. 12.4. It is customary to output the payment numbers as shown, as well as the other three amounts. Mortgage companies use forms for their output which will already have some of the above information printed on them. For example, the headings, like PAYMENT NUMBER, may be already printed on the forms. For our project we assume that the forms are blank to begin with.

We must make decisions about the format for the three numbers which are input. The amount of the mortgage can be in dollars (that is, no cents) and need not exceed $99,999. The interest rate is often expressed in ¼ percent units, as in 6¼ percent, or 6¾ percent. We should therefore allow at least two decimal places in the input, as in 6.25 or 6.75. We would need three decimal places if we anticipate interest rates involving ⅛ percent, as in 6⅜ percent. We must allow for a monthly payment in dollars and cents, but we need not allow for more than $999.99.

Some decisions must be made about rounding. The most serious involves what we should do when we divide by 12 to get the monthly interest rate. We should carry several decimal places in the result of this division. If we round the result up to this number of places we obtain a result that benefits the company slightly, rather than the person who is taking out the mortgage.

A major difficulty with the program we require is to arrange for the output of dollar signs, commas, and decimal points in the right places. You should make sure that dollar signs are printed, although you may find it is too much trouble to have them placed immediately to the left of the numbers. You may also wish to omit the commas, but the decimal points must be included in your output.

Special provision must be made for stopping the calculation. The simplest thing to do is to test the new prin-

cipal balance after each calculation to see if it has become negative. When it is negative the principal payment must be changed so that the new principal balance becomes exactly zero. The final payment is reduced accordingly and the final payment should be printed out at the end of the table. For example, the table could terminate with

| 250 | 7.25 | 87.89 | 57.11 |
| 251 | 2.86 | 57.11 | 0.00 |

FINAL PAYMENT IS $59.97

One further point can be investigated. It would be interesting to know what effect different decisions about rounding can have on the final payment.

It should be pointed out that we have avoided one rather difficult problem, that of determining what the monthly payment should be. In arranging for a mortgage we begin with the amount of the mortgage, the interest rate, and the number of payments. This information is used to determine what monthly payment comes closest to paying off the mortgage in the required number of payments. Only then can our program be used to work out the table of payments. The problem of determining the monthly payment requires either techniques of the kind discussed in Section 8.3 or those described in Section 11.1.

12.5 DECISION TABLES

The purpose of this section is to introduce a new way of describing procedures. Procedures can be described by means of flow charts, or pseudo-code, and so on, but *decision tables* can also be used in some situations, and there are circumstances in which decision tables are the most convenient way of describing procedures. These circumstances seem to arise most frequently in data-processing applications.

Decision tables can be illustrated with the following simplified version of a university admission procedure. An applicant is admitted to the university if he or she has taken at least six subjects in the final year of high school and has obtained (1) an average of at least 70 percent or (2) no failures and an average of at least 60 percent. A student with an average of 80 percent or more is awarded a scholarship. This procedure is described by the flow chart in Fig. 12.5.

The same procedure is described by the decision table in Fig. 12.6. In this example there are four *conditions*. The *condition statements* are placed to the left of a heavy line and above another heavy line. (This first condition statement is "Average ≥ 80 percent.") The *condition entries* are placed to the right of the condition statements and they consist of Y, N, and −, for Yes, No, and Don't care, respectively. There are three *actions*. The *action statements* are in the lower left part of the table. (The first action statement is "Award Scholarship.") The *action entries* are to the right of the action statements and they consist of X, and −, for Take action and Don't take action, respectively.

```
          RELIABLE MORTGAGE COMPANY
        SCHEDULE OF MORTGAGE PAYMENTS FOR
   A.B.WENTWORTH,LOT83,PLAN14,TOWNSHIP OF AJAX
   AMOUNT $15,000   RATE 6.00   PAYMENT $95.14

   PAYMENT   INTEREST   PRINCIPAL  NEW PRINCIPAL
   NUMBER    PAYMENT    PAYMENT    BALANCE

      1      $75.00     $20.14     $14,979.86
      2       74.90      20.24      14,959.62
      ⋮         ⋮          ⋮           ⋮
```

FIG. 12.4 A portion of a table of mortgage payments.

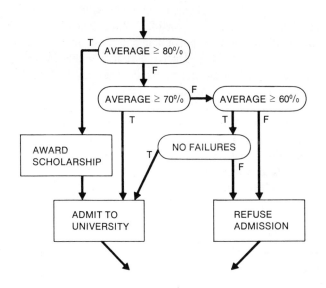

FIG. 12.5 University admission procedure.

	Rule 1	Rule 2	Rule 3	Rule 4
Average percent	≥ 80	≥ 70	≥ 60	< 60
Number of failures	—	—	0	—
Admission	Yes, with scholarship	Yes	Yes	No

FIG. 12.7 An extended-entry decision table for the university admission procedure.

The interpretation of the decision table is fairly straightforward. Rule 1 is followed when the average is greater than or equal to 80 percent. Rule 1 consists of awarding a scholarship and admitting to university. Rule 2 is followed when the average is not greater than or equal to 80 percent, but is greater than or equal to 70 percent, and similarly for the other rules.

A table in which the entries are limited to Y, N, X, and − is called a *limited-entry* table. Other tables are *extended-entry* tables or *mixed-entry* tables. An extended-entry table for the university admission procedure of Fig. 12.6 is shown in Fig. 12.7. Note that limited-entry tables have statements in the left-hand column, whereas extended-entry tables have variable names in the left-hand column. The entries in extended-entry tables are the values of the variables (including "Don't care").

Decision tables have two advantages over flow charts. The first is that they are more easily changed. If a university decides to change its admission procedures, the decision table can be adjusted fairly easily. Changing a flow chart, on the other hand, can often lead to quite serious complications. The other advantage of a decision table is that it makes it easier to see whether all possible cases have been taken into account.

There are special compilers for translating decision tables into other programming languages. Such compilers will, of course, cause the various tests to be carried out in a certain order. The decision table itself does not impose any particular order, although we could agree that the rules be tried in the order in which they appear in the table and that the conditions be tested in the order in which they appear. Some difficult questions about efficiency can arise in connection with the problem of translating decision tables into machine or assembly languages. The frequency with which the different rules are likely to be used would be an important factor in determining an efficient translation.

One other property of decision tables should be mentioned. It is possible to develop subtables that can be used in somewhat the same way as subprograms. One of the actions in a table could then cause control to be transferred to another table. We will not make use of this idea, but it does suggest that the subject of decision tables is more extensive than was indicated by the discussion given earlier in this section.

	Rule 1	Rule 2	Rule 3	Rule 4
Average ≥ 80 percent	Y	N	—	—
Average ≥ 70 percent	—	Y	—	—
Average ≥ 60 percent	—	—	Y	N
No failures	—	—	Y	—
Award scholarship	X	—	—	—
Admit to university	X	X	X	—
Refuse admission	—	—	—	X

FIG. 12.6 A decision table description of the university admission procedure given in Fig. 12.5.

EXERCISE 12.5

1. Give a flow chart and two decision tables (like the ones described in this section) for a procedure for determining whether or not a person should be issued a driver's license. The conditions should include passing a test and paying the proper fee. The actions should include granting a license without restriction and granting a license that restricts the driver to cars with automatic transmissions.

2. Construct decision tables and a flow chart for determining the cost of car insurance. The conditions should include the age and sex of each driver, as well as accident records. The actions should include additional premiums for male drivers under 25 and for drivers with poor records.

3. Give decision-table descriptions of the procedure described in the program of Fig. 11.6 for following cars through an intersection.

4. Give decision-table descriptions of one of the file management procedures you have developed in earlier sections of this chapter.

5. Invent a procedure that lends itself reasonably well to a description in terms of decision tables, and develop suitable tables. It is suggested that you consider the rules needed for managing an inventory. Another example to consider is the specification of priorities for determining the order in which jobs are scheduled on a computer.

6. Develop a program for translating decision tables into programs. Specify very carefully the format required for the input of the table.

12.6 FURTHER REMARKS

With the small-scale problems considered in this chapter, it has not been possible to illustrate the special difficulties caused by size alone that arise in large data-processing problems. These difficulties, of course, are not restricted to data-processing problems; they exist in any large problem. The main requirement in any large programming task is to develop and follow a well-defined and well-organized plan. The entire process must be very carefully supervised, from the first steps in identifying and defining the problem, through the design of the system, the coding and testing, to the documentation and, finally, the operation of the system. With large problems, many people will be involved. Each person must know exactly what he or she is to produce and provision must also be made for changes in personnel. The examples in this chapter are not large enough to illustrate all aspects of data-processing problems that occur in practice. They do cover many of the most important aspects, however, and it is hoped that they at least point to the others.

One other aspect of data-processing applications has not yet been mentioned in any detail. This concerns one of the major advantages of getting information into machine-readable form, which is that the information

can often be used several times to provide a variety of results. As an example, consider what happens when the information about a particular purchase in a store is available on a punched card. Recording this information on a card would not be justified if the only purpose in doing so was to have the computer store that information in a file for billing purposes. However, once the information is on the card, it can be used in many other ways as well. For example, the computer can use the card, along with similar ones for other purchases, to update the inventory file and, if commissions are paid, to update the payroll file. It may also be possible to develop programs for analyzing costs, producing progress reports, forecasting sales, and so on.

Different files can be used for more than one purpose as well. For example, the inventory file is used to order new shipments when needed. It can also be used to prepare reports on the most active items in the inventory, items that might be dropped from the inventory, and so on. The inventory file could also be used to prepare an analysis of the costs of running the warehouse.

The fact that information is used many times for many different purposes, whether it is information about a particular transaction or the information kept in a large file, merely reinforces the importance of planning. To gain maximum benefit from a data-processing system, it is extremely important to plan for a variety of uses for that system. Of course, this in turn leads to a complex system and to an even greater need for careful planning and organizing.

Before leaving the subject of data processing, we should mention the fact that special programming languages have been developed for the description of procedures in this area. The best known is COBOL (COmmon Business Oriented Language), but there are others. Special languages for handling decision tables have also been developed, including an extension of COBOL.

Finally, it should be noted that much attention has recently been directed toward the organization of files and information retrieval. Data Base Management Systems, which attempt to divorce the application programmer from the way in which files are physically organized, have been developed. This has allowed greater attention to be focused on how files are logically organized for various applications.

CHAPTER 13

Nonnumerical Applications

We have already introduced a variety of calculations described as numerical. The distinguishing feature of these calculations is the presence of truncation or roundoff error that can have a serious effect on the final results. Applications in which such errors do not appear are said to be nonnumerical. According to this distinction between numerical and nonnumerical calculations, some important kinds of problems do not belong entirely to either category. For example, neither statistical calculations nor simulations can be classified as being entirely one or the other. However, almost all the data-processing problems in the preceding chapter are nonnumerical in the sense in which we use the term. Problems involving searching and sorting, even if they involve numbers, are nonnumerical since they do not involve truncation or roundoff errors. Financial calculations can involve roundoff error but usually only in a very minor way. They should be classified as nonnumerical.

There are several other sources of nonnumerical problems. In the next section we consider a number of problems that arise in connection with networks of various kinds, such as transportation networks. Puzzles and games are a source of nonnumerical problems, and many aspects of computer graphics are nonnumerical. In the fourth section of this chapter, we also consider some nonnumerical problems that involve the manipulation of strings of symbols.

The extremely rapid development of computer science itself has produced a large number of interesting nonnumerical problems. Many of these are associated with the development of interpreters, and language translators such as assemblers and compilers. The next chapter is devoted to a study of special nonnumerical problems of this kind.

13.1 NETWORKS AND GRAPHS

A very brief preview of what we are about to describe was given in Section 1.4 when a simple example of a graph was used to help illustrate the variety of data structures that might arise in practice. Another example of such a graph, or network, is shown in Fig. 13.1. In

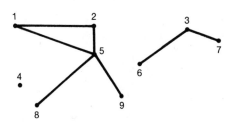

FIG. 13.1 Example of a network or graph.

this case, there are nine nodes, or points, numbered 1, 2, ..., 9. Some pairs of nodes are joined by edges, or arcs; for example, 1 and 2 are joined but 1 and 4 are not.

There are many obvious interpretations of a network or a graph. For example, the points can be interpreted as points in a maze and the lines as tunnels connecting the points, or the points can be cities while the lines are highways connecting the cities. Graphs can also be interpreted as telephone circuits. Another possibility is to interpret the points as boxes in a flowchart, although in this case we would want to attach a direction to each line and thus produce an example of a *directed graph*. There are many other interpretations and a few more will be introduced later in this section.

We need a convenient way of representing a graph such as the one shown in Fig. 13.1. The diagram itself is very convenient for many purposes. For example, when the diagram represents a highway system it is easy to determine how to get from one point to another. However, as indicated in Section 1.4, there are other ways of representing graphs that are more convenient for manipulation on a computer, or when certain mathematical questions are being considered. One of these is to represent a graph by a matrix. For example, the graph in Fig. 13.1 can be represented by a matrix whose elements are 1's and 0's, the (i,j)th element being 1 if there is an edge joining the ith point to the jth point, otherwise 0. Elements on the main diagonal can be taken to be 0, unless there is a loop in the graph that forms an edge connecting the corresponding node to itself. Thus, the graph in Fig. 13.1 is represented by the matrix in Fig. 13.2. If the graph is a directed graph, the (i,j)th element is 1 if an edge connects points i and j in the direction from i to j, whereas the (j,i)th element is 1 if an edge connects these points in the opposite direction. Matrices for representing graphs or directed graphs are called *adjacency matrices*.

A variety of questions can be asked about graphs. For example, we can ask if there is a path connecting two points in a graph. If there is at least one path, we can ask which are the shortest paths, that is, which are the paths consisting of the smallest number of edges. We can also ask how many distinct paths connect two points. The first two questions are discussed in the exercise at the end of this section, but the third question is more difficult and will not be considered here.

Other problems arise in which a number is attached to each edge of a graph. For example, if the graph represents a highway system, the numbers can represent distances between cities. Then a natural problem is to determine the minimum distance between two cities. Alternatively, the numbers might represent transportation costs, in which case an interesting problem is to determine the minimum cost. The graph can also represent a pipeline and the numbers can represent capacities of various pipes joining particular points. In this case, we might wish to determine the maximum flow that can be achieved between two points. This last question is quite difficult and we will not consider it any further, but the minimum-distance and minimum-cost problems will be considered in Questions 6 and 7 of Exercise 13.1.

Graphs with numbered edges also are conveniently represented by matrices. The (i,j)th element of such a matrix is the number attached to the edge joining the points i and j. The (i,j)th element can differ from the (j,i)th, for example, if the matrix represents a highway system and the distances are different because of detours or one-way streets. Other elements can be assigned in any convenient way. In the case of distance or cost the diagonal elements should be zero, while the off-diagonal elements corresponding to points not directly connected to each other should be infinite.

One further point should be considered in connection with procedures for solving problems that involve graphs. As with many other procedures, it is important to assess the efficiency of a particular method that is used in practice. If the problem involves n points, we usually want to know how rapidly the amount of work grows with n. With useful procedures we usually find that the amount of work is proportional to a low power of n, such as n^2 or n^3. If the amount of work is proportional to $n!$, the procedure is impractical, at least for large values of n. The value of $n!$ grows so rapidly with n that the amount of work soon becomes prohibitive, even for a high-speed computer.

$$\begin{pmatrix} 0 & 1 & 0 & 0 & 1 & 0 & 0 & 0 & 0 \\ 1 & 0 & 0 & 0 & 1 & 0 & 0 & 0 & 0 \\ 0 & 0 & 0 & 0 & 0 & 1 & 1 & 0 & 0 \\ 0 & 0 & 0 & 0 & 0 & 0 & 0 & 0 & 0 \\ 1 & 1 & 0 & 0 & 0 & 0 & 0 & 1 & 1 \\ 0 & 0 & 1 & 0 & 0 & 0 & 0 & 0 & 0 \\ 0 & 0 & 1 & 0 & 0 & 0 & 0 & 0 & 0 \\ 0 & 0 & 0 & 0 & 1 & 0 & 0 & 0 & 0 \\ 0 & 0 & 0 & 0 & 1 & 0 & 0 & 0 & 0 \end{pmatrix}$$

FIG. 13.2 The adjacency matrix that represents the graph in Fig. 13.1. The (i, j)th element is 1 if an edge joins point i and point j, otherwise 0.

EXERCISE 13.1

1. a) Suppose there are n points in a maze, numbered 1, 2, ..., n, and suppose that a_{ij} are the elements of its adjacency matrix. (See Fig. 13.2.) A new matrix with elements b_{ij} is defined by

$$b_{ij} = \max \, (a_{i1}a_{1j}, \, a_{i2}a_{2j}, \, \ldots, \, a_{in}a_{nj}).$$

Note that $b_{ij} = 1$ if and only if points i and j are connected by a path of length 2. Show how this idea can be generalized to produce matrices for paths of length 3, 4, and so on. Write a program or subprogram based on this idea that will start with an adjacency matrix, along with a pair of points, and that will determine whether or not there is a path connecting the two points. The minimum number of connecting edges should also be determined.

b) What changes need to be made in the definition of b_{ij}, and in the corresponding program if the 1 and 0 of the adjacency matrix are replaced by "true" and "false" respectively?

2. Another approach to the maze problem of Question 1(a) is the following. We start as before with an adjacency matrix and two particular points denoted by i and j. We then begin to construct a list of n items where the kth item is to be the minimum number of edges for a path connecting point i to point k, if there is a path between them, and 0 otherwise. To construct such a list, we first make all items 0, except those that correspond to points adjacent to point i, which we make 1. Then we examine each 0 element to see if it is connected to i by a path of length 2; if it is, the 0 is changed to 2. Then we examine each remaining 0 to see if it can be replaced by 3, and so on. We can stop the process as soon as the value of the jth element is changed, assuming that a path exists. One form of this procedure is outlined in Fig. 13.3. Write a program or subprogram based on this idea. Can you improve on the efficiency of what is presented in Fig. 13.3?

3. Another way of representing a graph is to use two subscripted variables, say L1 and L2. The components of the first variable are used as pointers to components of the second. If the value of L1(I) is J and the value of L1(I+1) is K, the points connected to the Ith point are given by L2(J), L2(J+1), ..., L2(K−1). This scheme

is illustrated below for the first five points in the graph of Fig. 13.1

Subscripts	1 2 3 4 5 6 7 8 9 10 11 ...
Components of L1	1 3 5 7 7 11 ...
Components of L2	2 5 1 5 6 7 1 2 8 9 ...

The number of points connected to the Ith point is L1(I+1)−L1(I). The number of components in L1 is one more than the number of points in the graph because L1(N+1) is needed to determine how many points are connected to the Nth point. Discuss the relative merits of using this scheme to represent a graph. Using two such lists in place of an adjacency matrix, write a program that uses the method outlined in Question 2 to determine whether or not two points in a given maze are connected.

4. Suppose the maze problem is to be solved by listing all possible sequences of points beginning with point i and ending with point j, and then testing each sequence to see if it corresponds to a path. What is the maximum number of sequences that would have to be tested? Approximately what is this number if $n = 10$? What if $n = 20$? How does the efficiency of this method compare with the efficiency of the methods described in Questions 1, 2, and 3, and how do the latter compare with each other?

5. The method described in Question 4 provides us with a path immediately, once it has been determined that there is a path. How could a path be determined if we use the methods of Questions 1, 2, or 3? Show how to modify the program or subprogram for one of the methods of Questions 1, 2, or 3 in order to determine a path that has the minimum number of connecting edges.

6. Suppose that d_{ij} is the distance along a single line connecting the points i and j, if there is such a line; otherwise, $d_{ij} = 0$ if $i = j$ and $d_{ij} = \infty$ if $i \neq j$. Suppose that e_{ij} is defined by

$$e_{ij} = \min \ (d_{i1} + d_{1j}, \ d_{i2} + d_{2j}, \dots, \ d_{in} + d_{nj}).$$

What does e_{ij} represent?   Suppose f_{ij} is defined by

$$f_{ij} = \min \ (d_{ij}, e_{ij}).$$

What does f_{ij} represent? Write a program based on this idea to determine the minimum distance between two given points. What does f_{ij} represent if d_{ij} is the cost of transportation between points whenever the two points are connected by a single line?

7. Develop another program for solving the minimum-distance problem of Question 6, using an idea similar to the one described in Question 2. Compare the efficiency of the two programs in Questions 6 and 7.

8. Suppose there are n individuals, numbered 1, 2, ..., n. Suppose that $a_{ij} = 1$ if individual i dominates individual j; otherwise, let $a_{ij} = 0$. We do not allow j to dominate i if i dominates j. (The matrix is therefore nonsymmetric and the graph associated with this situation is a directed graph in which at most one directed line is allowed between any two points.) However, the possibility that i dominates j, j dominates k, and k dominates i is not ruled out. Suppose that for every pair (i,j), exactly one of a_{ij} and a_{ji} is 1, so that one individual in every pair dominates

```
/The given adjacency matrix has the components of aᵢⱼ/
/The list to be constructed has the components lᵢ/
Set lᵢ to be initially the same as the ith row of aᵢⱼ
For pathlength = 2,3, . . . , n − 1
    For m = 1, 2, . . . , n
        For k = 1, 2, . . . , n
            If (lₘ = 0, lₖ = pathlength − 1, aₘₖ = 1 and m ≠ i)
            lₘ = pathlength
. . . . . . . . . . If (lⱼ ≠ 0) exit outer for
        End for
    End for
End outer for
If (lⱼ ≠ 0)
        there is a path of length lⱼ
    (lⱼ = 0)
        there is no path
End if
```

FIG. 13.3 Outline of a program for determining the minimum length of path, if any, between nodes i and j. The method followed is the one outlined in Question 2 of Exercise 13.1. (No attempt has been made to make it efficient.)

the other. Under these circumstances, it can be shown that at least one individual dominates all others, either directly or indirectly. (We say that *i* dominates *j* indirectly if there is a *k* such that *i* dominates *k* and *k* dominates *j*.) Can you prove this result? Write a program that will find all such natural leaders, given a particular dominance matrix. What do you believe is the corresponding situation with regard to followers?

9. Problems in project planning can sometimes be represented by a graph. An example is shown in Fig. 13.4. The jobs that must be completed before a house is built are represented by directed edges. The number on an edge is the number of days required to complete the job. Figure 13.4 indicates that the excavation requires two days. The edges are joined in a way that indicates which jobs must be completed before others are started. In the example shown, the excavation must be completed before the foundation is started. The foundation, in turn, must be completed before the framing is begun. The foundation must also be completed before the sewer can be laid. This latter fact is indicated by a directed edge marked with a zero. The problem is to determine the shortest time required to complete the entire project. This shortest time is the sum of the times along the longest path through the graph. Such a path is called a *critical path* and a method used to solve problems of this kind is called a *Critical Path Method*. Write a program for such problems.

10. In planning large projects it is not very convenient to represent the problem as a directed graph for input to a computer. It is more likely that the requirements would be presented as lists of specifications for the different jobs. With each job there would be a list of the other jobs that would have to be completed before it could be started, along with an estimate of the time needed for its completion. Describe a suitable input format and develop a computer program that will accept such input and find a corresponding critical path.

11. A town called Blizzardville has 10 east-west streets and 10 north-south avenues. Joe lives at the corner of 1st Street and 1st Avenue while his girl friend, Forlornia, lives at the corner of 10th Street and 10th Avenue. After each snowstorm, Joe's friends phone him to tell him which blocks are open to traffic and which are closed. He uses this information as input for a computer program which he uses for determining whether or not there is a path clear for him to drive to Forlornia's house. Write a program that will find such a path, if there is one.

13.2 PUZZLES AND GAMES

Puzzles sometimes lead to situations in which the solution is only one of a large number of possible arrangements. We can consider using the computer to search among these many different arrangements for the desired solution. Often a clever argument can help us find the solution, or at least reduce the number of possibilities that must be searched. It can also happen that we first find the solution as the result of a search and then, once a solution is known, develop a clever argument to show how it could have been found more quickly. All of this is intended to suggest that a combination of careful reasoning and computer searching may well be the best way to attack certain problems. Of course this remark applies to many kinds of problems and not merely to puzzles. (A combination of reasoning and computer searching, both on a very extensive scale, was used recently to solve the famous four-color map problem. The solution was announced in 1976, after the problem had remained unsolved for more than 100 years.)

A good illustration of these ideas occurs in the puzzle known as Instant Insanity, in which four cubes

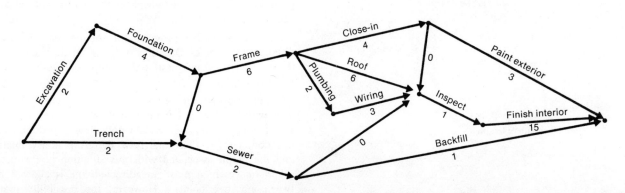

FIG. 13.4 Representation of a problem in critical path scheduling. The excavation must be completed before the foundation is begun. The foundation requires four days to complete and must be finished before framing can be started. It must also be finished before the sewer pipe can be installed.

have colored faces as shown in Fig. 13.5. The objective of the puzzle is to stack the four cubes in such a way that the four faces showing on each side are all of different colors.

A straightforward approach to this puzzle is to test every possible arrangement of the blocks. Each block has six faces and any one of these faces can be on the bottom. The first block can be placed in position in six different ways. Once the bottom face of each of the other blocks has been chosen there are four different positions into which each of them can be rotated. Each of the others can therefore be placed in $6 \times 4 = 24$ different ways, and all four blocks can be stacked in $6 \times 24^3 = 82944$ different ways. A computer program to test each of these arrangements can be used to solve the puzzle.

The straightforward approach just described can be carried out without undue difficulty. The programming required is not trivial but it can be done in a reasonable length of time, and the machine time should not be excessive, at least on a fast machine. However, it is interesting to consider ways in which the procedure can be made more efficient in terms of machine time. There are various ways in which the number of possibilities can be reduced, although the resulting programs may be more complicated.

It should be noted that even the straightforward approach does not include every conceivable arrangement. The positions of the blocks relative to each other obviously do not affect the final test, and the straightforward approach has already taken this fact into account. However, there are other aspects of this puzzle that can be used to reduce the total number of arrangements that need to be tested. A discussion of these reductions is asked for in Questions 4 and 5 of Exercise 13.2.

Games are another source of nonnumerical problems. Some games (such as Tic-tac-toe) are simple in that only a relatively small number of possibilities can arise and they can all be stored in a computer's memory, together with the best move to make in each case. These problems are trivial in principle, although they are not so trivial in practice because a considerable amount of ingenuity may be required to store the necessary information in an efficient way. Some other games (such as Nim) are simple in that there is an easy rule to follow in order to play the game well.

Other games (such as Checkers, Chess, Oware, and so on) are extremely difficult to program. Writing a program to follow the rules of such games is not too difficult, at least in principle, although it can be quite challenging to devise effective ways of representing the necessary information. The main difficulty in developing such programs is to make them play reasonably well. Programs have been developed to play some of these games as well as good human players, but a great deal of effort has been required to develop such programs.

One intriguing possibility arises when the program for playing a game depends on a "weighted" assessment of the result of each move that can be taken at any particular stage. For example, each move might be judged according to a number of criteria (such as the number of squares being threatened in a game of chess), and these criteria might be weighted together in a certain way to produce a single measure of the strength of the move. One could then adjust the weights in an attempt

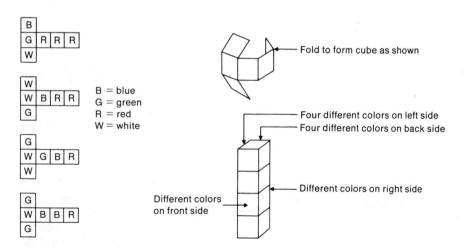

FIG. 13.5 Four cubes are used in the puzzle known as Instant Insanity. Their faces are colored as shown. The purpose is to stack the cubes so that the four faces on each side are different colors.

to improve the program's playing ability. It is intriguing to consider having the program itself do the adjusting of the weights in some systematic way, and thus appear to be improving its ability in the course of playing a number of games.

Games can often be represented by trees, each node being a situation that can arise in the course of playing the game (the root of the tree is the opening situation), and each edge being a move from one situation to another. Figure 13.6 shows a portion of the game tree for Tic-tac-toe. With more complicated games, it can be helpful to think of them this way, and to develop strategies for "looking ahead" to situations that might arise as the result of particular moves, and for deciding on which branches of the tree should be "pruned."

EXERCISE 13.2

1. There is a famous puzzle about a census taker who called at a particular house where his knock was answered by a man. In reply to questions the man informed the census taker that four people lived in the house, including himself, and he told the census taker his age. When asked the ages of the other three, the man replied that the sum of their ages was equal to the house number, while the product of their ages was 1296. The census taker then said he needed one more piece of information, namely whether or not the man was the eldest. The man said he was, and the census taker was able to leave, knowing what he wanted to know. The problem is to determine the ages of the other three.

At first it may appear that the information provided in this problem is not sufficient. There are three unknowns, but only one equation is given, namely, that the product of these unknowns is 1296. Admittedly, the census taker has one other equation because he has been told that the sum of the unknowns equals the house number and he knows the house number. This means the census taker is trying to determine three positive integers that satisfy two equations, since it is natural to assume that the ages must be positive integers. Such a problem will often have a unique solution. However, the census taker needed more information, so his particular problem must have had more than one solution.

In this way, we conclude that there must be two different ways of factoring 1296 and obtaining the same sum for each set of factors. Write a program that will find the required factors, and use the results to obtain the solution to the original puzzle.

2. An Italian mathematician named Leonardo of Pisa, better known as Fibonacci, proposed the following problem more than seven hundred years ago. Suppose that two adult rabbits, one male and one female, are brought together to breed. Suppose that a pair of rabbits gives birth to another pair each month, beginning two months after their own

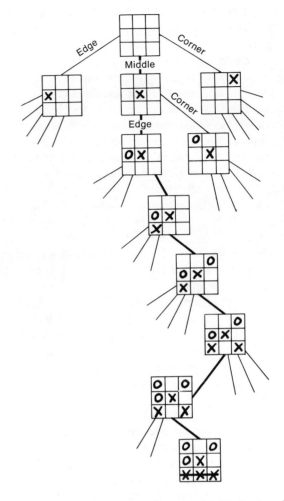

FIG. 13.6 A portion of the game tree for Tic-tac-toe. The heavy path represents a game in which X wins.

birth, and assume that every pair produced in this way consists of one male and one female. How many rabbits will there be at the end of 24 months?

3. Write a program to carry out the straightforward approach to the Instant Insanity problem and use it to determine the solution or solutions, if any.

4. Describe a few modifications in the straightforward approach to Instant Insanity that will reduce the computer time required. Write a program to carry out your modified approach.

5. Can you find all possible solutions of the Instant Insanity puzzle without the help of a computer?

6. Write a program for playing Tic-tac-toe. It is difficult to implement such a program in an interesting way, unless you are able to use an interactive computer facility. However, even without such a facility, the program can be tested by being played against simple-minded strategies such as choosing the next move in some random fashion.

7. Write a program for playing Nim. This game begins with three piles of counters. The players take turns removing counters and the player who picks up the last counter loses. Any number of counters can be picked up in each turn, as long as at least one counter is picked up and provided all are chosen from the same pile. Test your program against another whose strategy is to make random moves.

8. Write a program for playing the game of Oware. This game is played on a board consisting of twelve squares as shown below:

Second Player's Squares

00 00	00 00	00 00	00 00	00 00	00 00
00 00	00 00	00 00	00 00	00 00	00 00

First Player's Squares

At the start of a game each square contains four men, as shown in the diagram. A player's turn consists of picking up all the men in one of his six squares and distributing them counterclockwise, one to a square, beginning with the next square. No men are placed in the square from which they are taken. Then, if the square in which the last man is placed is one of his opponent's squares, and if there are exactly two or three men in that square, all the men in that square are removed. The same rule is applied to the square in which the second last man is placed, then the third last man, and so on, until a square is reached for which the rule does not permit removal of the men. For example, with the following situation:

Second Player's Squares

00		0	00	00 00	0
0	0 0 0	00 00	00	00 0 00	0 0

First Player's Squares

the first player can move the five men in his fifth square. If he does so, he would then leave the following situation for his opponent:

Second Player's Squares

00				00 0 00	00
0	0 0 0	00 00	00		00 00

First Player's Squares

The objective of the game is to capture as many men as possible. The game ends when one player cannot move.

9. A famous puzzle, known as the Towers of Hanoi, involves three posts with a number of discs on one of them, in decreasing order of diameter, as shown in Fig. 13.7. The goal is to move the discs one at a time, from one post to another, so that the discs on any one post are always in decreasing order of diameter, and to end up with all the discs on a post other than where they first began. Write a program that will output a sequence of moves for solving this problem for any given number of discs.

13.3 COMPUTER GRAPHICS

There are many applications in which we would like to display our final results in pictorial form. For example, we may wish to plot a graph, draw a wiring diagram, or make a blueprint. It would be very helpful if the computer could output the results directly in the required form, or at least in a form that can be converted easily to what we want.

The computer can of course be programmed to output graphs on a printer. Only rather simple graphs can be obtained on such devices, however, and special equipment has been developed to produce more satisfactory output. One such piece of equipment is a *plotter,* which is a machine that can trace out the required lines on paper or film according to specifications recorded on

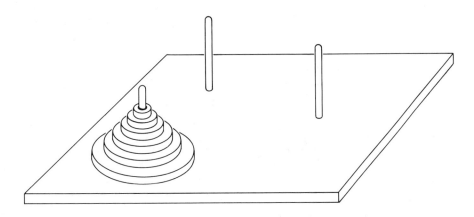

FIG. 13.7   Towers of Hanoi puzzle. (See Question 9.)

magnetic tape. The computer is used to write the specifications on the tape. The tape is then moved from the computer to the plotter and the plotter proceeds to make the required diagram. Other kinds of equipment make it possible to output graphical information directly from the computer. The graphs, line drawings, and so on, are output on special display tubes that look like television screens. If the output displayed in this way is to be preserved, it can be photographed.

Computer graphics can be used in many different areas. One important area is in the production of engineering drawings and another is in the production of movies and art. Cartoon-like movies produced by a computer can be used as a teaching aid. Other computer movies, and computer art as well, can be used merely to produce pleasing results. Most of us tend to overemphasize the economic advantages of computers. We should not ignore the possible direct benefits in terms of making life more pleasant. Perhaps one important reason for planning to have terminals in our homes is to provide artistic experiences, a fourth for bridge, or something to talk with on occasion!

In some of the applications mentioned above it is important to be able to interact with the computer during the development of the results. For example, in many problems of engineering design the user must see part of the design before he can decide what he wants next. He may also want to change some earlier part of the design after some of the other parts have been completed. This kind of interaction is not possible with a plotter, but other graphical display devices make it possible for the designer to see the results of his decisions almost immediately, so that he can make adjustments as he is proceeding. (See Fig. 13.8.) Some devices are considerably more flexible than others. We will not pursue any further the details of how these devices are used. These matters have been mentioned only to provide some motivation for the main purpose of this section, which is to introduce some of the basic ideas needed to develop programs for computer graphics.

Two main problems must be considered. First, the diagrams that are developed must be stored in the computer's memory, which means that we must invent a code for representing the information contained in a diagram. For example, we can represent a point by its coordinates, or a line segment by the coordinates of its endpoints. We must also have a convenient way of representing more complicated pictures.

The second problem that must be considered is the way in which the diagrams are handled. For example, if we already have a diagram, we must have programs for adding lines to it or for changing it in other ways, such as shifting its position, rotating it, or changing its scale. Various aspects of these two main problems will be considered in Exercise 13.3.

FIG. 13.8 Interactive computer graphics. The picture on the TV-like screen can be adjusted by the designer with the help of the computer.

Many other requirements must be considered in a full discussion of computer graphics. For example, in many applications it is necessary to place lettering in the diagrams, and, in fact, the diagram may consist almost entirely of lettering, punctuation, and so on. It is therefore necessary to have programs that can handle such information in a convenient way.

Another requirement in some applications is to handle three-dimensional information. This means, first of all, that we must be able to represent three-dimensional diagrams in the computer's memory and, second, that we must have programs to manipulate such representations. In addition to shifting position, scaling, and so on, we must be able to rotate in three dimensions and to form perspectives and other projections of three-dimensional diagrams. One very interesting problem in this area is the "hidden line" problem. For example, suppose we have a representation of a three-dimensional object, such as a cube, and we wish to output its projection in a particular plane. How do we determine which lines are hidden from view, so that we can omit them from the output?

In many of the important areas of computer graphics, the programs can become quite large and cumbersome. It is likely that a relatively large amount of computer time will be required to solve any realistic problems with these programs. Using computer graphics can therefore be quite expensive, a fact that must be kept in mind. On the other hand, the costs involved in other methods of preparing engineering drawings, in producing movies, and so on, are also very high. Moreover, once the computer method is established, it is much faster than more conventional methods. It is generally believed that computer graphics has an important role to play and that this role is likely to increase considerably as more suitable equipment and better programs and programming languages become available.

EXERCISE 13.3

1. A program is required that will plot points for the graph of a function. It should begin with two numbers, for instance A and B where $A < B$, an increment, and a definition of the function to be plotted, that is, $y = f(x)$. It should output points on the graph for values of x between A and B, in steps of the given increment for x.

The graph should be constructed so that the x values correspond to a position measured vertically down the page and the y values correspond to one of the print positions across the page. The scaling of the y values can be accomplished by determining both the maximum and minimum of the y values and using the known number of print positions. An example of the sort of output that is required is shown in Fig. 13.9. Your documentation should explain very clearly how your program is to be used. In particular, it must explain exactly how the user can specify the values of A, B, the increment, and his choice of function.

2. Suppose that diagrams to be represented are made up entirely of points and line segments in a plane. Describe how you would represent such diagrams in the programming language you are using. Give one representation based on each of the following suggestions:

a) a list of line segments, where each line segment is represented by the coordinates of its endpoints;

b) a list of points, together with an adjacency matrix to indicate which points are joined and which are not;

c) a square array, in which the (i,j)th entry in the array indicates whether or not there is a dot at that point (such a representation is sometimes called a *digitized picture*);

d) a list of triples, where the first two numbers in each triple are the coordinates of a point, and the third

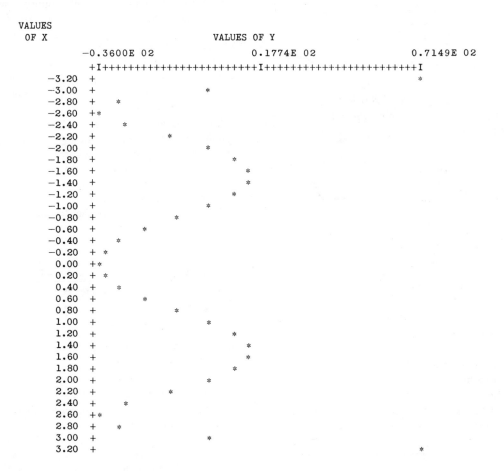

FIG. 13.9 A graph of the function $y = (x^2 - 1)(x^2 - 4)(x^2 - 9)$. Values at $x = -3.2$, -3.0, -2.8, $\ldots$, 3.2 are plotted. Thus $A = -3.2$, $B = 3.2$, and the increment is .2 in this example.

number indicates whether or not there is a line joining this point to the previous one in the list.

3. Write a program or subprogram that will produce a circle, given the desired center and radius. Solve this problem for each of the representations described in Question 2. For (a), (b), and (d), assume that a circle is represented by a regular polygon with 48 sides.

4. Write a program or subprogram that will carry out each of the following operations on diagrams:

a) translate by a specified amount;
b) rotate about a given point by a specified amount;
c) scale by a specified factor, with respect to a specified point; this last operation enables us to shrink diagrams toward, or expand them from, the particular point.

Develop programs for each of the representations described in Question 2 and discuss the relative convenience of the different representations.

5. Develop a program for finding the enclosing rectangle of a diagram and state which of the representations in Question 2 is most convenient for this purpose. The enclosing rectangle of a diagram is the smallest rectangle with sides parallel to the axes that contains the diagram.

6. Suppose that a line segment is represented by the coordinates of its endpoints.

a) Indicate how you would determine whether or not two given line segments intersect.

Intersection   No intersection

b) Develop a program for determining whether two given polygons intersect or not.

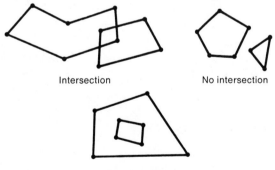

Intersection   No intersection

No intersection

Would knowing the enclosing rectangles be of any help?

c) Develop a program for determining whether or not a given point is inside a given polygon. Assume that the polygon does not cross itself.

7. A problem that arises quite often is that of determining when two diagrams overlap. Discuss the difficulties you see in trying to develop a program for solving this problem. Assume that the diagrams are relatively simple. Does knowing the enclosing rectangles help make the procedure more efficient?

8. Some diagrams can be reproduced reasonably well as output on a printer. Describe the format you would choose and develop programs that will output diagrams that are stored as described in Question 2.

9. Describe one or more ways of representing three-dimensional objects, and give programs for translating, rotating, and scaling such objects.

10. Give a program that will start with a three-dimensional object and a plane, and that will produce the projection of the object in the plane, in terms of one of the representations of Question 2.

11. Discuss one or more ways of representing lettering and punctuation. Your representations can be tested by scaling them to a rather large size and then having them output on the printer with the help of the program developed in Question 8.

12. Write a program that will rotate a given cube in a specified way and then remove the hidden lines.

13. Suppose that we have a digitized picture in which, for simplicity, we assume that there is only one region of dots and that the dots do not surround any other region without dots. This means the region has an outline, the interior of which is entirely filled with dots. Write a program that will begin with such a picture and find the outline.

14. Write a program that will produce a sequence of pictures, where the pictures are successive scenes a few seconds apart, of some particular action. For example, the scenes might show a wheel rolling across the floor or a truck going off in the distance. (For simplicity the truck can be represented by something not much more complicated than a rectangle. Note that 24 frames are needed for each second of a movie film.)

15. A program is required to follow the steps in a solitaire game called Life and to output the resulting sequence of patterns. At the start of the game a number of cells (like the squares on a checkerboard) are occupied by "organisms" (like checkers on the checkerboard). We assume that the checkerboard has a very large number of rows and columns, not just eight. The following are examples of possible beginning patterns:

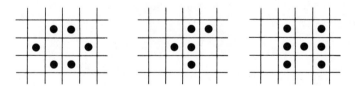

Note that any particular organism can have as many as eight neighbors, including the diagonal ones.

Subsequent patterns (or "generations") are formed according to the following rules:

Survival. Each organism with two or three neighboring organisms survives.

Death. Each with four or more neighbors disappears (dies from overcrowding), while each with zero or one neighbor also disappears (dies from loneliness).

Birth. Each empty cell with organisms in exactly three neighboring cells becomes occupied by a new ornism.

It is easy to determine what happens in some situations. For example, the first one shown above does not change at all—it is a stable population. Another simple example starts with three organisms in a row (horizontal or vertical)—it repeats itself every second generation. However, other sequences of patterns are more complicated and the program can be quite helpful, as is the case with the other two beginning patterns shown above.

This game was invented by the Cambridge mathematician J. H. Conway. For more information and many more examples the reader should consult the October 1970 issue of *Scientific American* (page 120). Further information also appeared in the January, February, and April issues of 1971.

13.4 STRING MANIPULATION

There are many situations in which we are required to handle strings of symbols, or characters. One example arises when we want to carry out relatively straightforward data-processing operations, such as sorting, or counting occurrences of particular substrings.

A second example arises when the string of symbols represents some text material that is eventually going to be printed (and therefore includes special symbols to mark the beginnings of paragraphs, to designate what parts are to be indented, and so on). In this example, we may first want to perform various *text editing* functions, such as insertion and deletion of portions of the text. We would also want to arrange for output of the final version in a convenient form. This last requirement would lead to the need for programs that could right justify the lines of the text, that could provide for the proper paragraphing, paging, page numbering, and so on.

Still another area in which we need programs for handling strings of symbols is in dealing with mathematical expressions. As an example, consider the expression

$$(5.01 + SIN(X))/(2.2 + X)$$

We certainly need programs that can translate such expressions into machine-language instructions for evaluating them. Alternatively, we may want programs that can find the derivatives of such expressions, i.e., that can produce other expressions which are the derivatives of the original expressions. Handling mathematical expressions in either of these two ways requires some analysis which we will not consider here. However, an example of a translator is considered in the following chapter.

Programming languages differ considerably in the ease with which they enable us to manipulate strings of symbols. With some languages it is relatively easy to search for required characters, to make insertions, to *concatenate* strings (that is, to make a single string by joining two separate strings together), and so on. With others, we just have to make do with what is available, and that often turns out to be both awkward and inefficient.

EXERCISE 13.4

1. How can strings of characters be input and output most easily with the programming facility you are using? Consider the input and output of strings of single characters and of strings of small groups of characters. Consider representations within the language itself both in terms of arrays and in terms of linked lists.

2. Describe how you would sort character data with the facility you are using.

3. Suppose that a rather large amount of text, such as the complete works of a particular author, is to be put into a machine-readable form. The purpose is to use the computer for various studies of the material. For example, the computer may be used to prepare a *concordance*, which is a cross-reference showing where particular words are used. A simple special case would be the preparation of an index for a book. Alternatively, it may be used to collect statistics about the frequency of use of certain words and certain word combinations, or about sentence lengths, and so on. Outline some subprograms that would be helpful in such studies. What advice would you give to the person responsible for preparing the machine-readable text? What would be required in the machine-readable material if the computer was expected to collect data which depended on knowing which words were verbs, which were nouns, and so on?

4. Show how to handle some of the basic string manipulation operations when the data is stored in arrays of single characters. In particular, write subprograms, if necessary, to

a) find the first occurrence of a specified character (if any),
b) count the number of occurrences of a specified character,
c) find the first occurrence of a specified substring (if any).

5. Do as in Question 4 when the data is stored in a linked list of single characters. Include subprograms for insertion and deletion in this case.

6. A program is to be developed for "right justifying" paragraphs of text. The program is to accept, as input, some sentences in the English language. All 80 columns of the input cards can be used for the sentences, but it is a good idea to reserve at least one column of each card for special codes to indicate when a new paragraph is to begin, when the input has terminated, or when some other special situation arises. For example, you may wish to have a special code to indicate that information is to be displayed in the middle of a line of output. The procedure should then arrange the characters in such a way as to make the output pleasing to the eye, with a certain number of characters allowed on each line. This number could be a part of the input so that the program could be used to justify type for columns of various widths.

Figure 13.10 shows an example of the sort of output that is required. In this case, only the first three lines are shown of what happens when the string of characters of the preceding paragraph are used as input, and 36 characters per line are specified for the output, with an indentation of 5 spaces at the beginning of each paragraph. Note that extra spaces have been inserted in the first and third lines to ensure that they are right justified. (The last line of a paragraph should not be justified.)

Whenever printed material is to be justified it is customary to hyphenate a word at the end of a line if this improves the appearance. However, it is extremely difficult to incorporate this feature in a program and we therefore do not suggest it as part of the project.

7. Write a program that will input several paragraphs of text material and that will then insert and delete portions of text as required by further input cards. It should also be capable of joining paragraphs together and splitting others into two. Once all such changes are completed, the program should right justify the paragraphs and output the final result. Indicate what changes could be made in your program so that it will also separate the output into numbered pages and provide a table of contents. A major requirement for this question is to provide clear specifications about how the program is to be used; for example, the computer could be expected to provide appropriate line numbers for the text material, but it is still necessary to decide on a convenient way for referring to individual positions within a particular line, in order to indicate exactly where insertions or deletions are to be made.

8. There must be some features of the programming language you are using that you would like to change. One possibility is to invent an improvement of your own, which can be fairly easily translated into an equivalent form in the language you are using. Such a translator is usually called a *preprocessor* and it is proposed that you develop

```
     A PROGRAM IS  TO  BE  DEVELOPED
FOR "RIGHT JUSTIFYING" PARAGRAPHS OF
TEXT.  THE PROGRAM IS TO ACCEPT,  AS
```

FIG. 13.10 The first three lines of output from a program for "right justifying" paragraphs of text. In this case the input started with the text of Question 6.

a small preprocessor for enhancing the facilities that are available to you, in some way that you consider to be helpful.

13.5 FURTHER REMARKS

The purpose of this chapter has been to show how computers can be used in four major areas that give rise to nonnumerical problems. The examples are an indication of the wide variety of computer applications in nonnumerical areas.

With numerical applications the emphasis is on techniques for analyzing the effects of truncation and roundoff errors and on the development of reasonably efficient procedures that attempt to minimize these effects. With nonnumerical applications the emphasis shifts to a study of how to represent the data and of how to develop reasonably efficient methods for manipulating the data. We are also interested in efficiency in both areas but the possibilities with nonnumerical problems are much more dramatic than they are with numerical ones. A typical nonnumerical problem is to find the best arrangement of a number of objects from among a very large number of possible arrangements. With n objects it often happens that a straightforward examination of all possible arrangements requires an amount of work proportional to $n!$. On the other hand, it may be possible to design an algorithm for which the amount of work is proportional to n^2 or n^3. The value of $n!$ is so much greater than the value of n^2 or n^3 for large values of n, even for moderately large values of n, that the straightforward method is likely to be completely unacceptable. By contrast, the relative efficiency of two different numerical methods is usually only a rather modest factor. One method might be twice as efficient as another, or even ten times, but only very rarely in proportion to $n!$ as compared to n^3.

Another important difference between nonnumerical and numerical problems is that the computer is not nearly as well adapted to nonnumerical calculations as it is to numerical ones. For example, in looking for arrangements or patterns of a special kind, the computer usually has to plod laboriously through large masses of data, whereas human beings often are able to discern a particular pattern almost immediately. On the other hand, with typical numerical calculations, a human being must follow steps substantially the same as those followed by a computer. The computer then has the advantage because of its much greater speed.

CHAPTER **14**

Interpreters and Translators

The final computer applications we consider are in the area of computer science itself. The main practical objective in this area is to make it easy for someone to write programs and have them implemented on a computer. If the programs are to be easy to write, the programming language must be convenient for the person writing the program. It must also be well suited to the problem being solved. The programming language is therefore not likely to be the machine's own language and some kind of *processor* is required before the program can be run.

In some cases the program being run is merely copied into the computer's memory and the processor causes the individual statements in that program to be analyzed and executed. We say that the statements are *interpreted* and the processor is called an *interpreter*. Otherwise, the program being run is first translated from the language in which it is written to some other language. The translation process may go through several stages. In the final stage of this process, the program usually appears in the machine's own language, although it can appear instead in a language which needs to be interpreted.

Interpreters are considered in the first section of this chapter. *Assemblers,* which are the simplest examples of translators, are considered in the second section. The next two sections are concerned mainly with *compilers,* which are processors that translate programs written in higher-level languages such as Fortran, Basic,

PL/I, Cobol, and so on, into machine- or assembly-language programs.

These topics are not treated in great depth. What we cover is intended only to convey some understanding of the basic ideas. This will enable us to appreciate some of the underlying problems and to see some of the ideas and techniques used by computer scientists in trying to solve these problems. We should also develop a better appreciation for the limitations of the processors we use.

To make good use of interpreters and translators it is necessary to have an *operating system* that keeps the computer working effectively on the various jobs required of it. The operating system connects each job to the appropriate processor, schedules work for the machine, looks after what has to be done when jobs run into trouble and have to be terminated, keeps accounting records, and so on. We will not discuss this topic any further. It is mentioned here only to help complete the overall picture of what is needed to make it easy and convenient for a user to write programs and have them implemented on a computer.

14.1 INTERPRETERS

A program to be interpreted is first placed in the memory of the computer. As each statement of the program is to be executed, the interpreter examines the statement to determine what has to be done. Then the interpreter carries out the necessary operation or operations.

For example, let us suppose we wish to write an interpreter for the simple hypothetical machine described in Appendix A. We require a program that will read in a sequence of statements like the following:

```
000  +0000030007
001  +0000030008
002  +0000010007
 .        .
 .        .
 .        .
```

and that will then proceed to carry out the instructions in this machine-language program. We would probably want to require an ID card as well, and some way of marking the end of the program, and hence the beginning of the data cards (if any), so that our interpreter would know when to stop reading in the program and to start execution. An outline of such an interpreter is given in Fig. 14.1.

We can also consider developing an interpreter for the machine language of a real machine, possibly one we are planning to build. The interpreter simulates the proposed machine and enables us to test it before construction begins. We can experiment with different designs in order to determine which is best for our purposes. One good feature of interpreters is that they are easy to modify, making it easy to try out different designs.

Another situation in which an interpreter for the machine language of a real machine is useful arises when a machine is being replaced. It often happens in practice that we want to run, on the new machine, programs that were written for the old one. The cost of converting the programs written for the old machine may be substantial and we may not want to run these programs very many times. In such a situation, interpreting programs on the new machine may be the least expensive method of having them run.

An interpreter can also be developed for programs written in a higher-level language to provide a means of testing the language before going to the trouble of developing a compiler for it. The main disadvantage of interpreters, namely their slowness in executing programs, is likely to be particularly noticeable with interpreters for higher-level languages. On the other hand, their slowness may not be a serious disadvantage when lower-level languages, such as the simple machine language of Appendix A, are being interpreted. In fact, interpreters can be the most efficient processors in some situations, especially if the programs being interpreted are very short.

```
/The program to be interpreted is first loaded; when com-
    pleted, only data cards (if any) will be left for subsequent
    reading. It is assumed that memory locations MEMORY
    (000), MEMORY (001),..., MEMORY (999) are available,
    along with the ACCUMULATOR and an instruction address
    register IAR./
Input ID card
Loop
      Input card
. . . If (end-of-program card) exit loop
      Store information in specified part of MEMORY
End

/Initialize IAR and proceed to execute program/
IAR = −1
Loop
.     IAR = IAR + 1
.     Pick up MEMORY (IAR) and determine OPCODE and
.          ADDRESS
.     If (OPCODE is 10)
.          ACCUMULATOR = MEMORY (ADDRESS)
.     (OPCODE is 11)
.          MEMORY (ADDRESS) = ACCUMULATOR
.     (OPCODE is 20)
.          ACCUMULATOR = ACCUMULATOR
.             + MEMORY (ADDRESS)
.          .                .
.          .                .
.     (OPCODE is 40)
. . . . . . . . Exit loop
.     (OPCODE is 50)
.          IAR = ADDRESS − 1
.     (OPCODE is 51)
.          If (ACCUMULATOR < 0) IAR = ADDRESS − 1
.          .                .
.          .                .
.     End if
End loop
Stop
```

FIG. 14.1 Outline of an interpreter for the hypothetical machine of Appendix A. Each OPCODE is defined in Table A.1. No provision has been made for any options, exceptional conditions, or errors in the program being interpreted.

It is fairly easy to write an interpreter, at least in principle. By this we mean that it is fairly easy to write a program that merely causes our computer to execute correct programs written in a specified programming language, such as the language of another machine, without first translating the programs to be executed. However, it is more difficult to write an interpreter that is going to be used in practice. The reason is that a useful interpreter must also cope with the many practical difficulties that arise because the programs being interpreted are likely to be incorrect. For example, the interpreter must detect invalid operation codes and output appropriate diagnostics. It must be able to terminate execution of a program that has run for too long a time. It must also be able to cope with a program that manages to destroy part of itself. It is generally much more difficult to develop an interpreter that is "fail safe" than it is to develop an interpreter that is merely capable of executing correct programs.

EXERCISE 14.1

1. Develop an interpreter based on the outline presented in Fig. 14.1. It is intended that the interpreter handle all correct programs based on the operation codes defined in Table A.1 of Appendix A.

2. Extend the interpreter developed in Question 1 so that it will handle the full SIMON Language, whose operation codes are summarized in Table B.2 of Appendix B.

3. Make changes in the interpreter of Question 1 or Question 2 in order to make it provide an optional listing of the program being interpreted, along with an appropriate heading, as well as headings for the beginning and ending of execution. Discuss what further changes you would make in order that the interpreter be as "fail safe" as possible. For example, how would you try to provide protection against invalid input, as might, for example, be caused by mispunched cards? What would you do about overflow, or attempts to divide by zero? Have you any suggestions about providing for limits on the number of instructions to be executed, limits on the number of lines to be output, or checking to make sure that IAR does not exceed 999? Are there other possibilities that you might provide for?

4. Incorporate as much as you think is reasonable from the discussion in Question 3 in the interpreter of Question 1 or of Question 2. The result should be a package that is reasonably useful for someone wanting to try out programs written in the machine language of Appendix A, or in the full SIMON language of Appendix B. A write-up for the user should be provided. It should include a clear indication of what error messages the user can expect and the circumstances under which he can expect them.

5. Provide a write-up of your interpreter for someone who intends to modify it. Include an explanation of how new instructions can be added and illustrate by showing how instructions for floating-point arithmetic can be added.

6. Develop an interpreter for the simple assembly language described in Section B.1.

7. Describe a simple higher-level language of your own invention and write an interpreter to execute programs written in this language. The purpose of this question is to illustrate the general idea of such an interpreter and no attempt need be made to produce a very extensive language. It is suggested that you choose an area, such as statistics, file maintenance, graphics, or text editing, and define a few statements of a kind that would be useful in the area. For example, a movie-making language might result in programs such as the following:

```
INPUT   P
OUTPUT  P
SCALE   P   90 10 05
MOVE R  P    4
OUTPUT  P
SCALE   P   90 14 05
MOVE R  P    4
        .
        .
        .
```

This program is intended first to input a picture and denote it by P. (We assume that a picture consists of a set of points on a grid of 50×50 points. An input format will have to be described.) Then a succession of pictures is output, beginning with a copy of the original. The original is followed by a sequence of pictures, each of which is obtained from its predecessor by scaling it by a factor of .90 and shifting it four units to the right. The point about which the scaling is to take place is (10,5) on the first occasion and it moves to the right with the picture on subsequent occasions.

14.2 ASSEMBLERS

When computers first began to be used it was realized that programming in machine language was an extremely tedious process. One of the most important steps in trying to make programming easier was to introduce mnemonic codes in place of the machine operation codes and addresses. The use of mnemonic codes leads to a programming language almost equivalent to machine language but very much easier to read. An example of such a language is described in Appendix B. A program for translating from such a language into the corresponding machine language is called an *assembler*.

As indicated in Appendix B the main task of an assembler is to translate assembly-language instructions into machine-language instructions that correspond almost one-to-one with what appears in the assembly-language program. The assembler uses a table to determine the appropriate operation codes and it must assign and keep track of addresses. It must also be able to handle the pseudo-operation codes of the assembly language. Most assemblers do even more; for example, they can usually provide the appropriate linkage with subprograms.

As with interpreters, the difficulty in writing an assembler is not so much in developing one that can translate correct assembly-language programs as in making it fail safe. It must be able to handle incorrect programs in some sensible way.

EXERCISE 14.2

1. Develop an assembler for programs written in the SAP assembly language described in Appendix B. The objective is to develop an assembler that will handle correct assembly-language programs.

2. Discuss what changes you would make to the assembler in Question 1 to make it fail safe. Describe each difficulty separately and show what you would add to the assembler to take care of the difficulty.

3. Develop a SAP assembler that is fail safe and provide a write-up for the user. The write-up should explain what error messages the user can expect.

4. Suppose that an assembler has portions of a program that it can copy into a machine-language program and thereby insert an open subprogram into what it is assembling. Show how this can be incorporated into the assembler developed in Question 1, and illustrate with an example for interchanging the values of two variables. This means, for example, that if the addresses of I and J are 624 and 732, respectively, and if the assembler has reached location 070, then it should translate

        INT I,J

into the following sequence:

```
070  +0000010624    Copy I into accumulator
071  +0000011077    Store I in temporary location
072  +0000010732    Copy J into accumulator
073  +0000011624    Store J in location for I
074  +0000010077    Copy I from temporary location
075  +0000011732    Store I in location for J
076  +0000050078    Jump over temporary location
077  +0000000000    Temporary location
078  ──────────
```

5. Consider the higher-level programming language you developed in Question 7 of Exercise 14.1 and write a program for translating from that higher-level language into the more familiar higher-level language that you are currently using.

14.3 POLISH NOTATION

The first stored-program computers became available beginning in the late 1940's. However, it was not until the mid-1950's that higher-level programming languages began to be widely used, following the introduction of the first version of Fortran. The purpose of this section and the one following is to give a brief indication of how a translator for such a higher-level language can be constructed.

One key problem in translating from higher-level programming languages into machine or assembly languages is the handling of expressions. The problem is to translate each expression into a sequence of machine- or assembly-language instructions that can evaluate the expression. For the sake of illustration, we will consider the problem of translating simplified expressions such as

$$(I-J)*K+L-M/N$$

into the assembly language of Appendix B. The expression is simplified in that each operand is a variable name consisting of a single letter, only binary arithmetic operators are used, and no blanks are allowed. We can drop some of these restrictions later.

An important preliminary step in the translation process is to convert the expression into what is called *Polish notation*. (A Polish mathematician, Lukasiewicz, was the first to use such a notation. The notation is currently used in some hand calculators. However, most hand calculators use the more familiar *algebraic* form.)

The Polish form of an expression can be introduced with a few examples. The Polish *postfix* form of $I-J$ is $IJ-$. (The *prefix* form is $-IJ$ but we will consider only postfix forms. The algebraic form, $I-J$, is called the *infix* form in this context.) The postfix form of $(I-J)*K$ is $IJ-K*$. The rule for converting a Polish postfix form back to its usual mathematical form is as follows:

Read the Polish postfix form from left to right. As soon as an operator is reached, it is placed between the preceding two variables and the resulting infix expression is enclosed in parentheses, if necessary. The resulting infix expression is then treated as a single variable and the scan continues until the conversion is complete.

Thus, when we scan $IJ-K*$, the first operator encountered is $-$. We place the $-$ between I and J to obtain $I-J$, which we enclose in parentheses. We now treat $(I-J)$ as a single variable. Continuing the scan we reach the operator $*$. We place $*$ between $(I-J)$ and K to obtain $(I-J)*K$ as required.

The rule can be used to show that

$$IJ-K*L+MN/-$$

is the Polish postfix form of the original expression. When the $-$ is encountered, we replace $IJ-$ with $(I-J)$ and treat the latter as a single variable, which leads us to

$$(I-J)K*L+MN/-$$

⎵

↑

Treat as single variable

We continue the scan and when the $*$ is encountered, we are led to

$$(I-J)*KL+MN/-$$

⎵

↑

Single variable

We could have enclosed $(I-J)*K$ in parentheses to obtain $((I-J)*K)$ but it is not necessary in this case. Encountering the $+$ leads to

$$(I-J)*K+LMN/-$$

Single variable

When the **/** is reached, the two preceding variables are M and N. According to the rule, we replace MN**/** with M**/**N and enclose in parentheses if necessary. The parentheses are not necessary here and we are led to

$$(I-J)*K+LM/N-$$

Single variable   Single variable

Finally, when the − is encountered we are led to

$$(I-J)*K+L-M/N$$

as required. It is obvious that parentheses are not needed in this last step.

The rule just described can be used to show that the following relationships are valid:

Usual Infix Form	*Polish Postfix Form*
I/J+K/L	IJ/KL/+
(I/J)+(K/L)	IJ/KL/+
((I+J)*K+L)*M+N	IJ+K*L+M*N+
(I/J)/K	IJ/K/
I/(J/K)	IJK//

Note that the Polish form contains no parentheses. It is a "parenthesis-free" notation for expressions.

The rule described above enables us to convert a Polish expression into an equivalent infix form. What we require is a rule that can be used to go the other way. We need a rule for converting expressions into corresponding Polish forms. (We continue to consider only simplified expressions.) An algorithm known as the *shunting-yard* algorithm can be used for this purpose. A pictorial representation of this algorithm is given in Fig. 14.2, where the expression I−(J+K)*L is shown as the input string waiting to be converted.

To explain the algorithm we think of the input string as a train. As the symbols in the input string reach the "Y" in the track, they are sent directly along the track to become part of the output string or they are shunted onto the siding. Symbols can also be moved from the siding to become part of the output string. The siding can obviously be represented by a stack.

All that is required to complete the explanation of the algorithm is to state the rules for determining how the symbols are to be moved. The rules are as follows:

1. Operands at the front of the input string go directly to the output string.

2. A left parenthesis at the front of the input string is stacked.

3. A right parenthesis at the front of the input string causes operators to be moved from the top of the stack to the output string, if necessary, until a left parenthesis appears at the top of the stack. The left and right parentheses are then discarded.

4. Operators at the front of the input string cause operators in the stack to be moved to the output string until the top item in the stack is one of lower priority than the operator at the front of the input string, according to the following table:

Symbol	Priority
(	0
+ −	1
* /	2

If the stack is empty or the top of the stack is an item of lower priority, an operator at the front of the input string is stacked.

5. When the input string is empty, all items remaining in the stack are moved to the output string.

The shunting-yard algorithm is illustrated in Fig. 14.3, using I−(J+K)*L as the expression.

EXERCISE 14.3

1. Write a program that will implement the shunting-yard algorithm to convert simplified expressions into their postfix form. Make a clear statement of exactly what input your program can handle properly and the format in which it must be presented.

2. Do you believe the shunting-yard algorithm does what it is supposed to do? Why? If you find a collection of successful examples reasonably convincing, you should state which ones you used. Then show how you could modify the program to work correctly on all the examples you have given, yet fail on some other example. If the examples alone are not completely convincing what else is

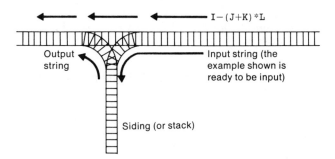

FIG. 14.2 The shunting-yard algorithm for converting expressions into their corresponding Polish postfix forms. The five rules given in the text are needed to complete the description.

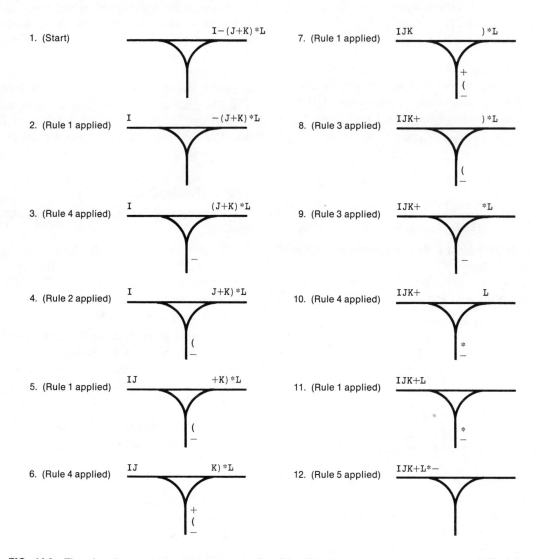

FIG. 14.3 The shunting-yard algorithm converts I − (J + K) *L into its Polish postfix form IJK+L*−.

there about the algorithm that makes you believe it to be correct? Do you think a proof of its correctness is possible?

3. Discuss ways in which you would modify the program in Question 1 so that it will do something sensible if the input is not a valid expression. Can you guarantee that your program will always produce either a valid Polish form if the input is valid or an error message if the expression is invalid?

4. Modify the program in Question 1 so that it will be able to handle more complicated expressions. State exactly what the new program can handle. It should at least be able to deal with inserted blanks, variable names of more than one character, and operands that are constants.

5. Modify the program in Question 1 so that it will handle exponentiation and assignment. Use whatever symbols you wish for these operators. For example, use $ for

exponentiation and = for assignment. One very elegant way to handle these two operators is to treat them like other operators except that exponentiation is given priority 3 and assignment, priority −1. As an example, the assignment statement

    I=J$L+K$L

should be converted into the following postfix form:

    IJLKL+=

14.4 COMPILERS

In the preceding section we described an algorithm for converting a simplified expression into its corresponding Polish postfix form. This is the first stage in translating an expression into a sequence of machine- or assembly-language instructions for evaluating the expression. The remaining stage is quite a bit less complicated because the rule for evaluating an expression is so simple when the expression is in Polish form.

To illustrate the final stage of the translation process we continue to restrict our attention to simplified expressions. This means they contain no constants, variable names consist of single alphabetic characters, and operators are binary. It also means that only the four arithmetic operators are used. Blanks are not permitted in simplified expressions but we can ignore this fact because we assume that the first stage of the translation process has already been completed. Any blanks that might have appeared in the original expression have therefore already been removed.

The task of the final stage of the translation process is to produce a sequence of machine- or assembly-language instructions for evaluating an expression that is already in its postfix form. To be specific, our objective will be to produce sequences of SAP assembly-language instructions. We will concentrate first on describing an algorithm that works correctly but is as simple as possible; that is, for the moment we will not worry about its efficiency.

An algorithm for translating postfix forms into suitable sequences of SAP instructions is shown in Fig. 14.4. The string of symbols in the postfix form is scanned from left to right. Variable names are placed in a stack until an operator is encountered. As soon as an operator is found, the following three assembly-language instructions are output:

L   v2 { v2 is the second variable name from the top of the stack.

op v1 { op is the mnemonic code for the operator and v1 is the variable name at the top of the stack.

ST Tn { n is the value of the counter N and Tn is the nth temporary variable name.

The process is illustrated in Fig. 14.5. The first operator to be encountered there is +. At this stage, K and J occupy the top and second from top positions in the stack, respectively. The instructions

```
L   J
A   K
ST  T1
```

are output. Once the appropriate three instructions have been output and the two variable names have been removed from the stack, the nth temporary variable name is placed on the top of the stack. The scan then proceeds as before. The process continues until the end of the postfix form is reached.

```
/Assume at the start that the sequence of symbols is in postfix
    form, followed by a symbol which is not a variable name
    or an operator. Begin by initializing the counter N, which
    will be used to designate names of temporary variables./
N = 1
Loop
.   Get new symbol
.   If (symbol is variable name)
.        Place symbol on top of stack
.   (symbol is an operator)
.        Output appropriate 3 instructions
.        Remove top two symbols from stack
.        Place Nth temporary name on stack
.        N = N + 1
.   else
. . . . . . . . . Exit loop
.   End if
End loop
Stop
```

FIG. 14.4 An algorithm for translating postfix forms into sequences of instructions for evaluating the expressions.

One of the first points to be noted about this process is that it does not produce particularly efficient programs. For example, the two instructions

```
ST  T1
L   T1
```

could have been eliminated entirely. Moreover, it was not necessary to use different temporary names in this example. However, the process does produce a valid

Output		n	Stack	Postfix form	Action just completed
		1		IJK+L*−	Ready to examine symbols from left to right
		1	I	JK+L*−	Next symbol was variable name so placed in stack
		1	J I	K+L*−	Next symbol was variable name so placed in stack
		1	K J I	+L*−	Next symbol was variable name so placed in stack
L A ST	J K T1	2	T1 I	L*−	Next symbol was operator so three instructions output and T1 placed in stack
		2	L T1 I	*−	Next symbol was variable name so placed in stack
L M ST	T1 L T2	3	T2 I	−	Next symbol was operator so three instructions output and T2 placed in stack
L S ST	I T2 T3	4	T3		Next symbol was operator so three instructions output and T3 placed in stack
		4	T3		Next symbol was neither variable nor operator so process was stopped

FIG. 14.5 The algorithm in Fig. 14.4 is applied to a postfix form to produce appropriate assembly-language instructions.

translation. Any process that produces more efficient results will probably be more complicated. It may therefore produce the translation more slowly and make it more difficult to ensure that the algorithm is correct.

With the algorithm of Section 14.3 and the one described here, we are able to translate simple mathematical expressions into assembly-language programs that will evaluate those expressions. This is an important part of a compiler, but it is only a very small part of a complete compiler. The algorithms described in these two sections need to be extended considerably if we wish to translate more general expressions. For example, we must be able to handle variables of different types and variable names of different lengths. We must also be able to handle subscripted variables and functions. Once assignment statements have been looked after, we must consider how to translate all other kinds of statements and how to organize the complete process. We have concentrated on expressions because it is easier to see, at least in principle, how the other statements should be translated than it is to see how expressions are translated.

It should be emphasized that an algorithm that merely translates correct programs is of very limited use. The algorithm must cope in some sensible way with incorrect programs. We may also require it to produce efficient translations.

EXERCISE 14.4

1. Write a program to carry out the algorithm described in Fig. 14.4 for translating postfix forms to assembly-language instructions.

2. Were you able to guarantee that only valid postfix forms would be produced by the program developed in Question 3 of Exercise 14.3? If not, show how you would modify the program in Question 1 of this exercise so that it can cope with invalid forms.

3. Develop a program for translating assignment statements into sequences of assembly-language instructions. Assume that all variable names are only single characters, that there are no blanks or constants, and that only the four binary arithmetic operations are used.

4. It has been pointed out that the algorithm described in this section produces sequences of instructions that can be inefficient. Two examples of such inefficiency were noted. Show how to overcome each of these inefficiencies. Can you indicate any other ways in which the resulting instructions might still be inefficient? Give an example of an expression for which an algorithm designed to produce efficient sequences of instructions requires three temporary variable names.

5. Show how you would extend the program in Question 3 so that it will be able to handle blanks, variable

length names, and constants. What other features would you require of such a program if it is to be useful in practice?

6. Write a program that will input expressions such as might be presented to a hand calculator (for example,

$$6/7 + 3*14/(25 - 734)$$

illustrates what might be considered) and that will calculate and output the corresponding value. State precisely what your program will accept as input. What precautions have you taken in case the input is not a valid expression?

7. Some compilers try to produce very efficient assembly-language programs. One often-used device is to remove common subexpressions from the expressions in the program being compiled. The result is equivalent to replacing an assignment statement such as

$$J = (K*L*M*N + 3)*7 + M/(K*L*M*N + 3)$$

with the following two statements:

$$I = K*L*M*N + 3$$
$$J = I*7 + M/I$$

A key step in this process is to find common subexpressions. Give a program that can find two common substrings in a given string of symbols whenever such substrings exist. State clearly exactly what your program is able to do.

8. Write a program that can translate logical expressions into corresponding assembly-language programs.

9. So far our discussion has been concerned almost entirely with the translation of expressions and assignment statements. Describe a few other features of the programming language with which you are most familiar and indicate how you would translate them into assembly-language programs. Write a program that is able to input another program written in your particular programming language and that will determine what feature is associated with each statement.

10. Describe a very simple higher-level programming language. Call it "Minilanguage" and write a minicompiler for it. The language can, for example, be a very simple subset of whatever language you are using. Only simplified expressions need be allowed, except that constants should be included. Only very much simplified versions of input and output statements need be allowed. Comment statements can be included without much extra trouble and so can inserted blanks. The format for all statements in Minilanguage should be very restricted so that the compiler is kept as simple as possible. The minicompiler should be able to compile most of the programs discussed in Chapter 2 of this book. Give a precise description of exactly what the compiler is able to handle.

14.5 CONCLUDING REMARKS

This chapter has been only a brief presentation of the problems and techniques that arise in the development of language processors, particularly interpreters and translators. As has been the case with all the application areas considered in this book, we have necessarily been restricted to presenting only an introductory treatment of the topic. In particular, it has not been possible to treat the ever present difficulties that arise in "real life" because of the much larger scale of problems that have to be handled in actual practice.

Nevertheless, we hope that we have given at least some idea of the intriguing and challenging problems that arise in the development of language processors. It is certainly an area in which a great deal of work still needs to be done, especially if we are to be able to develop better programming languages in the future, and to depend on the construction of dependable processors —hopefully, processors which are correct, which are able to fail safe in helpful ways, and which are at the same time reasonably efficient.

Answers to Selected Questions in Part III

CHAPTER 8

Exercise 8.1

1. A bound on the error when the first 12 terms of the series for e are used as an approximation for e is $(1/12!) \times (13/12)$, which is less than 3×10^{-9}. With 13 terms our bound is approximately 1.7×10^{-10}, and with 14 terms it is approximately 1.2×10^{-11}, so we would need 14 terms to guarantee an error of no more than 10^{-10}.

2. We could guarantee a truncation error of no more than 10^{-3} in $\pi/4$ if the first neglected term is $1/1001$, which would mean using the first 500 terms.

3. In the following graph

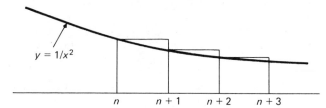

we note that the sum of the rectangular areas is greater than the corresponding area under the curve, i.e.,

$$\frac{1}{n^2} + \frac{1}{(n+1)^2} + \frac{1}{(n+2)^2} + \cdots > \int_n^\infty \frac{1}{x^2}\, dx = \frac{1}{n}.$$

Similarly, it can be seen that

$$\frac{1}{n^2} + \frac{1}{(n+1)^2} + \frac{1}{(n+2)^2} + \cdots < \int_{n-1}^\infty \frac{1}{x^2}\, dx = \frac{1}{n-1}.$$

The required result can be derived from these two inequalities. The resulting bound on the error, $1/(n(n-1))$, is approximately 1.008×10^{-3} when $n = 32$ and 9.5×10^{-4} when $n = 33$, so we would have to take $n = 33$ to be able to guarantee an error bound of no more than 10^{-3}.

5. In the example of Fig. 8.2 it is probably not worthwhile arranging to take fewer terms when x is small; there aren't very many terms anyway, and the cost of making tests to determine when to stop would probably cancel any savings that might result from reducing the number of terms. (An example where savings can be obtained from this idea is given later in Question 8.) However, precomputing the coefficients and using Horner's rule would provide a real increase in speed. This would be especially true if the approximation is evaluated directly, without using any explicit loop structure. If the precomputed coefficients are denoted by a, b, c, d, and e, and the value of x^2 is also precomputed, and denoted by y, then the program can simply evaluate the expression

$$(((ey + d)y + c)y + b)y + a.$$

The coefficients would of course be different for the two functions, and the polynomial approximation for the sine would also require a final multiplication by x.

6. The main source of difficulty arises in reducing the value of x to an interval near the origin. If we use the interval $[0, 2\pi]$, the equation which causes the difficulty is $x - 2n\pi = x'$. If x is large, there can be a cancellation of several significant digits in calculating x'. For example, if x is greater than 1000, there could be a loss of about 3 significant decimal digits in calculating x'. Any small relative error originally present in x (such as a roundoff error), and any relative roundoff errors in calculating x' could be magnified by a factor of 1000 or so. By the mean value theorem, $\Delta\sin(x') = \cos(\xi)\Delta x'$, so the error in $\sin(x')$ could be comparable to the error in x'. For large x, this is likely to be the major source of error in the approximation to $\sin(x)$.

7. The remainder term is bounded in magnitude by $2^n/n!$, for x in the interval $[0,2]$. By trying a few values of n, it can be seen that 10 is the smallest value of n for which this bound is no more than $.0005$.

8.
```
/Given x, tolerance/
sum = 1
i = 1
nextterm = −x
Loop while (|nextterm| > tolerance)
    sum = sum + nextterm
    i = i + 1
    nextterm = −(nextterm × x)/i
End loop
/"sum" approximates e⁻ˣ to within specified
    "tolerance"/
```

9. For work with decimal arithmetic, we can write $e^x = e^{n\log_e 10 + x'} = 10^n e^{x'}$. We can therefore reduce the problem of approximating e^x to the problem of approximating $e^{x'}$. By choosing n in an appropriate way, we can make sure that x' is in a small interval over which we have an adequate polynomial approximation.

11. It can be shown that, over the interval given, the error in this case is bounded in magnitude by the first term neglected.

Exercise 8.2

2. With a subinterval of length $1/2^3$ the approximation is 2.30192; with $1/2^4$ it is 2.30237. Incidentally, the rule for estimating the error ($1/3$ of the difference between two approximations to the integral is an approximation to the error) is the same for the midpoint method as it is for the trapezoidal method.

3. The result is an obvious one, based on geometrical considerations, for any integrand that is concave upward. The reverse rule is true if the integrand is concave downward.

4. The expression for the error in applying the trapezoidal rule does not hold for (d) and (e) because f'' does not exist at one point in each of the intervals of integration. (In fact, even f' fails to exist.) However, it is still possible that the calculated results are reasonably good approximations; in any event, a modification of the theoretical analysis would be needed before any definite conclusions could be drawn.

5. A straightforward application of the formulas in this section will show that h must be no larger than about .004 if we are to guarantee that the error in $\int_1^{20} dx/x$ does not exceed .00005. By adding up the separate contributions from the subintervals [1,2], [2,3], [3,4] . . . , this value of h can be improved to about .015.

8. The force is proportional to $1/r^2$, where r is the distance from the center of the earth. The work done is therefore $C\int_{6500}^{7000} 2000 \, dr/r^2$ where C is a proportionality factor. With the units we have chosen, it can be shown the C is approximately 4×10^{18} in order to produce a result in ergs. However, the main point of the question is to find an approximation to the integral $\int_{6500}^{7000} dr/r^2$. This particular integral can be evaluated exactly (it is $1/6500 - 1/7000 = 1/91000$), and this can be used as a check on the numerical integration; in many applications, the integrals cannot be evaluated exactly, and we are forced to calculate approximations.

9. A trapedoizal rule could be used with each subinterval in an obvious way, except that some modification will be needed in the first and last subintervals if the force has not been measured at the endpoints. We cannot guarantee anything about the accuracy unless we are willing to make some assumption about the smoothness of the force between points of measurement, and of course about the accuracy with which the force and distance measurements are made.

Exercise 8.3

1. /Method of bisection, given A,B, the function F, and a TOLERANCE.
Assume F(A) and F(B) have opposite signs.
Purpose is to use bisection until obtaining a subinterval for which F = 0 at its midpoint, or whose length is less than or equal to TOLERANCE./
X1 = A
X2 = B
Loop
    If(F((X1 + X2)/2) = 0 or |X1 − X2| ≤
                    TOLERANCE)
. . . . .Exit loop
    (F((X1 + X2)/2) and F(X1) differ in sign)
        X2 = (X1 + X2)/2

else
    X1 = (X1 + X2)/2
  End if
End loop
/Value of (X1 + X2)/2 is required result/

With regard to accuracy, the slope of F at the result can be quite informative. For example, with (c) we can take the function F to be $x - \cos(x)$. Its slope is $1 + \sin(x)$, which will certainly be >1 near the solution point, since it can easily be seen from graphs of x and $\cos(x)$ that the solution point must be between 0 and $\pi/2$. With a slope >1, the zero of F is known to within TOLERANCE, provided of course that we can neglect the small inaccuracies in evaluating F itself.

2. Provision must be made in the program to avoid using a denominator that is zero, or even one that is extremely small.

3. The method of functional iteration converges with each of the suggested functions.

4. In making comparisons, the points to be considered should include ease of choosing starting values and of coping with exceptional conditions (such as zero denominators), ease of extending to situations in which values for which F has opposite signs are not known and also of extending to complex roots, ease of proving the program works correctly, and efficiency.

8. We can eliminate y between the two equations to obtain

$$x^2 + x + 4/x^2 - 10 = 0.$$

This equation has four roots.

9.

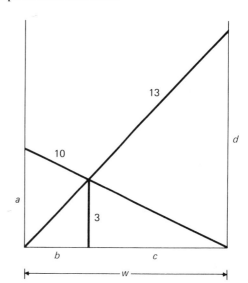

The required width is w. We have $w = b + c$. Two other equations follow from the theorem of Pythagoras, namely $a^2 + w^2 = 10^2$ and $d^2 + w^2 = 13^2$. Two equations can also be obtained using similar triangles, namely $3w = ac$ and $3w = bd$. A fourth degree equation for w^2 can be derived by eliminating a, b, c, and d from these five equations.

13. The equation to be solved for the rate of interest, i, is

$$(1 + i)^{10} + (1 + i)^9 + \cdots + (1 + i)^2 + (1 + i) = 20.$$

Summing the series, this can be rewritten as

$$(1 + i)((1 + i)^{10} - 1) = 20i.$$

By experimenting with a few values of i, it can be shown that the required root lies between .1230 and .1231, so that the required rate of interest is just over 12.3 percent. A more exact result can be obtained by the methods of this section.

Exercise 8.4

1. The calculus can also be used to solve this problem. It leads to an elegant result known as Snell's Law, which states that $u/v = \sin i/\sin r$, where u is the speed in the first medium and i is the angle of incidence, while v is the speed in the second medium and r is the angle of refraction.

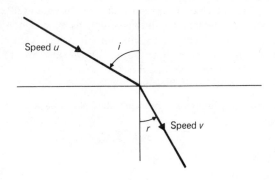

2. Let x represent the length of one side of the rectangle. Then find the area as a function of x, and determine a value of x that maximizes this function. (The calculus, which can be applied to this problem, leads to a solution where the rectangle is 25m × 50m. The calculus cannot solve the problem when the fence must be constructed of certain fixed lengths.)

4. The volume of a cylinder of radius r and height h is $\pi r^2 h$. Its total surface area is $2\pi rh + 2\pi r^2$. The cost should be found as a function of r.

6. The profit should be expressed as a function of h or r. The problem then is to find where this function is a maximum. The unreasonable aspect of the problem as stated is that the profit function becomes infinite as the radius approaches zero. Clearly it is not this maximum that we are trying to find.

8. Suppose the man heads initially for a point x meters downstream. If there were no current, he would require

$$\sqrt{100^2 + x^2}/3000$$

hours to reach the shore. The effect of the current is to cause him to reach a point that is further downstream by the distance he would drift in this period of time, that is,

this period of time multiplied by 3000. The function to be minimized is therefore

$$\sqrt{100^2 + x^2}/3000 + $$
$$\sqrt{300^2 + (500 - x - \sqrt{100^2 + x^2})^2}/4000.$$

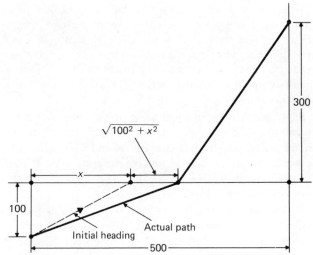

9. If x cm of wire are used for the circle, the sum of the two areas is

$$\frac{x^2}{4\pi} + \left(\frac{25 - x}{4}\right)^2.$$

If the calculus is used, and a value of x is found which makes the derivative zero, the sum of the two areas will be a minimum, rather than a maximum. The maximum occurs when $x = 25$, i.e., when all of the wire is used for the circle and none for the square.

10. Using the calculus, it can be shown that the minimum value of the cost function occurs when $x = 10\sqrt{10}$.

11–12. The methods of the calculus cannot be used on these examples because the functions are not differentiable.

13.

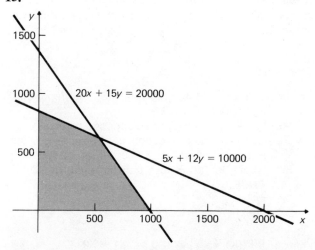

The shaded area in the accompanying graph represents the feasible solutions, which means that each point in the region corresponds to a choice of x and y that satisfies all the inequalities $5x + 12y \leq 10000$, $20x + 15y \leq 20000$,

$x \geq 0$, $y \geq 0$. The problem is to find which of the feasible values cause $x + y$ to be a maximum, first if x and y must be integers and second if they can be fractions. (This problem is an example of a linear programming problem.)

To justify making nothing but Weejees, he would have to find that the maximum profit occurred at the point where $x = 1000$ and $y = 0$. For this to happen the profit function must be proportional to $px + qy$ where $p/q \geq 20/15$. He would therefore have to make a profit per Weejee that is at least one third larger than the profit per Wumper.

CHAPTER 9

Exercise 9.1

1. The largest hexadecimal number is $(1 - 16^{-6}) \times 16^{63} \approx 7.2 \times 10^{75}$, and the largest binary number is $(1 - 2^{-24}) \times 2^{63} \approx 9.2 \times 10^{18}$. The smallest (in magnitude) nonzero hexadecimal number is $(1/16) \times 16^{-64} \approx 5.4 \times 10^{-79}$, and binary is $(1/2) \times 2^{-64} \approx 2.7 \times 10^{-20}$.

6. If $A = 10$ and $B = 2^{-30}$, $\text{fl}(A + B) = A$ for the binary representation of this section. A would be represented as $(.101)_2 \times 2^4$, and the largest B such that $\text{fl}(A + B) = A$ in chopped binary arithmetic would be $(.\text{twenty-four 0's followed by twenty-four 1's})_2 \times 2^4 = (.\text{twenty-four 1's})_2 \times 2^{-20} \approx 9.5 \times 10^{-7}$.

7. Floating-point arithmetic is commutative, but neither associative nor distributive. In decimal arithmetic with 3 decimal digits in the fraction parts, consider $A = .501$ and $B = .502$. Then $\text{fl}(A + B) = 1.00$, and $\text{fl}((A + B)/2) = .500$, which is less than both A and B.

8. a) The error in $\text{fl}(A + B) = (A + B)(1 + \epsilon)$ is $(A + B)\epsilon$, and $|(A + B)\epsilon| < (2 + 4)u = 6u$.

d) If A and B are not machine-representable, we have to allow for conversion errors as well, in which case

$$\text{fl}(A + B) = (A(1 + \epsilon_1) + B(1 + \epsilon_2))(1 + \epsilon_3).$$

The error is

$$A(1 + \epsilon_1)(1 + \epsilon_3) + B(1 + \epsilon_2)(1 + \epsilon_3) - A - B.$$

Neglecting u^2, this is bounded by $|A|2u + |B|2u$, which is $< 12u$.

9. The error bound is smaller if the sum is taken from the smaller number to the larger. The situation is illustrated more clearly again in the next section; see the remark following Eq. (1) of Section 9.2.

10. The second approach involves one more arithmetic operation, and the resulting error bound has $2i - 3$ in place of $2i - 4$.

11. Chopping before normalizing can cause the loss of at most one digit on multiplication. The main difficulty arises when two nearly equal quantities are subtracted. If this happens when a shift of one of the quantities is required before the subtraction takes place, there can be a considerable loss of accuracy. For example, with 6-digit arithmetic, $1.00000 - .999666$ yields 0.000554 but the 4 is chopped, resulting in a very large relative error in the result. In the most extreme case, i.e., $1.00000 - .999999$ we obtain 0.000001, but the 1 is chopped! In this latter case $\epsilon = -1$, so that $|\epsilon| = 1$.

13. In this example, $\text{fl}(x\sqrt{1 + x}) = x(\sqrt{(1 + x)(1 + \epsilon_1)} \times (1 + 3\epsilon_2))(1 + \epsilon_4)$. Neglecting u^2, and noting that $\sqrt{1 + u}$ is then $(1 + \frac{1}{2}u)$, the error turns out to be bounded by $x\sqrt{1 + x}(9u/2)$. The largest value occurs when $x = 2$, so that the error is bounded by $2\sqrt{3}(9u/2) < 1.6 \times 10^{-6}$.

14. The mean value theorem asserts that $f(y) = f(x) + f'(\xi)(y - x)$ for some ξ in $[a,b]$. When $f(x) = x^3$, $f'(x) = 3x^2$ and, assuming that y differs only slightly from x, the error in $f(x)$ due to not knowing x exactly is approximately $3x^2 \times$ (error in x). The additional error due to the calculation of x^3 in floating-point arithmetic is $x^3(1 + \epsilon_1)(1 + \epsilon_2) - x^3$ which is bounded approximately by $x^3(2u)$. The total error in the final result is therefore bounded approximately by $3x^2 \times$ (bound on error in x) + $x^3(2u)$.

Exercise 9.2

1. a) The value of $(1 + 2^{-23})^{40000} - 1$ is slightly less than 1.0048, whereas the value of $1.01 \times 40000 \times 2^{-23}$ is slightly greater than this quantity.

4. The values of k_i under the circumstances described in this question are $k_1 = 0$, and $k_i = 2i - 4$ for $i > 1$. These can be substituted into Eq. (3), and we can note that $n - (i - 1) + k_i$ is bounded by $2n$ for each value of i. From here we can proceed as in the example following Eq. (3) and obtain $1.01 \times u \times 2n \times e^x$ as a bound on the total roundoff error.

5. From the answer to Question 7 of Exercise 8.1 we note that a bound on the truncation error is $2^n/n!$. From the answer just obtained to Question 4 of Exercise 9.2 we note that a bound on the roundoff error is $1.01 \times u \times 2n \times e^2$. For a given value of u it now remains to determine the smallest value of n for which the sum of these two bounds is less than or equal to the accuracy that has been prescribed.

We have assumed that the accuracy was to have been prescribed in advance, and that the corresponding value of n was to have been fixed in advance. Other possibilities could be considered, along the lines suggested in the answers to Questions 5 and 8 of Exercise 8.1, but they are if anything even less attractive under the present circumstances when roundoff error is included in the analysis.

There is an important limitation on the value of the prescribed accuracy. As n increases, the total error decreases at first, but the roundoff error eventually dominates and the total error will begin to increase with increasing n. For a given value of u, there is a limit to the accuracy we can require. For example, with $u = 10^{-6}$, the sum of the two error bounds given above reaches a minimum value of approximately $.000098$ when $n = 12$. We therefore cannot prescribe an accuracy of less than about 10^{-4}.

7. Continuing with the following steps

$$fl(a_n x + a_{n-1}) = a_n x (1 + \epsilon)^2 + a_{n-1}(1 + \epsilon)$$
$$fl((a_n x + a_{n-1})x + a_{n-2}) = a_n x^2 (1 + \epsilon)^4$$
$$+ a_{n-1} x (1 + \epsilon)^3 + a_{n-2}(1 + \epsilon),$$

we eventually obtain

$$fl((\cdots((a_n x + a_{n-1})x + a_{n-2})x \cdots) + a_0)$$
$$= a_n x^n (1 + \epsilon)^{2n} + a_{n-1} x^{n-1}(1 + \epsilon)^{2n-1}$$
$$+ \cdots + a_1 x (1 + \epsilon)^3 + a_0(1 + \epsilon).$$

Except for the first term, the exponent of $(1 + \epsilon)$ with a_i is $2i + 1$. If the polynomial is evaluated directly, without the use of Horner's rule, and if the terms are added in order, beginning with the term $a_n x^n$, then the corresponding exponents of $(1 + \epsilon)$ are exactly the same. The corresponding error bounds would therefore be the same. (But adding terms in a different order in the second case would lead to a different error bound.)

However, the direct approach is less efficient. Even if care is taken to compute each power of x only once ($n - 1$ multiplications), it is still necessary to multiply by the coefficients (n more multiplications), and it is thus seen that $2n - 1$ multiplications are needed, compared to n with Horner's method. A program for the direct approach will also probably be slightly more complicated than one based on Horner's rule.

8. a) The exact value is $\pi/4$.

9. The difficulty is that the derivative of the integrand (and hence its second derivative) does not exist at one point $(x = 0)$ in the interval of integration. This means that the theoretical basis for the error estimate with the trapezoidal rule is not valid. However, the theory is applicable in all subintervals that do not contain that particular point, and one suspects that the error estimate ought not to be particularly misleading in this example.

To get around the difficulty, some preliminary mathematical analysis might be tried. For example, the change of variable $x = u^2$ gets rid of the difficulty in this case.

Exercise 9.3

5. To eliminate x_1 from all equations except the first requires $n(n - 1)$ multiplications, because there are n multiplications per row and $n - 1$ rows. (No multiplication is needed for the first column, but one is needed for the right side of the equations.) Similarly, to eliminate x_2 from all equations after the second requires $(n - 1)(n - 2)$ multiplications. The elimination process therefore requires

$$n(n - 1) + (n - 1)(n - 2) + (n - 2)(n - 3) + \cdots$$
$$+ (2)(1)$$
$$= n^2 + (n-1)^2 + (n - 2)^2 + \cdots + 2^2 + 1^2$$
$$- n - (n - 1) - (n - 2) - \cdots - 2 - 1$$
$$= n(n + 1)(2n + 1)/6 - n(n + 1)/2$$

multiplications altogether. This is equal to $n^3/3$, except for some terms proportional to n^2, and some to n, and a constant. The terms proportional to n^2, etc., are negligible when n is large. It can be shown that the additional multiplications required for the back substitution are also negligible. A similar argument applied to the method of Jordan leads to $n^3/2$ in place of $n^3/3$.

To solve 100 equations in 100 unknowns by the method of Gauss requires approximately $100^3/3$ multiplications, i.e., approximately one third of a million multiplications. It is not unusual for a machine to be able to execute that many multiplications in one second. Even if this requires approximately 10 percent of its time, solving 100 equations requires only 10 seconds.

When n is large, storage of the coefficients can become an important factor, along with the time required to carry out the calculations.

6. The value of $n!$ is approximately 1.55×10^{25} when $n = 25$. Even with a machine that can execute one million multiplications per second, it would require $1.55 \times 10^{25}/(10^6 \times 60 \times 60 \times 24 \times 365)$ years to carry out this many multiplications, which is approximately 4.9×10^{11} years. By contrast, $n^3/3$ is approximately 5208 when $n = 25$, and this many multiplications could be carried out in about $1/200$ of a second.

9. Probably the most natural way in which we would want to consider a program for solving equations to be correct is simply to say it is correct if it produces the correct result. Of course we would add qualifications to this requirement to allow for the possibility that there is no solution, or that there are infinitely many solutions.

As long as a method includes some kind of pivoting to avoid zero divisors, and if all arithmetic is done exactly, we can expect a method to be correct in this sense. However, we are normally not able to avoid roundoff errors in practice, and this introduces errors in the "solution" produced by a program. It would then be natural to consider a program correct if it produces good approximations to the exact solutions. However, as is discussed in more detail in the next section (Section 9.4), it turns out that some solutions can be very sensitive to the presence of roundoff errors, and it may therefore be expecting too much to require a method to produce good approximations in all cases.

Another approach is to consider a method correct if it produces approximations that come very close to satisfying the original equations, regardless of whether they are good approximations to the solutions of those equations. The distinction between these two approaches is discussed more fully in the next section.

A final approach, and one that we can reasonably apply at this stage, is to consider the program to be correct if it follows faithfully the algorithm we had in mind. This may appear to be avoiding the real issues, and it is certainly true that the major difficulties are at least being postponed if we adopt this point of view. However, it *is* a legitimate point of view, and it *is* worthwhile insisting that the program be correct, at least to this extent. For the purposes of this section, we can therefore assume that we have a clear, unambiguous description (in words and using mathematical symbols) of what it is we want our program to do, and we can consider the program to be correct if it does exactly what we want it to do. To convince ourselves of even this much still requires very careful programming, and a thorough testing of the final product!

Exercise 9.4

1. Consider $a = 1$, $b = 10^{-50}$, and $c = -1$. Then

$$\text{fl}((a + b) + c) = 0 \text{ while } (a + b + c) = 10^{-50}.$$

The relationship given in the question cannot be true for any small value of ϵ. In fact, it is clear that the relationship can be true only for $\epsilon = -1$. The worst possible magnitude that ϵ must be allowed to have is 1, which is exactly what is required with the example just presented.

2. We can easily show that

$$\text{fl}(x_n y_n + x_{n-1} y_{n-1} + \cdots + x_1 y_1)$$
$$= x_n y_n (1 + \epsilon)^n + x_{n-1} y_{n-1}(1 + \epsilon)^n + \cdots + x_1 y_1 (1 + \epsilon)^2$$

where the exponent of $(1 + \epsilon)$ with $x_i y_i$ is $i + 1$, except in the first term. (We have assumed that the sum begins with $x_n y_n$, then $x_{n-1} y_{n-1}$, etc., down to $x_1 y_1$.) We can interpret this result in a variety of ways. For example, we can say it is the exact scalar product of x' and y' where x'_i, y'_i differ from x_i, y_i by factors of no more than $(1 + \epsilon)^{(i+1)/2}$. Or we can say it is the exact scalar product of x and y' where y'_i differs from y_i by a factor of no more than $(1 + \epsilon)^{i+1}$.

4. The graphs of the two equations are shown below. The

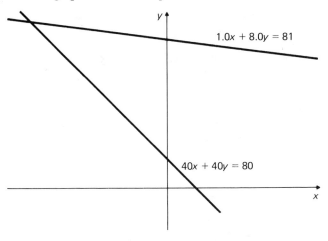

effect of eliminating x from one of the equations is to replace its line with a line whose graph is parallel to the x-axis. Without roundoff error the new line must of course go through the same point of intersection as did the line it replaces. The effect of roundoff error is to produce a slightly different equation, and hence a slightly different graph that is parallel to the x-axis, and hence a different point of intersection.

If x is eliminated from the second equation, we obtain what is shown below. However, if x is eliminated from the

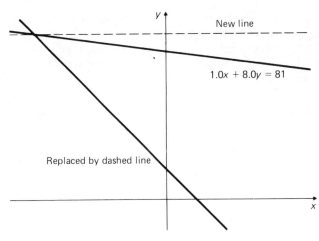

first equation, that is, if we use partial pivoting, we obtain the next graph. It should be obvious that the effect of small

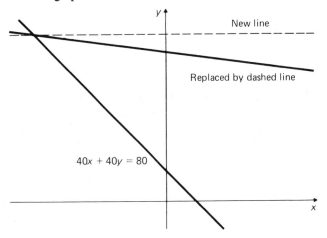

changes in the position of the dashed line in the second of these cases is more drastic than in the first. The effect would be even more pronounced if we were to begin with a line that is more nearly horizontal than $1.0x + 8.0y = 81$.

5. The "exact" solution must lie in the shaded portion shown in the diagram given below. The required intervals

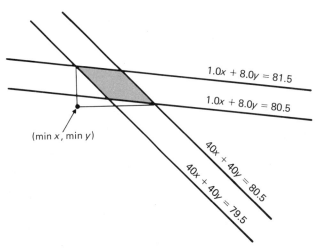

for x and y can be obtained by finding the points of intersection of the different pairs of equations in this diagram. The point referred to in the question (min x, min y) obviously cannot satisfy any pair of equations within the range of possibilities.

6. Direct computation of the various roots will show that the roots (1 and 3) of the first equation are much less sensitive to small changes than is the double root (2) of the second equation. Drawing graphs of $y = x^2 - 4x + 3$ and $y = x^2 - 4x + 4$ can suggest geometrically (as was done in the answer to Question 4 of this section) why simple roots can be expected to be less sensitive to small changes than multiple roots.

7. The change in $\sin(x)$ due to a relative change in x of 10^{-5} is

$$\sin(x + x \times 10^{-5}) - \sin(x)$$

which, according to the mean value theorem, is $(x \times 10^{-5})\cos(\xi)$, where ξ is in the interval $[x, x + x \times 10^{-5}]$. If x is near to 1 we can guarantee that this error is no more than about 10^{-5}. However, the situation worsens as x increases, and for x near 10000, the best we can do is to guarantee an error of no more than about 10^{-1}.

8. If c is very small, there will be cancellation of significant digits in the numerator of the formula for x_1 or the formula for x_2, depending on the sign of b. The corresponding root is small but, because of the cancellation, will not be known accurately to as many decimal places as one might wish. The alternative approach suggested in the question gets around this difficulty. However, the alternative fails in the case when both b and c are zero, since then the "first root" is zero and an attempt to divide by that "first root" will cause an error condition.

Another concern arises when $b^2 - 4ac$ overflows or underflows, even though the value of $\sqrt{b^2 - 4ac}$ would not.

Altogether it is quite difficult to write a program for solving quadratic equations that is able to cope sensibly with all possible cases. An ideal program would be one that produced accurate results whenever the exact solutions were close to machine-representable numbers, and otherwise appropriate error indications. The correctness of a program would be concerned mainly with a statement about what class of problems the program is able to handle correctly in this sense.

CHAPTER 10

Exercise 10.1

2. The modification is straightforward. However, there is one detail that could cause trouble. Because the percents have to be rounded off in some way (e.g., to the nearest percent, or the nearest tenth of a percent), they may not add up to exactly 100 percent. Making adjustments that remove this possibility would require some careful attention to detail; moreover, there is no obviously best way to make those adjustments. (For example, what should be done if three percents are exactly 33⅓?)

3. Using the data in the last column of Fig. 10.1, the output could appear as follows:

```
INCOME        NUMBER
   0 - 2000   **********************************
2001 - 4000   ****************************
4001 - 6000   *********************
6001 - 8000   ********************
8001 -        ***************
```

In this example each asterisk represents 3000 people.

5. The documentation should state clearly how to use the program and what its limitations are. For example, if no provision has been made for answers other than those stated in the question (including those caused by keypunch errors), this fact should be clearly acknowledged. Of course, it would be better to have the program handle such exceptional cases in some reasonable way, such as not including them in the final totals in any way, but printing out a message about them instead; the message should at least indicate how many were rejected. Another possibility is to extend the bivariate table to include counts of such invalid values.

6. The items would have to be input as strings of characters. After being tested for validity, they would have to be converted to their numerical values for further processing. The details depend to a considerable extent on the programming language being used, and perhaps to some extent on the machine as well.

7–8. The following table contains the results required for Question 7:

Tenth	1	2	3	4	5	6	7	8	9	10
Number	98	102	98	102	98	102	98	102	98	102

It is easily seen that these values are fairly close to the expected values. However, the values follow a rather regular pattern and are probably not a suitable source of the "random" numbers alluded to in Question 8.

9. The following table was produced using the generator in Question 7:

```
32  34  32   0   0   0   0   0   0   0
 0   0   0  34  34  34   0   0   0   0
 0   0   0   0   0   0  32  34  32   0
34  34   0   0   0   0   0   0   0  34
 0   0  32  34  32   0   0   0   0   0
 0   0   0   0   0  34  34  34   0   0
32   0   0   0   0   0   0   0  32  34
 0  34  34  34   0   0   0   0   0   0
 0   0   0   0  32  34  32   0   0   0
 0   0   0   0   0   0   0  34  34  34
```

This table shows very clearly that the numbers are not very "random" since, for example, a number in the first tenth is never followed by a number in the fourth tenth of the interval, or the fifth tenth, etc.

10. The expected number of runups in a truly random sequence is given by the following table, which does not include "end" runs:

Length of runup	1	2	3	4	5	6
Number of runups	166	208	91	26	6	1

With n numbers, it can be shown that the expected number of runups of length r (excluding end runs) is

$$\frac{(r^2 + r - 1)(n - r - 1)}{(r + 2)!}$$

The following is an outline of a program for determining the number of runups of different lengths in a sequence of numbers. It assumes that succeeding numbers in the sequence must be distinct (as is the case with all generators that will be of interest to us).

> Initialize an array called length-counter to zero, the first component to be the number of runups of length 1, etc.
> Generate the first two or more numbers in the sequence until a number is reached which is less than its predecessor; then set old = down. /The variable "old" represents the preceding change in numbers and will be "up" or "down"; the current change will be represented by the variable "new"./
> Loop through remaining numbers
> > Generate next number
> > Set new = up or down accordingly
> > If (old = down & new = up)
> > > Set length = 1 /this is the beginning of a new run/
> > > (old = down & new = down)
> > > Do nothing
> > > (old = up & new = up)
> > > Add 1 to length
> > > (old = up & new = down)
> > > Add 1 to appropriate component of length-counter/this is the end of a runup/
> > End if
> > Set old = new
> End loop
> /Required components of length-counter are now available/

Exercise 10.2

1. a) The advantage is that the mean and variance can be computed while examining each data item only once. With the formula given earlier, it would be necessary to examine each item twice—once to compute the mean and once to compute the variance. The disadvantage is that the needed sum of squares of data items may become very large, and perhaps even cause overflow, even though the variance itself is not particularly large.

b) The disadvantage here is that the formulas are quite a bit more complicated.

2. Many hand calculators, even some nonprogrammable ones, are able to carry out such calculations automatically.

3. Suppose we determine that the median must lie in the range 5601–5700 and that 57 numbers lie in this range. If 14 of the numbers in this interval must lie below the median and 42 above, the median can be estimated to be $5601 + (14/(14 + 42))99$ which, to the nearest integer, is 5626.

6. The average of the magnitudes of the deviations is computationally inconvenient because it would require two passes through the data to calculate.

10. It would be advantageous to use a formula which requires only one pass through the data. It can be shown that

$$\sum_{i=1}^{n} (x_i - m_x)(y_i - m_y) = \sum_{i=1}^{n} x_i y_i - n m_x m_y.$$

13. The result is .0835.

14. The program should not save more than k items of data at any one time. To minimize the amount of moving of information when k is more than 2 or 3, the data should be stored in an array of length k which is treated as "circular." New items are added in turn, until the end of the array is reached, after which the next item is placed at the beginning of the array, and so on.

Exercise 10.3

2. The regression coefficients for the data in Fig. 10.5 are $a = .6960$ and $b = 25.04$. If the variables are interchanged, the values are $a = 1.118$ and $b = 11.93$. We do not get the same line because the distances that are squared are different. In the first case they are measured vertically from the sample points to the line; in the second case they are measured horizontally.

6. Part (a) is similar to the problem discussed in the text in that the function is linear in the unknown parameters. This means that linear equations can be found for the parameters, and such equations are easily solved. Parts (b) and (c) are more difficult, and methods like those in Section 8.3 must be used. Part (c) is particularly difficult because four parameters must be found. Searching for the minimum in this case may take a relatively large amount of computer time.

Exercise 10.4

2. The chi-square statistic is about 30, which is certainly much larger than anything shown in the table for 1 degree of freedom. In fact, it can be shown that the probability of obtaining a statistic as large as this, purely by chance with an unbiased die, is .0000002. (The results quoted in this experiment were actually obtained by an English biologist named Weldon, although his experiment was somewhat different. He used 12 dice, rolling them simultaneously, rather than 1 die.)

3. Suppose that the number of heads obtained in 500 tosses is $250 + x$. Then the number of tails is $250 - x$, and it can be shown that the chi-square statistic is $x^2/125$. With 1 degree of freedom, the 1-percent level is 6.6. We therefore become suspicious when the statistic exceeds 6.6, that is, when x exceeds $(125 \times 6.6)^{1/2}$, which is approximately 28.5. According to the criteria used in this question, we become suspicious if the number of heads is 279 or more. Of course we also become suspicious if the number is 221 or less.

4. The value of the chi-square statistic for the generator in Question 7 of Exercise 10.1 is .4, which is well below even the 10-percent level (14.7) for 9 degrees of freedom. We therefore have no reason to be suspicious of the generator, at least on the basis of this test. Of course, we might argue that the statistic is suspiciously small! But see the answer to the next question.

5. The value of χ_2^2 for the generator in Question 7 of Exercise 10.1 turns out to be 2336, so that the value of $\chi_2^2 - \chi_1^2$ is very much larger than even the 1-percent level (124) for 90 degrees of freedom. The generator in Question 7 of Exercise 10.1 is therefore not acceptable as a random number generator, despite the fact that it passed the test discussed earlier. This conclusion is of course consistent with what we observed when we obtained the bivariate table in Question 9 of Exercise 10.1. This example is rather extreme; in other cases the lack of randomness is not so obvious and further tests are usually necessary.

6–9. The midsquare method will not pass very many statistical tests, even if a fairly large number of digits are used. Lehmer's method is better. Some methods based on the techniques suggested in Question 9 can be very good. Further details are discussed in Chapter 11.

CHAPTER 11

Exercise 11.1

1. The answer for part (a) can be expressed as $\$1000 \times (1.12)^{10}$. Of course this can be evaluated with the help of a computer, but many hand calculators can provide the result quite easily. The result is $\$3105.85$, to the nearest cent. The answer for part (b) is $\$1000 \times (1.01)^{120}$, which is $\$3300.39$ to the nearest cent. The result for (c) is the same as the result for (a) in this case. It would not be the same in general, but the difference will usually be small. (If only $\$10$ is invested the difference turns out to be 2 cents at the end of 10 years.)

2. The first $\$100$ will amount to $\$100 \times (1.10)^{10}$ at the end of 10 years, the second to $\$100 \times (1.10)^9$, and so on. We therefore require the sum

$$100 \times (1.10)^{10} + 100 \times (1.10)^9 + \cdots + 100 \times (1.10).$$

A computer program could be used to find the sum. Alternatively, this is a geometric series and the sum can be expressed in the form $1100 \times ((1.10)^{10} - 1)$, after some simplification. The value turns out to be 1753.12.

3. Suppose the interest rate is i. If the man's debt at the end of n months is D_n, his debt at the end of $n + 1$ months is $D_{n+1} = D_n(1 + i/12) - 90$. We know that $D_0 = 1000$ and that D_{12} must be 0. We could write a program to try different values of i, until we found one that satisfied these conditions.

Once again, some preliminary analysis might simplify the calculations somewhat, as was illustrated in the preceding question. But it should be clear that, as problems of this sort become increasingly complicated, they lend themselves more conveniently to a direct approach with the help of a computer.

6. The present value of the first payment is $\$500 \times (1 + .043/12)^{-1}$, of the second payment $\$500 \times (1 + .043/12)^{-2}$, and so on, up to the 12th, which is $\$500 \times (1 + .043/12)^{-12}$. The present value of the 13th is $\$500 \times (1 + .047/12)^{-13}$, etc. The present value of the annuity is the sum of the present values of all such individual payments.

8. /Euler's method for decay process/
   Initialize decay constant, to .01 in this case
               total time, to 60 minutes in this case
               number of lines, to whatever is wished
   Loop over time intervals
      Initialize mass, to 2 in this case
      Loop over steps: number of steps
               = total time/time interval
         mass = mass − decay constant
               × time interval
      End loop
      Output time interval, mass
      If this is not the first time interval
         Calculate first difference
         Output first difference
      End if
      Save value of mass
   End loop
   Stop

10. A geometrical description of Euler's method can help provide the information required for this question. The results produced by Euler's method are too small for growth processes, as well as for decay processes. If the time interval is taken to be much too large with a decay process, the calculated mass can become negative, and its magnitude can actually begin to increase.

11. Since Euler's method gives results that are too small, the calculated values will reach half of the original mass too soon. The estimate of the half-life will therefore be too small.

The main practical difficulty in this question is to find the time at which the substance reaches a particular mass, such as half of its original value, because the sequence of values obtained in the course of a calculation are likely to skip over the desired particular value. One way of coping with this difficulty is to modify the program so that it interrupts itself just as it is about to step over the desired point. It can then interpolate to find an approximation to the desired point; that is, it can choose a point inside that last interval, whose distances from the end of that interval are in proportion to the amounts by which the values of the mass at the endpoints differ from the desired value.

The approach just described is quite general. However, in the special circumstances of this example, the solution can also be found analytically with the help of the calculus. For example, it can be shown that the half-life is exactly $(\log_2 e)/.01$ minutes in this example, which is 693.147 minutes, to three decimal places.

16. The velocity v can be determined in a way analogous to what has been done in preceding examples. The distance can also be obtained at the same time, because the rate of change of distance is equal to the velocity, and the distance can be treated as just another quantity to be computed along with the velocity. We use Euler's method, or the trapezoidal method, or any other we happen to have available, on two rate equations at the same time.

17. Here is an example involving two quantities, x and y, which are quite analogous to the velocity and distance of the preceding question. The program is straightforward. For example, with Euler's method, the two rates of change at the beginning of the interval are calculated and then the new values of x and y at the end of the interval are obtained.

It should be obvious that the technique is easily extended to handle any number of quantities, as long as an expression is known for the rate of change of each of the quantities.

18. At time t, the man has reached a point $5t$ north of his starting point, as shown in the diagram below, where we

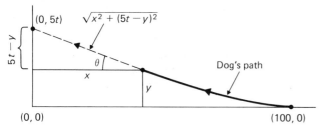

have placed the man's starting point at the origin, and denoted the position of the dog at time t as (x,y). The dog's speed in the direction of his master is 20 meters per second. The component of his speed in the x-direction is this quantity multiplied by $\cos\theta$. Thus, the rate of change of x is $-20x/\sqrt{x^2 + (5t - y)^2}$. (The minus sign appears because x is decreasing.) The rate of change of y is 20 multiplied by $\sin\theta$, i.e., $20(5t - y)/\sqrt{x^2 + (5t - y)^2}$. With these two rates of change we can write a program to calculate an approximation to the dog's path. We have to make provision for stopping the calculation at the point where the dog reaches his master, which is at the point where x becomes equal to zero.

With foresight, and with further help from the theorem of Pythagoras, the dog could catch his master in $20/\sqrt{15}$ seconds, which is approximately 5.16 seconds.

Exercise 11.2

2. The result in part (c) should appear to be statistically quite good. However, it can provide only about 10000 numbers before the cycle repeats.

3. Suppose that the generator we use produces results in the interval $(0,1)$. Then a natural way to simulate the rolling of a die is to denote the number generated by x

and use $[6x] + 1$ as the number rolled ($[6x]$ is the greatest integer less than or equal to $6x$). For this to work properly we have to be sure that the generated value of x cannot be exactly equal to 1; otherwise $[6x] + 1$ could equal 7.

On the other hand, if the generator we use produces integers in a large interval $(0,N)$, we can denote an integer by i and use $[i/j] + 1$ as the number rolled, where j is the smallest integer $\geq N/6$.

Theoretically, it can be shown that, when two dice are rolled 1000 times, the number of 7's should be 167 on the average, while the number of 11's should be 56 on the average.

4. The approximation to the normal distribution given in the question is quite a good one for many practical purposes.

5. We obtained 100 approximations to $\pi/4$ by the method described in this question. The average of these approximations was .7842, which differs from the true value (.7854) by .0012.

6. For the 100 approximations mentioned in the answer to Question 5, the standard deviation from the mean of .7842 was .0188. The value of $(2/\sqrt{n})$ times the standard deviation is therefore $(2/\sqrt{100}) \times (.0188)$, which is .0038. We therefore expect the true value of $\pi/4$ to lie in the interval $(.7842 \pm .0038)$, with probability 95 percent. The true value $(.7854)$ lies well within this interval and the statistical theory referred to in this question seems to be reasonable. Intervals such as the one just obtained are known in statistics as "confidence intervals." We have found a 95-percent confidence interval.

7. The modification should lead to more accurate results. The reason, in general terms, is that the randomness is being confined to a smaller part of the expected value we are trying to determine. The $1/2$ is calculated exactly, and only the value of $\pi/4 - 1/2$ is being determined by the Monte Carlo method.

We used this approach to obtain 100 new approximations to $\pi/4$. We obtained a mean of .7839 with a standard deviation of .0112. Although the mean is not quite as good as before, the main point is that the confidence interval has been reduced substantially.

The idea illustrated here is one that is generally applicable. With Monte Carlo methods it is advantageous to reduce as much as possible the part of the result that is "left to chance," as it were. Of course, there is usually a price to pay in that the individual calculations will usually become more costly, and a decision must be made as to how much reduction is worthwhile.

8. It can be shown theoretically that the probability is $1/4$.

10. It can be shown theoretically that Mr. B and Mr. C have equal chances of surviving.

11. In one experiment with 100 trials that we carried out, the average number of rolls was 12.53. The smallest number of rolls was 3 and, except for one trial that required 37 rolls, the largest number was 27.

14. Games like Snakes and Ladders are easy to simulate because their outcome depends entirely on chance. However, games like Monopoly require decisions on the part of the players, and are therefore much more difficult to simulate, at least if the simulation is to be at all reasonable.

15. Use a random number generator to determine a point where the midpoint, *M*, of the needle falls. Then use the generator to obtain two values which can be used as the ratio *a*:*b*.

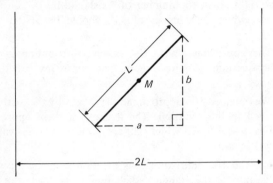

If the needle is of length *L* and the lines are *A* units apart, it can be shown that the probability $p = 2L/\pi A$. It is reported that a student used a needle of length 2.75 inches and lines that were 3.5 inches apart. He made only two tosses and the needle crossed the line on one of them. He then substituted 1/2 for the probability in the formula and obtained 3.143 as an approximation to π! What is your comment on this result?

16. We do not know the exact answers for this question.

Exercise 11.3

1. A maximum of 25 cars can get through the intersection during each minute. The system will therefore become saturated if the arrival rate exceeds 25/60, which is approximately .416. A variety of arrival rates should be tried, including one or two slightly larger than this value, for which we can expect the average waiting time and maximum queue length to grow indefinitely as the length of the simulation run grows. For one experiment, with a program based on Fig. 11.7 but with a simulation run of only 4000 seconds, we obtained the following results:

Arrival rate	Maximum queue length
.1250	12
.1875	15
.2500	16
.3125	17
.3750	23
.4375	111

To determine the average waiting time, we would have to add to what is outlined in Fig. 11.7. The simplest change would be to introduce a "total waiting time," which is set initially to zero. Then, with each arrival it would be possible to calculate the waiting time, since the number currently in the queue is known and the status of the lights is known. This waiting time can be added to the total wait-ing time. A count of the total number of cars will also have to be kept. These two values can be used at the end to compute the average waiting time.

2. The queue will consist of a list of records, each record corresponding to one car in the queue and containing all items pertaining to that car. For example, the list could be simply some consecutive locations in an array, each location giving the arrival time for the corresponding car. In this case, a pointer to the head of the queue would be needed (which could be set to zero when the queue is empty) and another pointer to the tail of the queue would also be needed. Provision would have to be made for treating the array as "circular," so that, when the end of the array is reached, it would be followed by the first component of the array. It may also be necessary to test the length of the queue to make sure that it never exceeds the length of the array.

Another possibility is to use a linked list to represent the queue. In this case each record will consist of two items: the arrival time and a pointer to the next item.

In either case, a program along the lines outlined below will carry out what is asked for in this question.

```
Initialize queue,
        total waiting time
        number of cars
        length of queue
        maximum length of queue
        random number generator
Input parameters needed for model
Loop for length of time of simulation
    Generate random number
    If (car arrives)
        Add 1 to length of queue
        Insert record in queue
        Add 1 to number of cars
    End if
    If (queue not empty & lights are O.K.)
        Calculate waiting time
        Add to total waiting time
        Remove record from queue
        Subtract 1 from length of queue
    End if
    If (length > maximum length)
        Assign new value to maximum length
    End if
End loop
Calculate average waiting time
Output this average and maximum length
Stop
```

3. As suggested in the question, special generators may be available for generating numbers from distributions which are nonuniform, such as would be required for the next arrival time, for example. However, if such a generator is not available, it is often possible to develop something which will do what is required, although perhaps less ef-ficiently. In the case of the next arrival time, we could use the following:

Set next arrival time = current time
Set arrival = false
Loop while (arrival = false)
    Generate random number
    If (random number < appropriate value)
        Set arrival = true
    End if
    Add 1 to next arrival time
End loop

Event-driven simulations are likely to be more efficient when there can be relatively long periods of time between events, although using generators such as the one just described will tend to cancel some of the advantages of event-driven models that can use more efficient generators for nonuniform distributions.

4. Very short cycle times cause long waiting times and long queues, because so much of each cycle is devoted to amber and red phases. On the other hand, very long cycle times will also cause long waiting times and long queues as well. Somewhere in between we expect to find optimum times (which of course may be different, depending on what we want to minimize).

With an arrival rate of .25 and simulation runs of 4000 seconds, we obtained the following results for average waiting times:

Cycle time	Average waiting time	Cycle time	Average waiting time
30	11.14	70	16.69
40	10.98	80	17.54
50	13.35	90	17.97
60	14.57	100	20.99

7. Here is an example where the probability distribution that is used depends on past experience. As more experience accumulates, the distribution may change and it is obviously a good idea to write the program so that a new table could be input before making additional simulation runs. The program should be designed so that new parameters are easily introduced, usually by input near the start of the program.

One way to handle the generation of orders, from such a nonuniform distribution is to determine the total of the second row (60 in this case) and then set up an array of this length with a 1 appearing in as many components as are given by the first number in the second row (2 in this case), 2 appearing in as many as are given by the second number (5 in this case), and so on. Using a random number to pick one of the components of this array will produce the required distribution. In this case, the random number would be uniformly from the set 1,2,3, . . . , 60, and two of the corresponding components would be 1, five would be 2, nine would be 3, and so on.

In an example we tried, which followed the simulation for 10000 days, we found the total number of orders to be 50535, of which only 9 had to be delayed.

9–10. Part (a) of Question 9 can be completed without having to manage a queue. However, it would be better to

introduce a queue, so that a uniform approach can be used in parts (a) and (b), and also in Question 10.

A record should be created for each new job that arrives. It is convenient to have the record contain at least four items. The arrival time is needed to calculate the total waiting time when the job is eventually completed. Two copies of the execution time are helpful, one to identify the type of job when it is finished, and a second one to be used for "counting down" when it reaches the head of the queue (to determine when its processing is finished). The fourth item would be a pointer for the linked list.

If all records are kept in a single queue, the main difference between parts (a) and (b), and Question 10, is the way in which new arrivals are inserted in the queue. In part (a), the new arrival is inserted at the end. In (b), the queue would be kept sorted on the execution times, and a new arrival would be inserted in such a way that this order is preserved. In Question 10, the queue is also kept sorted, and a new arrival is inserted accordingly, as with part (b) of Question 9, except that now the new arrival can interrupt the job being processed if the new arrival's execution time happens to be less than that of the job being processed.

Provision should be made for the possibility that the queue is full when a new job arrives. Probably the most practical action to take under such circumstances is to refuse to accept the job, i.e., to "flush" it out of the system, along with an appropriate message of course.

The following is a very brief overview of how the program might be organized. (Much of the detail has been omitted.)

Initialize, including a determination of all the
        parameters to be used in the simulation
Loop over simulation time
    If (queue not empty)
        Update data; e.g., reduce the time remaining for the job at the head of the queue, and delete the corresponding record if that job is finished
    End if
    Get random number
    If (job arrives)
        If (queue not full)
            Determine execution time
            Insert record into queue at appropriate place
            Update data
        else
            Flush job, with message
        End if
    End if
End loop
Calculate required statistics
Output results
Stop

The data provided with Question 9 is reasonably realistic, but it covers such a wide range of execution times that a considerable amount of computer time is required to complete the simulation. The program should be written so that it can handle other tables of data, including tables with different numbers of columns. It can be tested on smaller examples. In some of our tests we used only the first 3 columns and ran the simulation for 5000 seconds at 5-second intervals, assuming the jobs could arrive only at times which were multiples of 5 seconds.

Exercise 11.4

1. Sorting a list of 52 random numbers takes a moderate amount of time. A somewhat faster alternative is as follows. A list of 52 random integers from the set $1,2,3,\ldots,$ 52 is generated (there may be duplicates). Suppose these are designated by $I(1), I(2), \ldots, I(52)$, respectively, and that the 52 cards in the deck are designated by $CARD(1)$, $CARD(2), \ldots, CARD(52)$. Then the shuffling consists of making 52 interchanges: $CARD(1)$ with $CARD(I(1))$, $CARD(2)$ with $CARD(I(2)), \ldots,$ $CARD(52)$ with $CARD(I(52))$. (Of course the 52 values, $I(1), I(2), \ldots,$ $I(52)$, need not be stored as the components of an array, unless we want to reuse those values in subsequent shuffles. It would have the same effect if none of these numbers were stored, as long as the corresponding interchange is made as soon as each of these numbers is generated.)

4. It can be shown that, if George has n girl friends and $n > 1$, the probability that not one letter is put in the correct envelope is

$$1/2! - 1/3! + \cdots + (-1)^n/n!$$

Thus, for $n = 5$, the probability turns out to be $11/30$. As n becomes large the probability rapidly approaches the value $1/e$, which is approximately .366. The value changes very little with n, unless the values of n are quite small.

5. The contents of the container can be represented by 15 numbers, say five 0's for the five white balls and ten 1's for the five black balls. Shaking the container would correspond to shuffling these 15 numbers. Drawing three balls without replacement then corresponds to taking three of these numbers, say the first three. The probability of drawing one white ball and two black balls is exactly $45/91$.

8. Blackjack is probably the only game one can play in gambling casinos in which the player has a better than 50-50 chance of winning, provided he has a good playing strategy. Most players cannot play that well. The strategy suggested in the question turns out to provide the player with a chance of winning that is close to 50-50. What do your simulations suggest? Is it just under 50-50 or just over? Thorp provides examples of winning strategies.

The program asked for in this question is a relatively complicated one. It is worthwhile trying to organize it carefully, so that it will be reasonably easy to understand. An overview will be essential for anyone else who tries to understand your program.

9–11. There are 2,598,960 possible poker hands. The following is a breakdown of the kinds of hands that can occur:

Straight flush	40
Four-of-a-kind	624
Full house	3,744
Flush	5,108
Straight	10,200
Three-of-a-kind	54,912
Two pairs	123,552
One pair	1,098,240
Other	1,302,540
Total	2,598,960

Since four-of-a-kind is so unlikely to occur, the chance of obtaining even one such hand in a few hundred trials is very small. Even a full house is expected to occur only once in 694 trials on the average.

Questions 9 and 10 are mainly exercises in writing programs to recognize patterns such as "full house," etc. Question 11 is for those who know the rules of a particular game and would like to try to devise a strategy for playing a reasonably good game.

"Poker tests" are sometimes used to test random number generators. They usually consider only 4-card hands and use chi-square tests to compare the observed number of hands that are three-of-a-kind, two pairs, etc., with the expected number.

13. One way to make this question more specific is to assume the section of street is divided into 150 one-meter lengths and to assume that each car occupies exactly 6 of these. (Or we could consider 300 half-meter lengths and assume each car occupies exactly 12, etc. Different assumptions will lead to only slightly different results.) Now let us concentrate on where the back ends of the cars can be placed. There are only 145 possible positions for the first car, and we choose one of these at random. Whichever is chosen causes the following 5 one-meter lengths to be ineligible for any other car's back end (perhaps fewer if the car is near the end of the section of street), as well as the preceding 5 (or fewer if the car is near the other end). These ineligible one-meter lengths can then be removed from our list in some way. Of the remaining eligible one-meter lengths, one is chosen at random. This causes another group of one-meter lengths to become ineligible. Then a third car is placed, and so on, until finally there are no eligible positions left. Meanwhile the number of parked cars is being counted. The whole process has to be repeated a number of times in order to obtain an average number of parked cars.

Exercise 11.5

1. If the total amount of money available to a gambler and a casino is a and the gambler's share is z (so that the casino has $a - z$), and if the probability that the gambler wins in a particular game is p, then the probability of the gambler's ultimate ruin can be shown to be

$$Q = \begin{cases} \dfrac{(q/p)^a - (q/p)^z}{(q/p)^a - 1}, & \text{if } q \neq p, \\ 1 - z/a, & \text{if } q = p, \end{cases}$$

where $q = 1 - p$. (For a proof, see *Probability and its Applications*, by William Feller, Wiley, New York, 1950, pp. 282–284.) The situation in Question 1 corresponds to $a = 15$, $z = 5$, and $p = q = 1/2$, which leads to a probability of 2/3 of reaching the barrier at -5 and 1/3 of reaching the barrier at $+10$. It should be noted that our chances of winning in a sequence of games is very much better if we begin with more capital than our opponent. (For interesting comments on random walks, see the sections on mathematical games in the May and June issues of *Scientific American*, 1969.)

2. The average number of steps before termination is

$$D = \begin{cases} \dfrac{z}{q-p} - \dfrac{a}{q-p} \times \dfrac{1 - (q/p)^z}{1 - (q/p)^a}, & \text{if } p \neq q, \\ z(a - z), & \text{if } p = q. \end{cases}$$

(See Feller, pp. 286–288.) With $a = 15$, $z = 5$, and $p = q = 1/2$, this means that the average duration will be 50 steps. Is this longer than you would have guessed?

3. It can be shown theoretically that the average distance approaches $\sqrt{2N/\pi}$ as the number of steps, N, becomes large. This is approximately $.8\sqrt{N}$.

5. The process described in this question is analogous to what happens when a barrier is broken between two gases at different pressures.

6. It can be shown theoretically that the value approaches $\sqrt{N}$ as N becomes large.

8. It can be shown that the required probability is approximately .3524. This means that one of the players will be ahead after every one of the twenty tosses in 17.62 percent of the games and similarly the other will be ahead throughout in 17.62 percent of the games, on the average. We suspect that most people would guess that these percentages would be quite a bit smaller.

Feller (p. 250) gives the following table of probabilities for a particular player to be ahead after exactly 0, 2, . . . , 20 of the twenty tosses:

N	*Probability one particular player is ahead after exactly N of the 20 tosses*
0	.1762
2	.0927
4	.0736
6	.0655
8	.0617
10	.0606
12	.0617
14	.0655
16	.0736
18	.0927
20	.1762

It is interesting to note that being ahead after exactly 10 of the tosses is the *least* likely outcome. (In the case of a tie it is convenient to say that the player who was in the lead after the preceding toss is still in the lead; other conventions could be adopted.)

9. There is one important difference between Question 8 and Question 9. In Question 8, the probability of each toss was completely independent of the others. In Question 9, the probability with each report will depend very much on the previous reports. For example, once a particular candidate has received 500 votes, it is certain that he will not receive any more.

The situation in Question 8 is analogous to random draws with replacement, whereas in Question 9 it corresponds to random draws without replacement. One way to simulate the process in Question 9 is to generate 500 1's and 500 0's. Then these 1000 "votes" can be shuffled, and finally counted. The shuffling and counting can be repeated any number of times.

The result should show that one of the candidates is quite likely to be ahead throughout most of the counting. The result that is asked for is the probability that one of the candidates (it does not matter which one) is ahead 90 percent of the time.

CHAPTER 12

Exercise 12.1

1. Another error that occurs quite frequently, but which can also be guarded against, is that of a character other than a digit appearing in place of a digit. Protection against this kind of error can be accomplished by reading all information into the computer as characters and checking those that are supposed to be digits, before making any further use of them.

3. It is impossible to prevent all errors, of course, since there obviously are situations in which it is impossible to detect errors that might have, for example, been introduced with the original data. However, checks of the kind being suggested in this section, along with checks for reasonableness of the sizes of numbers, etc., will catch a very large percentage of the errors that appear in the information being processed.

5. Question 2 required the development of a basic program which works properly only in the (unlikely!) event that the input is correct. Question 3 required the introduction of some data verification, and Question 4 the introduction of some check on other aspects of the input, such as its being in the proper order, having proper identification codes, etc. If an input record does not pass the tests, the program should output an appropriate message and go on to the next record.

Question 5 is intended to do more, and will require a major modification to the original program. In particular, it should be able to cope with more than one change record for an individual master-file record. It is reasonable to assume that change records for one master-file record should appear in the order stated: insertion, modifications, deletion. It is also reasonable to assume that the modifications should appear in chronological order. But the program must be designed to cope with the possibility that these assumptions are not satisfied.

7. If a linked list is kept in sorted order, one good way to speed up searching for a record in such a list is to maintain an array of entry points in place of a single header. For example, if the linked list is sorted alphabetically, the array of entry points could provide pointers to the beginning of the A's, the beginning of the B's, and so on. Then, to find a particular record, a search would first be made in the list of pointers to determine where in the linked list of records a second search, the search for the record itself, should be started.

Maintaining such a file would of course be somewhat more complicated than maintaining a simple linked list with a single pointer to its first record, but the extra trouble would be worthwhile if the list has to be searched frequently.

If the array of pointers is very long, it may be important to use faster techniques than a straightforward linear search to find the appropriate pointer. One such technique is described in Question 1 of Exercise 12.3.

12. The program must make provision for insertion and searching, and possibly for deletion as well. For example, to add a record to such a file, we assume that the records are stored as an array and that all unoccupied records are marked in some special way (such as a negative value for the key) which makes it possible to identify them easily. Then the portion of the program for adding a new record can be as follows:

```
Obtain the key
Use the hashing function to compute the
        corresponding location in the array
Loop while this location is occupied
        Add 1 to this location, modulo the length
                of the file
End loop
Insert new record in this location
```

An analogous portion of program is needed to search for a particular record. Of course, in trying to add a new record provision should be made for doing something sensible if the array is already full. It would be simplest to keep a separate count of the number of entries in the table. In searching, it may be wise to provide for the possibility that the record cannot be found.

Deletion is more complicated. Once a specified record has been found and deleted, it may be necessary to shift some of the records between the one that has been deleted and the next unoccupied record in the array, in order to ensure that future searches need only proceed as far as the first unoccupied record. The solution is not unique, but one way of carrying out appropriate shifts is as follows:

```
/Assume that i is the location just made vacant and
        that j is the next unoccupied location/
Loop
        Search locations j − 1, j − 2, ..., i + 1, modulo
                the length of the file, for the first record,
                if any, whose hash code is ≦i or >j
        If (there is no such record)
........Exit loop
```

```
        else
                Move this record to the ith location
                Set i = old location of this record
                Mark new ith location unoccupied
                If (i = j − 1)
.........Exit loop
                End if
        End if
End loop
Stop
```

Exercise 12.2

2. The maximum number of comparisons needed by the bubble sort is approximately $n^2/2$ when n is large. However, the average number is only $n^2/4$.

4. The disadvantage of the insertion sort is that, on the average, a large number of records have to be shifted in order to make room for those that are inserted in their appropriate locations.

7. If $n = 1000$, $n \log_2 n$ is approximately 10,000 whereas $n^2/2$ is 500,000. Thus, with this value of n, a merge sort requires 50 times fewer comparisons than more straightforward methods. On the other hand, a merge sort requires more storage, if it is carried out entirely within the memory of the computer. It is also true that more time may be required per comparison for a merge sort. However, the advantage of $n \log_2 n$ over $n^2/2$ more than compensates for these disadvantages in most applications, especially when n is large.

If the programming language being used allows recursion, it will be convenient to describe the merge sort in terms of recursive procedures. In any event, a "merge" statement such as the following:

Merge $A_i \leq A_{i+1} \leq \cdots$ with $B_j \leq B_{j+1} \leq \cdots$ to
        produce $C_1 \leq C_2 \leq \cdots$

will be needed. A suitable refinement for this statement is as follows:

```
Where "Merge ..." means
        Set ii = i, jj = j
        Determine length of array C
        Set n = 1
        Loop while n ≦ length of array C
                If (finished with array A)
                        C(n) = B(jj)
                        jj = jj + 1
                (finished with array B)
                        C(n) = A(ii)
                        ii = ii + 1
                (A(ii) < B(jj))
                        C(n) = A(ii)
                        ii = ii + 1
                else
                        C(n) = B(jj)
                        jj = jj + 1
                End if
                n = n + 1
        End loop
End where
```

8. It can be shown that sorting cannot be carried out with fewer than $n \log_2 n$ comparisons.

Exercise 12.3

1. With each comparison the number of possibilities is reduced by 1/2 approximately. Therefore, if k comparisons are made the number of possibilities has been reduced to approximately $(1/2)^k n$. We want this to be only 1, so we must take k large enough so that n is approximately 2^k. That is, we must take k to be approximately $\log_2 n$.

How should the program be modified to take some appropriate action if it turns out that X is not one of the entries in the table? How should it be modified to find the item in the table that is nearest to X?

3. The modification of the insertion sort suggested in this question leads to a program that requires at most $n \log_2 n$ comparisons to sort n items. However, it still has the disadvantage of having to move items to make the insertions themselves, and the number of moves can be quite large.

4. The following are some of the possibilities: owner's name and address, the make, year, model number, and color of the car, license number, serial number, owner's driver's license, and whether or not the car has been stolen. Can the file be organized so that it can be searched efficiently in a number of alternative ways, such as by name of owner or by license number? Would it be possible to obtain reasonably efficiently a list of all records for cars of a given make, model, and color?

5. This question is closely related to what was discussed in Section 10.1.

6. What are your views concerning the selling of lists of names and addresses to companies that use these lists to send out unsolicited advertising? Should government agencies be allowed to search medical files to obtain information that might be helpful in planning medical services or to determine, for example, if some diseases are being treated in radically different ways by different doctors?

7. How should an airline handle the situation when people make reservations on 2 or 3 flights? Is the file you have described organized in such a way that it would be easy to determine that a person has made more than one reservation? Should overbooking be allowed? Could information about the number of meals to be prepared for a particular flight be obtained easily from your file?

9. In estimating the cost you should include the initial cost of keypunching and the cost of verifying the correctness of what has been keypunched. The cost of maintaining the file must also be considered. It would be interesting to try to compare the costs of setting up and using a relatively modest file, such as a student record file, with a very large one that might be useful to the medical or legal profession. Even the "relatively modest" one may turn out to be surprisingly expensive!

Exercise 12.4

1. The updates for the file would include information concerning additional purchases made by particular cus-

tomers, payments received from particular customers, and information as to whether or not the account was in arrears, as well as information concerning the return of unwanted goods.

5. Provision should be included in your program for the possibility of current meter readings that are less than the last meter reading. For example, if the meter reading is a five-digit number, the current meter reading might be 00123 whereas the last meter reading might have been 99906.

9. Does the order in which the transactions for a particular day are processed have any effect on the outcome? For example, does it matter whether the notice of a new shipment is processed before or after the orders are processed?

11. One approach to the problem of being fair would be to make a preliminary calculation of each dividend and at the same time keep track of the roundoff errors. Then the preliminary calculations could be adjusted to distribute the total of all the roundoff errors over all the payments in some equitable manner. This approach is not really acceptable because it would require more than one pass through the data.

A much simpler approach is to keep a running total of all roundoff errors and to use this total at each stage to determine the rounding procedure. The general idea is to be generous if the roundoff errors are running in favor of the company, but to be less generous if the total of the roundoff errors has been in favor of the employees. To be specific, we begin by calculating the first payment to the nearest cent, but record the roundoff error. We then calculate the next payment exactly, but add the roundoff from the first payment before rounding the result to the nearest cent. We record the resulting roundoff error to use in the same way to adjust the next payment. This process is repeated with each payment.

This procedure ensures that the total of all roundoff errors at any stage in the calculation is never more than half a cent in magnitude. Moreover, everyone is treated equally.

Exercise 12.5

6. The problem becomes harder if we want the resulting programs to be efficient. It should be mentioned that it might also be useful to have a program that will use a decision table to determine its course of action, without bothering to translate the table into a program. This would be particularly useful if the decision table is likely to be changed frequently.

CHAPTER 13

Exercise 13.1

3. The representation introduced in this problem usually requires less storage. If n is large, the saving may be substantial. With an adjacency matrix, n^2 storage locations are required and many of these locations store information to the effect that a path of length 1 between two points does not exist. The scheme introduced in this problem requires only $(n + 1) + 2\times$(number of paths) storage locations, which in most cases is considerably less than n^2. A second point worth noting is that, given any point I in the graph, it is not necessary to search through n items to determine what points, if any, are connected to point I.

This representation can also be extended to problems in which a number is associated with each edge of a graph. The components of a third subscripted variable, L3, would give the number associated with the path specified by the corresponding components of L2.

The main disadvantage in using the representation suggested in Question 3 arises when we wish to know whether or not two particular points are connected by a path of length 1. The adjacency matrix gives this information immediately, whereas the representation of Question 3 requires a search, although the search is quite short if the graph is relatively sparse. Which representation is to be preferred depends upon storage requirements and whether we prefer working with the ith row of an adjacency matrix or a list of the points that are connected to point I.

4. With n points, and assuming that we do not double back, there is 1 possible path of length 1, $n - 2$ possible paths of length 2, $(n - 2)(n - 3)$ of length 3, ..., $(n - 2)(n - 3)(n - 4) \ldots (n - p)$ of length p. The total number of possible paths is therefore

$$1 + (n - 2) + (n - 2)(n - 3) + \cdots + (n - 2)(n - 3)(n - 4) \ldots (2)(1).$$

Reversing the order of the terms, this series is equal to

$$(n - 2)!(1 + 1 + 1/2! + 1/3! + \cdots + 1/(n - 2)!)$$
$$\approx (n - 2)!e \approx (n - 2)!(2.7).$$

An approximation for the sum of the series is therefore

$$8!(2.7) \approx 10^5 \quad \text{if} \quad n = 8,$$

and

$$18!(2.7) \approx 5 \times 10^{15} \quad \text{if} \quad n = 20.$$

The value of $n!$ grows very quickly as n increases. Any method in which the amount of work is proportional to $n!$ requires too much time, even with the fastest machines, when n is moderately large.

The method of Question 1 requires at most $n - 1$ matrices to be constructed. Each matrix has n^2 elements, and each element requires n multiplications to be performed. The method therefore requires at most $(n - 1) \times n^2 \times n \approx n^4$ multiplications.

The method of Question 2 is even more efficient, especially if some care is taken to improve the efficiency of the program outlined in Fig. 13.3.

The method of Question 3 is the same as the method of Question 2 except that the one in Question 3 does not usually require as many items to be searched to determine if the path can be extended. The reason is that it needs to search only those elements with which the point in question is connected. If the matrix is sparse, the saving is considerable. The method of Question 3 is, in general, much more efficient than the method in Question 2. This is a good illustration of how the choice of data representation can have a profound effect on efficiency.

5. As an example, consider once again the method outlined in Fig. 13.3. To be able to determine the path itself, as well as whether or not one exists, it is convenient to use an additional array, say p (for path). Then, whenever l_m is set equal to pathlength, the corresponding component, p_m, is set equal to k. Thus, when the node m is reached, we can determine from p_m the node, namely k, from which it is reached. Then, knowing k, we can in turn determine from p_k the node from which k was reached, and so on, back to the original node i.

8. For a given dominance matrix a_{ij}, computing

$$b_{ij} = \max(a_{i1} \times a_{1j}, a_{i2} \times a_{2j}, \ldots, a_{in} \times a_{nj})$$

leads to a matrix in which $b_{ij} = 1$ if individual i dominates individual j indirectly through a third person; otherwise $b_{ij} = 0$. This leads to computing

$$c_{ij} = \max(a_{ij}, b_{ij})$$

so that $c_{ij} = 1$ if individual i dominates individual j directly, or indirectly through another person. In this matrix, if all entries in the ith row (except possibly the ith element) are one, then the ith person is a natural leader.

A corresponding situation exists with regard to followers. It can be shown that at least one individual follows all others, either directly or indirectly.

It is fairly easy to prove by induction that there is at least one natural leader under the circumstances stated in the question. The result is obviously true for small numbers of individuals such as 2 or 3. Let us assume it is true for k individuals and show that it must then be true for $k + 1$ individuals. We choose some k of the $k + 1$ individuals and pick out one leader amongst these k. All others, of these k individuals, can be divided into two classes: one consists of individuals who are dominated directly by the leader, the other of individuals who are dominated indirectly. (Some individuals can belong to either class but it does not matter in which class we place them.) If the leader dominates the $(k + 1)$st individual directly, or if anyone in the first class dominates him directly, the leader of the k individuals is also a leader of the $k + 1$ individuals. If none of these circumstances hold, the $(k + 1)$st individual must dominate the former leader directly, as well as all individuals in the first class. Since he dominates all in the first class directly, he must dominate all in the second class indirectly (just as the former leader did) and the $(k + 1)$st individual qualifies as a natural leader of the enlarged group. We have therefore shown that either the leader of the k individuals or the $(k + 1)$st individual must be a natural leader of the $k + 1$ individuals. In either case, there is a natural leader, and the proof is complete.

9. The methods of Questions 6 and 7 are easily modified to determine the longest path length, which gives the minimum time that is required to complete the project. Use t_{ij} to represent the time associated with the edge joining point i to point j, if there is an edge; otherwise $t_{ij} = 0$ if $i = j$ and $t_{ij} = -\infty$ if $i \neq j$.

Using the method of Question 6, we then find

$$r_{ij} = \max(t_{i1} + t_{1j}, t_{i2} + t_{2j}, \ldots, t_{in} + t_{nj})$$

for the maximum times for paths of length 2, and

$$s_{ij} = \max(t_{ij}, r_{ij})$$

for the maximum times for paths of length less than or equal to 2. After $n - 1$ steps, s_{be}, where the starting point is b and the final point is e, is the time for the longest path.

The method of Question 7 can also be modified in order to determine the critical path.

11. There are 100 intersections in Blizzardville. An excessive amount of memory is required if an adjacency matrix is used to represent which streets are open and which streets are closed. Each intersection can be connected to at most four other intersections, and the representation you choose for storing the information about which streets are open and which streets are closed should make use of this fact.

Exercise 13.2

1. The two factorings of 1296 which produce the same sum are 1, 18, 72, and 2, 8, 81, the sum being 91.

2. Let us denote the number of pairs at the end of the Ith month by $N(I)$. Then $N(0) = 1$ and $N(1) = 1$. For $I = 2, 3, \ldots$, we calculate the values of $N(I)$ by means of the following recurrence formula:

$$N(I) = N(I - 1) + N(I - 2).$$

The first term on the right side, $N(I - 1)$, simply indicates that the pairs at the end of the $(I - 1)$st month survive to the end of the Ith month. The second term represents the number of births that take place at the end of the Ith month; the only pairs that can produce such births are those that were alive at the end of the $(I - 2)$nd month. It turns out that there are 121,393 pairs at the end of 24 months. (Many interesting properties of the Fibonacci sequence, along with several references on the subject, are given in an article by Martin Gardner in *Scientific American*, March, 1970, pp. 116–120.)

5. We will not describe a complete proof here, but will give only an indication of how to get started. First of all, it is not too difficult to determine which position must be used for the first cube. It is one of the positions in which both the top and bottom are red. (It doesn't matter which of these two positions you choose because the other choice will simply lead to the same relative positions of the different cubes.) The reason that the other positions must be rejected are outlined in the following paragraph.

We cannot stack the first cube with 3 Red faces showing on the sides. If we did, there could be only 1 more Red face and this would have to be provided by the second cube (which cannot avoid having at least 1 Red face showing on the sides of the stack). There are two ways in which this can be done. The first way leads to 5 White faces showing, while the other way leads to 5 Green faces. Since neither of these possibilities can provide a solution, we conclude that the first cube cannot have all 3 Red faces showing. We can also show that the first cube cannot have 2 Red faces showing, although to obtain this result we have

to follow through and test some trial arrangements. The difficulty is to carry out these tests in a systematic way and make sure that all distinct possibilities have been accounted for.

Once we have established that we need consider only one position for the first cube, the problem is very much reduced in size and it is much easier to test possibilities for the remaining cubes.

An entirely different approach is to first represent the problem as shown in the following diagram:

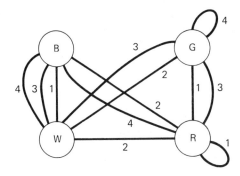

The 1 on the edge connecting B and W indicates that cube No. 1 has a Blue face opposite a White face. The other edge numbers have similar interpretations. The Instant Insanity problem can now be rephrased as one of finding two subgraphs of the given graph, each subgraph having four edges numbered 1, 2, 3, and 4, and having vertices of degree 2, and such that the subgraphs have no edges in common.

The following are two such subgraphs:

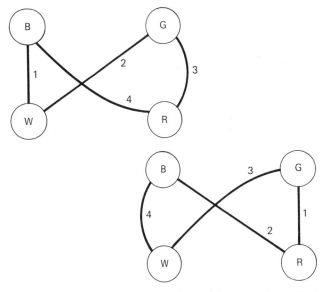

You should check to see that these subgraphs do in fact correspond to a solution to the problem. Are there any others?

6. A variety of suggestions are discussed in an excellent treatment of Tic-tac-toe as a computer application in a book entitled *Basic Programming* by John G. Kemeny and Thomas E. Kurtz (Wiley, New York, 1967). An interesting chapter on the game is contained in the *Scientific*

American Book of Mathematical Puzzles and Diversions by Martin Gardner (Simon and Schuster, New York, 1959).

7. There is a strategy for playing Nim that guarantees a win whenever it is possible to do so. We will not describe the strategy in detail, but simply illustrate the idea with an example. We first require the number of counters in each pile to be expressed in *binary* form and then we add the columns, in decimal, as shown below. In this example we assume that the three piles contain 35, 86, and 103 counters; these numbers are larger than what one would usually have in an actual game, but it is a little easier to explain the strategy with such numbers.

$$
\begin{array}{r}
35 = 100011 \\
86 = 1010110 \\
103 = \underline{1100111} \\
2210232
\end{array}
$$

The following is a strategy for winning the game when the purpose is to pick up the last counter. The idea is to leave our opponent with three piles whose binary representations give a total that consists entirely of even digits (0 or 2). It happens that: (1) if the digits are not all even, we can always make a move that will make them all even, and (2) if the digits are all even, *any* move will make them not all even. Because of these two facts, if we can once present our opponent with an "all-even" situation, we will be able to do so in all subsequent moves of the game. If we start with a situation that is not all-even, we are therefore sure to win. If we start with one that is all-even, we can make a random play in the hope that our opponent will make a mistake. Since most arrangements of counters are not all-even, we have a good chance of winning against a player who does not know the strategy.

To return to our example, it is easy to see what move will lead to an all-even situation. We must do something to change the 1 and the 3 in the sum. This is easily accomplished by subtracting 10010 from the second row. Since 10010 is 18 (in decimal) we remove 18 counters from the second pile. This leads to

$$
\begin{array}{r}
35 = 100011 \\
68 = 1000100 \\
103 = \underline{1100111} \\
2200222
\end{array}
$$

Whatever move is now made by our opponent, he will introduce at least one odd digit in the sum, and we can then make a move that restores the all-even property. By considering examples with only a few counters left, it can be seen that preserving the all-even property is a winning strategy.

Further information about Nim is given in the references at the end of the preceding question.

8. Games like Oware are known in many parts of the world, especially in Africa where it is said to be particularly well known. A number of different variants of the game are described by Charles H. Goren in *Goren's Hoyle: Encyclopedia of Games,* Greystone Press, Hawthorn Books, New York, 1961, pp. 410–412. The game given in the text

is a version described by W. W. Sawyer, who first learned about it in Ghana. The players can agree to terminate a game if each player has only a few men left. There are several different rules for deciding how to divide the men remaining at the end of the game between the two players.

Some suggestions regarding this game, including some ideas for developing a good strategy, are given in a text entitled *Introduction to Electronic Computers* by Fred J. Gruenberger and Daniel D. McCracken, Wiley, New York, 1961.

9. A solution to the Towers of Hanoi problem can be described in a particularly simple manner if the programming language being used allows recursion. In this case, if we denote the three pegs by A, B, and C, the statement

    Move N discs from A to B using C

can be refined as follows:

    Where "Move N discs from A to B using C" means
      If (N = 1)
          Move one disc from A to B
      (N > 1)
          Move N − 1 discs from A to C using B
          Move one disc from A to B
          Move N − 1 discs from C to B using A
    End if
  End where

The two occurrences of "Move one disc from A to B" can include output of a description of the move, and the final result will be a sequence of outputs that specify a complete solution of the problem.

It can be shown that a total of $2^N - 1$ individual moves is needed, and it should be noted that this number is impractically large unless N is quite small.

Exercise 13.3

3. In (a), (b), and (d) the required coordinates can be obtained from

$$
\begin{aligned}
x &= a + r \cos \theta \\
y &= b + r \sin \theta
\end{aligned}
$$

where (a,b) is the center and r the radius of the circle. To produce 48 points, we should find the coordinates for $\theta = n\pi/24$, $n = 0,1,\ldots,47$. Computing time can be reduced by taking advantage of the symmetry of the diagram, but the program will become longer and more complicated. For some applications it may be worthwhile testing the results of the calculations to make sure they do not correspond to points outside the range of permitted values.

More care must be taken in (c). One good way to handle this case is to find the "coordinates" (I,J), which should be represented by dots or asterisks, for the first octant only and then find the others by means of the symmetries of the circle. This means finding the values of y that correspond to the lines on the printer (that is, to the proper values of J) and then calculating the corresponding values of x from the formula $x = \sqrt{r^2 - y^2}$. These values of x must be rounded to their nearest integer values in order to produce values of I. The values of y should be all those lying between b and $b + r/\sqrt{2}$.

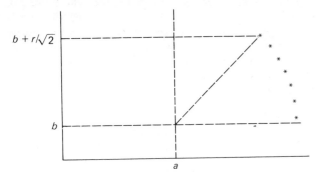

4. b) If we rotate the point (x,y) about the point (a,b) by an angle θ, we obtain the point (x',y'), where

$$x' - a = (x - a) \cos \theta - (y - b) \sin \theta,$$
$$y' - b = (x - a) \sin \theta + (y - b) \cos \theta.$$

c) If we scale the point (x,y) with respect to the point (a,b) by the scale factor s, we obtain the point (x',y'), where

$$x' - a = s(x - a),$$
$$y' - b = s(y - b).$$

6. a) One approach is to determine the equations of the two lines and solve the equations to find their point of intersection. Then it would be necessary to determine whether or not this point was on both line segments. (If it lies on the extensions of either or both, the line segments do not intersect.) Provision would have to be made for the possibility of parallel or coincident lines.

Another approach, and probably the better of the two, is to find the equations of the lines in the form $Ax + By + C = 0$ as before, but this time make use of the fact that $Ax' + By' + C$ is positive for (x',y') on one side of the line and negative for (x',y') on the other side. The line segments intersect if and only if the endpoints of each line segment are on opposite sides of the line determined by the other segment.

b) One possibility is to determine whether or not any edge of one polygon intersects any edge of the other. A preliminary check to determine whether or not the minimum enclosing rectangles overlap can be done relatively quickly and, if they do not overlap, it can be concluded that the polygons do not intersect and a considerable amount of further computation can be avoided. Such a preliminary check could be worthwhile in some circumstances.

c) Choose any point that is definitely outside the polygon, such as a point on the boundary of the allowed region. We then imagine a line segment being drawn from the given point to the outside point, and we count the number of intersections that this line segment makes with the sides of the polygon. If this number is even, the original point is outside the polygon; if odd, it is inside.

8. Representation (c) is much easier to output on a printer. To output other representations on a printer, it is simplest to convert them to (c). This means that we must have a way of converting a line segment into a sequence of dots or asterisks in appropriate entries of a matrix. If the slope of the line is less than 1 in magnitude, we should compute values of x that correspond to columns on the printer, and then compute the corresponding values of y from the equation of the line segment. The latter must be rounded to correspond to the lines on the printer.

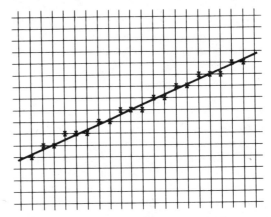

Vertical lines in the figure represent columns on the printer; horizontal lines represent lines on the printer. If the slope of the line segment is greater than 1 in magnitude, we should compute the values of y first and then find the corresponding values of x from the equation.

One of the difficulties that arises stems from the fact that the spacing of columns on a line is not the same as spacing of the lines themselves. For the purposes of this question it is probably best to ignore this difference and proceed as if the two spacings were the same. The resulting pictures will be distorted, of course, but it may not be worth the trouble to compensate for the distortion.

9. Translation and scaling of three-dimensional objects are easily handled. Rotation is quite a bit more complicated. One of the simplest ways of viewing this process is to imagine the rotation carried out in several stages. We first translate the origin to a point about which we wish to have the rotation take place. Then we perform the rotation in three stages as explained below, after which we translate back to the origin.

To perform the required rotation we perform three separate rotations, one in each of the three planes. For example, to rotate the vector (x,y,z) by an angle θ in the $x - y$ plane, we obtain the result (x',y',z') by means of the matrix-vector product given below:

$$\begin{pmatrix} x' \\ y' \\ z' \end{pmatrix} = \begin{pmatrix} \cos \theta & -\sin \theta & 0 \\ \sin \theta & \cos \theta & 0 \\ 0 & 0 & 1 \end{pmatrix} \begin{pmatrix} x \\ y \\ z \end{pmatrix}$$

To perform a second rotation by an angle ϕ in the $x - z$ plane, we obtain the result (x'',y'',z'') by means of

$$\begin{pmatrix} x'' \\ y'' \\ z'' \end{pmatrix} = \begin{pmatrix} \cos \phi & 0 & -\sin \phi \\ 0 & 1 & 0 \\ \sin \phi & 0 & \cos \phi \end{pmatrix} \begin{pmatrix} x' \\ y' \\ z' \end{pmatrix}$$

Similarly a third rotation can be performed in the $y - z$ plane.

It is a relatively straightforward matter to program these transformations. However, it may not be the most convenient way of carrying out the kind of transformations required in a practical application. There are at least two possible objections. One is that the user may prefer to think of rotations in terms of an axis of rotation and an angle. He would then be forced to transform his specifications into the point and angles required by the program. Secondly, it is uneconomic to recompute sines and cosines every time they are needed if the arguments do not change. The program should be organized in a way that enables it to take advantage of such a situation.

10. The simplest way to get a result of the kind required in this question is to perform two rotations, like those described in the preceding question, with the purpose of making the projection plane end up in a position parallel to one of the coordinate planes. The projection of the object is then easily obtained by making the remaining coordinate equal to zero. Thus, if we rotate into a plane parallel to the $x - y$ plane, we make all z coordinates equal to zero. Once again, this may not be as convenient to the user as he would wish. He may prefer to define the direction of projection in another way.

Another complication arises if we wish the projection to be from a point (such as one's eye), rather than along lines that are perpendicular to a given plane.

12. Let z be the coordinate measured out from the plane of the page. There is a simple rule for determining which of the 12 line segments that make up a cube cannot be seen. We search the corners of the cube for the corner whose z-coordinate is least. The three lines issuing from that corner cannot be seen. This rule may work satisfactorily even in the special cases where we have a two-way or even a four-way tie for the corner with the minimum z-coordinate. When there is a tie, it may not matter which corner we choose. For example, this is the case if we are using representation (c). Otherwise, special steps may have to be taken in case there is a tie. For example, we may want to ensure that a pen does not try to retrace a line on a plotter, lest the line appear to be too thick.

The "hidden-line" problem is in general a very difficult one. It is quite a bit easier if we know that the object is a cube.

13. A major problem in many applications is that of recognizing patterns. The purpose of this question is to introduce the idea in a relatively simple situation, where the problem is to find the outline of a certain region. The general problem is more complicated because the region is not usually so simple and also because the outline may not be sharply defined. Consider, for example, the problem of identifying interesting regions in a chest X-ray.

There is one relatively simple approach to this problem. It is to scan every point in the matrix and to apply the following rule: remove every dot that has 4 other dots that are located North, South, East, and West of it. The main disadvantage of this program is that it requires the examination of every point, and may therefore require an excessive amount of computer time.

It is a much more challenging problem to write a program that is capable of following an outline. Suppose that some preliminary scanning has located a dot on the boundary of the given region. An "edge following" program would then be able to work its way around the outside edge of the region, identifying those dots that lie on the edge and producing a new figure consisting only of the dots on the outline.

Exercise 13.4

3. The main programming requirement is for a portion of a program that can search through text material and locate the occurrence of a specified word. It would have to be able to find the word regardless of whether it occurs in the middle of a line of text (possibly followed by a punctuation mark, or next to a left or right parenthesis), or if it occurs at one end of a line. The word may also be hyphenated, unless it has been arranged in advance that such hyphens have been removed during some sort of pre-editing of the material.

Concordances are used increasingly for research by scholars in a number of areas. Statistical studies of various texts are also of interest in quite a few areas. For example, in some situations very strong evidence regarding the authorship of ancient texts can be derived from such statistical results. The results can often differ quite noticeably between two different authors.

Putting text into machine-readable form can be extremely costly. It is easy to underestimate the cost of getting such a task done, especially if not enough allowance is made for getting dependable results.

In general, a program cannot be expected to recognize nouns, verbs, and so on. Even in very special circumstances the rules would be extremely complicated. But in general circumstances no rules are available that, to mention just one difficulty, would be able to resolve the ambiguities that occur so frequently in the language of ordinary text material. Pre-editing with special symbols to mark verbs, nouns, etc., would be necessary if the program was to take these properties into account.

6. A key part of this problem is the justification of a line of text. Once the words to be fitted onto one line have been determined, extra blanks will usually have to be inserted between some of the words. One possibility is to insert one after the first, another after the second, and so on, until the right number have been inserted. If a blank has been inserted after the second last word and the right number have still not been inserted, the process could be started again with another blank after the first word, then after the second, and so on. To give a balanced appearance to the paragraphs, the program could insert blanks from the left, as just described, only with alternate lines, inserting them from the right with the other lines.

For this question it is quite difficult to write a program that does a good job in a wide variety of circumstances. For example, should the program be able to handle the case where only two words can be fitted onto one line? What if only one word can be squeezed in (as could happen, for example, with one long chemical term on a short line such as is used in a newspaper column)? It is usually considered a good idea to have two blanks following a period at the end of a sentence. But can such a period be distinguished from a period in e.g., or from the periods following someone's initials?

One of the main difficulties that arises in organizing a program for this question is that the input and output steps are not synchronized. Only part of the first line of input may be needed to complete the first line of output. But the second line of input may have to be obtained before the second line of output is completed. A good way to handle this complication is to start with an overall design of a program which assumes that the input is simply a stream of characters, without regard, at least at first, to the fact that the characters may most conveniently be input in groups, such as one card at a time.

It will, of course, be necessary to refine a statement such as "Get character." If cards are used for input, this refinement can simply count characters and input a new card whenever the count reaches a multiple of 80.

CHAPTER 14

Exercise 14.1

1. Since this question does not require the interpreter to handle incorrect programs, the outline given in Fig. 14.1 can be completed in a straightforward way to produce the required solution. One complication that may be encountered is that some programming languages do not allow subscripts to be zero. This difficulty can be overcome by representing MEMORY(000) as MEMORY(1), MEMORY(001) as MEMORY(2), and so on.

2. Since the hypothetical machine of Appendix A does not have any index registers, it is necessary to provide for this feature. A subscripted variable XREG can be used for this purpose.

One major change that must be made concerns effective address computation. With the machine of Appendix A, it is easy to compute an address, since we need only find the remainder when the instruction being interpreted is divided by 1000. However, with SIMON programs, the computation of effective addresses is more complicated. The following portion of a program outline shows how this can be done, where it is assumed that INSTRUCTION represents the instruction being interpreted.

```
ADDRESSTWO = digits 2,3,4 of INSTRUCTION
INDEX      = digit 5 of INSTRUCTION
OPCODE     = digits 6,7 of INSTRUCTION
ADDRESS    = digits 8,9,10 of INSTRUCTION
If(OPCODE < 60 and indexing specified)
    ADDRESS = ADDRESS + appropriate
                 component of XREG
If(indirect addressing specified)
    ADDRESS = last three digits of MEMORY(ADDRESS)
/ADDRESS contains the effective address at this
                 point/
```

Note that indexing is allowed only when the operation code is less than 60, and that indexing is performed before an indirect address is determined.

The additional operation codes 32, 33, 60, 61, 62, and 63 must also be provided for in an interpreter for SIMON programs. A sequence of tests can easily be inserted to test operation codes for these possibilities. In order to interpret operation codes 32 and 33, which provide alphanumeric input and output, it is necessary to establish a table of equivalences between the allowed characters and their corresponding SIMON codes. A table look-up can be used to convert each character from one representation to the other. Interpreting operation codes 60–63 is not difficult.

3–4. The first requirement mentioned in Question 3 can be handled within the first Loop-End in the outline of Fig. 14.1. This portion of the interpreter is often referred to as the "loader," since its purpose is to load the instructions to be interpreted into the memory of the machine.

In order that the interpreter be fail safe, provision for the following situations must be included:

i) Invalid input, which can be encountered by the loader, as well as when operation codes 30 or 32 are interpreted.

ii) Invalid operation codes, or improperly specified instructions.

iii) Invalid addresses, especially when address modification with index registers is required.

iv) Other suggestions specified in Question 3.

The loader cannot detect invalid operation codes, since it must be possible to load constants and other data that the program may wish to use.

A final suggestion concerns the interpretation of operation codes 60–63. The tests for invalid instructions must be carefully designed. For example, it is necessary to specify an index register with operation codes 60–63. Overflow is a possibility with operation code 62. Tests to detect these possibilities must be included if the interpreter is to fail safe.

5. The purpose of this question is to require a different type of documentation than that required with most problems. In order to be used effectively a programming language requires documentation of various kinds. First of all, the interpreter must be documented. This is the type of documentation required with Questions 1 and 2 and emphasized in earlier sections. A User's Manual must also be available and it is this type of documentation that was required for Question 4. Finally, a system programmer's manual must be provided for those people who are to maintain the system. These various kinds of documentation must be "tailored" for prospective users, and these problems illustrate the variety of purposes for which documentation is required.

In preparing documentation of the first-mentioned type, some emphasis must be placed on explaining the algorithm. The second type must emphasize how to use the program, but need not explain how it works. Finally, the third type must explain how to modify the program so that various features can be added or deleted, or so that corrections can be made when necessary.

Providing for floating-point arithmetic is not recommended as an exercise, but explaining how it can be provided for will reinforce the concepts involved. In addition to providing for the four floating-point arithmetic operations, some discussion as to how the input and output could be handled is worthwhile.

7. An interpreter for the movie-making language could make substantial use of the subprograms that were developed for the questions in Exercise 13.3. Similarly, subprograms that were developed for the other application areas mentioned would be useful if one of these other application areas is selected.

Exercise 14.2

1. This question is difficult; the development of an assembler for the simple assembly language introduced in Section B.1 is a simpler problem. Such an assembler could then be extended to incorporate the additional features of the SAP assembly language.

The first portion of an assembler for "simple SAP" is described by the program outline given below. As indicated below, one method that can be employed is to perform the translation in two stages, or "passes" through the source code. (It is possible, but not straightforward, to develop a one-pass assembler.) In the first pass, the operation codes can be translated to their SIMON counterparts (the table should include the blank opcode as well as L, ST, etc.), a table of defined symbols and their locations can be constructed (this is often referred to as the "symbol table"), and any additional information required for the second pass is saved.

In the program outline given below, it is assumed that the end of the simple assembly-language program is indicated by END in the operation code field.

```
Initialize Locationcounter and symbol table
Loop
    Input NAME, OPCODE, ARGUMENT
...If (OPCODE = END) exit loop
    Increment Locationcounter
    If (NAME is not blank)
        Save the name and its location in the
            symbol table
    End if
    Translate OPCODE, using a table look-up, and
        store result in MEMORY(Locationcounter)
    Save ARGUMENT for pass 2
End loop
/End of pass 1/
```

The second pass completes the translation to machine language. The arguments must be translated into addresses using the symbol table constructed in the first pass. If an argument is not found in the symbol table, it must be

added to the table, as indicated in the following outline for pass 2.

```
/Second pass/
Loop for J = 0,1, . . . , Locationcounter
    If (ARGUMENT(J) is a name or literal)
        Look it up in symbol table
        If(name or literal was not found)
            Add name or literal to symbol table,
                and assign next available address
                for its location
        End if
        Use appropriate address to complete the
            translation of the instruction in
            MEMORY(J)
    End if
End loop
Loop for J = Locationcounter + 1, . . . , Location-
                counter + number of symbols added
                to symbol table
    If(symbol added was a literal)
        MEMORY(J) = value of literal
    End if
End loop
/End pass 2/
```

Finally, following execution of the assembler, control can be handed over to an interpreter so that the machine-language program can be executed. The interpreter in this case would be identical to that outlined in Fig. 14.1, except that the loader is no longer required.

The following suggestions may be helpful in extending the assembler given above to handle SAP programs:

- Pseudo opcodes must be detected in pass 1, since the location counter must be increased by more than 1 with most RES instructions.
- The additional operation codes must be added to the table used to translate opcodes.
- The translation of arguments must detect commas, and be able to separate arguments into the various parts, which then must be dealt with individually.

2–3. Some of the difficulties that should be handled are as follows:

duplicate names in name field,
invalid operation codes,
undefined names (with branch instructions),
invalid address fields (for example, an address missing with BIX or no index register specified when required).

Refer to the answer given for Question 5 of Exercise 14.1 regarding documentation.

4. This question introduces one way in which assemblers create a number of machine-language statements corresponding to only one statement in the assembly-language program. To handle the statement INT I,J the assembler must have the following sequence of numbers available in a block.

```
10000
11007
10000
11000
10007
11000
50008
    0
```

The address of I is then added to the first and fourth of these numbers, the address of J is added to the third and sixth, and the value of the location counter when the statement was encountered must be added to the second, fifth, and seventh numbers. In this way, a block of instructions, such as those illustrated in the text, can be generated whenever INT is encountered.

Exercise 14.3

2. In order to be convinced that the shunting-yard algorithm converts from infix to postfix forms, it is necessary to convince ourselves that operators are placed following the operands to which they apply, that parentheses are discarded, and generally that the input and output are equivalent expressions. Proving that algorithms do what they are supposed to do can be extremely difficult.

An algorithm that works correctly on a particular set of examples can always be modified so that it will fail on others. For example, if none of the particular set has an input string of a certain length, we can modify the algorithm so that it will examine the length of the input string and do something ridiculous whenever that certain length is encountered. The point of all this is simply to prove that a set of successful examples can never, by themselves, prove the correctness of a program.

A rigorous proof of the correctness of a program such as the shunting-yard algorithm is a bit too complicated to consider here. We shall have to be content with testing the algorithm on a number of carefully chosen examples, and examining the algorithm itself in detail. Such a detailed examination would constitute a proof, if done carefully enough, but a complete proof for the shunting-yard algorithm involves a rather complicated use of induction and is beyond the scope of this text.

In actual practice, there are additional difficulties that must be considered when we are concerned about the correctness of programs, especially with regard to what they do on invalid input. We must also make provision for exceeding the capacity of our resources. For example, in the case of the shunting-yard algorithm, we must make sure that the capacity of the stack is not exceeded.

3. Invalid use of parentheses can be detected quite easily. If a right parenthesis appears at the head of the input string and a left parenthesis is not found in the stack, or if a left parenthesis is moved to the output string when the input string is empty, then the parentheses are not properly matched in the input expression.

The other kinds of errors that can be detected are those in which the following rules are not adhered to. Diagnostic messages can be given whenever these rules are broken.

i) the first item must be a variable or a left parenthesis,
ii) a variable must be followed by a right parenthesis or an operator,
iii) a left parenthesis must be followed by a left parenthesis or a variable,
iv) an operator must be followed by a left parenthesis or a variable,
v) a right parenthesis must be followed by a right parenthesis or an operator,
vi) the last item must be a right parenthesis or a variable.

In order to detect situations in which these rules are not followed, it is necessary to perform a test each time the next item at the head of the input string is examined. (The initialization can include setting the value of a variable to indicate that the last item examined was an operator.) One extra test is necessary at the end of the procedure.

4. One way of dealing with inserted blanks, variable names of more than one character, and operands that are constants is to edit the input string and construct an input string equivalent to that allowed as input for the algorithm described in Question 1. This can be accomplished by scanning the input string from left to right, discarding blanks as they are encountered, and searching for the beginning and end of variable names and constants. When a variable name of more than one character is encountered, it is entered in a symbol table (if it is not already in the table) and replaced in the input string by a single item—namely its address. Constants can be handled in a similar way. Thus, an input string such as

$$INT - (INT/100)*100 + 1$$

might be edited into the following sequence of items 999, −, (, 999, /, 997,), *, 997, +, 996, where it is assumed that INT corresponds to memory location 999, and locations 997 and 996 contain 100 and 1, respectively.

The unary operators + and − can be detected since they can appear only at the beginning of the string or immediately after a left parenthesis. (Binary + or − cannot appear in these positions.) A unary + can simply be ignored. A unary − can be handled by inserting a preceding constant of zero and then treating the − as if it were a binary operator, although it would obviously be more convenient to have a "change sign" operator available.

Function operators can also be handled. One way of doing this is to assign these operators a priority in such a way that the operators are stacked until the argument, or arguments, appear in the output string, and to then cause the operator to be unstacked. For example,

$$\sqrt{(A*A + B*B)} - F$$

(where $\sqrt{}$ is the symbol for square root) should be transformed to the following form:

$$AA*BB*+\sqrt{}F-$$

(When a pair of parentheses disappear, the top item in the stack is examined. If it is a function operator, then that operator should be unstacked into the output string.)

5. Using the suggestion given in this question, the only additional item to be considered concerns the detection of invalid forms. With assignment statements, the first item must be a variable and cannot be a constant. In addition, the second item must be an equals sign.

Exercise 14.4

1. Assume that the length of the postfix string is known in advance, since it was probably generated using the technique outlined in Section 14.3. As in earlier questions, it is more useful to construct a subprogram, rather than a program, for this question. The parameter list should include the input string, the length of the input string, and the array into which the assembly-language instructions are to be placed.

2. Ordinarily, the detection of errors would have been performed during the process of obtaining the Polish form. If this is not the case, an invalid Polish form can be easily detected, especially if unary operators are not allowed. One counter is required. Its value is initialized at 0. When an operand is encountered, the counter is incremented by one; if an operator is encountered, the counter is decremented by one. If the value of the counter ever goes below 1, the expression is invalid. The final value of the counter must be zero. (A separate test must also be done at the beginning. The first two items must be operands.)

3. Combining the solutions for Question 5, Exercise 14.3, and Question 1 of this exercise leads to the required result with one modification. The operator $=$ produces only a sequence of two instructions, and not three, as is the case with the four binary operations. (To produce efficient code, only one instruction, a store instruction using the argument on the bottom of the stack, need be generated. This instruction would replace the last store instruction that placed the value of the expression in a temporary location.)

4. The redundant store and load instructions can be deleted by testing the last generated instruction when an operator is encountered in scanning the postfix form from left to right. In many situations, it will be necessary to output only the two instructions *op v*1 and ST *Tn*. (Additional testing can detect situations in which the commutative property of $+$ and $*$ can be used to produce more efficient code. For example, the infix expression D*(A+B) is transformed to the Polish form DAB+*, which leads to

L	A
A	B
ST	T1
L	D
M	T1

when the algorithm of Fig. 14.4 is used. Clearly, it is more efficient to have the following code executed,

L	A
A	B
M	D

but it is also expensive to detect such situations.

The number of temporary locations required can be minimized by noting that whenever a load instruction specifies a temporary location as its argument, the content of that temporary location is no longer required and the location is free for other use.

Three temporary variable names are required for the following expression:

$$(A/B)/((A-B)/(B/A))$$

5. A solution to this problem involves a discussion of the answer for Question 4, Exercise 14.3. Blanks can be discarded, and variable names and constants can be replaced by single character addresses before the shunting-yard algorithm is performed. By so doing, such items will not appear in postfix forms, and thus they in no way affect the code-generation technique of this section.

6. The ideas of Questions 1, 3, and 4, Exercise 14.3, in addition to those of Question 1, Exercise 14.4, are required for a solution to this problem. In this case, however, the values of the constants can be used, instead of addresses, when the postfix form is being produced. Then, when the algorithm of Fig. 14.4 is used, the stack will contain values, rather than symbols, and the arithmetic operations can be performed, rather than "outputting appropriate three instructions." In order to work with values, it will be necessary to convert strings of numerals to fixed-point values. Invalid constants can be detected when this conversion is performed. Other invalid inputs (such as misuse of parentheses, an operator followed by a right parenthesis, etc.) can be detected using the ideas of Question 3, Exercise 14.3. Finally, it should be remembered that situations in which an attempt is made to divide by zero must be avoided.

8. Boolean expressions can be handled in an elegant way by simply assigning the correct priorities to the logical operators, so that the shunting-yard algorithm can be carried out with input strings that are Boolean expressions. The following table gives values of priorities that could be used for handling such expressions.

Symbol	*Priority*
(	0
$\vee$ (or)	1
$\wedge$ (and)	2
$\neg$ (not)	3
$>, \geq, =, \neq, <, \leq$	4
$+, -$	5
$*, /$	6
\$ (exponentiation)	7

APPENDIX

A Stored-Program Computer

The role played by the computer itself was discussed briefly in Section 1.2, and reasons were given there to indicate that some familiarity with the nature of a "stored-program" computer could be helpful to the user. Some knowledge of the ultimate form in which a user's program is executed on a computer can be helpful in a number of ways, in terms of an awareness of what can or cannot be accomplished, an appreciation of various questions related to efficiency, an understanding of roundoff error, and so on.

The purpose of this appendix is to explain the nature of a stored-program computer and to emphasize those features which are most important from the user's point of view. To accomplish this, we will describe one particular machine in detail. We want to avoid most of the details that are needed to describe any of the machines in actual use. We therefore consider a simple hypothetical machine, but one which, nevertheless, has the main features needed to understand the ones used in practice. The basic ideas are quite similar, whether the machine is a large-scale one or a so-called minicomputer, or a "programmable" hand calculator. For anyone wishing to pursue this topic in still further detail, a number of additional features are introduced in Appendix B, together with a more convenient "lower-level" programming language for the hypothetical machine.

A.1 GENERAL DESCRIPTION

To understand the steps which a computer is able to carry out, the first idea we explain is that of a computer *memory*. This is a device for storing information, and the important points about it are as follows:

1. The information stored in the memory consists of two kinds: the instructions to be followed by the machine (in coded form) and the data to be handled by the machine (numbers to be added, alphabetic information to be printed out, and so on).

2. The machine is able to record new information in its memory. For example, after adding two numbers it records the result. It can also receive new information from an input device (such as a card reader or a typewriter) and record this information in its memory. Whenever new information is recorded in some part of a computer's memory, any information previously in that part is lost. The recording of information is therefore similar to what happens with a tape recorder. As new information is recorded on the tape of a tape recorder, any previously recorded information is erased. In fact, special tape units are often used as memory units, but tapes are too slow to be used for the main memory of a computer.

3. The machine can read any information it requires from its memory. In doing so it does not erase the in-

formation in the memory. This again is analogous to what happens with a tape recorder. When a tape recorder is used to produce the information stored on its tape, it does not erase that information.

There is a variety of devices which can be used as memory units for computers. Since there is no need for the user to understand what physical processes are involved, we will not consider any details as to how they are constructed. However, the user must know about the instruction codes and the way data is stored. In practice he may also have to take into account a number of factors such as size and speed of the memory of the particular machine he is using.

Let us now suppose that the instructions for a particular algorithm have already been stored in the memory of a computer. The next idea to be explained is that the computer can then proceed to carry out these instructions. It reads the first instruction from its memory and carries it out. Then it reads the second instruction and carries it out, and so on. One instruction may cause it to perform an addition; another may cause it to get new information from the next punched card and record it in memory. Once started, the machine proceeds through the sequence of instructions without any further intervention on the part of the operator.

This indicates in a general way how a computing machine is capable of carrying out algorithms for us. We first make out a list of instructions for the machine to follow. This list is then stored in the machine's memory, after which the machine begins to carry out the instructions for us.

EXERCISE A.1

1. What two different kinds of information are stored in a computer's memory?

2. In discussing computer memories, one sometimes hears the phrase *destructive read-in* and *nondestructive read-out.* Explain why these phrases are appropriate.

3. The phrase *automatic computer* is sometimes used to distinguish the kind of computer we are discussing from something much simpler, like a desk calculator. A desk calculator will automatically add, multiply, etc., and so will our computer. What is it about the computer we are discussing that makes it deserve the term automatic more than a desk calculator does?

A.2 INSTRUCTION CODES AND DATA

We will now consider what kinds of instructions and data may be stored in a computer's memory. We illustrate with the details for a hypothetical machine. A schematic diagram of the hypothetical machine is shown in Fig. A.1.

Computer memories are made up of a large number of relatively small units, which are sometimes called *words,* or *storage locations,* or *memory locations,* and each memory location has an *address.* We assume that our hypothetical machine has 1000 such memory locations, and that their addresses are 000, 001, 002, ..., ..., 999. We also assume that the computer has two other special storage locations, one called the *accumulator* and the other called the *instruction address register* (IAR).

The instruction address register can store the value of any three-digit nonnegative number, its purpose being to store the address of the next instruction to be executed. We assume that its initial value is 000 whenever the computer starts to execute instructions. In general, just after each instruction is executed, the value of the instruction address register is incremented by one. Instructions in the stored program may also alter its value, as will be discussed later.

Each of the 1000 memory locations and the accumulator are assumed able to store a sign and ten decimal digits. Thus, for example, the memory locations beginning at 000 may store the following information:

Address

	Content
000	+0000010073
001	+0000020074
002	+0000011075
...	...
...	...
...	...

while the three memory locations beginning at 073 are as follows:

073	+0000001234
074	+0000001111
075	−9876543210

and the accumulator is storing

+0000202020

One point should be emphasized. If we know only what is stored in a particular storage location, we usually do not know whether it is an instruction or some data. For example, +0000010073 is stored in memory location 000. This could represent an instruction, as we shall see in a moment, or it could be simply the number 10,073. However, the information stored in location 075, namely −9876543210, must be a number because instructions cannot be of this form.

All instructions considered in this appendix for our hypothetical machine will be of a special form. One

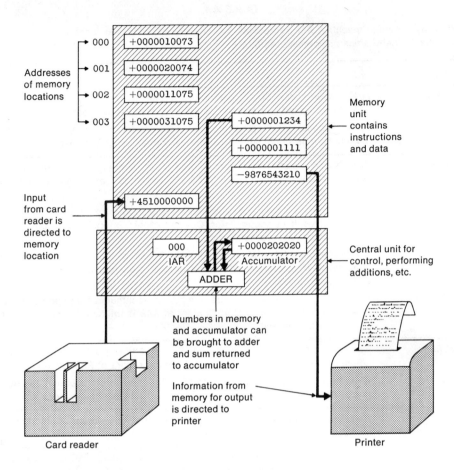

Addresses
of memory
locations

000 +0000010073
001 +0000020074
002 +0000011075
003 +0000031075

+0000001234
+0000001111
−9876543210

Memory
unit
contains
instructions
and data

Input
from card
reader is
directed to
memory
location

+4510000000

000
IAR

+0000202020
Accumulator

Central unit for
control, performing
additions, etc.

ADDER

Numbers in memory
and accumulator can
be brought to adder
and sum returned
to accumulator

Information from
memory for output
is directed to
printer

Card reader

Printer

FIG. A.1 Schematic diagram of computer showing different ways in which information can flow to or from the memory unit.

storage location can store one instruction. The properties of an instruction are summarized as follows:

1. the sign is positive;
2. the first five digits are zero;
3. the next two digits are a code determining the *operation* to be performed, according to Table A.1;
4. the last three digits give the address of the memory location that is needed by the operation, if any; otherwise, the last three digits are zero.

As a first example of an instruction, consider the one in location 000, namely, +0000010073. The sign is positive and the first five digits are zero as required. The operation code is 10. According to Table A.1 this is the code for copying information from a memory location to the accumulator. The memory location needed in this case is 073. The first instruction therefore causes the machine to copy the number in memory location 073 into the accumulator. The content of location 073 is not changed, but the original content of the accumulator is lost. The new content of the accumulator is

+0000001234

Consider now the second instruction, the one in location 001, which is +0000020074. According to Table A.1, 20 is the code for adding, and the number in location 074 is therefore added to the number in the accumulator. The content of 074 is unchanged, but the content of the accumulator is changed. The sum of +0000001234 and +0000001111 replaces what was in the accumulator, so that we now have

+0000002345

in the accumulator.

The third instruction, +0000011075 in 002, causes the machine to copy the number in the accumulator into storage location 075. This time the accumulator is unchanged, but the original content of 075 is lost. After carrying out the three instructions in order, the contents of the computer's memory locations are unchanged, except that 075 and the accumulator now both contain

+0000002345

and the IAR contains 003.

TABLE A.1

Instruction codes for the hypothetical machine. AAA represents the address of a storage location in memory; for example, AAA can be 073 or 074. Additional instructions are considered later.

Instruction	Meaning
+0000010AAA	*Load accumulator.* Copy content of location AAA into accumulator. Content of AAA is unchanged, but former content of accumulator is lost.
+0000011AAA	*Store accumulator.* Copy content of accumulator into location AAA. Content of accumulator is unchanged, but former content of AAA is lost.
+0000020AAA	*Add to accumulator.* Add number in AAA to number in accumulator and store result in accumulator. Content of AAA is unchanged, but former content of accumulator is lost.
+0000021AAA	*Subtract from accumulator.* Subtract number in AAA from number in accumulator and store result in accumulator. Content of AAA is unchanged, but former content of accumulator is lost.
+0000022AAA	*Multiply accumulator.* Multiply number in AAA by number in accumulator and store result in accumulator. Content of AAA is unchanged, but former content of accumulator is lost.
+0000023AAA	*Divide into accumulator.* Divide number in accumulator by number in AAA and store quotient in accumulator. Content of AAA is unchanged, but former content of accumulator is lost.
+0000030AAA	*Read.* Input number to location AAA. Sign and 10 digits of number are read from columns 1–11 of the next data card. Former content of AAA is lost.
+0000031AAA	*Write.* Output number from location AAA. Sign and 10 digits of number are printed in positions 1–11 of the next line. Content of AAA is unchanged.
+0000040000	*Halt.* This causes machine to stop. Notice that no address is needed with this instruction.
+0000050AAA	*Branch.* The value of the instruction address register IAR is changed to AAA. Thus, the next instruction to be executed is in memory location AAA.
+0000051AAA	*Branch on negative.* The value of IAR is changed to AAA if present content of accumulator < 0; otherwise, there is no effect and the normal sequencing continues.
+0000052AAA	*Branch on zero.* The value of IAR is changed to AAA if present content of accumulator $= 0$; otherwise, there is no effect.
+0000053AAA	*Branch on positive.* The value of IAR is changed to AAA if present content of accumulator > 0; otherwise, there is no effect.

The steps just described are typical of what a computer does. Of course, the instructions and data with which the machine begins must be prepared and placed in the computer's memory before the computer can begin to execute the instructions. We will assume that the machine is equipped with a special button that, when pressed, causes the instructions and data to be read from cards and stored in specified memory locations. When the program has been loaded, the content of the IAR is set to 000 and the computer begins to execute instructions. It copies the first instruction into its control unit and executes that instruction. It repeats this process with the second and third instructions, and so on, until instructed to stop.

The instructions and data which are placed initially in the computer's memory are together called the *program*. One way to prepare a program for a computer is to know its operation codes, like those in Table A.1, and to write out all the instructions and data that are required. This is called machine-language programming, and it was the method originally used with the early machines. However, it is obviously an extremely tedious process.

A much easier way to prepare programs for a machine is to write them in a programming language such as Fortran, Basic, or PL/I. When this is done, another program, called a *compiler,* is used to translate the program so written into a machine-language program. The computer is then able to carry out the translated program.

To understand programming languages thoroughly, one should know more about machine-language programming than what has been discussed so far. This is the purpose of the rest of this appendix.

EXERCISE A.2

1. What is the largest number that can be stored in a single memory location of our hypothetical machine?

2. Which of the following can represent instructions for the hypothetical machine?

a) +0000032045   b) +0000101234
c) +0000030000   d) −0000021365
e) +0000052999   f) +0330012321

3. Describe the changes that take place as the machine carries out the three instructions in locations 000, 001, and 002, in each of the following:

a)
000 +0000010200
001 +0000011201
002 +0000011202
...   ...
...   ...
...   ...
200 +0000000000
201 +1234567890
202 +1234567890
...   ...
...   ...
...   ...

b)
000 +0000010350
001 +0000020351
002 +0000011350
...   ...
...   ...
...   ...
...   ...
...   ...
350 +0000000013
351 +0000000001
...   ...
...   ...

4. What two instructions in locations 000 and 001 will cause the computer to copy the content of location 120 into location 125?

5. Suppose that the number 1 is stored in location 300. What sequence of instructions, beginning in location 000, will cause the computer to reduce the number stored in location 400 by 1?

6. Give a sequence of instructions that will cause the computer to replace the content of the accumulator by its square.

7. What happens if the accumulator holds

+0000000000

and the machine proceeds to carry out the following instructions:

000 +0000011000
001 +0000011001
002 +0000011002
...   ...
...   ...
...   ...

8. a) In attempting to interchange the numbers in memory locations 075 and 076, a programmer wrote the following sequence of instruction:

000 +0000010075
001 +0000011076
002 +0000010076
003 +0000011075
...   ...
...   ...
...   ...

Why does this sequence of instructions fail to produce the required result?

b) Write a sequence of instructions to interchange the contents of memory locations 075 and 076.

9. It is possible for a machine-language program to make up its own instructions. Consider, for example, the following sequence of instructions:

000 +0000010026
001 +0000020027
002 +0000011003
003 +0000000000
...   ...
...   ...
...   ...
026 +0000031000
027 +0000000500
...   ...
...   ...
...   ...

What is the content of location 003 immediately after the first three instructions have been executed, and what instruction does it represent?

A.3 EXAMPLES OF PROGRAMS

The example shown in Fig. A.2 is a program for finding the sum of two numbers, and a flowchart is shown beside the program to help explain it. Comments are given beside each instruction to help with the interpretation. Note that there is nothing in the machine-lan-

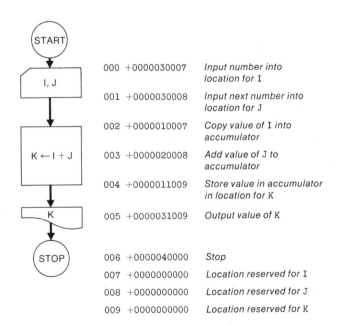

000	+0000030007	*Input number into location for I*
001	+0000030008	*Input next number into location for J*
002	+0000010007	*Copy value of I into accumulator*
003	+0000020008	*Add value of J to accumulator*
004	+0000011009	*Store value in accumulator in location for K*
005	+0000031009	*Output value of K*
006	+0000040000	*Stop*
007	+0000000000	*Location reserved for I*
008	+0000000000	*Location reserved for J*
009	+0000000000	*Location reserved for K*

FIG. A.2 Machine-language program for finding the sum of two numbers. A flowchart is also shown to help with the explanation and, incidentally, to show the correspondence between two ways of describing the same algorithm.

guage program to correspond to the start box of the flowchart. We assume that the machine always starts with whatever instruction is in location 000.

The first instruction is +0000030007. According to Table A.1 this causes the computer to input a number and store its value in location 007. We assume that our machine reads the sign and 10 digits of the number from columns 1–11 of the next data card. Once the number has been read and stored, the card reader passes on to the next card. The next input instruction will cause the next number to be read in and stored. In the example considered here the next input instruction appears in location 001. It causes the second number to be input and stored in location 008. The next three instructions (in locations 002, 003, and 004) cause the number in 007 to be copied into the accumulator, the number in 008 to be added to it, and the result to be stored in 009. The instruction in 005 then causes the result stored in 009 to be output. Finally, the instruction in 006 causes the machine to halt.

An important point to notice is that I, J, and K do not appear explicitly anywhere in the machine-language program. However, these names do have counterparts in the program. They correspond to addresses: I to 007, J to 008, and K to 009. Thus, each reference to I is a reference to the number stored in location 007. This situation is typical of the relationship between the two ways of describing algorithms. It should be clear that it does not matter which address corre-

sponds to I: the two references to 007 could be replaced just as well by references to 010, as long as all references to I are the same. (Of course, they cannot be replaced by references to 000, 001, . . . , or 006.)

One point remains to be discussed. We have stated that the flowchart and the machine-language program are two different ways of describing the same algorithm. This statement requires some qualification. The magnitudes of the numbers I, J, and K are not restricted in the flowchart, whereas they cannot exceed +9999999999 in the machine-language program. Differences like this can be avoided by assuming that our flowcharts are restricted in the same way that our machine is restricted. But the difference is a simple illustration of the distinction between an algorithm and a program that was mentioned in Section 1.2.

A second example of a program, one for finding the larger of two numbers, is shown in Fig. A.3. It is similar to the program we have just discussed, except that it illustrates the use of the operation codes 50 and 51. The first two instructions cause two numbers to be input and stored in locations 009 and 010. The next two instructions cause the difference between these two numbers to be found and the value of this difference, namely I−J, to be left in the accumulator.

According to Table A.1 the instruction in 004, namely +0000051007, causes the machine to go to 007 for its next instruction if the number in the ac-

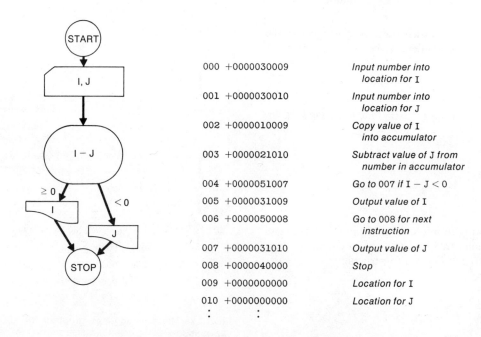

FIG. A.3   Machine-language program for finding the larger of two numbers.

cumulator is less than zero. In 007 there is an instruction for the output of the value of J, as required when the value of I−J is less than zero. Then, in 008, there is a stop instruction. On the other hand, if the value of I−J turns out to be greater than or equal to zero, the instruction in 004 allows the machine to continue in the normal sequence of instructions. This means it will go to the instruction in 005, that is, to the output of the value of I, as required when the value of I−J is greater than or equal to zero. Then the instruction in 006, which is +0000050008, causes the machine to go to 008 for its next instruction. In other words, it skips over the instruction in 007 and goes on to 008 where it finds the stop instruction.

The next example is more complicated because it is a program for a repetitive procedure. The example shown in Fig. A.4 describes an algorithm for finding the sum of any number of nonnegative integers. The program should be tested with specific input numbers, such as 2, 5, 7, −4. It is a good idea to work through a few such examples "by hand" as a check on the correctness of the program.

The difference between the name of a variable and the value of a variable can be noted once again. For example, the variable K represents the sum. Its *name* is K and this name corresponds to the *address* of a storage location, which is 012 in this case. On the other hand,

the *value* of a variable corresponds to the *content* of the memory location. The value may change, but the name remains the same. For example, each time the instruction in location 007 is executed, the content of location 012 may change.

There is one further point that should be made about the machine-language program in Fig. A.4. Three instructions in that program (in locations 005, 006, and 007) correspond to the assignment statement K ← K + N. They copy K into the accumulator, add N, and then store the result in the location for K. However, the value of N is in the accumulator just before these instructions are to be executed. They can, therefore, be replaced by only two instructions: one that adds K to the accumulator and another that stores the result in the location for K. We prefer, nevertheless, to leave the machine-language program the way it is, so that the relationship between the flowchart and the machine-language program is as simple as possible, but of course the shorter program would be the more efficient "translation" into machine language.

Three examples of complete programs have been presented in this section, and in some of the remaining exercises in this appendix you will be asked to give machine-language programs for certain procedures. Each program should be tested very carefully to make sure that it does exactly what it is supposed to do. You are

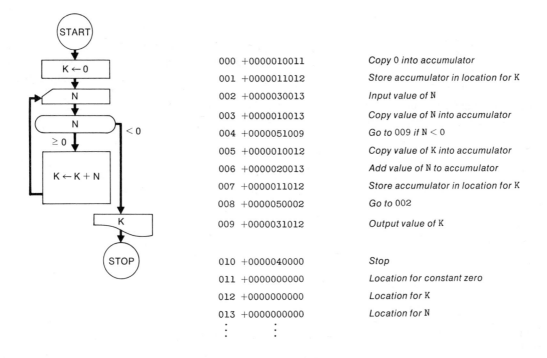

000	+0000010011	*Copy 0 into accumulator*
001	+0000011012	*Store accumulator in location for K*
002	+0000030013	*Input value of N*
003	+0000010013	*Copy value of N into accumulator*
004	+0000051009	*Go to 009 if N < 0*
005	+0000010012	*Copy value of K into accumulator*
006	+0000020013	*Add value of N to accumulator*
007	+0000011012	*Store accumulator in location for K*
008	+0000050002	*Go to 002*
009	+0000031012	*Output value of K*
010	+0000040000	*Stop*
011	+0000000000	*Location for constant zero*
012	+0000000000	*Location for K*
013	+0000000000	*Location for N*

FIG. A.4 Machine-language program for finding the sum of any number of nonnegative integers.

also strongly advised to run a few machine-language programs on a computer. A way of doing this on any computer you happen to be using is described in Section 14.1. The program discussed there causes a machine to imitate our hypothetical machine. The program developed in Section 14.1 may already be available for your computer, and can therefore be used to enable you to try out a few programs for the hypothetical machine.

EXERCISE A.3

1. Suppose that the first instruction in Fig. A.2 is replaced by +0000030015. What other change needs to be made in the program so that it will continue to work properly?

2. If the instruction in 004 of Fig. A.3 is replaced by +0000053007, what other changes would have to be made in the program so that it will continue to work properly?

3. What change is needed in the program of Fig. A.3 in order that it find the minimum rather than the maximum of two numbers?

4. What does N correspond to, and what does the value of N correspond to, in the program of Fig. A.4?

5. What restrictions are there on the inputs to the machine-language programs in (a) Fig. A.2, (b) Fig. A.3, and (c) Fig. A.4?

6. What sequence of instructions will cause the computer to go to location 100 if the number in the accumulator is negative, to 200 if zero, and 300 if positive?

7. Give machine-language programs that will find each of the following:

a) the sum of three numbers,
b) the absolute value of a number,
c) the largest of three numbers,
d) the smallest of three numbers.

Describe the tests you would make for each program.

8. Give a machine-language program that will find the larger magnitude of two numbers. What inputs do you consider are adequate to test this program?

It should be clear by now that writing programs directly in machine language can be extremely tedious. An easier way of producing machine-language programs is explained in Section B.1. If you wish to write many more such programs you will find it helpful to use the technique outlined there.

In each of the following questions a program is required to solve a certain problem. For at least one of these questions a brief report should be prepared. The report should contain the following information:

a) Title of report.
b) Name of author.
c) Date.
d) Purpose of program.

e) Statement of how to use the program, or a statement of what the program has already done, whichever is appropriate.
f) A flowchart, or a description of the algorithm using the pseudo-code notation of Section 1.3.
g) Description of tests made on the program.
h) Other comments about the program's limitations, efficiency, accuracy, and so on, if appropriate.
i) A listing of the program, together with the output.

9. Write a program that will find the largest number in a sequence of any number of positive integers.

10. A hydroelectric company charges 8 cents per kilowatt-hour up to the first 100 kilowatt-hours, and 5 cents thereafter. The number of kilowatt-hours for each customer is punched on a data card in the required format. Write a program that will cause the computer to read a card and then calculate and output the cost in cents, along with the number of kilowatt-hours. It is then to repeat this process with succeeding cards until a negative number is read.

11. Construct a machine-language program that will begin with the input of two positive integers, say I and J, and that will calculate and output the value of I^J. Assume that I^J is not too large for one memory location. What does your program do if $I \leq 0$ or $J \leq 0$?

12. Suppose that five hundred numbers are stored in memory locations 500-999. Construct a portion of a machine-language program that finds and outputs the sum of these five hundred numbers.

A.4 MACHINE ARITHMETIC

We have assumed that our machine can add, subtract, multiply, and divide integers, but it is necessary to discuss division in more detail. Division of two integers produces two new integers, one being the quotient and the other the remainder. For example, 25/7 yields a quotient of 3 and a remainder of 4. Some machines have two accumulators, leaving the quotient in one and the remainder in the other. Since our machine has only one accumulator, only the quotient is available.

When either of the integers being divided is negative, different definitions of the quotient and remainder are possible. For example, both

$$\frac{-5}{3} = -1 - \frac{2}{3} \quad \text{and} \quad \frac{-5}{3} = -2 + \frac{1}{3}$$

are correct, but give different quotients and remainders. For our purposes the first form is preferable, so that the quotient is -1 and the remainder is -2.

We will assume the following rules for determining the quotient and remainder in each case. Our equations are of the form

$$\frac{\text{Numerator}}{\text{Denominator}} = \text{Quotient} + \frac{\text{Remainder}}{\text{Denominator}}$$

The first rule is that the magnitude of the remainder must be less than the magnitude of the denominator. The second rule is that the sign of the remainder must be the same as the sign of the numerator of the original fraction. It is left as an exercise to show that these two rules determine the result uniquely. (See Question 12 of Exercise A.4.)

The results of our rules for all possible combinations of +5 or −5 in the numerator and +3 or −3 in the denominator are given below.

$$\frac{5}{3} = 1 + \frac{2}{3} \qquad \frac{-5}{3} = -1 + \frac{-2}{3}$$

$$\frac{5}{-3} = -1 + \frac{2}{-3} \qquad \frac{-5}{-3} = 1 + \frac{-2}{-3}$$

On our hypothetical machine the remainder is not available following an instruction for division. However, the form given above leads to

Remainder = Numerator − Quotient × Denominator

as a formula for evaluating the remainder. It is left as an exercise to show that a suitable sequence of instructions may be constructed to generate the remainder. (See Question 3 of Exercise A.4.)

There are two exceptional cases in our hypothetical machine's handling of the four basic operations. One exception occurs when the result of an operation is too large in magnitude to be stored in one memory location. For example, this can happen if we try to add +9876543210 and +9998887776, or if we try to multiply +0005556667 by −0003336669. When the result is too large we say it *overflows*. Different machines handle overflow in different ways. Some machines have a second accumulator into which the result of a multiplication can overflow. We will not make up any rules for our hypothetical machine to follow in case of overflow. However, it can be very important to know how overflow is handled by the particular machine you happen to use.

A second exceptional case arises when the result of an arithmetic operation is zero. Although no difficulty is likely to arise, we should be aware of the fact that there are two zeros on our hypothetical machine, +0000000000 and −0000000000. In general, the difference between the two is unimportant.

Handling fractions on our machine is awkward. For example, to store the number 3.14, we would have to store the integer 314 (+0000000314) and remember that this integer represents the number of hundredths. To multiply 3.14 by 1.7, we would have to multiply +0000000314 by +0000000017 and realize that the result, +0000005338, represents the number of thousandths in the answer.

Keeping track of fractions in this way is called *scaling,* and the arithmetic is called *fixed-point* arithmetic. Except in very simple calculations, it is an intolerable nuisance. Fortunately, a much easier method of calculating with fractions has been developed, called *floating-point* arithmetic. It is accomplished by special programs on some machines, but it is so important that most machines now have special instructions for handling this kind of arithmetic.

Fortunately, we do not usually need to write machine-language programs, and, in particular, we do not need to write instructions for doing calculations in floating-point arithmetic. However, we do need to know the basic idea of this kind of calculation, and so we devote the next section to it.

EXERCISE A.4

1. Give the quotient and the remainder, according to our definition of these numbers, for each of the following fractions:

a) $\frac{15}{4}$ b) $\frac{-15}{4}$ c) $\frac{15}{-4}$ d) $\frac{-15}{-4}$

2. Suppose that three memory locations are as follows:

```
048  +0000000012
049  +0000000123
050  +0000000010
```

where the first number represents the number of tenths in 1.2, the second represents the number of hundredths in 1.23, while the third is the constant 10. What is the content of location 051 after each of the following sequences of instructions has been carried out, and what does it represent?

a)		b)	
000	+0000010048	000	+0000010048
001	+0000022049	001	+0000022050
002	+0000011051	002	+0000020049
		003	+0000011051

3. Give a program that will input two integers and find and output their quotient and remainder.

4. Construct a machine-language program that will input a number and output 1 or 2, depending on whether the number is odd or even.

5. Give a machine-language program that will input two positive numbers and find and output their average.

6. Give a program that will input three positive integers and find and output their average, rounded to the nearest integer.

7. Write a machine-language program that will input a natural number N, and find and output its natural number divisors. For example, if the input is 12, the output is 1, 2, 3, 4, 6, 12. [*Hint:* Divide N by each of 1, 2, 3, ..., N, and determine if the remainder is zero.]

Prepare a brief report on the program you develop for one of the following four questions.

8. In finding the divisors of a number in Question 7, the program can be made more efficient, for if we find one divisor, we have automatically found another. Give a machine-language program that utilizes this fact.

9. A machine-language program is required that will input a natural number and output its prime factors. Thus, if the input is 12, the output is 2, 2, 3.

10. Write a machine-language program that inputs a sequence of positive integers and finds and outputs their average to the nearest tenth.

11. Give a machine-language program that will input two integers I and J, representing the numerator and denominator of the fraction $\frac{I}{J}$. The program is to find and output an integer representing the nearest number of hundredths in this quotient. For what possible inputs will your program work properly?

12. Consider the following equation:

$$\frac{\text{Numerator}}{\text{Denominator}} = \text{Quotient} + \frac{\text{Remainder}}{\text{Denominator}}$$

We suppose that the numerator and denominator are given integers. This equation then helps to define two other integers, the quotient and the remainder. Show that:

a) There are infinitely many quotients and remainders that satisfy the equation for any given numerator and denominator.

b) If we insist that the remainder be less in magnitude than the denominator, there are never more than two quotients and remainders to choose from.

c) If we insist further that the sign of the remainder be the same as the sign of the numerator, there is only one quotient and one remainder satisfying the equation.

A.5 FLOATING-POINT ARITHMETIC

Since many problems deal with numbers other than integers and scaling with fixed-point arithmetic can be very tedious, we turn now to another method, called floating-point arithmetic, for handling numbers on our hypothetical machine. It must first be explained how numbers are stored in memory locations of our machine in floating-point form. The number 12.345 is rewritten as $.12345 \times 10^2$. The fraction part, 12345, is stored in the last eight digits of the storage location, with enough zeros being added to the string of digits to fill eight positions. The sign is stored in the sign position. Finally, the exponent, 2, is added to 50 and stored in the first two digits, so that the final result is +5212345000. This is typical of how numbers are stored in floating-point form. The steps in getting this form are as follows:

1. The decimal point is moved to a position immediately to the left of the most significant digit. Thus with 12.345 the decimal point is moved two places to the left.

2. The result is then multiplied by a power of 10, to compensate for the change in value caused by moving the decimal point. For example,

$$12.345 \quad \text{becomes} \quad .12345 \times 10^2$$
$$.0163 \text{ becomes} \quad .163 \times 10^{-1}$$
$$-3.14 \quad \text{becomes} \quad -.314 \times 10^1$$

Numbers in this new form are said to be *normalized*.

3. The sign is stored in the sign part of the storage location, the fraction part is stored, left justified, in the last eight digits, and the power of 10 is added to 50 and stored in the first two digits. For example,

$$12.345 \quad \text{is stored as} +5212345000$$
$$.0163 \text{ is stored as} +4916300000$$
$$-3.14 \quad \text{is stored as} -5131400000$$

The reason for adding 50 to the power of 10 is that this provides an easy way of storing negative powers (like −1 in the second example) as well as positive ones.

There is one number that cannot be treated the same as the above examples, namely, the number zero. It is stored as +0000000000 or as −0000000000. These are the only floating-point forms that are allowed to have zero as the third digit.

Some of the computer's instructions may be used with data stored in floating-point form just as well as with data stored in fixed-point form. For example, the instructions for copying numbers into and out of the accumulator work equally well on either form. However, new instructions are needed to do the arithmetic with numbers in floating-point form. For example, instructions of the form +0000025AAA could cause the machine to do floating-point addition. They would cause the machine to add the number in location AAA to the number in the accumulator, and leave the result in the accumulator. The numbers in AAA and the accumulator must be in floating-point form, and the result is left in the accumulator in floating-point form. To illustrate what the machine would have to do, consider adding the two floating-point numbers +5212345000 and +4916300000, which were introduced earlier in this section. The machine would have to line up the fraction parts properly and find their sum:

$$\begin{array}{r} 12345000 \\ 16300000 \\ \hline 12361300 \end{array}$$

Then the exponent must be properly accounted for and the final result is +5212361300. As a second example consider adding +5212345000 to +5290000000. We first obtain

$$\begin{array}{r} 12345000 \\ 90000000 \\ \hline 102345000 \end{array}$$

which leads to +5310234500 as the final result. Note that the exponent had to be changed from 2 to 3 to compensate for the carry with the addition.

It should be obvious that the result of a floating-point calculation can be so large (exponent > 49) that it cannot be represented in our standard floating-point form. This is an example of *floating-point overflow*. It is also possible that the result is so small (exponent < −50) that it cannot be represented. This is called *underflow*. Different machines handle floating-point overflow and underflow in different ways, and options are usually made available to the user.

As you might imagine, the circuitry needed for the machine to carry out floating-point addition is quite a bit more complicated than that needed for fixed-point addition. Nevertheless, most machines have instructions for all the floating-point arithmetic operations.

Our reason for learning about floating-point arithmetic is to appreciate exactly the kind of arithmetic the machine is doing, after our programs have been translated into machine-language programs, so that we can understand what takes place and what limitations there are. One of the most important aspects of floating-point arithmetic concerns roundoff error. Consider the two numbers 12.345 and 1.00001. These are easily stored as floating-point numbers, but their product, 12.34512345, cannot be stored in this way. The best that can be done is to store 12.345123 and lose the last two digits. It is usual for machines to discard digits in this way. The digits that cannot be stored are simply dropped. On our hypothetical machine only the first eight digits of a result can be saved; as a consequence, the results are not rounded. For example, the sum of +5140000004 and +5010000008 is +5141000004 rather than +5141000005. We often refer to this kind of arithmetic as *chopping* arithmetic rather than *rounding* arithmetic. But other rules are also possible, and the general term usually used to describe all the rules collectively is *rounding,* so that this latter term has two meanings, one specific and one general. (This is also referred to in Chapter 9.)

EXERCISE A.5

1. State what each of the following can represent. (The possibilities are fixed-point number, floating-point number, and instruction.)

a) +0000011057   b) −0000011057
c) +0000101010   d) +5012340000
e) −5012340000   f) +5201919191
g) +4387600000   h) +0012300000

2. What is the largest number that can be stored in a memory location of our hypothetical machine in floating-point form?

3. What is the number of smallest magnitude, other than zero itself, that can be stored in floating-point form?

4. Give the floating-point form in which each of the following is stored:

a) 5.55   b) 1.0   c) −17.
d) .0063   e) −.0063 f) 10^{13}

5. What is the floating-point form of the number whose value is closest to each of the following?

a) $\frac{1}{3}$ b) $\frac{2}{3}$ c) π

6. Give the ordinary decimal equivalents of each of the following floating-point numbers:

a) +5412340000   b) −5412340000
c) +4798000000   d) −4798000000

7. Give the result in floating-point form of each of the following calculations:

a) +5044400000   added to   +5011100000
b) +5044400000   added to   +5111100000
c) +5044400000   added to   +4811100000
d) +5044400000   added to   −4811100000
e) +5211000000   multiplied by   +5211000000
f) +5211000000   multiplied by   −4711000000

8. Give the result of each of the following when chopping arithmetic is applied:

a) +5044400000   added to   +4911111111
b) +5211000000   multiplied by   +4722222222
c) +5044300000   added to   +4799999900
d) −5044300000   added to   +4799999900
e) +5230000300   multiplied by   +5056560000

9. Show that floating-point arithmetic on a machine is not associative. The simplest way to prove this is to give examples of three floating-point numbers A, B, C, such that (A + B) + C is not equal to A + (B + C) when these expressions are evaluated by machine.

10. Is floating-point arithmetic on a machine commutative? Is it distributive? Give examples to illustrate your answers.

11. Can you think of a way in which fixed-point arithmetic on a machine can fail to satisfy the usual commutative, associative, and distributive laws of arithmetic?

12. For our hypothetical machine, give examples of nonzero floating-point numbers A and B such that A + B = B, when A + B is evaluated by the machine.

A.6 OTHER MACHINE FEATURES

The hypothetical machine described in this chapter has been kept as simple as possible. Our purpose has been to explain the basic idea of a computer, without introducing any unnecessary details. We also wanted to explain two different ways in which numbers can be stored, that is, in fixed-point or floating-point form.

Machines used in practice are more complicated. They usually have larger memories, as well as auxiliary memories, such as disk files and magnetic tape units. In addition, they usually have many more instructions. These facilities make them more convenient for many purposes, but they do not enable them to do anything essentially new. For example, it would certainly be convenient to have an instruction for comparing numbers directly rather than subtracting them and comparing the result to zero. (Incidentally, comparing numbers directly also avoids any possibility of overflow or underflow with the subtraction.) Another special feature that is available on most machines is that of *index registers,* which we will refer to again in Sections B.3, B.4, and B.5.

We should also discuss briefly the storage of data other than numbers. It is often necessary to input and output words and punctuation marks. This is accomplished by having special codes for storing such information and special instructions for input and output. One example of such a code is to have A, B, C, D, . . . represented by 10, 11, 12, 13, . . . and to use two digits of each storage location for each letter or punctuation mark. Thus the word BAD could be stored as +1110133636, assuming that 36 represents a blank. It should be pointed out that we now have altogether four different kinds of information that can be stored in a memory location: an instruction, a fixed-point number, a floating-point number, and nonnumerical data such as alphabetic information. (The handling of nonnumerical data is discussed in more detail in Section B.2.)

Another point worth noting is that many machines do not store information in the form of decimal digits. Some are binary or hexadecimal, rather than decimal (examples are discussed in Chapter 9 and in Appendix C). Others are character machines, which means that the basic unit is an alphabetic or numeric character, rather than just a binary or decimal digit.

It should be quite clear by now why this appendix is entitled *a stored-program computer,* since the computer we have been discussing has its programs stored in its memory. Another term used to describe this kind of computer is *digital.* This term is appropriate because these computers work with information in the form of digits. Some use decimal digits, others binary, and still others use characters (alphabetic and others) that are equivalent to digits for a base other than 10 or 2. However, the term digital does not correctly distinguish the computers we are studying from all other kinds. A desk calculator is a digital computer, for example, but it does not have a stored program.

The term digital is used mainly to distinguish digital computers from another type known as *analogue* computers. The latter use physical quantities, like voltages and currents, or lengths, to represent numbers. The physical quantities are *analogous* to the numbers. The simplest example of an analogue computer is a slide rule, where lengths are proportional to the logarithms of numbers.

More complicated examples are usually electronic. Analogue computers have important applications, but they are not *general-purpose* in the sense that digital computers are. Moreover, analogue computers do not carry out algorithms in the precise sense in which we use the term.

The popular hand calculators are digital computers. And they carry out calculations internally in a floating-point form, although they display numbers in a more readable form than has been described in this section. Some hand calculators—the so-called programmable calculators—can execute stored programs, as well as carry out individual calculations as they are keyed in from the keyboard. The early versions of these programmable calculators are about as much trouble to program as is the hypothetical machine described in this appendix, but there is no doubt that improved versions will be programmed in higher-level languages.

EXERCISE A.6

1. What four kinds of information can be stored in one memory location? Can one particular piece of information have all four interpretations with our hypothetical machine?

2. Which of the following properties of computers distinguishes them from other calculating devices?

a) high-speed   b) automatic
c) electronic   d) stored-program
e) general-purpose   f) digital

3. What features distinguish digital computers from analogue computers?

4. Is a desk calculator an automatic computer?

5. Which of the properties given in Question 2 are applicable to all hand calculators? Which only to some?

APPENDIX

Assembly-Language Programming and the SIMON Computer

Some of the problems in the exercises of Appendix A involve the preparation and testing of machine-language programs for a hypothetical machine. Unfortunately, this process is extremely tedious. For one thing, it is easy to make mistakes in machine-language programming and, once made, the mistakes are usually difficult to correct. Moreover, frequent reference to Table A.1 may be necessary to determine the numeric operation codes. It is also tiresome to assign and keep track of all storage locations for variables and constants in the program, as well as all locations to which transfers must be made.

The purpose of this appendix is to explain a technique, called assembly-language programming, that is equivalent to machine-language programming but very much easier to use. In the first section we explain a simple assembly language that corresponds exactly to the machine language in Appendix A. This assembly language can be used to solve the programming problems in Appendix A.

In the second section we begin to describe a number of features that can be added to the simple machine of Appendix A. The corresponding additions to the assembly language are also described. Finally, in Section B.6, we combine these new features together with the machine described in Appendix A to make a new hypothetical machine. We call this new machine SIMON (because it is still very simple!) and we call its assembly language SAP (because it can be translated by a SIMON Assembler Program).

It is not absolutely necessary that a beginning programmer know very much about machine- or assembly-language programming. However, we believe that a knowledge of at least *some* machine- and assembly-language programming is essential for a proper understanding of programming in higher-level languages. Exactly how much is needed is a matter of taste, of course, but we have included what we believe to be a reasonable minimum of machine language in Appendix A and a corresponding minimum of assembly language in Section B.1. The material in later sections of this appendix is recommended to anyone wishing to pursue further the subject of machine- and assembly-language programming. The material described in those later sections can be helpful in understanding several important features of higher-level languages such as the handling of alphanumeric data, repetition (or looping), subscripting, and linking with subprograms.

B.1 SIMPLE ASSEMBLY LANGUAGE

The basic idea in assembly-language programming is to write programs in a language equivalent to machine language but easier to read. Once a program is written in this way, the corresponding machine-language version is easily produced and the program can then be executed by a computer. To illustrate assembly-language programming, consider the first example of an algorithm in Appendix A, the one for finding the sum of two numbers. Three languages have been used in Fig. B.1 to describe this algorithm: a flowchart language, our hypothetical machine language, and the new assembly language.

Note that in the assembly-language version, mnemonic operation codes have been used. For example, the letter L is used for "load" and ST is short for "store." Thus, the meaning of the statements in the assembly-language program should be obvious. Table B.1 gives a list of the mnemonic codes we have chosen for our simple assembly language, together with the corresponding machine-language operation codes.

The main point about the example in Fig. B.1 is that the assembly-language program is related in a straightforward way to the machine-language version. If we start with the program written in assembly language, it is a straightforward matter to translate it into machine language. As a beginning, we can easily assign addresses for all the variables in the program. Each statement in the assembly-language version can then be translated. For example, R must be translated into the operation code 30, I must be translated into· an address, and so on. The use of assembly language simplifies the task of coding in machine language.

A second example of an assembly-language program is given in Fig. B.2. It describes a procedure for finding the sum of any number of nonnegative integers and corresponds to the program described in Fig. A.4. Two new features of our assembly language have been introduced in this program.

TABLE B.1

Mnemonic code	Numeric code	Effect
L	10	Load accumulator
ST	11	Store from accumulator
A	20	Add to accumulator
S	21	Subtract from accumulator
M	22	Multiply accumulator
D	23	Divide into accumulator
R	30	Read
W	31	Write
H	40	Halt
B	50	Branch
BN	51	Branch on negative
BZ	52	Branch on zero
BP	53	Branch on positive

1. The first statement in the program demonstrates a method of referencing constants in an assembly language program. The constant can be recognized because it is preceded by an equals sign. In such a case the translation from assembly language to machine language requires not only that we reserve a memory location for the constant, but also that we assign to that location the value of the constant. Constants referenced as the 0 is in this example are called *literals*.

2. Two of the statements in the program are labeled, using the names BACK and ANS. The instructions with these labels are referenced by the transfer instructions BN   ANS and B   BACK. We can use names such as ANS and BACK, which identify the purpose or location of a statement, in order to make the program easier to follow.

Once again, you should convince yourself that the translation from assembly language to machine language is straightforward. Since this translation is straightforward, it must be possible to construct an algorithm for doing the translation. A program for carrying out such a translation is called an *assembler*. Once an assembler has been prepared, programs can be written in the easier-to-use assembly language. The computer can be directed to translate the programs into machine language and then to execute the assembled version.

Another advantage of an assembler arises when a program is being tested. It is often useful to output intermediate results, as well as the required answers, to follow the course of the calculations in detail. The output obtained is similar to the information provided by a checking table. Extra output instructions must be inserted in the program to provide this information. These additional instructions can easily be removed from an assembly-language program once the program is working properly. The assembler can then create a new machine-language version without any further effort

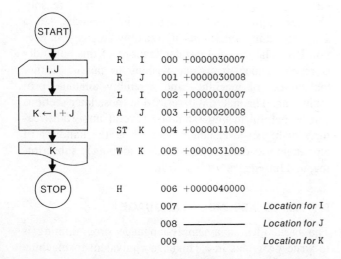

FIG. B.1 Three descriptions of an algorithm for finding the sum of two numbers.

R	I	000	+0000030007
R	J	001	+0000030008
L	I	002	+0000010007
A	J	003	+0000020008
ST	K	004	+0000011009
W	K	005	+0000031009
H		006	+0000040000
		007	——————— Location for I
		008	——————— Location for J
		009	——————— Location for K

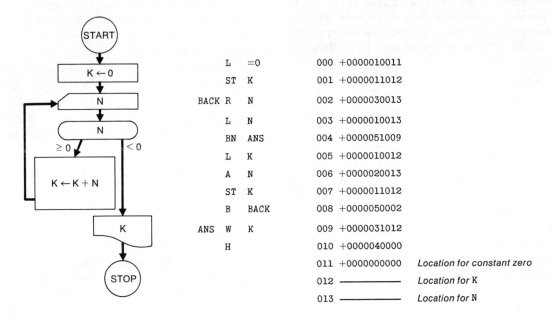

	L	=0	000 +0000010011
	ST	K	001 +0000011012
BACK	R	N	002 +0000030013
	L	N	003 +0000010013
	BN	ANS	004 +0000051009
	L	K	005 +0000010012
	A	N	006 +0000020013
	ST	K	007 +0000011012
	B	BACK	008 +0000050002
ANS	W	K	009 +0000031012
	H		010 +0000040000
			011 +0000000000 *Location for constant zero*
			012 —————— *Location for K*
			013 —————— *Location for N*

FIG. B.2 Three descriptions of an algorithm for summing nonnegative integers.

on the part of the programmer. On the other hand, to remove extra instructions directly from a machine-language program and to make other adjustments that then become necessary is extremely tedious and is likely to introduce new errors into the program.

It is an interesting project (see Section 14.2) to develop a program in a higher-level language that will translate assembly-language programs, like the ones described in this appendix, into machine-language programs for the hypothetical machine of Appendix A. Once such a program is developed it can be used to produce machine-language programs, which can then be run on a computer with the help of the interpreter referred to in Appendix A and discussed in detail in Section 14.1.

To be specific, we assume that the names must be left justified in columns 1–4. Similarly, the operation codes must appear in columns 6–8, beginning in column 6, and the address part must begin in column 10.

Even without an assembler it is helpful to write our machine-language programs initially in assembly language. Once the program has been written this way and carefully checked, it can be translated quite easily into machine language by hand.

EXERCISE B.1

1. Translate the following assembly-language program into an equivalent machine-language program:

```
READ R    N
     L    N
     BN   QUIT
     M    =575
     ST   A
     W    N
     W    A
     B    READ
QUIT H
```

2. Most assembly languages provide a second way of handling literals. In Fig. B.2, we would replace =0 by a name, such as CONS, that we choose for the constant. Then we insert the statement CONS DC 0 at an appropriate place in the program, which, in the program of Fig. B.2, would be immediately after the halt instruction. DC (for Define Constant) does not correspond to a machine-language operation code and we therefore call DC a *pseudo-operation code*, rather than an operation code. The address part of the corresponding pseudo-instruction can be any constant. It is 0 in this example but it could be 75, −23, or +222, etc. (It can also be blank, in which case we assume the assembler treats it as a zero.) Show how you would use DC in the program of Question 1.

Show also how DC can be used to reserve storage locations for variables such as K and N in Fig. B.2. The main difference between allowing the assembler to reserve such locations by itself and using DC to instruct the assembler to do so is that we are able to initialize the values stored in the locations if we use DC. (It should be pointed out that most assemblers are not able to reserve such locations by themselves and require the programmer to reserve the locations explicitly with a pseudo-operation code like DC.)

Another difference is that using DC enables us to specify where in the program we want the location to be reserved. (Most assemblers would allow us to use a pseudo-operation code like DC to initialize more than one storage location. For example,

```
LIST DC  20*0
```

could be used to place 0 in 20 locations beginning with location LIST. However, we will not need to use such a feature.)

Write assembly-language programs to carry out each of the following tasks:

3. Input a number and find and output its square and cube.

4. Input a sequence of positive integers and find and output the largest. How do you propose the end of the sequence be indicated?

5. Input a sequence of positive integers and find and output the second largest. How have you interpreted "second largest"?

6. Input a sequence of marks obtained on a test and find and output the number of failures.

B.2 ALPHANUMERIC INPUT-OUTPUT

The purpose of this section is to describe features that can be added to the simple machine of Appendix A so that it can handle *alphanumeric* information. The term *alphanumeric* describes alphabetic characters, numerals, punctuation, and other special characters such as the dollar sign, asterisk, and blank character. Instruction codes for these features are included in a complete list near the end of this appendix (Table B.2).

To handle alphanumeric information, the machine must be able to store such information and it must be able to input and output the corresponding characters. One simple way of storing the information is for each alphanumeric character to be represented by a pair of decimal digits in the memory of the computer. For example, the alphabetic characters A, B, C, . . . , Z can be represented by 10, 11, 12, . . . , 35, followed by 36, 37, . . . for the blank, the punctuation marks, and so on. Digits may be mixed with other alphanumeric characters on input and output and it is convenient to represent them by such two-digit codes as well, even though they already have the obvious representations by one-digit codes. It is natural to use 00, 01, . . . , 09 to represent the digits 0, 1, . . . , 9. Thus AB4 is represented by 101104.

Five alphanumeric characters can be stored in a single memory location. According to the scheme suggested above, the five characters in GO TO would be stored as 1624362924, if we assume that 36 is used to represent the blank character. It is an important advantage that the letters of the alphabet are represented by codes whose numerical values are steadily increas-

ing in value as we move through the alphabet from A to Z. This fact enables us to sort alphabetic information into proper order with the help of programs for sorting numeric information.

Operation codes for the input and output of alphanumeric information are also required. According to Table B.2, code 32 is used for input and its assembly language equivalent is RA (for Read Alphanumeric). The complete specification of this operation code is as follows:

Operation code 32 (RA) causes the 80 alphanumeric characters punched on a card to be read into the 16 memory locations beginning at the specified memory location, 5 characters being stored in each location. The signs of these locations are left unchanged.

Thus the instruction +0000032444 causes characters to be read into locations 444, 445, . . . , 459. Operation code 33 is used for output and its assembly-language equivalent is WA (for Write Alphanumeric):

Operation code 33 (WA) causes the 80 characters in the 16 locations beginning at the specified location to be printed in one line of output. The signs of these locations are ignored.

We also introduce a new feature in assembly-language programming that enables us to reserve memory locations for certain purposes. For example, we may want to reserve 16 locations into which the alphanumeric information on a card can be read. To do so we can use a statement such as the following:

```
INFO RES 16
```

Here INFO is the name that will be given to the first of the 16 locations. RES is another example of a pseudo-operation code. (The first was DC, which was introduced in Question 2, Exercise B.1.) As an illustration of how RES is used, the following sequence of instructions causes the information on two cards to be used and then printed out:

```
     RA   INFO
     RA   MORE
     WA   INFO
     WA   MORE
     H
INFO RES 16
MORE RES 16
```

It is also convenient to be able to define the initial content of the locations reserved by RES. This is illustrated in the following example:

```
MESS RES 4'THE RESULTS ARE'
```

With this example, four consecutive locations will be reserved. The first location, named MESS, is to contain THE R, the second location ESULT, and the third S ARE; the fourth location will contain five blanks, which means that its numeric representation will be +3636363636, if we assume that 36 is used to represent the blank character. We are assuming that all characters in the locations reserved by RES statements that are not specified between the quotation marks are specified as blank by the assembler.

It is now easy to make our programs output phrases such as THE SMALLEST NUMBER IS or PLEASE PAY THE AMOUNT SHOWN. Of course, we must also develop ways of including the results of calculations together with such phrases. For example, if we wish to output THE SMALLEST NUMBER IS and follow this with the number itself in the same line, we must have a way of converting the number in its numerical form into its corresponding alphanumeric form. Thus, if the number is +0000000023, we must convert it to

$$+3636360203, \quad \text{or to} \quad +3636020336,$$

and so on, depending on just where we want blanks to appear.

If our machine has only the operation codes we have assumed thus far, it is rather awkward to carry out conversions from numeric to alphanumeric forms. However, it can be done, and the programming required is typical of much of the detailed programming that sometimes must be done with computers. It is therefore a worthwhile problem to consider developing portions of programs to do such tasks.

The introduction of features for handling alphanumeric information has made the hypothetical machine complete in one important respect. The machine is now able to input assembly-language programs and, at least in principle, it can be used to translate such programs into machine language. In other words, an assembler can be developed for the hypothetical machine we now have and it can be run on that machine. However, the memory of the machine is too small for an assembler that would be of any use and the repertoire of instructions that have been described so far is also too small for the assembler to be of any practical interest.

EXERCISE B.2

1. The following is an example of how certain information is punched onto each card in a file:

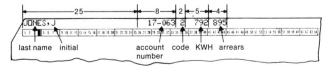

Write a program that reads such a file and lists the infor-

mation from each card for which the account is in arrears.

2. The following is another example of how certain information is punched onto each card in a file:

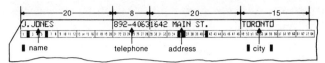

a) Write a program that inputs each card and prints a label for mailing letters to each person.

b) Write a program that inputs each card and lists the name and telephone number of each person whose telephone exchange is 483.

3. Explain how a portion of a program can be made to determine whether or not the information in certain columns is numeric. Can you suggest situations in which such a determination might be useful?

4. The immigration department has on file a large number of cards on which information about people entering the country during a particular year has been recorded. This information includes the person's name, the country from which he came, and the date on which he entered the country. Write a program that inputs the name of a country and then searches the card file and lists all persons immigrating from that country. Discuss what would have to be done if the information is required only for a specified part of the year, such as the period between June and September inclusive.

5. Write a portion of a program that converts a positive number less than 10^5 to its alphanumeric representation.

6. Indicate how you would output two numbers side by side, when you know that each number is less than 10^5, assuming that they are to be right justified in print positions 1–5 and 11–15, respectively.

B.3 REPETITION

Index registers are among the most interesting features of existing machines. They can be used to control repetition or looping, to modify addresses, and to provide links with subprograms. Their use in connection with repetition is discussed in this section. The other uses are discussed in the next two sections.

Index registers are special storage locations. The information they hold is usually related to addresses and they are normally just large enough to hold an address. We therefore assume that our machine has index registers consisting of three decimal digits (without a sign). In most of our discussion, we need only one index register, which we denote as number 1, but it will be obvious how index registers numbered 2, 3, and 4 can be used as well.

We need instructions that will cause information to be copied into and out of index registers. As indicated in Table B.2:

Operation code 60 (LX) causes information to be copied from the address part of the specified memory location into the specified index register. The index register is specified by the fifth digit of the instruction.

Thus +0000160444 causes the address part of location 444 to be copied into index register 1. We also have:

Operation code 61 (STX) causes the content of the specified index register to be stored in the address part of the specified memory location. The index register is specified by the fifth digit of the instruction.

We also require operation codes for adding to or subtracting from the contents of index registers and for transferring control in ways that depend on the index registers. There are many possibilities. Operation code 62 is just one such possibility. It was chosen because its use leads to a relatively simple way of handling repetition in machine language.

Code 62 (BIX) causes the content of the specified index register to be increased by 1 and then compared to the number whose address is specified by digit positions 2, 3, and 4 of the instruction itself. If the former is less than or equal to the latter, control is transferred to the memory location specified by positions 8, 9, and 10. Otherwise the normal sequence is followed.

These three new operation codes are illustrated in Fig. B.3, where the correspondence between a repetitive loop and machine language is emphasized. The purpose of the machine-language instruction containing operation code 61 is to copy the value of I to a memory location so that it can be used during the calculations inside the loop. If the value of I is not used, the instruction with operation code 61 is not required in Fig. B.3.

A new feature of the assembly language is shown in Fig. B.3. Information contained in the first five digits of a machine-language instruction is placed *after* the address part of the assembly-language instruction and separated from the address part by a comma. With LX

and STX, the address part is followed by a comma and the specification of the index register, as in LX =1,1 and STX I,1. With BIX, the address part must be followed by a comma, then the name of the number used in the comparison, then another comma followed by the specification of the index register. (The name of the number used in the comparison can be a literal such as =50. We could also allow the name to be replaced by an absolute address, such as 014, but we will not make use of this possibility.) No blanks are allowed between the beginning of the address part and the end of the specification of the index register.

The main shortcoming of the operation codes we have chosen is that they provide no simple way of incrementing the index register by more than 1. However, these codes are sufficient to illustrate the general idea of how index registers can be used, not only for looping but also for indexing, as explained in the next section. They would also enable us to explain why there often are restrictions associated with repetition constructs, or loops, in higher-level languages.

EXERCISE B.3

In each of the following questions a program is required to solve a certain problem. For at least one of these questions a brief report should be prepared, as outlined in Exercise A.3.

1. Write an assembly-language program that generates and outputs the first 50 terms of the Fibonacci sequence, which is defined as $t_1, t_2, t_3, \ldots$, where

$$t_1 = t_2 = 1; \ t_n = t_{n-1} + t_{n-2}, \ n \geq 2.$$

2. Write a program that will input a number N and find and output the sum of the first N terms of the sequence

$$1, \ 3, \ 5, \ 7, \ldots$$

3. Give a program that will calculate and output a table of numbers and their squares for all numbers between 50 and 100 inclusive.

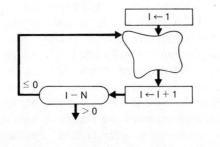
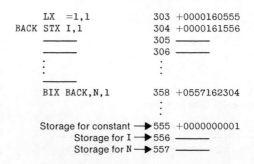

FIG. B.3 Loop control using an index register.

4. The program is to input a natural number N that indicates how many data cards are to follow, and then find and output the sum of the N numbers on these cards, assuming that one number is punched on each card.

5. The first number to be input is the number of students who wrote a certain aptitude test. The cards following the first contain the scores obtained, each card containing the score for one student. A program is required that will read these cards and count the number of scores below 50, the number between 50 and 65 inclusive, the number between 66 and 74 inclusive, and the number above 74. The program is to output the final counts and the total number of students.

6. One number is to be input. The computer is to then output the same number followed by YES or NO, depending on whether or not the number is a perfect square.

7. After input of one number the computer is to output that number followed by YES or NO, depending on whether or not the number is the sum of two squares.

8. Find and output all three digit integers with the property that each integer is equal to the sum of the cubes of its digits.

9. Suppose that the value of N is input, followed by N cards with one number on each card representing the grade obtained by a student in a particular class. Assume that no two grades are the same and write a program that will find the top three grades.

10. Give an assembly-language program that calculates and outputs the sum of all terms of the form xy, where x and y each take all values between 1 and 25 inclusive.

B.4 INDEXING

Index registers have a second important use in what is called *automatic address modification,* or *indexing.* This occurs when the address of an instruction is modified, just before the instruction is executed, by having the content of an index register added to it. The index register is specified by the fifth digit in the machine-language instruction.

As an example, suppose that index register 1 contains the number 033, and suppose that the instruction +0000120600 is about to be executed. Without the 1 in the fifth digit position, this instruction would cause the number in location 600 to be added to the accumulator. However, with the 1 in the fifth digit position, the content of index register 1 is first added to the specified address so that the number in location 633 is added to the accumulator.

The use of automatic address modification is illustrated in Fig. B.4. The flowchart refers to a subscripted variable named M with 20 components named M(1), M(2), . . . , M(20). The first time the loop is ex-

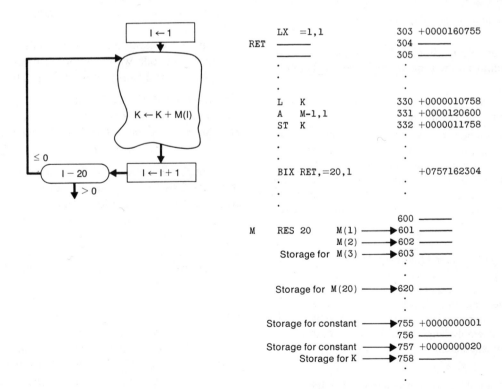

FIG. B.4 Automatic address modification using an index register.

ecuted, the first component, M(1), is added to K. The second time, M(2) is added to K, and so on. In the corresponding machine-language program, it has been assumed that the components of M are stored in locations 601, 602, ..., respectively. With the value of I in index register 1, that index register can be used both for loop control and for automatic address modification.

Another new feature of assembly-language programming has been introduced in Fig. B.4. The address part of one of the instructions is M−1. This has the obvious meaning that it corresponds to an address equal to 1 less than the address of M. It is an example of *address arithmetic,* which will be described in more detail later. It is needed in this example because RES causes 20 locations to be reserved and M is the name of the first location. The address of the add instruction is modified, first by adding 1, then 2, and so on. The address of the add instruction must therefore be M−1.

The use of index registers for address modification is illustrated in some of the questions given below. It is worthwhile considering how much more complicated the resulting programs would have to be if index registers were not available.

EXERCISE B.4

1. Write an assembly-language program that inputs a sequence of 50 positive integers into a sequence of 50 memory locations. When the input has been complete, the program is to find and output the sum of the numbers that were input.

2. Modify your solution in Question 1 so that instead of summing the numbers, the program finds the maximum of the numbers.

3. Do as in Question 2, except that the output should also include the position of the maximum.

4. a) The instruction A   M−1,1 has been used in Fig. B.4 for adding components of the array M to the content of the accumulator. Address arithmetic is required because storage is reserved for M by the statement M   RES 20. What changes are required in Fig. B.4 if storage is reserved instead by the following sequence of two statements:

```
M     DC  20
      RES 20
```

b) If storage is reserved for arrays in the manner illustrated in Question 4(a), it is possible to arrange for *execution-time* checking of subscripts. This means that the value of a subscript is tested, before it is used, so that a message can be given if the subscript exceeds the maximum value. Write a sequence of assembly-language instructions corresponding to the assignment statement:

$$K \leftarrow K + M(I)$$

and arrange for an appropriate message to be output if the value of I exceeds the maximum, that is, if the value exceeds the number stored in location M.

5. Write an assembly-language program that inputs SAP mnemonic operation codes and that finds and outputs the corresponding numeric operation codes (see Table B.2). The program should output the message

> nnn IS NOT A SAP OP-CODE

whenever the input *nnn* is not a valid SAP operation code.

6. Construct a program that inputs an assembly-language program and constructs a table of the statement names in that program along with their corresponding locations. When the last card of the assembly-language program has been read, the table should be output. For example, if the assembly-language program displayed in Fig. B.2 is input, the output should be as follows:

```
NAME      LOCATION
BACK      002
ANS       009
```

7. Write an assembly-language program that inputs a sequence of five-letter words and then sorts this list of words into alphabetical order. The sorted list is then to be output. (One method of sorting is discussed in Chapter 1.)

B.5 SUBPROGRAM LINKAGE

The third way in which index registers are used is in helping to provide the link between a subprogram and the program, or subprogram, from which it is called. A special operation code is required to record the address to which control must be returned, or at least an address from which the return address can be easily calculated.

There are many different possibilities. The particular operation code we have chosen to use is 63 or BAL (for Branch And Link). It is defined as follows:

Operation code 63 (BAL) *causes the address of the location following the one in which the* 63 *operation code is located to be placed in the specified index register and control to be transferred to the specified location.*

Thus, if +0000163500 is found in location 065, it causes 066 to be placed in index register 1 and control to be transferred to location 500.

One of the main advantages of subprograms is that they can be designed to carry out some specific task and are then available whenever required. For example, suppose that we have constructed a sequence of instructions for converting a numerical value less than 10^5 to its corresponding alphanumeric representation, as in Question 5 of Exercise B.2. Such a sequence of instructions could assume that the numerical value was initially in the accumulator. The resulting alphanumeric representation could be loaded into the accumulator when the conversion is finished. The BAL instruction, together with an indexed branch instruction, provides a method of linking to and from such a conversion routine from any point within memory. This is illustrated in Fig. B.5.

The instructions in Fig. B.5 illustrate how the conversion routine can be used on two different occasions. On each occasion, the number to be converted is loaded into the accumulator and a BAL instruction is then executed. This saves the address of the following instruction in an index register (number 1 in this example). Control is then sent to the first instruction in the conversion routine (CONV in this example). When the conversion has been completed, an indexed branch instruction (B   0,1) causes control to be returned to the instruction following the BAL instruction. (Note that the address part of an assembly-language instruction may be constant, i.e., an *absolute address*. It is 0 in the branch instruction.) The alphanumeric representation of the number that was converted can then be stored in an appropriate location, to be output at a later time. In Fig. B.5 the two numbers are output in the same line.

The linking described in this first example can be used whenever one value is to be passed on to a subprogram and one value is to be returned. It could, for example, be used when some of the common arithmetic functions, such as square roots, sines, cosines, etc., are required. (Of course, we would want to perform floating-point operations in such cases.) However, this method of linking to subprograms is not general enough, since we may want to pass on several values to a subprogram and have more than one value returned.

A more general method of subprogram linkage is shown in Fig. B.6, where, to illustrate, a subprogram is provided with the locations of three variables. (For example, we could suppose that there are two values to be passed on to the subprogram and a third value is to be returned.) The BAL instruction in this case is followed by a list of addresses. Note that a blank appearing in the position of an operation code in the assembly language corresponds to 0 in machine language. Indexed "load-accumulator" instructions are shown being used to pick up the addresses of the arguments and an indexed branch instruction is used to return control to the calling program. Note that in this example the return address is 3 more than the content of index register 1.

The subprogram in Fig. B.6 can now be completed as an exercise (see Question 6 in Exercise B.5). The machine-language program is much simpler, however, if use is made of indirect addressing, which is discussed in the next section.

It should be pointed out that there are many different ways in which a program can be translated into machine language, and, in particular, there are many variants of the way in which a subprogram can be linked to a calling program. For example, in some cases

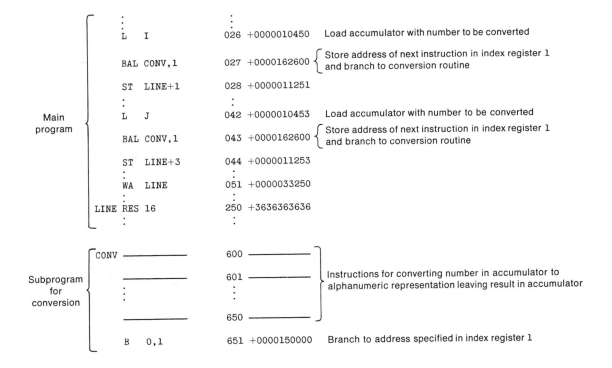

FIG. B.5 The BAL instruction is used twice in the main program to branch and link with a subprogram.

Main program:

The subprogram is called with the arguments L1,L2,M	BAL SUB,1	065 +0000163500	
	L1	066 +0000000200	Address of L1
	L2	067 +0000000201	Address of L2
	M	068 +0000000225	Address of M
		069 ———————	(Return from subprogram)

Subprogram:

A subprogram with 3 parameters is defined	SUB	500 ———————	
	L 0,1	. +0000110000	Copy address of L1 to accumulator
	L 1,1	. +0000110001	Copy address of L2 to accumulator
RETURN	B 3,1	. +0000150003	Return

FIG. B.6 Example of how a subprogram can be linked to the program from which it is called. Note how an instruction in the subprogram can be indexed to copy the address of an argument into the accumulator.

the linkage may provide the values required by the subprogram, rather than the locations of those values. Also, some of the techniques for providing the linkage may be quite different from the one introduced in this section; and they can also be much more elegant.

For completeness we should also mention that it is sometimes important to have a method of linkage that permits a subprogram to call itself (permitting what is called *recursion*), which would of course mean that the required addresses (including the return address) would have to be saved. But this is a topic we will not pursue further in this appendix, although the idea of recursion is used occasionally where appropriate elsewhere in this text.

EXERCISE B.5

1. Assume that the accumulator contains a positive number less than 10^5. Write a sequence of instructions to convert this number to its corresponding alphanumeric representation.

2. Write a program that produces the following table. The sequence of instructions developed in Question 1 will be useful.

NUMBER	SQUARE	CUBE
1	1	1
2	4	8
3	9	27
.	.	.
.	.	.
.	.	.
20	400	8000

3. Assume that the accumulator contains the alphanumeric representation of a number less than 10^5. Write a

sequence of instructions that converts this representation to the corresponding numeric representation.

4. Write an assembly-language program that inputs a sequence of cards. Each card contains the license number of a car and the speed at which it was observed to be traveling. The penalty for speeding is given in the following table:

speed ≤ 50	no penalty
50 < speed < 60	$2 per km over 50 km/h
60 ≤ speed < 70	$3 per km over 50 km/h
70 ≤ speed	$4 per km over 50 km/h

The output is to be a list of the license numbers of cars that were speeding, together with the observed speed at which they were traveling and the penalty to be assessed. The subprograms of Question 1 and 3 can be useful.

5. When more than one value is to be passed on to a subprogram, a common procedure is to provide a list of their addresses following the BAL instruction, as illustrated in Fig. B.6. This list of addresses can be used by the subprogram to pick up the values that it requires. A subprogram is required for finding the maximum of two values. The calling sequence is

BAL MAX2,1	Branch and link to MAX2
A1	Address of first argument
A2	Address of second argument

and the result is to be returned via the accumulator. The subprogram might then begin as follows:

MAX2 L	0,1	Load address of first argument
A	LOAD	Add "load" operation code to address
ST	N1	Store instruction just formed
N1 DC		in next location

—————

—————

LOAD L

When the instruction in location N1 is executed, the value of the first argument is loaded into the accumulator. Write the remaining instructions for the subprogram MAX2.

6. Write a subprogram for finding the greatest common divisor of two values. The calling sequence should be as illustrated in Fig. B.6. (As mentioned in this section, indirect addressing can provide a convenient way of picking up values of the argument. However, it is instructive to attempt this question without the use of indirect addressing.)

B.6 THE SIMON COMPUTER

The purpose of this section is to summarize the machine and assembly languages for our hypothetical computer. The basic machine language was explained in detail in Appendix A. A few additional features were only mentioned at that time since the purpose of Appendix A was to provide no more than the bare essentials needed to understand the nature of a stored-program computer and, at least in a general way, to appreciate the correspondence between programs in higher-level languages and machine language. Some additional features have been described in this appendix. Their purpose has been twofold. First, the ability to handle alphanumeric characters is necessary if the idea of an assembler or a compiler is to be credible. Second, the use of index registers is needed to make the machine reasonably like real machines.

The process of adding new features to the hypothetical machine can be continued almost indefinitely. For example, we could introduce numerous operation codes that cause branching on different conditions such as overflow, or on various conditions of the index registers. We could also consider operation codes to shift the accumulator left or right, or to handle parts of words (to copy addresses, for example). We resist the temptation to add a large number of new features. We consider only one.

The new machine feature is *indirect addressing*. We assume that SIMON has this feature and that instructions are forced to use indirect addresses whenever 5 is added to the fifth digit of the instruction. For example, suppose that the number in location 444 is +0000633222. Then the instruction +0000010444 causes this number to be copied into the accumulator, whereas the instruction +0000510444 causes the number in location 222 to be copied into the accumulator. Adding 5 to the fifth digit in the instruction has caused the address part of the instruction (444 in this case) to be used as the address of the required address, rather than as the required address itself. We assume that only the address part of the memory location referred to is used and that the other part (+0000633 in this case) is ignored.

According to what has been stated so far, it is possible to require the address of an instruction to be modified by the content of an index register and to be indirect at the same time. It is necessary to state which of these two modifications takes place first and we choose to require the indexing to be first. For example, suppose the instruction +0000110000 in the subprogram of Fig. B.6 is replaced by +0000610000. (Note that 5 has been added to the fifth digit.) During execution, the address is first modified by adding the content (066) of index register 1, so that the address becomes 066. Then the address part of 066 (namely 200) is used in carrying out the instruction. Thus, the instruction is equivalent to +0000010200 and would cause the value of L1 to be copied into the accumulator. In a similar way, replacing +0000110001 with +0000610001 in the subprogram of Fig. B.6 causes the value of L2 to be copied into the accumulator.

We see that indirect addressing can be quite helpful in the implementation of subprograms. Although convenient, it turns out that indirect addressing is often not the most efficient way of making values of arguments available to subprograms, because some machine time is consumed each time the indirect address is obtained. However, indirect addressing can be helpful in other ways as well, and it is generally considered to be a useful feature of any machine language.

A simple way to specify indirect addressing in assembly-language programs is to add 5 to the specification of the index register, just as we add 5 to the fifth digit in the machine-language instruction. Thus we have the following correspondences:

```
ST   3,1      +0000111003
ST   3,6      +0000611003
A    246,5    +0000520246
```

The third of these examples specifies indirect addressing without address modification.

Most assembly languages make provision for what is called *address arithmetic,* and it is convenient to include this feature in SAP. Specifically, we allow the address part of an assembly-language instruction to be a name, plus or minus an unsigned integer. Thus we allow instructions such as

```
A    LAB+3
ST   POS-2
```

Blanks are not allowed, so that LAB + 3 is invalid. As is suggested by the notation, LAB+3 corresponds to the machine-language address that is 3 more than the address of LAB and similarly POS−2 corresponds to the address that is 2 less than the address of POS. It should be clear that this device enables us to avoid an excessive number of names for different memory locations. Another use was illustrated in Fig. B.4.

Many instructions refer to memory locations near to where the instructions themselves are located. For example, we might wish to refer to the memory location 3 locations further along in memory, or to one 5 locations back. It is therefore convenient to have a symbol that is equivalent to the name of the current instruction and an asterisk is usually used for this purpose. We will therefore allow instruction such as

```
HERE L    *+3
     B    *-5
```

In the first of these, *+3 is equivalent to HERE+3.

We could continue to add new features to SAP. However, the features already described are sufficient for our purposes. We conclude this section with a summary of the main properties of the SIMON machine and its SAP assembler.

The standard format for assembly-language statements is as follows:

In columns 1–4, name field can consist of:
  name
  blank
In columns 6–8, operation code field can consist of:
  operation code
  pseudo-operation code
  blank
In columns 10– , address field can consist of:
  with all but DC, RES, LX, STX, BIX, BAL
    address
    address,digit
    blank
  with DC
    signed or unsigned integer
    blank
  with RES
    unsigned integer
    unsigned integer 'character string'
  with LX, STX, BAL
    address,digit
  with BIX
    address,address,digit

Columns 5 and 9 must be blank. Each of the three fields must be left justified. Each *name* consists of at most 4 alphabetic and numeric characters, the first of which must be alphabetic. Each *address* consists of

  name
  = signed or unsigned integer
  name ± unsigned integer
  ** ± unsigned integer*
  absolute address

Except for RES, if the operation code field or address field is blank, the assembler places zeros in the corre-

sponding digit positions. With RES, unspecified character positions are filled with blanks.

The only exception allowed in the above requirements is that an apostrophe can appear in column 1. When this happens, the statement is not translated into machine language. It will, however, be printed along with the rest of the assembly-language program. Such statements can be used to insert comments in the program. Other special symbols can be placed in column 1 to mark control cards. In particular, a special symbol in column 1 can be used to mark the end of the program.

The operation codes for SIMON and SAP are summarized in Table B.2. It must be admitted that the meanings of these codes are still not completely specified. For example, we have not stated what will happen in case of overflow or if an invalid address arises (as it can with indexing), or if an invalid operation code is encountered. Such questions must be settled if a machine is built, if an interpreter is constructed, or if an assembler is developed. It is best to specify such details only when considering a particular implementation.

Floating-point operations are not included in the table. They were mentioned earlier in order to empha-

TABLE B.2

Operation codes for the SIMON *computer:* The organization and programming of the basic machine is described in detail in Appendix A. All additional features are described in this appendix.

Operation codes and pseudo-operation codes for the SAP *assembler:* Details of the SAP assembler are described in this appendix.

Numeric code	Mnemonic code	Brief explanation
10	L	Load accumulator
11	ST	Store accumulator
20	A	Add to accumulator
21	S	Subtract from accumulator
22	M	Multiply accumulator
23	D	Divide into accumulator
30	R	Read
31	W	Write
32	RA	Read alphanumeric
33	WA	Write alphanumeric
40	H	Halt
50	B	Branch
51	BN	Branch on negative
52	BZ	Branch on zero
53	BP	Branch on positive
60	LX	Load index
61	STX	Store index
62	BIX	Branch on incremented index
63	BAL	Branch and link
	DC	Define constant
	RES	Reserve space

size some of the properties of roundoff error. They would not be particularly useful to SIMON because, to be reasonably realistic, we would also have to develop rather complicated subprograms for the input and output of floating-point numbers.

EXERCISE B.6

1. Write an assembly-language program that inputs 80 characters from a punched card. The program is to search for the first right parenthesis on the card and output its position.

2. Write an assembly language program that inputs 80 characters from a punched card, followed by a pair of numbers, I and J, from the next card. The program is to output YES or NO depending on whether or not the first card contains only numeric information between columns I and J inclusive.

3. Two numbers less than 10^5 have been punched somewhere on a card. A portion of a program is required to search the 80 card columns to find the numbers and then to convert the numbers to their numeric representation.

4. A subprogram for finding the greatest common divisor of two numbers is required. The calling sequence is

```
BAL IGCD,1      Branch and link to IGCD
    I           Address of first argument
    J           Address of second argument
```

and the result is to be returned via the accumulator. The subprogram should make copies of the values of I and J before finding their greatest common divisor. In this way the values of I and J in the calling program are not altered by the subprogram.

5. Do as in Question 4, except that the subprogram should not copy the values. Rather, the subprogram should use the addresses of these values whenever it refers to them.

6. A subprogram for finding the greatest common divisor of two numbers is required. The calling sequence is

```
BAL GCD,1
    I           Address of first argument
    J           Address of second argument
    K           Address of result argument
```

so that the subprogram does not return the result via the accumulator.

7. A sequence of cards is to be input. On each card, there is a telephone number and a person's name. A program is required to produce the following:

a) a list of names and telephone numbers, with the names in alphabetical order;

b) a list of telephone numbers and names, with the telephone numbers in increasing order.

Number Representations

All of our explanations as to how numbers are handled by the hypothetical computer of the preceding two appendixes have assumed decimal number representations, although we have studied both integer and floating-point representations of decimal numbers.

It is the purpose of this appendix to describe other number representations, especially binary and hexadecimal numbers, and to show how to convert from one representation into another.

C.1 INTEGERS

Our first objective is to learn how to represent integers with different number bases. We are of course most familiar with base 10. To emphasize what it means to represent an integer in this way, we consider 159 as an example. We can write

$$159 = 1 \times 10^2 + 5 \times 10^1 + 9 \times 10^0$$

This emphasizes the fact that the digit 1 is the number of hundreds (10^2), 5 is the number of tens (10^1), and 9 is the number of units (10^0).

The same number can be written equally well in terms of powers of any number base other than 10. For example, in terms of base 6, it is easy to verify that

$$159 = 4 \times 6^2 + 2 \times 6^1 + 3 \times 6^0$$

We can therefore write the base 10 number 159 as 423 in base 6. We denote this by writing

$$159 = (423)_6$$

We could have written $(159)_{10}$ in place of 159, but we will assume that the base is 10 whenever the base is not specified explicitly.

We now describe an algorithm for converting from one base to another. Let us first assume we are converting from base 10 to base b. Then, for a given integer i the problem is to find $a_n, a_{n-1}, \ldots, a_1, a_0$ so that we can write

$$i = a_n \times b^n + a_{n-1} \times b^{n-1} + \cdots + a_1 \times b^1 + a_0 \times b^0$$

In the example where $i = 159$ and $b = 6$, we see that $n = 2$ and $a_2 = 4$, $a_1 = 2$, $a_0 = 3$. From the general form, it is fairly easy to see how one can proceed. If i is divided by b, the quotient is

$$a_n \times b^{n-1} + a_{n-1} \times b^{n-2} + \cdots + a_1$$

while the remainder is the digit a_0. If the quotient is divided by b, the new remainder is the digit a_1. This process can be repeated to give the digits $a_2, a_3, \ldots, a_n$ as remainders, until a quotient is zero.

We illustrate this algorithm using 159 and base 6:

First quotient is 26, first remainder is 3
Second quotient is 4, second remainder is 2
Third quotient is 0, third remainder is 4

Thus, the digits 4, 2, 3 are produced as remainders, in reverse order, and this agrees with the earlier result.

Consider this algorithm using 159 with the base 2. We divide repeatedly by 2 and obtain the following:

Division	Quotient	Remainder
1st	79	1
2nd	39	1
3rd	19	1
4th	9	1
5th	4	1
6th	2	0
7th	1	0
8th	0	1

The base 2 or *binary* representation therefore is

$$159 = (10011111)_2$$

To represent numbers in base 10 we need 10 digits, 0 through 9. To represent numbers in base b we need b digits, 0 through $b - 1$. Thus, with base 6, we need the digits 0, 1, 2, 3, 4, 5, and with base 2 we need only the digits 0 and 1. These binary digits are frequently referred to as *bits*. Something special will obviously have to be done if $b > 10$. One base that is frequently used with computers is 16. In this case we use the 16 digits 0, 1, . . . , 9, a, b, c, d, e, f. Thus, since

$$159 = 9 \times 16^1 + 15 \times 16^0$$

we write $159 = 9 \times 16^1 + f \times 16^0$ or $(9f)_{16}$. Numbers expressed in base 16 are usually called *hexadecimal* numbers.

We have so far considered only the problem of converting from base 10 into some other base. To convert from base b into 10 is even easier. An example with base 6 is as follows:

$$(1234)_6 = 1 \times 6^3 + 2 \times 6^2 + 3 \times 6^1 + 4 \times 6^0$$
$$= 216 + 72 + 18 + 4$$
$$= 310$$

You might expect the algorithms for conversion to be the same, whether the conversion is from one base to another or vice versa. The reason they are not the same is that we tend to think in terms of base 10. If we insist on doing our calculations in base 10 arithmetic, we must expect our algorithms to be different, depending on whether we are converting from base 10 to base b or vice versa. The algorithm for converting from base 10 to base 6 could be just as easy as the one for converting from base 6 to base 10, if we were prepared to

do all of our arithmetic in base 6. Since $10 = (14)_6$ we would obtain

$$159 = (1)_6 \times (14)_6^2 + (5)_6 \times (14)_6^1 + (13)_6 \times (14)_6^0$$
$$= (244)_6 + (122)_6 + (13)_6$$
$$= (423)_6$$

which is easy and straightforward for anyone who just naturally does arithmetic in base 6!

There is only one important fact to keep in mind about the way in which integers are represented in the machine. This concerns the largest magnitude that can be represented. On our hypothetical machine the largest magnitude is 9999999999 or $10^{10} - 1$. Similarly, on a binary machine in which 35 binary digits are used for the magnitude of the number, the largest number that can be represented is 34359738367 or $2^{35} - 1$. On a hexadecimal machine in which 8 hexadecimal digits are used for the magnitude, the largest integer that can be represented is $16^8 - 1$.

Until now we have considered only the possibility of representing a number by its sign and magnitude. There is another possibility used on some machines in which a *2's-complement* representation is used for negative numbers. For nonnegative numbers the first bit is zero and the remaining bits represent the magnitude in the usual way. Thus if one storage location consists of 12 bits,

159 is represented by 000010011111

In this way all the numbers 0, 1, 2, . . . , $2^{11} - 1$ are represented. On the other hand, negative numbers are first added to 2^{12} and the result is represented in the usual way by the 12 bits, as illustrated in the following:

Number	Added to 2^{12}	Representation
-1	$2^{12} - 1$	111111111111
-2	$2^{12} - 2$	111111111110
-3	$2^{12} - 3$	111111111101
-159	$2^{12} - 159$	111101100001
-2^{11}	$2^{12} - 2^{11}$	100000000000

In this way the negative numbers $-1, -2, -3, . . . ,$ -2^{11} are represented.

The notation is called *2's-complement* because, except for the last negative number, -2^{11}, all the representations of the negative numbers can be obtained from the representations of the corresponding positive numbers in the following way. Each digit in the representation of the positive number is *complemented,* that is, 1's are replaced by 0's and 0's by 1's, and then 1 is added to the result. Thus,

159 is represented by	000010011111
complementing yields	111101100000
adding one yields	111101100001

The only effect of all this extra complication for a programmer is that the maximum magnitudes allowed for integers are 1 more for negative numbers than for positive numbers. Thus, when one word consists of 12 bits, the maximum magnitude for a sign-and-magnitude representation is $2^{11} - 1$. However, with a 2's-complement representation, the negative numbers can have magnitudes as large as 2^{11}. The saving, if you would like to call it that, comes about because there is only one 2's-complement representation of zero. With sign-and-magnitude there are two representations of zero, $+0$ and -0.

It is important to determine exactly how integers are represented in the machine you intend to use. It is particularly important to know what are the largest magnitudes allowed. If possible, one should also find out what happens when overflow occurs, that is, when an attempt is made to exceed these maximums.

EXERCISE C.1

1. Verify the following:

a) $1000 = (13000)_5$
b) $171 = (ab)_{16}$
c) $39 = (100111)_2$
d) $574 = (23e)_{16}$

2. a) Show that the 2's-complement representation of -39, when one storage location consists of 12 bits, is 111111011001.

b) What is the sign-and-magnitude representation of -39 with a 12-bit word?

3. Write a program or subprogram to convert base 10 integers into base b integers, where $b < 10$. Write another to convert back. Assume the integers are denoted by single variable names.

4. Repeat Question 3, but denote the integers by subscripted variables, one digit per component.

5. Another approach to the problem of converting from base 10 integers to base b integers is based on the following steps. Divide the original integer repeatedly by b, until b^{n+1} is found, that is, until the first power of b is found that is larger than the original integer. Divide the original integer by b^n. The quotient is a_n. The remainder is then divided by b^{n-1} to produce a_{n-1}. The new remainder is then divided by b^{n-2} to produce a_{n-2}, and so on. Write a program or subprogram to implement this algorithm.

6. Give a program or subprogram to convert from base b_1 to base b_2, where $b_1, b_2 \leq 10$.

7. Give a program or subprogram to convert from base 10 to base 16, and another to convert back.

C.2 FRACTIONS

We turn now to the problem of converting a fraction from one base to another. We can write the fraction .125 in the form

$$.125 = 1 \times 10^{-1} + 2 \times 10^{-2} + 5 \times 10^{-3}$$

and this emphasizes the fact that 1 is the number of tenths, 2 the number of hundredths, and 5 the number of thousandths.

In general, we can express a fraction f to base b as follows:

$$f = a_{-1} \times b^{-1} + a_{-2} \times b^{-2} + a_{-3} \times b^{-3} + \cdots$$

where $a_{-1}, a_{-2}, \ldots$ are digits from 0 through $b - 1$. In the example with $f = .125$ and $b = 10$, we see that $a_{-1} = 1$, $a_{-2} = 2$, and $a_{-3} = 5$. Once again the general form suggests an algorithm for finding the digits. We first multiply f by b. This produces the integer a_{-1}, plus the fraction

$$a_{-2} \times b^{-1} + a_{-3} \times b^{-2} + \cdots$$

If we now multiply this fraction by b, we produce the integer a_{-2}, plus a new fraction, and so on.

Consider converting the fraction .125 to base 6:

multiplying .125 by 6 yields the integer 0 plus the fraction .750

multiplying .750 by 6 yields the integer 4 plus the fraction .50

multiplying .50 by 6 yields the integer 3 plus the fraction .0

We therefore conclude that $.125 = (.043)_6$

On the other hand, if we express .125 to base 5, we find that $.125 = (.030303 \ldots)_5$, where 03 is repeated indefinitely. This is an example of something that happens quite frequently. A fraction which terminates in one number base frequently has a repeating expansion in another base. Another example of this situation occurs when we express .1 in binary form. We obtain

$$.1 = (.000110011001100 \ldots)_2$$

where 1100 repeats indefinitely.

Again, converting back from base b to base 10 is quite straightforward. For example, consider

$$(.213)_6 = 2 \times 6^{-1} + 1 \times 6^{-2} + 3 \times 6^{-3}$$

Since it is easier to work with integers we rewrite this as

$$(.213)_6 = (2 \times 6^2 + 1 \times 6^1 + 3 \times 6^0) \times 6^{-3}$$
$$= 81/216$$
$$= .375$$

Finally, we can now use our algorithms for converting integers and fractions to convert numbers which have both integer and fraction parts. For example, to write the number 159.375 in base 6, we first obtain

$$159 = (423)_6$$
$$.375 = (.213)_6$$

and combining these results we conclude that

$$159.375 = (423.213)_6$$

EXERCISE C.2

1. Verify the following:

a) $.875 = (.513)_6$
b) $.375 = (.011)_2$
c) $.2 = (.001100110011\ldots)_2$
d) $.1 = (.19999\ldots)_{16}$

2. Verify the following:

a) $17.25 = (10001.01)_2$
b) $7.1 = (111.00011001100\ldots)_2$
c) $25.1 = (19.19999\ldots)_{16}$
d) $25.8 = (19.cccc\ldots)_{16}$

3. Write a program or subprogram for converting decimal numbers (including both integer and fraction parts) to binary. Write another to convert back. Assume the numbers are denoted by subscripted variables, one digit per component. Assume that the number of places to the right of the decimal point is fixed, and that the number to the right of the binary point is also fixed.

4. Repeat Question 3, replacing binary by hexadecimal.

C.3 FLOATING-POINT REPRESENTATION

In Section A.5 we described how numbers are represented in floating-point form on our hypothetical machine. In that case the representation used floating-point decimal numbers. For example, the number 6.25 was rewritten as

$$6.25 = .625 \times 10^1$$

and this in turn was stored as +5162500000. Note that 50 has been added to the exponent.

The situation is similar with binary machines. The number 6.25 would first have to be converted to binary form, which leads to

$$6.25 = (110.01)_2$$

Then the binary number must be normalized, which leads to

$$(110.01)_2 = (.11001)_2 \times 2^3$$

Let us suppose now that 12 bits are available altogether. This word length is too short for practical purposes, but it can be used to illustrate the basic ideas.

Let us also suppose that the first bit is used to denote the sign (0 for +, 1 for −), and that the next 3 bits are used for the exponent. This leaves 8 bits for the fraction part of the number.

We can now represent 6.25 in the following way:

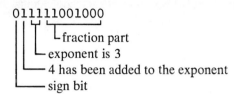

Note that the quantity added to the exponent is $\frac{1}{2} \times 2^3$ when 3 bits are available for the exponent. Compare this with $50 = \frac{1}{2} \times 10^2$ when two decimal digits are available. Generally, if d digits are available for the exponent, and the base is b, we add $\frac{1}{2} \times b^d$ to the exponent. This enables us to store approximately as many positive exponents as negative exponents.

As an example of how negative exponents appear, consider

$$.15625 = (.00101)_2 = (.101)_2 \times 2^{-2}$$

which is represented by

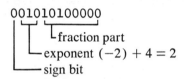

Here the three bits following the sign bit represent the exponent −2 with 4 added, which is 2.

We may find that the number we are considering cannot be represented exactly on a binary machine. For example, 6.25 could not have been represented exactly if we had had fewer than 5 bits for the fraction part of the floating-point number. This difficulty also arises whenever we have a repeating binary fraction. For example, we already know that

$$7.1 = (111.0001100110011\ldots)_2$$

Then we have

$$(111.000110011\ldots)_2 = (.111000110011\ldots)_2 \times 2^3$$

so we would represent this number as

011111100011

where we have chopped off all digits beyond the first 8 significant digits. In this case rounding to the nearest digit in the last place and chopping produce the same result; in other cases they may be different.

Zero is the only floating-point number we allow that cannot be properly normalized. It is represented either by 000000000000 or by 100000000000.

In hexadecimal notation we have

$$6.25 = (6.4)_{16} = (.64) \times 16^1$$

This means that the fraction part of the floating-point form begins with 64. If these two hexadecimal characters are expanded into their binary equivalents, we find that the fraction part begins with

01100100—binary

6   4 —hexadecimal

This example shows that a normalized hexadecimal fraction may begin with leading zeros when expressed in terms of its binary equivalent. A hexadecimal representation may therefore not be as accurate as a binary representation that uses the same number of bits.

One other possibility with hexadecimal notation should be mentioned. The sign and the exponent can be combined and represented by 1 or 2 hexadecimal characters. For example, with a word length of 12 bits we could let the first bit represent the sign as before, and the next 3 bits represent the exponent plus 4. These 4 bits can then be represented by one hexadecimal character, and the remaining 8 bits can be represented by two hexadecimal characters that give the fraction part of the number. Thus, 6.25 is represented by the bits

010101100100
exponent is 1
4 is added to exponent
sign bit

which in turn are represented by the hexadecimal digits 564. For −6.25, the first bit is changed to 1, and the hexadecimal form becomes d64, as shown in the following:

110101100100

d   6   4

It is important that a programmer know how numbers of this type are stored in the machine he is using. He should in particular know the largest and smallest magnitudes that can be stored, and what happens in his compiled program if results are encountered which are too large or too small. He should also know about the roundoff errors that can occur, a topic which is discussed in considerable detail in Chapter 9.

EXERCISE C.3

1. Assume the floating-point binary representation described in this section for storage locations of 12 bits, and verify each of the following repersentations:

a) 1.25 by 010110100000
b) −4.2734375 by 111110001000 if chopped, but by 111110001001 if rounded
c) .65 by 010010100110 whether chopped or rounded

2. Show that the largest magnitude that can be represented in binary floating-point form with the 12-bit word discussed in this section is 7.96875.

3. Suppose that 8 bits are used for the exponent (plus $\frac{1}{2} \times 2^8$) in place of 3, and that 27 bits are used for the fraction part of a number. Show that the largest magnitude that can be represented is approximately 2^{127}.

4. Show that the smallest nonzero magnitude that can be represented with the 12-bit word, assuming the number is properly normalized, is .03125.

5. Show that the smallest nonzero magnitude that can be represented under the assumptions of Question 3 is 2^{-129}.

6. Assume the floating-point hexadecimal representation described in this section for storage locations of 3 hexadecimal digits and verify that:

a) 170 is represented by 6aa.
b) −170 is represented by eaa.
c) .1 is represented by 419 if chopped but by 41a if rounded.
d) 4080 is the largest magnitude that can be represented.
e) 16^{-5} is the smallest nonzero magnitude that can be represented consistent with Question 1.

7. Suppose that a storage location consists of 32 bits and can therefore be represented by 8 hexadecimal digits. Suppose also that the first two of these digits represent the sign and the exponent (plus $\frac{1}{2} \times 2^7$), and that the remaining 6 hexadecimal digits are for the fraction part of the number. Show that the largest magnitude in this case is approximately 16^{63}, while the smallest nonzero magnitude is 16^{-65}.

8. Show that multiplication and division by 2 can be carried out exactly with binary floating-point numbers (provided the result does not become too large or too small). However, show that this is not the case with hexadecimal floating-point numbers.

9. Suppose we wish to design a binary machine, and we want decimal numbers that are converted back on output to exactly the same as what was input. If this requirement is to hold for all decimal numbers having 8 or fewer "significant" digits, what is the minimum number of binary digits that we would have to have in the fraction part of the internal representation?

Answers to
Selected Questions in Appendixes

APPENDIX A
Exercise A.1

1. Instructions for the computer to follow and data to be used in the calculations.

2. *Destructive read-in:* whenever new information is stored in a part of the memory, the information previously stored in that part is destroyed.

Nondestructive read-out: whenever information is retrieved from the memory, it is not destroyed but only copied from the memory.

3. Once the machine is started, it executes the instructions automatically, one after the other, without operator intervention, whereas a desk calculator must be given a new instruction after each arithmetic operation. The newer "programmable calculators" are much more automatic than desk calculators. The term "automatic" is not sharply defined and we have to admit that it has a different meaning when applied to desk calculators than it does when applied to computers.

Exercise A.2

1. $+9999999999$ is the largest number that can be stored in a single location. Larger numbers can be stored using the floating-point representation outlined in Section A.5.

2. (c),(e).

3. a) The instruction in 000 causes the content of location 200 to be copied into the accumulator. When the instructions in 001 and 002 are executed, the content of locations 201 and 202 will become zero.

4.

000 +0000010120	Copy content of location 120 into accumulator
001 +0000011125	Store content of accumulator in location 125

5.

000 +0000010400	Copy content of location 400 into accumulator
001 +0000021300	Subtract content of location 300 from accumulator
002 +0000011400	Store content of accumulator in location 400

6. Two instructions are necessary: the first copies the content of the accumulator into an available location and the second multiplies the content of the accumulator by the number just stored in the available location.

8. a) The first two instructions cause the original content of location 075 to replace the original content of location 076. Thus, these two instructions cause the original content of location 076 to be lost.

Exercise A.3

1. The instruction in location 002 must be changed to $+0000010015$.

2. The following two changes would be required:

005 +0000031010
007 +0000031009

A second solution is as follows:

002 +0000010010
003 +0000021009

3. The most likely change is

004 +0000053007

but the following changes could also be used:

005 +0000031010
007 +0000031009

4. N corresponds to location 013 whereas the value of N is the value of each number as it is input and becomes the *content* of location 013.

5. a) I and J must (i) be integers;
     (ii) be less than 10^{10} in magnitude;
     (iii) have a sum of less than 10^{10} in magnitude.

b) I and J must (i) be integers;
     (ii) be less than 10^{10} in magnitude;
     (iii) have a difference of less than 10^{10} in magnitude.

c) Each value of N must (i) be an integer;
     (ii) be less than 10^{10} in magnitude.

Also, each partial sum must be less than 10^{10} in magnitude.

7. b)

000 +0000030009	Input value of N
001 +0000010009	Copy value of N into accumulator
002 +0000053007	Go to 007 if N>0
003 +0000052007	Go to 007 if N=0
004 +0000010009	Copy value of N into accumulator
005 +0000022010	Multiply accumulator by −1
006 +0000011009	Store accumulator in location for N
007 +0000031009	Output value of N
008 +0000040000	Stop
009 +0000000000	Location for N
010 −0000000001	Location for constant −1

7. c)

000	+0000030017	Input value of I
001	+0000030018	Input value of J
002	+0000030019	Input value of K
003	+0000010017	Copy value of I into accumulator
004	+0000011020	Store accumulator in location for M
005	+0000010020	Copy value of M into accumulator
006	+0000021018	Subtract value of J from accumulator
007	+0000053010	Go to 010 if accumulator > 0
008	+0000010018	Copy value of J into accumulator
009	+0000011020	Store accumulator in location for M
010	+0000010020	Copy value of M into accumulator
011	+0000021019	Subtract value of K from accumulator
012	+0000053015	Go to 015 if accumulator > 0
013	+0000010019	Copy value of K into accumulator for M
014	+0000011020	Store accumulator in location for M
015	+0000031020	Output value of M
016	+0000040000	Stop
017	+0000000000	Location for I
018	+0000000000	Location for J
019	+0000000000	Location for K
020	+0000000000	Location for M

Exercise A.4

1.

	Quotient	Remainder
a)	3	3
b)	−3	−3
c)	−3	3
d)	3	−3

3.

000	+0000030014	Input value of I
001	+0000030015	Input value of J
002	+0000010014	Copy value of I into accumulator
003	+0000023015	Divide accumulator by value of J
004	+0000011016	Store accumulator in location for Q
005	+0000010016	Copy value of Q into accumulator
006	+0000022015	Multiply accumulator by value of J
007	+0000011017	Store accumulator in temporary storage
008	+0000010014	Copy value of I into accumulator
009	+0000021017	Subtract temporary location from accumulator

010	+0000011018	Store accumulator in location for R
011	+0000031016	Output value of Q
012	+0000031018	Output value of R
013	+0000040000	Stop
014	+0000000000	Location for I
015	+0000000000	Location for J
016	+0000000000	Location for Q
017	+0000000000	Temporary storage (for product Q×J)
018	+0000000000	Location for R

This program does not work properly if J = 0. How should it be modified to handle this possibility?

5.

000	+0000030019	Input value of I
001	+0000030020	Input value of J
002	+0000010019	Copy value of I into accumulator
003	+0000020020	Add value of J to accumulator
004	+0000011021	Store accumulator in location for K
005	+0000010021	Copy value of K into accumulator
006	+0000023022	Divide accumulator by 2
007	+0000011023	Store accumulator in location for M
008	+0000010023	Copy value of M into accumulator
009	+0000022022	Multiply accumulator by 2
010	+0000011024	Store accumulator in temporary location
011	+0000010021	Copy value of K into accumulator
012	+0000021024	Subtract temporary location from accumulator
013	+0000052017	Go to 017 if accumulator = 0
014	+0000010023	Copy value of M into accumulator
015	+0000020025	Add 1 to accumulator
016	+0000011023	Store accumulator in location for M
017	+0000031023	Output the value of M
018	+0000040000	Stop
019	+0000000000	Location for I
020	+0000000000	Location for J
021	+0000000000	Location for K
022	+0000000002	Location for constant 2
023	+0000000000	Location for M
024	+0000000000	Temporary location (for product M×2)
025	+0000000001	Location for constant 1

Note that the program rounds the result up if the sum of the two numbers is odd.

Exercise A.5

1. a) can represent the fixed-point number 11,057 or instruction to store accumulator in location 057

b) can represent fixed-point number −11,057

c) can represent fixed-point number 101,010

d) can represent fixed-point number 5,012,340,000 or floating-point number $.1234 \times 10^0$

e) can represent fixed-point number $-5,012,340,000$ or floating-point number $-.1234 \times 10^0$

f) can represent fixed-point number 5,201,919,191

g) can represent fixed-point number 4,347,600,000 or floating-point number $.876 \times 10^{-7}$

h) can represent fixed-point number 12,300,000 or floating-point number $.123 \times 10^{-50}$

2. $.99999999 \times 10^{49}$

3. $.1 \times 10^{-50}$, if the number must be properly normalized.

4.
a) +5155500000
b) +5110000000
c) −5217000000
d) +4863000000
e) −4863000000
f) +6410000000

5.
a) +5033333333
b) +5066666667
c) +5131415927

6.
a) 1234.
b) −1234.
c) .00098
d) −.00098

7.
a) +5055500000
b) +5115540000
c) +5044511000
d) +5044289000
e) +5312100000
f) −4812100000

Exercise A.6

1. Instructions, fixed-point numbers, floating-point numbers, and character information (in coded form).

It is not possible for one memory location of the hypothetical machine to be storing information that can have all four interpretations at the same time, since instructions and floating-point numbers are mutually exclusive.

2. The notion of a stored program distinguishes computers from most other calculating devices. Some calculators (often referred to as programmable calculators) have a stored program but it is not usual for them to be able to modify their programs as they are being executed. (See Question 9, Exercise A.2.) The term general-purpose is also applied to the computers discussed in this book but it is not applicable to any other calculating device. The other terms are not peculiar to general-purpose, stored-program computers. Analogue computers can be high-speed, electronic, and automatic. A desk calculator is digital.

3. Digital computers operate with information that is stored in the form of digits whereas analogue computers use physical quantities to represent numbers. A digital computer will give the same result each time, if it is started off

in the same way a number of times, whereas an analogue computer may give slightly different results each time because the various voltages and currents can be expected to fluctuate slightly.

Analogue computers are not general purpose to the extent that digital computers are. Analogue computers are faster but less accurate.

Hybrid computers are computers that are partly digital and partly analogue, in an attempt to combine the best features of both.

4. Desk calculators "automatically" compute sums, products, and so on, but they do not have stored programs. Since each computation is followed by operator intervention, desk calculators are not automatic in the sense that computers are. On the other hand, programmable calculators do use stored programs and in this sense they are more automatic than desk calculators, since they can carry out sequences of instructions. (See also Question 3, Exercise A.1.)

APPENDIX B

Exercise B.1

1. A solution is as follows:

```
000  +0000030009
001  +0000010009
002  +0000051008
003  +0000022010
004  +0000011011
005  +0000031009
006  +0000031011
007  +0000050000
008  +0000040000
009  +0000000000      Location for N
010  +0000000575      Location for constant 575
011  +0000000000      Location for A
```

2. The program could be as follows:

```
READ  R    N
      L    N
      BN   QUIT
      M    CONS
      ST   A
      W    N
      W    A
      B    READ
QUIT  H
CONS  DC   575
```

3.
```
      R    NUM
      L    NUM   ⎫
      M    NUM   ⎬ Determine square of input
      ST   SQAR  ⎭
      M    NUM   ⎫ Determine cube of input
      ST   CUBE  ⎭
      W    NUM   ⎫
      W    SQAR  ⎬ Output results
      W    CUBE  ⎭
      H
```

```
NUM  DC  0
SQAR DC  0
CUBE DC  0
```

4. Suppose that the end of the sequence is indicated by a card on which a negative number has been punched. The following program could then be used:

```
        L   ZERO  ⎫ Initialize maximum to zero
        ST  MAX   ⎭
LOOP R  NUM       Input number
        L   NUM   Copy number into accumulator
        BN  DONE  Branch to DONE if negative
        S   MAX   Subtract current maximum
        BN  LOOP  Branch back if not new maximum
        L   NUM   ⎫ Store new maximum
        ST  MAX   ⎭
        B   LOOP  Branch back
DONE W  MAX       Output maximum
        H         Stop
ZERO DC  0
MAX  DC  0
NUM  DC  0
```

Since we have defined the value of MAX using the statement

```
MAX  DC  0
```

it is not really necessary to have the first two instructions in the program given above. (The purpose of the first two instructions given above is to *initialize* the value of MAX.) With the first two instructions, the initialization is performed at *execution-time;* with the DC statement, it is performed at *translation-time.*

5. An interpretation of "second largest" should include provision for sequences such as

$$6 \quad 8 \quad 3 \quad 8$$

in which the largest occurs more than once. What should your program do if the sequence contains only one number?

Exercise B.2

1. Assume that the last card in the sequence contains END in columns 1–3 and that columns 4, 5 are blank. The following program could be used.

```
NEXT RA  CARD ⎫
        L   CARD ⎬ Test for last card
        S   END  ⎪ in sequence
        BZ  QUIT ⎭

        L   ARER ⎫
        D   HUN  ⎬ Determine whether or not
        S   BLNK ⎪ account is in arrears
        BZ  NEXT ⎪
        WA  CARD ⎪
        B   NEXT ⎭
QUIT H
CARD RES  8   ⎫
ARER RES  1   ⎬ 16 locations reserved for
     RES  7   ⎭ card image
```

```
END  RES  1'END'
HUN  DC   100
BLNK RES  1'0'
```

Note that it is necessary to remove the information from column 45 that is contained in location ARER prior to deciding whether or not the account is in arrears.

With the program given above, it is assumed that the account is in arrears if columns 41–44 are not blank. Is this a reasonable assumption?

3. One way in which this can be accomplished is for the program to first of all "separate" the information so that the two-digit representation for each column is stored in separate (consecutive) storage locations. Using the representation for character information given in this section, the program can then test the value stored in each location to determine whether or not it is numeric. Leading blanks, as well as plus or minus signs, can also be checked.

In practice, this type of data screening is often required. As well as working when the program is presented with correct data, a program should also do something sensible when it is presented with invalid data.

4. The way in which the information is organized on each card is not specified. You should first of all specify a convenient way for organizing this information. With the representation we have chosen for character information, it is likely that you will want to have groups of 5 card columns used for the various fields. If this is done, the second part of this problem will be fairly easy to handle.

Exercise B.3

1. The following program uses index register 1 to control the number of times the loop will be executed. Note that the first two terms are output prior to the loop, and also that the last term and the second last term (LAST and SEC) are initialized with the values of t_1 and t_2 at translation-time.

```
        W   =1
        W   =1
        LX  =3,1
LOOP L  LAST ⎫ Next term = Last term +
        A   SEC  ⎬         Second last term
        ST  NEXT ⎭
        W   NEXT  Output next term
        L   LAST ⎫ SEC ← LAST
        ST  SEC  ⎬
        L   NEXT ⎫ LAST ← NEXT
        ST  LAST ⎭
        BIX LOOP,C50,1
        H
LAST DC   1
SEC  DC   1
NEXT DC   0
C50  DC   50
```

It is not necessary to use an index register to control the number of times the loop will be executed; a variable that represents the number of times can be used to accomplish this task.

2. The simplest program is as follows:

```
     R    N
     L    N
     M    N
     ST   ANS
     W    ANS
     H
```

This program uses the fact that the sum of the first N terms of the specified sequence is N^2.

3. The output should be arranged with suitable headings and with more than one number on each line. Thus, it will be necessary to convert the numbers to their character representation and to use the WA instruction to output each line of the table.

4. Since the format of the data cards is not specified, it is possible to specify that each data value will be punched so that the R instruction can be used to input each value. This makes the program straightforward.

Exercise B.4

1.
```
        LX   =0,1     ⎫
INP     R    N,1      ⎬  Input the 50 numbers
        BIX  INP,=49,1 ⎭
        L    =0       ⎫
        LX   =0,1     ⎪
ADD     A    N,1      ⎬  Form the sum in accumulator
        BIX  ADD,=49,1 ⎭
        ST   SUM      ⎫
        W    SUM      ⎬  Output the sum and stop
        H             ⎭
N       RES  50          Locations for numbers
SUM     DC   0
```

2–3. A solution for Question 2 is given below. Note that, in the case of a tie, the program outputs the "last" maximum that is encountered. This interpretation can be used for Question 3.

```
        LX   =0,1     ⎫
INP     R    N,1      ⎬  Input the 50 numbers
        BIX  INP,=49,1 ⎭
        L    N        ⎫  Assign first number
        ST   MAX      ⎭  to maximum
        LX   =1,1     ⎫
TEST    L    MAX      ⎪
        S    N,1      ⎪
        BP   DOWN     ⎪
        L    N,1      ⎬  Find the maximum
        ST   MAX      ⎪
DOWN    BIX  TEST,=49,1 ⎭
        W    MAX
        H
N       RES  50
MAX     DC   0
```

4. b)
```
        .
        .
        .
        STX  I,1   ⎫
        L    I     ⎬  Test the value of the subscript
        S    M     ⎪
        BP   ERR   ⎭
        L    K     ⎫
ADD     A    M,1   ⎬  K ← K+M(I)
        ST   K     ⎭
        .
        .
        .
ERR     WA   MESS
        W    I
        H
MESS    RES  6'ERROR — SUBSCRIPT I EXCEEDS MA'
        RES  5'XIMUM PERMISSIBLE VALUE A'
        RES  5'T ADD INSTRUCTION. I ='
```

The portion of program given above assumes that the value of I is available in index register 1. Note that the error message indicates the name of the instruction that would have been in error if the subscript exceeded the maximum value. The portion of program given above does not test to determine if the subscript is less than the minimum permissible value. How can this be accomplished?

Exercise B.5

1.
```
        LX   =1,1    
BACK    ST   NUM     
        D    DIV-1,1  ⎫
        M    DIV-1,1  ⎪
        ST   TEMP     ⎬  Compute remainder on division
        L    NUM      ⎪  by 10, $10^3$, $10^5$, or $10^7$
        S    TEMP     ⎪
        ST   REM      ⎭
        L    TEMP    
        M    DIV     
        A    REM     
        BIX  BACK,=4,1
```

(at this point, the accumulator contains the required result)

```
        .
        .
        .
NUM     DC 0
DIV     DC 10
           1000
           100000
           10000000
TEMP    DC
REM     DC
```

With the sequence of instructions given above, it is assumed that the number in the accumulator is less than 10^5. When this sequence of instructions is used as a subprogram by a calling program, it may be (inadvertently) presented with a number that is not less than 10^5. What precautions can be built in to the sequence of instructions to make it "fail-safe"?

2. The BAL instruction can be used three times for each line of output. The sequence of instructions developed for Question 1 must have provision for returning to the calling program. (See Fig. B.5.)

3. Is it safe to assume that the representation initially in the accumulator is of the form +000d0d0d0d where the d's represent digits? Can you form a sequence of instructions that will always work, in the sense that it handles invalid data in some sensible way?

5.

```
MAX2 L   0,1  ⎫
     A   LOAD ⎬  Store value of first
     ST  N1   ⎪  argument in location TEMP
N1   DC       ⎪
     ST  TEMP ⎭
     L   1,1  ⎫
     A   LOAD ⎬  Store value of second
     ST  N2   ⎪  argument in location TEMP+1
N2   DC       ⎪
     ST  TEMP+1⎭
     L   TEMP ⎫
     S   TEMP+1⎪
     BP  DOWN ⎪  Determine largest, load largest
     L   TEMP+1⎬ into accumulator, and return to
     B   2,1  ⎪  calling program
DOWN L   TEMP ⎪
     B   2,1  ⎭
LOAD L
TEMP RES 2
```

Exercise B.6

```
1.   RA   CARD
     WA   CARD
     LX   =0,1
LOOP BAL  GET,2
     S    LPAR
     BZ   GOT
     BIX  LOOP,=79,1
     WA   DONE
     H
GOT  STX  I,1
     L    I
     A    =1
     ST   I
     WA   MESS
     W    I
     H
CARD RES  16
DONE RES  16'SEARCH COMPLETED'
MESS RES  4'PARENTHESIS FOUND AT'
     RES  12'FOLLOWING COLUMN NUMBER'
LPAR RES  1'0000('
```

With the program given above, a sequence of statements beginning with the name GET is required to return the next

character via the accumulator in the tens and units position. This could be done with a subprogram, or, as in this solution, the refinement could appear later in the program. This latter approach avoids passing the parameter CARD to a subprogram.

```
GET  STX  TEMP,1 ⎫
     L    TEMP   ⎪
     D    =5     ⎪
     ST   QUOT   ⎬  Compute quotient and
     M    =5     ⎪  remainder when index
     ST   TEM2   ⎪  register 1 is divided by 5
     L    TEMP   ⎪
     S    TEM2   ⎪
     ST   REM    ⎭
     LX   QUOT,3
     LX   REM,4
     L    CARD,8
     D    TABL,4
     ST   TEM3    ← Result is last two digits
                     of TEM3 at this point
     D    =100   ⎫
     M    =100   ⎪  Determine remainder of
     ST   TEM4   ⎬  TEM3 divided by 100
     L    TEM3   ⎪
     S    TEM4   ⎭
     B    0,2      Return
TABL DC   100000000
     DC   1000000
     DC   10000
     DC   100
     DC   1
```

2–3. A portion of the answer given for Question 1 will be useful.

4. The subprogram IGCD could start out as follows:

```
IGCD L  0,6  ⎫
     ST NUM1 ⎬  NUM1 ← value of first argument
     L  1,6  ⎫
     ST NUM2 ⎬  NUM2 ← value of second argument
```

The remaining part can be a straightforward application of Euclid's algorithm, followed by

```
     B    2,1
```

to return to the calling program, after ensuring that the accumulator contains the greatest common divisor.

5. The use of indirect addressing, as well as the value stored in the index register specified in the BAL instruction, allows Euclid's algorithm to be rendered in SAP in a straightforward way.

APPENDIX C

Exercise C.1

3. /Convert Number from base 10 to base B, B<10.
Assume Number and B are available./
Value = 0
L = 1

Loop while(Number>0)
    R = remainder of Number/B
    Number = quotient of Number/B
    Value = Value + R×L
    L = L×10
End loop
/Value is the number in base B/

/Convert Value from base B to base 10,(B<10).
Assume Value and B are available/
Number = 0
L = 1
Loop while(Value>0)
    R = remainder of Value/10
    Value = quotient of Value/10
    Number = Number + R×L
    L = L×B
End loop
/Number is the number in base 10/

4. /Purpose is to convert the number represented by N10, a singly subscripted array with n components containing the digits of N10, into its equivalent base B representation. The result is to be stored in BK, a singly subscripted array with m components, containing the digits of the result. Assume N10, n, B, m are available./
Loop for L = m,m−1, . . . ,1
    Rem = 0
    Loop for I = 1,2, . . . ,N
        J = N10(I) + Rem×10
        N10(I) = quotient of J/B
        Rem = remainder of J/B
    End loop
    BK(K) = Rem
End loop
/BK contains the required result/

The number of components of BK that will be required depends on n and on B. For example, with $n = 10$ and $B = 2$, we must have $m \approx 33$, while with $n = 5$ and $B = 16$, $m \approx 5$ will suffice. In general, the relationship $10^n = B^m$ can be used to determine an appropriate value for m.

5. The solution given below assumes that the integers are denoted by single variable names and that overflow will not arise. If overflow is a possibility, the digits in the integers can be assigned to components of arrays, similar to the conditions imposed in Question 4.

/Purpose is to convert Number in base 10 to its value in base B. Assume that Number and B are available./
L = B
Loop while (quotient of Number/L > 0)
    L = L×B
End loop
Value = 0
Loop while L > B
    L = L/B
    R = remainder of Number/L
    Number = quotient of Number/L
    Value = Value×10 + Quotient
End loop
Value = Value×10 + R
Stop

Exercise C.3

9. For values greater than 1, it is obvious that we must have at least n binary digits such that $10^9 \leq 2^n$. However, in order to also accommodate values less than 1, a greater number of digits will be required, since the conversion process (from base 10 to base 2 for fractions) can lead to nonterminating binary fractions. The rounding procedure used for the conversion processes will also play an important role in determining how many "extra" binary digits will be required.

Index